D0236569

THE STABILITY AND GROWTH PACT

Also by Marco Buti

ECONOMIC POLICY IN EMU *(co-edited with André Sapir)*
THE WELFARE STATE IN EUROPE: Challenges and Reforms
(co-edited with Daniele Franco and Lucio R. Pench)
TAXATION, WELFARE AND THE CRISIS OF
UNEMPLOYMENT IN EUROPE *(co-edited with Paolo Sestito
and Hans Wijkander)*

Also by Daniele Franco

THE WELFARE STATE IN EUROPE: Challenges and Reforms
(co-edited with Marco Buti and Lucio R. Pench)
INDICATORS OF STRUCTURAL BUDGET BALANCES
(co-edited with Sandro Momigliano)
FISCAL SUSTAINABILITY *(co-edited with Fabrizio Balassone)*

The Stability and Growth Pact

The Architecture of Fiscal Policy in EMU

Edited by
Anne Brunila
Marco Buti
and
Daniele Franco

palgrave

Selection, editorial matter and Chapter 1 © Anne Brunila, Marco Buti and Daniele Franco 2001

Individual chapters (in order) © Roel Beetsma; Matthew B. Canzoneri and Behzad T. Diba; Juergen Stark; Declan Costello; António J. Cabral; Jonas Fischer and Gabriele Giudice; Michael J. Artis and Marco Buti; Thomas Dalsgaard and Alain de Serres; Ray Barrell and Karen Dury; Matti Virén; Sixten Korkman; Massimo Rostagno, Paul Hiebert and Javier Pérez-García; Alessandro Missale; Fabrizio Balassone and Daniele Franco; Alessandra Casella 2001

All rights reserved. No reproduction, copy or transmission of this publication may be made without written permission.

No paragraph of this publication may be reproduced, copied or transmitted save with written permission or in accordance with the provisions of the Copyright, Designs and Patents Act 1988, or under the terms of any licence permitting limited copying issued by the Copyright Licensing Agency, 90 Tottenham Court Road, London W1T 4LP.

Any person who does any unauthorised act in relation to this publication may be liable to criminal prosecution and civil claims for damages.

The authors have asserted their rights to be identified as the authors of this work in accordance with the Copyright, Designs and Patents Act 1988.

First published 2001 by
PALGRAVE
Houndmills, Basingstoke, Hampshire RG21 6XS and
175 Fifth Avenue, New York, N.Y. 10010
Companies and representatives throughout the world

PALGRAVE is the new global academic imprint of
St. Martin's Press LLC Scholarly and Reference Division and
Palgrave Publishers Ltd (formerly Macmillan Press Ltd).

ISBN 0–333–96145–5

This book is printed on paper suitable for recycling and made from fully managed and sustained forest sources.

A catalogue record for this book is available from the British Library.

Library of Congress Cataloging-in-Publication Data
The stability and growth pact: the architecture of fiscal policy in EMU
edited by Anne Brunila, Marco Buti and Daniele Franco.
     p. cm.
     ISBN 0–333–96145–5 (cloth)

     1. Fiscal policy—European Union countries. 2. Monetary policy—European Union countries. 3. Economic and Monetary Union.
4. European Union countries—Economic integration. I. Brunila, Anne. II. Buti, Marco. III. Franco, Daniele, 1953–

     HJ1000.5 .S7 2001
     339.5′2′094—dc21   2001031519

10   9   8   7   6   5   4   3   2   1
10   09   08   07   06   05   04   03   02   01

Printed in Great Britain by
Antony Rowe Ltd, Chippenham, Wiltshire

Contents

PART IV 'CLOSE TO BALANCE OR IN SURPLUS': THE MEDIUM-TERM BUDGETARY TARGETS

PART V   FISCAL POLICY COORDINATION UNDER THE PACT

PART VI   PUBLIC DEBT UNDER THE STABILITY AND GROWTH PACT

PART VII   WERE THERE POSSIBLE ALTERNATIVES?

List of Tables

List of Figures

Acknowledgements

The discussions and negotiations on the Stability and Growth Pact were a stepping stone in the establishment of EMU and it is widely believed that the implementation of the Pact will deeply affect the functioning of this new institutional setting. In short, the public finance commitments undertaken by EU countries in the context of the Pact are possibly the clearest evidence that EMU is more than a simple currency reform.

The preparation of this book has involved several 'actors' of the Pact. We are particularly indebted to Giovanni Ravasio, Director-General of Economic and Financial Affairs of the European Commission. His experience as chief negotiator on the Commission side in the 1995–97 period and supervisor in the implementation of the Pact since 1999 has been invaluable to us in devising and shaping this volume. We are also grateful to Antonio Cabral, Director of the Economies of Member States, and Hervé Carré, Director of the Euro Area at the European Commission, for their insights on the working of the Pact and their encouragement in carrying out this project.

The Pact has aroused a large and controversial debate. All contributors to the book have played a role in this debate, either at the policy and institutional level or at the academic level. We are grateful to all of them for enduring graciously the repeated requests of 'intrusive' editors. An early version of Chapters 3, 8 and 15 were originally published in *Empirica, Public Finance and Management* and *Fiscal Studies*, respectively. We thank the editors of those journals for their permission to use this material.

We are also indebted to Tue Fosdal who compiled the glossary, Pietro Rizza for his excellent research assistance, Chris Neenan for help in editing the text, and Maria Davi-Pilato and Aliki Drossou for secretarial support.

Finally, the assistance of Zelah Pengilley of Palgrave was paramount for the rapid publication of the book.

Brussels and Rome

Anne Brunila
Marco Buti
Daniele Franco

List of Contributors

Michael J. Artis   Professor of Economics, European University Institute

Fabrizio Balassone   Research Department, Bank of Italy

Ray Barrell   Senior Research Fellow, National Institute of Economic and Social Research, and Visiting Professor at Imperial College

Roel Beetsma   Professor of Macroeconomics, Department of Economics, University of Amsterdam

Anne Brunila   Economic Adviser, European Commission

Marco Buti   Economic Adviser, European Commission

António J. Cabral   Director, Directorate-General for Economic and Financial Affairs, European Commission

Matthew B. Canzoneri   Professor, Department of Economics, Georgetown University

Alessandra Casella   Professor of Economics, Columbia University

Declan Costello   Directorate-General for Economic and Financial Affairs, European Commission

Thomas Dalsgaard   Senior Economist, Economics Department, Organisation for Economic Co-operation and Development

Behzad T. Diba   Professor, Department of Economics, Georgetown University

Karen Dury   Senior Research Officer, National Institute of Economic and Social Research

Jonas Fischer   Directorate-General for Economic and Financial Affairs, European Commission

Daniele Franco   Director of Public Finance Division, Bank of Italy

Gabriele Giudice   Directorate-General for Economic and Financial Affairs, European Commission

Paul Hiebert   Economist, Fiscal Policies Division, European Central Bank

Sixten Korkman   Director-General, General Secretariat of the Council of the European Union

Alessandro Missale   Professor of Economics, Faculty of Political Science, University of Florence

Javier Pérez-García   Economist, Fiscal Policies Division, European Central Bank

Massimo Rostagno   Senior Economist, Monetary Policy Strategy Division, European Central Bank

Alain de Serres   Senior Economist, Economics Department, Organisation for Economic Co-operation and Development

Juergen Stark   Deputy Governor, Deutsche Bundesbank

Matti Virén   Professor, Department of Economics, University of Turku and Bank of Finland

1 Introduction

*Anne Brunila, Marco Buti and
Daniele Franco*

1.1 THE AIM OF THIS BOOK

Sound public finances are at the core of European Monetary Union (EMU). Fiscal discipline contributes to maintaining an economic environment in which monetary policy can effectively pursue price stability.

The fiscal framework of EMU has been developed gradually. The Treaty of Maastricht in 1992 set the fiscal criteria for joining Monetary Union. The Stability and Growth Pact (SGP), adopted by the European Council in Amsterdam in June 1997, developed these criteria with a view to permanently restraining deficit and debt levels while allowing room for fiscal stabilisation. The Pact also strengthened the monitoring procedures complementing the quantitative rules.

The Stability and Growth Pact represents a new historical development. For the first time a number of sovereign countries adopt a set of common fiscal rules and an elaborated multilateral surveillance mechanism. This new institutional setting has extensive implications for the European economies. Apart from the conduct of fiscal policy, it affects the relationships between European Union (EU) member states and the relationships between the different levels of government. It affects intergenerational redistribution and the way demographic ageing is dealt with. It may imply the end of public debt. The allocation and distribution functions of government, although not covered by the agreed rules, are indirectly influenced.

Some aspects of the framework of EMU are still to be completely specified. Several implications are far from being fully examined and understood. Some criticisms to the Pact still require adequate answers. The new fiscal regime has not yet had to face critical challenges.

The editors of the volume are convinced that fiscal rules can in the end be successfully implemented over a long period of time only if public opinion considers them a valuable contribution to policy-making.

1

They are also convinced that accurate analysis of the implications of the SGP and open discussions about its problematic aspects can contribute to meeting the policy challenges ahead.

This volume aims at providing a comprehensive overview of the fiscal architecture of EMU. It examines the development, rationale and implementation of the SGP, and covers both its institutional aspects and its economic implications. Problematic issues and the aspects still to be clarified are evaluated. Alternative fiscal frameworks are also examined.

The authors of the chapters have extensively contributed to the preparation of the Pact, to its implementation, and to the academic debate around its rationale. Some of them took part in the negotiations. The different angles covered by the chapters provide a comprehensive view of the academic and policy debate concerning the Pact.

This introduction highlights the main aspects of the studies. In particular, it outlines the conclusions reached by the authors and their contribution to the policy debate.

1.2   WHY FISCAL RULES IN EMU?

The need for fiscal rules has been at the core of the debate on EMU since the early 1990s. The discussion has focused on the rationale and the effectiveness of the SGP. The arguments put forward in favour of and against fiscal rules in the EMU context are discussed extensively in the chapters by Roel Beetsma (Chapter 2) and by Matthew Canzoneri and Behzad Diba (Chapter 3). While investigating thoroughly the existing literature, the two chapters reach somewhat different conclusions as to the desirability of the SGP. Beetsma finds the Pact necessary and desirable, although susceptible to improvements. Canzoneri and Diba, while not opposing in principle the introduction of fiscal rules in EMU, judge that the Pact imposes unnecessary and harmful constraints on fiscal policy.

The debate on fiscal rules in EMU is grounded on the wider debate about the role of fiscal institutions and procedures in shaping budgetary outcomes. While certain political configurations, such as weak coalition governments, have been recognised as conductive to budgetary misbehaviour or to hampering attempts to redress the budgetary situation, inadequate budgetary institutions and procedures may also contribute to a lack of fiscal discipline. In this context, institutional reforms in the fiscal domain have been discussed and introduced in several countries. As noted by Beetsma, these reforms come in two main categories: (a) the introduction of procedural rules conducive to a responsible fiscal behaviour and (b) the introduction of a fiscal rule, that is, a permanent constraint on domestic fiscal policy in terms of an indicator of the overall fiscal performance (budget balance, borrowing, debt, reserves) of central and/or local government. In practice, both types of measures have proved to be effective tools in containing political biases in fiscal policy-making and in achieving and sustaining fiscal discipline. It has, however, been noted that fiscal rules may have costs in terms of stabilisation policies and may hamper the achievement of allocative and distributive objectives.

Beetsma argues that procedural or fiscal rules are necessary because the factors that in the 1970s and 1980s have determined fiscal profligacy in several countries have not disappeared. He notes that the EMU dimension is likely to increase the need for such rules. Without strong rules, the legal independence of the European Central Bank (ECB) may turn out to be an empty shell because of pressure by high-debt countries for *ex ante* bail-out (refraining from raising interest rates in conditions of inflationary tensions) or *ex post* bail-out (debt relief through unanticipated inflation). EMU may also raise interest rate spillovers. It can induce unilateral fiscal expansions since governments may feel less inclined to preserve fiscal rectitude, as they individually face a less steep interest rate schedule in a monetary union than under flexible exchange rates.

Canzoneri and Diba examine the need for rules protecting the ECB from the pressure of governments to reduce interest rates. They also evaluate the implications of the ECB having to interact with several fiscal authorities. They note that these factors do not provide strong arguments in favour of permanent constraints on the deficit. The multiplicity of fiscal authorities may actually dilute the pressure on a central bank. In their view, the case for fiscal rules to protect the central bank is actually less strong in the EU than in the USA where the problem is not considered important. According to Canzoneri and Diba, a more relevant case for fiscal rules is provided by the so-called fiscal theory of price determination. In this context, a deficit constraint is important to underpin the 'functional', as opposed to the 'legal', independence of the central bank: without a credible deficit criterion ensuring government fiscal solvency, the central bank would not be able to keep control of the price level. However, they note that the need for fiscal rules for monetary stability in EMU may be temporary. Once the ECB has established its credibility, the

Pact would no longer be needed, provided fiscal solvency is guaranteed.

The two chapters also question the structure of the SGP. First, they examine the approach taken by the EU which is predominantly rule-based, while in most countries fiscal discipline largely depends on budgetary procedures. Beetsma notes that the first-best strategy would have been that of dealing with the factors leading to excessive deficits at the national level. However, the adoption of harmonised tight budgetary procedures would have led to fundamental problems from the point of view of national sovereignty. Moreover, institutional reforms are more difficult to monitor centrally, compared to numerical targets. The latter are also simpler to evaluate and easier to grasp by public opinion and policy-makers. Canzoneri and Diba reach similar conclusions. They stress that the credibility of fiscal rules is of the utmost importance. For this reason, there is a need for manageable and transparent rules that facilitate the monitoring process and make sure that fiscal solvency is guaranteed. Excessively stringent rules may be counterproductive. If the Pact leads to an unduly tight fiscal stance in one or more countries, pressure may mount on the ECB to deliver a monetary offsetting. Otherwise, the credibility of the Pact may be endangered.

The specific solutions adopted in the SGP – less flexible than those in federal countries – are also considered: the rules are defined on the basis of established numerical parameters; *ex post* compliance with the parameters is required each year; margins of flexibility are envisaged only in connection with exceptional events; no allowance is considered for investment expenditure; tight monitoring procedures are envisaged; non-compliance triggers the application of preestablished monetary sanctions; overshoots must be rapidly dealt with.

In particular, Canzoneri and Diba criticise the central role attributed to actual rather than structural (or cyclically adjusted) deficits. They believe that this may severely hamper counter-cyclical stabilisation. In their view, the SGP does not represent an adequate balance between fiscal discipline and the flexibility required for stabilisation purposes. Reference to cyclically adjusted balances or debt levels would greatly help in dealing with this problem. Beetsma, although less critical on the Pact, has similar suggestions concerning the fiscal variables to be considered. In particular, he notes that the debt provides a better measure of fiscal solvency problems and of the potential pressures on the central bank to relax monetary policy. Reference to the debt ratio would improve the credibility of the Pact and would reduce the constraints to stabilisation policies.

1.3 FROM MAASTRICHT TO THE STABILITY AND GROWTH PACT

1.3.1 The German Initiative

The requirements of achieving fiscal discipline to join the single currency are at the core of the Maastricht Treaty. Although the Treaty also attempts to ensure that fiscal discipline is maintained after entering EMU, there were doubts especially on the German side whether it was stringent enough. By leaving several issues open and subject to interpretation, the Treaty allows a significant degree of discretionary powers at various levels of decision-making which could weaken the confidence in the continuation of fiscal discipline in monetary union. As outlined by Juergen Stark (Chapter 4), these worries finally led the German Finance Minister, Theo Waigel, to put forward a proposal in November 1995 to complement the provisions of the Treaty. Waigel's proposal for a 'Stability Pact for Europe' presented a number of initiatives to make fiscal prudence watertight in EMU: to this end, member states should commit themselves to a uniform medium-term deficit target of 1 per cent of GDP and a system in which sanctions would be automatically applied when an 'excessive deficit' (that is, a budget deficit higher than 3 per cent of GDP) occurred. In addition, the proposal put forward the idea of creating a European Stability Council to ensure a strict application of the Pact.

Stark, who headed at the time the German Ministry of Finance, discusses the underlying rationale for the original German proposal and presents the arguments raised by other member states and the Commission during a series of negotiations and ECOFIN meetings in 1996 and the first half of 1997 before the final agreement was reached. After initial hesitation and even resistance on the part of some member states, the proposal found broad acceptance throughout the EU. However, as to specific issues, views were more diverging. In particular, there were wide controversies about how sanctions should be imposed and how to define 'exceptional conditions' under which the 3 per cent deficit limit would be allowed to be breached without triggering the Excessive Deficit Procedure of the Maastricht Treaty. After almost a year of negotiations on the contents and format of the Pact, the political agreement on the difficult issue of the 'exceptional' conditions was reached at the European Council in December 1996. The SGP was finally adopted by the European Council in Amsterdam in June 1997.

While Stark's perspective is essentially that of the German fiscal authorities, Declan Costello (Chapter 5) looks at the negotiations from the perspective of the European Commission. He considers various legal aspects and the difficulties in reconciling these with the proposed content and format of the Pact. Specifically, the role of the European Commission in shifting the debate from the German call for disciplinary elements in the form of automatic rules towards an emphasis on preventive elements is established. The Commission questioned *inter alia* the economic desirability of a uniform medium-term target, the possibility for imposing 'automaticity' of sanctions, and the scope for creating a Stability Council outside the Treaty framework. As a result of the negotiations, it was agreed that countries should select medium-term targets of 'close to balance or in surplus', rather than imposing a uniform deficit level and – also on legal grounds – the automaticity of sanctions as well as the proposal of establishing a Stability Council were dropped. By stressing the need to find the solutions within the existing Treaty, the Commission focused on the development of the early-warning mechanism and surveillance procedure involving the adoption of Stability Programmes (for euro area members) and Convergence Programmes (for the other EU countries).

1.3.2   What Is the SGP? How Is It Implemented?

In Chapter 6, António Cabral provides an extensive analysis of the contents of the Stability and Growth Pact. The Pact consists of two Council Regulations which are complemented by two European Council resolutions. The essential feature of the Pact is that it enforces fiscal discipline while recognising the need for flexibility at the national level by setting country-specific 'medium-term objectives of budgetary positions close to balance or in surplus'.

Cabral explores in detail both the 'preventive' and the 'dissuasive' aspects of the Pact. The preventive function is carried out by regular surveillance of budgetary positions. To this end, a Council Regulation strengthening the multilateral surveillance of budget positions and the coordination of economic policies was adopted. Stability and Convergence Programmes, which member states have to submit annually, represent the key feature of the enhanced surveillance procedure and an early-warning mechanism. The programmes specify national medium-term budgetary objectives of 'close to balance or in surplus' which would allow member states to respect the 3 per cent deficit ceiling even during economic downturns. The Council, after having examined the programmes, can issue a recommendation to a member state to take adjustment measures should significant slippage from the set targets be identified. The Pact applies to all EU countries but it stops short of imposing sanctions on the non-euro area members.

The dissuasive function of the Pact requires member states to take immediate corrective action in the event the 3 per cent reference value is being breached. If necessary, it allows for the imposition of sanctions, such as non-interest-bearing deposit, that can be transformed into fines. These elements are contained in the Council Regulation on speeding up and clarifying the implementation of the Excessive Deficit Procedure. In order to avoid the imposition of sanctions, the member state which finds itself in excessive deficit would need to take immediate action and complete correction of the deficit in the year following its identification unless special circumstances apply. The Pact does not specify what these special circumstances are, but it is widely accepted that the clause could be called upon in case of protracted or very severe recessions.

In order to strengthen SGP credibility, the legal provisions are supplemented by a political commitment by all parties involved in the SGP – the Commission, member states, the Council – to the full and timely implementation of the budget surveillance process. This element is contained in two Resolutions agreed at the Amsterdam European Council in June 1997. This political commitment ensures that effective peer pressure is exerted on a member state failing to live up to its commitments.

The practical implementation and the actual working of the Pact is discussed by Jonas Fischer and Gabriele Giudice (Chapter 7). Their attention is mainly focused on the Stability and Convergence Programmes. On the basis of the experience of the first years, the authors conclude that the implementation of the SGP has been successful and progress towards balanced budgets has continued, albeit at a slower pace than during the run-up to EMU. Moreover, the obligation to submit Stability and Convergence Programmes annually has enhanced policy coordination by increasing the transparency of budgetary policies in Europe. In most countries, the programmes provide an overall framework for expenditure and revenue choices. The medium-term budgetary targets are considered guiding principles for the budget process over a multi-annual interval.

However, as Fischer and Giudice point out, the Pact does not give a fully satisfactory answer to all important fiscal policy issues, notably: the use of cyclically adjusted figures in budgetary surveillance; the importance of the composition of the fiscal retrenchment; and the role of the long-run sustainability of public finances in the budgetary surveillance. Also, it remains unclear how different levels of government are involved and how to integrate the Stability and Convergence Programmes with the existing national budgetary procedures. After discussing these topics, the authors conclude that the programmes can become an effective instrument to trigger more integrated budgetary procedures at the national level and better policy coordination at EU level, thereby going well beyond the core assignment of the Pact.

1.4 DISCIPLINE, FLEXIBILITY AND COORDINATION

The debate on EMU during the 1990s has largely converged on the three principles which should govern fiscal policy in a currency area: discipline, autonomy and coordination. Budgetary discipline would prevent unsustainable debt and deficit paths to endanger the independence of the ECB and its commitment to price stability; in line with the traditional findings of the Optimal Currency Area literature, budgetary autonomy would allow fiscal policy to respond to country-specific disturbances in the absence of national monetary independence; finally, fiscal policy coordination would allow the internalisation of demand and interest rate externalities thereby ensuring an appropriate fiscal stance in the member countries and in the euro area as a whole. Therefore, 'to supply the adequate mix of autonomy, discipline and co-ordination is the challenge the fiscal regime of the Community has to meet' (European Commission, 1990, p. 102).

The SGP translates these broad principles into policy orientations: budgetary discipline should be preserved by making sure that the Maastricht reference value of 3 per cent of GDP becomes a 'hard' ceiling, which could be exceeded only in exceptional circumstances and for a limited period of time; fiscal autonomy/flexibility, that is, the ability to respond to country-specific shocks, would be ensured by selecting a medium-term budgetary target allowing sufficient room for manoeuvre and letting the automatic stabilisers play freely; finally, in the light of the previous two principles, budgetary coordination would be essentially rule-based. It would largely be the consequence of rules aiming at preventing budgetary misbehaviour.

Three chapters of the volume deal with the choice of the appropriate medium-term budgetary target by euro area members and two chapters examine the issue of fiscal policy coordination under the SGP.

1.4.1 Fiscal Discipline and Fiscal Flexibility

The underlying philosophy of the SGP is that countries set appropriate medium-term targets of 'close to balance or in surplus' and let automatic stabilisers play symmetrically over the business cycle. Such choice is important for several reasons. First, maintaining medium-term fiscal positions of 'close to balance or in surplus' would ensure that there is no repeat of the past fiscal policy mistake of high and persistent structural deficits which contribute to the accumulation of public debt. Second, it would provide room for automatic fiscal stabilisers to operate fully during normal economic downturns, thereby helping economies to adjust to economic shocks in the absence of the exchange rate instrument. Third, it would reinforce credibility in the commitment to fiscal discipline in EMU, as breaches of the 3 per cent reference value would be allowed only during very severe economic downturns or in exceptional occurrences.

As stressed by Mike Artis and Marco Buti (Chapter 8), unlike the numerical rules of the Maastricht Treaty – which set a common upper limit for the government deficit for all member states – the Pact introduces an element of country specificity. The Pact *de facto* relies on the concept of the cyclically adjusted budget balance, a measure considered by several commentators as a more appropriate policy target than the actual deficit. In identifying a 'safe' medium-term budgetary position, the first worry is to create sufficient room for manoeuvre to accommodate the budgetary effects of cyclical fluctuations. Calculations based on the business cycles of the post war period point to a deficit target between 0 and 1 per cent of GDP for most of the EU countries, and a surplus for the Nordic countries which, traditionally, have experienced a larger cyclical component in their budgets. Artis and Buti present also estimates that show that an additional safety margin of the order of 0.5 to 1 per cent of GDP would be necessary to cover unforeseen fiscal developments not directly linked to the working of automatic stabilisers, such as the risk of unexpected shortfalls in tax revenues or spending overruns and interest rate shocks. This would bring most countries of the euro area towards a balanced budget or a small surplus.

Similar conclusions have been obtained by applying more sophisticated methodologies. Thomas Dalsgaard and Alain de Serres (Chapter 9) estimate a structural VAR model capturing the effects on the budget deficits of shocks having prevailed historically in EU countries. In order to capture the shift in the deficit stemming purely from the working of automatic stabilisers, all other aspects of fiscal behaviour have been assumed unchanged. the authors show that for a majority of EU countries a structural deficit of around 1 per cent of GDP would help to avoid breaching the 3 per cent of GDP threshold with a 90 per cent certainty over a three-year horizon. However, such deficit levels imply only a 50 per cent likelihood of not exceeding the 3 per cent limit if the time horizon is extended from three to ten years. More ambitious targets obviously imply a lower risk of moving into 'excessive deficits'. Balanced budgets in structural terms would provide most countries with a 90 per cent likelihood of keeping the deficit within the 3 per cent threshold over a five-year horizon. For the three countries not belonging to the euro area (the UK, Denmark and Sweden) small surpluses are required to obtain such outcome.

The authors conclude that, for most of the EU countries, achieving the budgetary objectives for 2003 set out in their Stability and Convergence Programmes would allow them to fend off the risk of breaching the 3 per cent Maastricht threshold without resorting to pro-cyclical policies in bad times. Dalsgaard and de Serres indicate that such targets – while being 'SGP-compatible' – may not be the most appropriate if one takes into account other considerations. For instance, countries like France, Italy and Austria could require more ambitious targets if one considers the budgetary implications of population ageing on pension and health care expenditure.

The above studies examine the likelihood of breaching the 3 per cent limit using retrospective evidence. Ray Barrell and Karen Dury (Chapter 10) extend this literature using a model (NiGEM) which tries to encompass the current and anticipated structure of European economies rather that simply relying on past cyclical experience. NiGEM uses a New Keynesian framework in which agents are forward-looking but nominal rigidities imply that adjustment to shocks does not occur instantaneously. The model is shocked repeatedly to evaluate the range over which variables, and notably the budget balance, may move.

Model simulations allow the analysis of the fiscal implications of different monetary regimes, an issue which was raised in Chapter 8. The latter shows that the preferences of the ECB over the output–inflation trade-off matter. In particular, a higher degree of 'activism' of the ECB – rather than the degree of conservatism as such – allows a reduction of the needed safety margin in the event of demand shocks, while the opposite holds in the case of supply shocks. Barrell and Dury compare three possible feedback rules for the interest rate:

a standard monetary targeting rule, a pure inflation-targeting rule and a mixed rule.

The findings by Barrell and Dury suggest that automatic stabilisers are generally lower than normally assumed. Their study confirms that, if the countries adhere to the budgetary targets laid down in their Stability and Convergence Programmes, the full working of automatic stabilisers and the respect of the 3 per cent deficit ceiling are expected to be compatible. They also show empirically that while the monetary policy regime of the ECB can have significant effects on the stability of member economies, the impact of this on the probability of defaulting the SGP criteria is small. The authors conclude that this leaves substantial room for fiscal activism in helping to reduce economic fluctuations.

All in all, there is a widespread consensus that broadly balanced budgets are right for most EU member countries in that they will allow discipline to be preserved without hurting fiscal flexibility. However, although an effort is made to anticipate the possible effects of EMU, such estimates inevitably rely on pre-EMU datasets. It is still uncertain what effect the move to the EMU regime will have on the cyclical behaviour of the EU economies, the origin and the degree of asymmetry of economic shocks, and the interplay between fiscal rules and monetary rules. Therefore, as the economic and policy environment adapts to the new EMU framework, the issue of the appropriate medium-term targets under the SGP will have to be addressed again.

1.4.2 A Rule-Based Policy Coordination

In EMU national budgetary policies will have an important role for macroeconomic stabilisation across the economic cycle and in the event of asymmetric shocks. In line with the traditional Optimal Currency Area literature, budgetary policy needs to pursue a twofold aim: first, perform a shock-absorption function at the national level and, second, allow the establishment of an optimal budgetary stance at the EMU level. In order to meet the first objective, a degree of flexibility has to be left to national budgets. Meeting the second objective requires that the issue of budgetary policy coordination be addressed.

For the supranational coordination of national fiscal policies, a number of requirements have to be fulfilled. As spelled out by Matti Virén (Chapter 11), the cyclical behaviour of the economies and the nature of shocks must be similar; countries must have reasonably similar automatic stabilisers; forecasts and the assessment of the current situations must be sufficiently accurate; effects of fiscal policy actions must be relatively similar and predictable; the effectiveness of coordinated policy actions must be much larger than uncoordinated actions; different countries must share the same policy view (in terms of the instruments and objectives of policy); and policy commitments must be enforceable in different countries.

A number of such requirements are not met in the euro area. Hence, it is likely that active fiscal coordination will be the exception, rather than the rule. For instance, in the event of a particularly severe negative common shock, there might be a need for a discretionary 'budgetary supplement'. However, each member country might refrain from taking the initiative, hoping to free-ride on other countries' stabilisation. This wait-and-see attitude might be compounded by the fear that moving alone could bring forward the threat of sanctions under the Stability and Growth Pact arrangement. In this case, fiscal coordination will be necessary to bring about an adequate policy response. However, as pointed out by Virén, apart from these extreme cases, 'negative' coordination aiming at preventing countries ending up in an excessive deficit position will remain the rule.

These conclusions are consistent with those of Sixten Korkman (Chapter 12) who introduces, alongside economic arguments, institutional, political and practical considerations related to the implementation of policy coordination. He points out that the present trend focuses on clarifying and reinforcing certain aspects of economic policy coordination within the institutional limits set by the Treaty. This implies that, for the foreseeable future, political and practical considerations suggest relying on the SGP and simple assignments of policies which are complemented by guidelines for fiscal policies and intense dialogue in the Euro Group. Korkman states that, provided that fiscal policy autonomy is preserved, there is no need in EMU for a mechanism for fiscal transfers at the Community level to help member states deal with the consequences of idiosyncratic developments. Such a scheme would risk giving wrong incentives to economic agents and policy-makers and could therefore be counterproductive.

Even if the SGP can be considered a sound framework for conducting fiscal policies in EMU, it may not, however, be sufficient to prevent budgetary misbehaviour over the economic cycle. Korkman notices that there is nothing in the SGP to prevent countries from undertaking pro-cyclical expenditure increases and tax reductions during periods of strong growth. While headline budget figures may not deteriorate, the underlying budgetary position will. And fiscal policy, instead of contributing to smooth business cycles, would actually accentuate the cyclical swings. Korkman concludes that the SGP could be usefully complemented by fiscal policy guidelines encouraging EMU members to avoid fiscal laxity in periods of upswing and buoyant activity.

1.5 PUBLIC DEBT UNDER THE SGP

The SGP does not mention the public debt, nor does it elaborate on the 60 per cent of GDP threshold set in the Maastricht Treaty. Nevertheless, the Pact has very substantial consequences for debt dynamics. Adherence to the close-to-balance requirement will gradually reduce debt/GDP ratios. Asymptotically, public debt would disappear or reach very low levels.

This trend will have significant effects on financial markets, pension funds and corporate governance. The supply of the most typical risk-free asset will gradually dwindle. It will also affect intergenerational distribution since current generations of taxpayers will carry the burden of the debt reduction. Moreover, the SGP also affects public debt management. Cost-minimisation targets have to be considered in a context in which deficit stabilisation is also important.

The chapters by Massimo Rostagno, Javier Pérez and Paul Hiebert, and by Alessandro Missale consider two aspects of public debt management in the future. While Rostagno *et al.* examine the rationale of the debt reduction process started by the SGP, Missale evaluates how the debt structure can contribute to deficit stabilisation.

1.5.1 The Rationale of Debt Reduction

Rostagno *et al.* (Chapter 13) consider the implication of the SGP for the definition of the optimal debt level and the optimal level of budgetary sensitivity to cyclical fluctuations. Their analysis is based on a dynamic overlapping generations framework, in which the economy is populated by infinitely-lived households and population grows because of a steady inflow of immigrants. The model is calibrated for most EU countries.

The chapter highlights the main costs and benefits attached to the reduction of public debt. On the one hand, present generations have to pay higher taxes than future generations. On the other hand, the 'core' tax rate needed to sustain the debt is permanently reduced. This has positive implications especially in unfavourable economic circumstances, in which liquidity-restrained households would greatly appreciate automatic and discretionary stabilisation policies. Debt reduction can therefore be considered a policy for providing self-insurance against income shortfalls in periods of distress. According to the authors, the decision concerning the desired debt ratio is tightly related to the one concerning the desired budgetary sensitivity.

Rostagno *et al.* estimate the optimal debt ratio and the optimal budgetary sensitivity both conditionally to and independently from the current fiscal positions. They show that in the latter case, that is, freed from the burden of inherited debts, electorates would select higher stabilisation effects; hence governments would have either a positive or a balanced net asset position. The authors argue that these results may explain the policies of debt reabsorption carried out by several European countries.

The chapter also considers the implications for the debt reduction process of the deficit constraint set by the Pact. Without this constraint, present generations could in principle choose to stabilise the debt at its existing level and rely on large stabilisation policies. This would avoid an excess burden for the current taxpayers, related to the debt reduction, but would also leave unaffected the current 'core' tax rate needed to sustain the debt.

1.5.2   Optimal Debt Structure

Missale (Chapter 14) looks at the SGP from the angle of public debt management. He considers that the Pact introduces a new objective for debt management, that of deficit stabilisation. In his view, interest payments can represent a buffer against the budget consequences of cyclical downturns and unexpected deflation. This would allow more room for stabilisation policies.

He argues that the optimal debt composition depends on the stochastic relations between output, inflation and interest rates, as determined by monetary policy. It also depends on the correlation of shocks across euro area countries, on differences in the size of the shocks and in the transmission mechanism of monetary policy. More specifically, a long-maturity structure is optimal if economies are hit by asymmetric shocks and the ECB is primarily concerned with inflation stabilisation rather than with output stabilisation. Short-term and floating-rate debt is useful if shocks are correlated and in countries in which output and inflation uncertainty is relatively high. Debt maturity should also be shorter in countries where the interest rate sensitivity of demand is relatively low. Inflation-indexed debt, which can be helpful in case of unexpected deflation, should be issued in a strict inflation regime.

Missale explores how the relationship between output, inflation and interest rates may have changed with EMU and, more specifically, with the changes in the weight the ECB places on output stabilisation compared to national monetary authorities. On the basis of correlation coefficients estimated for EU countries and the USA, Missale argues that long-term debt is the best solution for most EU countries. Only a few countries should issue short-term and floating-rate debt. He concludes that the present structure of public debt can provide an adequate insurance against macroeconomic shocks and reduce the risk of deficits exceeding the 3 per cent threshold. He also notes that, while the optimal share of inflation-indexed debt should be relatively large for its positive role in stabilisation policies, its actual share on total public debt in EU countries is extremely limited.

1.6   WAS THERE ANOTHER WAY TO ENSURE FISCAL DISCIPLINE IN EMU?

The Maastricht Treaty and the SGP aim at ensuring fiscal discipline by setting numerical constraints on budgetary variables. In particular, they set an upward ceiling on the overall budget deficit. The two final chapters of the volume examine alternative approaches to the issue of guaranteeing fiscal discipline. The chapter by Fabrizio Balassone and Daniele Franco considers whether the so-called 'golden rule' of deficit financing could represent a feasible alternative to the overall rigid deficit limit. The chapter by Alessandra Casella explores a more radical option, namely that of replacing numerical constraints for individual countries with a market mechanism of allocating a pre-defined euro area budget deficit.

1.6.1   The 'Golden Rule'

Under the 'golden rule', governments are only allowed to borrow in order to finance government investment. The rule implicitly assumes that public investment spending leads to the accumulation of a stock of assets, which yields a stream of future returns beyond the current accounting period. Moreover, it assumes that tax financing would negatively affect investment decisions by removing the possibility of spreading investment costs over the generations benefiting from investment. The golden rule of deficit financing, which implies a dual budget, has been introduced in some countries as a fiscal discipline device to control budgetary policy at the national level. It is also widely used for regional and local authorities. Could the golden rule have been introduced into the EMU fiscal framework to constrain deficits without reducing public investment?

In Chapter 15, Balassone and Franco acknowledge that a broadly balanced budget, like that required by the SGP, may negatively affect the public investment level and they note that this effect can be especially relevant during the transition to the low debt levels consistent with the chosen structural balance. The double burden determined by this transition can be assimilated to that arising from the transition from a pay-as-you-go to a funded pension system. However, they put forward two lines of arguments against the introduction of the golden rule.

First, they note that a dual budget may distort expenditure decisions in favour of physical assets compared with spending on intangibles that can give a relevant contribution to economic growth, for example, those increasing human capital. They also note that the possibility of borrowing without strict limits in order to finance investments can lower the attention paid when evaluating the costs and benefits of each project. Moreover, there is no clear evidence in the empirical literature that investment in public infrastructure always leads to significant positive growth effects. Some studies suggest that government investment may be subject to rapidly decreasing returns.

Second, Balassone and Franco note that in the EMU context the golden rule would be an obstacle to deficit and debt reduction. In particular, given the ratio of public investment as a percentage of GDP, the long-run equilibrium level of government debt could be very high, especially in an environment of low inflation. This could imply that the debt ratio would rise in low-debt countries, while in high-debt countries there would be a very slow pace of debt reabsorption. The golden rule would also meet with practical difficulties, such as the evaluation of amortisation, and would make the multilateral surveillance process more complex, by providing leeway for opportunistic behaviour. Governments would have an incentive to classify current expenditure as capital spending.

1.6.2 A Market for Deficit Permits

Alessandra Casella (Chapter 16) proposes a system of tradable budget deficit permits as an efficient mechanism for implementing fiscal constraints in EMU (for example, the current 3 per cent of GDP deficit or a lower figure). The basic idea is that, having chosen an aggregate target for the Union and an initial distribution of deficit permits, EMU countries could be allowed to trade rights to deficit creation. While this system keeps the aggregate area-wide deficit unchanged, it allows individual member states to deviate from the initial allowances in case of idiosyncratic shocks. The proposal combines the belief that markets are unable to ensure fiscal discipline with the appreciation of the role of markets in the allocation of resources.

Comparing the negative externality produced by member states running excessive deficits to that of pollution, Casella suggests applying the experience of environmental economics to the question of fiscal discipline within the EMU. Externalities are dealt with by creating appropriate ownership rights and allowing free trade in them. Once the initial allotment of rights is set, market incentives would produce, through free trade, the most efficient allocation in relation to the financial needs of the various governments in any given year. The total volume of permits issued could be related to the European economic cycle, so as to absorb the cyclical impact on the budget. Deficits above the amount of permits would result in a cut in the permits assigned the following year. The mechanism would minimise the aggregate cost of compliance with the aggregate targets and provide rewards for countries running surpluses in favourable cyclical conditions. It would also reduce the room for political manipulations.

In order to compensate for the fact that the deficits of the various governments may generate different externalities, that is, different risks of triggering a financial crisis, the amount of permits required per unit of deficit can be proportional to the stock of debt of each government.

At present, the scheme outlined by Casella does not appear a feasible alternative to the current numerical rules, the main reason being that radical changes in the EMU fiscal rules could undermine the credibility of the SGP, which is still in an early stage of implementation. In a later stage, when the Pact has become a permanent feature of the EU fiscal framework and debt levels have been considerably reduced, a market-based solution may be considered. However, before introducing the mechanism at the EU level, it would be useful to experiment with it at country level. At that level, the number of market operators would be greater and the allocation of permits may raise smaller political problems. A market in deficit permits for regional and local governments could help combine the limits set by the SGP for the general government balance with the flexibility required to allow for different investment needs. Moreover, the permit system seems better suited to financing investments than to buffering the budgetary effects of the business cycle.

1.7 FINAL REMARKS

At the time of writing, the Stability and Growth Pact has been in operation for three years. It is still too early to draw definitive conclusions on its effectiveness in shaping the fiscal policy of euro area members. Nevertheless, experience up to now indicates that the EMU fiscal policy framework is working. Gloomy predictions of an 'opportunistic' budgetary consolidation by prospective euro area members during their run-up to EMU, followed by a return to fiscal profligacy once in the single currency proved wrong. The improvement in budgetary positions has continued in recent years and the 3 per cent of GDP reference point has come to be seen as a 'hard ceiling'.

While the Pact is so far working as predicted, a number of issues remain to be addressed:

(a)   The SGP tends to function asymmetrically. While an excess over the 3 per cent ceiling is sanctioned, there is no apparent reward for appropriate budgetary behaviour in 'good times'. In particular, the political temptation to give away the automatic fruit of growth by curbing the operation of the automatic stabilisers may prove irresistible. Furthermore, the SGP does not encompass incentives for carrying out structural reforms (such as pension reforms) which may be costly in the short run, but enhance discipline in the longer period. The feasibility of alternative rules, such as the tradable deficit idea, remains untested.

(b)   The extent to which the SGP will function as an effective coordination device between fiscal authorities and between them and the single monetary policy is an open question. It also remains to be seen whether the SGP model of 'negative', rule-type coordination will evolve into a more active form of coordination.

(c)   The SGP's underlying philosophy is to choose an appropriate budgetary target and then let automatic stabilisers work freely. While such an 'automatic pilot' version of fiscal policy would avoid the pitfalls of Keynesian fine-tuning, it is not clear that it would provide a sufficient degree of cyclical smoothing, especially in countries with relatively low automatic stabilisers, in view of the larger requirements of fiscal stabilisation in EMU.

(d)   On more technical grounds, the issue of the most appropriate methodology for estimating cyclically adjusted budget balances remains open to discussion. National and international economic institutions have so far adopted different solutions and there is no consensus in academic circles. The uncertainty related to the estimation of the cyclically adjusted budget balance raises the issue of not only how to evaluate a situation in which the headline deficit drifts towards the 3 per cent of GDP threshold while the underlying budget balance may not show any significant deterioration, but also, conversely, how to prevent or correct a pro-cyclical loosening of fiscal policy in cyclical upswings 'masked' by the offsetting impact of automatic stabilisers.

(e)   The focus of the Pact is on making sure that budget balances provide a sufficient safety margin under the 3 per cent threshold. As deficits are credibly reduced, new priorities come to the fore. Incorporating long-run sustainability concerns, especially in view of the expected budgetary impact of ageing populations, and improving the 'quality' of public finances (reduction in the tax burden, restructuring of public spending) will be the next frontier for the implementation of the SGP.

(f)   Multilateral surveillance and peer pressure at the EU level proved effective in triggering the process of fiscal consolidation in the 1990s. However, budgetary procedures and institutions at the national level do not fully incorporate the constraints imposed by the new EU framework. While a number of countries have introduced 'domestic stability pacts', the degree to which local governments internalise the SGP discipline constraints varies across countries.

(g)   The gradual decline in public debt/GDP ratios represents a positive development, also in view of the looming budgetary pressures arising from population ageing. However, in the longer term, the disappearance of public debt as the typical risk-free asset may raise adjustment problems in financial markets.

(h)   Finally, particularly in the perspective of the enlargement of the
       EU, reconciling the 'close to balance' rule of the Pact with the
       high public investment needs of the new members – most of
       whom are still in a catching-up phase – may prove difficult.

The introduction of a single currency in many sovereign countries
poses new major challenges to fiscal policy. The SGP responds to
these challenges by setting a complex framework of rules and procedures. It aims at reconciling the concern for budgetary discipline with
the recognition of the need for fiscal stabilisation. It strikes a balance
between general rules applying at the EMU level and room for
manoeuvre at the national level. This book gives an extensive account
of these problems and developments.

By pointing to the issues which still remain open, the analyses
included in this volume also show that the definition of the fiscal
architecture of EMU is still in progress. Many aspects will be clarified
only as time goes by. The economic implications of the new rules are
also far from being fully understood. Identifying key issues and relevant trade-offs is essential for designing appropriate policy responses
at the EMU and at the national level. The aim of this book is to
provide the theoretical, empirical and institutional foundations to
undertake such a crucial task.

Part I
Does EMU Need Fiscal Rules?

2 Does EMU Need a Stability Pact?*

Roel Beetsma

2.1 INTRODUCTION

Fiscal rules are at the centre of the public policy debate. For example, in the United States, some years ago an attempt to impose a federal balanced-budget requirement only very narrowly failed to win Senate approval. New Zealand has its Fiscal Responsibility Act and the United Kingdom has its Code for Fiscal Stability. For the European Union members, the Maastricht Treaty imposes budgetary entrance criteria for participation in European Monetary Union (EMU). In particular, budget deficits should not be higher than the reference level of 3 per cent of GDP and (gross) public debt should not be higher than its reference level of 60 per cent of GDP. When these limits are exceeded, the actual values of the deficit or debt ratio should be close to their reference values and falling at a satisfactory pace. In fact, countries are supposed to adhere to these criteria not only before they enter EMU, but also when they already participate in EMU.

Of course, once a country has been admitted into EMU, it is much more difficult to enforce these fiscal rules upon that country, simply because it can no longer be excluded from participation. The Maastricht Treaty does not allow for countries to be expelled from EMU, neither does it specify how countries can be forced to adhere to the fiscal criteria. The fear that, once in EMU, countries might fall into fiscal profligacy again has led the (then) German Finance Minister, Theo Waigel, to propose a so-called Stability Pact.[1] The original proposal envisaged automatic fines for countries with excessive deficits. However, this idea was dropped and the eventual result, adopted at the Amsterdam Summit in 1997 as the Stability and Growth Pact

* I thank Anne Brunila for detailed comments on an earlier version of the chapter. I also thank the European Commission for providing me with data. The usual disclaimer applies.

(SGP), sets out a number of steps, starting from the observation of an 'excessive deficit', in which the severity of the sanctions gradually increases. In particular, if the European Council of Economics and Finance Ministers (ECOFIN Council) concludes that a country has an excessive deficit and it fails to adopt the appropriate measures to correct the deficit, then it may be required to submit a non-interest-bearing deposit. The deposit may be turned into a fine if the country remains in an excessive deficit position (see also Chapters 4 and 6).

Most commentators, especially those from the academic world, view the SGP with much scepticism.[2] Essentially, there are two sets of criticisms. The first set of criticisms questions the seriousness of the problem that the SGP is trying to address. In particular, the claim is that any potential cross-country spillovers of individual countries' budgetary policies cannot be very large. However, there is much uncertainty about the strength of international spillovers from fiscal policy, which, moreover, can take on different forms. For example, there may be direct spillovers on demand in other countries or on the interest rate, as well as indirect spillovers via the common monetary policy. It is also often argued that, even if these spillovers were serious, capital markets would discipline profligate governments by raising the interest rates on the debt they issue. However, the effectiveness of capital markets in disciplining governments is at best ambiguous (see Restoy, 1996, for a brief overview). Moreover, as Corsetti and Roubini (1993) note, higher interest rates did not prevent countries from pursuing unsustainable fiscal policies in the 1980s.

The second type of criticism concerns the specific design of the SGP itself. It is often argued that the numerical reference deficit level of 3 per cent is rather arbitrary. More important is that this upper bound is more likely to be binding when a country is in recession. As a result, people argue (for example, Eichengreen and Wyplosz, 1998) that such targets could hamper the operation of the automatic stabilisers and thus increase the volatility of output. This argument fails to do justice to the fact that the SGP also commits countries to balance their budgets in the medium run, thereby restoring fiscal flexibility. Once this is achieved, full use can be made of the automatic stabilisers (Buti and Sapir, 1998).

Another objection to the design of the Pact is that, given the numerical upper bound on the deficit, there is no prescription for how an excessive deficit is supposed to be corrected. The importance of this is underlined by some of the methods that countries have used to meet the budgetary criteria imposed by the Maastricht Treaty. In particular, many countries have resorted to 'creative accounting', for example, by reducing interest payments by issuing zero-coupon bonds (see Milesi-Ferretti, 1998). Of course, the fear is that countries would resort to similar measures to produce deficits that fulfil the requirements of the SGP. However, a Pact that imposes detailed rules on how budgetary corrections are to be achieved can be easily seen as further intrusion 'from Brussels' into national affairs. Moreover, the adherence to more detailed rules will be more difficult to monitor. In fact, the figures for the years preceding the take-off of EMU reveal that, although 'creative accounting' may have played a role, the bulk of the fiscal retrenchment reflected a genuine effort. It should be noted, though, that Italy and Belgium, the most heavily indebted countries, owe their spending reductions largely to reduced interest payments on their public debt.

This chapter tries to evaluate the overall usefulness of the SGP. The argument is developed in a number of steps. Section 2.2 assesses the danger of renewed fiscal profligacy in the future. This section also discusses the cross-country spillovers from more expansionary fiscal policies and how the failure to internalise these spillovers may exacerbate fiscal profligacy. Section 2.3 reviews some of the existing theoretical models of the SGP, as well as their incompleteness. Section 2.4 assesses the empirical evidence on the effectiveness of the fiscal rules that are used in practice (in particular, balanced-budget rules at the US state level). While section 2.5 evaluates the SGP in its current format, section 2.6 discusses potential improvements of the existing SGP as well as alternatives for the SGP. Finally, section 2.7 concludes this chapter.

2.2   RATIONALES FOR FISCAL RULES

By definition, the source of an *excessive* deficit must be some type of distortion. Generally speaking, then, the best way to get rid of excessive deficits is eliminate the underlying distortions. This requires the reform of political and economic institutions that are responsible for these distortions. However, such reforms are often hampered by public resistance, because it is usually specific groups in society that stand to lose from these reforms, while the benefits of reform are dispersed across society.

An alternative to attacking distortions head-on is to resort to some kind of fiscal rule. Such rules do exist and one of the most prominent examples is the balanced-budget rules at the state level in the USA.

These are self-imposed and there is no formal authority to enforce them. Nevertheless, experience suggests that, depending on their specific format, they exert a restraining influence on fiscal profligacy. Because of the absence of any formal enforcement mechanism, enforcement has to rely on the public support for these rules and the potential reactions of financial markets to the violation of these rules.

The SGP is quite different from the US state-level rules. It is imposed at a supranational level (because it has been adopted through a mutual agreement of all EU members) and, in principle at least, it will be supported by external enforcement. Because it comes into full force with sanctions once a country enters EMU, many commentators perceive a rationale for the SGP only if monetary unification exacerbates or causes adverse international spillovers from national fiscal policies. However, this view does not do sufficient justice to the SGP, because it may bind the hands of profligate domestic politicians even in the absence of any international fiscal spillovers.[3]

The remainder of this section briefly discusses the pattern of public debt since the end of the 1970s and asks whether there is a danger of renewed fiscal profligacy in the future. This is followed by a discussion of the potential cross-country spillovers arising from expansionary fiscal policies.

2.2.1   Are Fiscal Excesses Something of the Past?

From the end of the 1970s until the mid-1990s, many industrialised countries saw large build-ups of public debt. Figure 2.1 shows the (unweighted) average of the gross public debt over this period for the

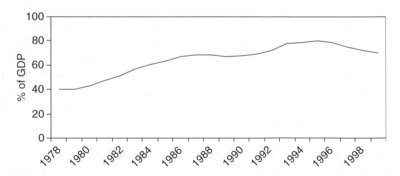

Figure 2.1   Average debt/GDP ratio

countries that participated in the year 2000 in EMU (excluding Luxembourg). Since the end of the 1970s the debt/GDP ratio doubled from around 40 per cent to a maximum of 80 per cent in 1995. Put in a wider historical perspective, this development was exceptional. Although large debt build-ups have occurred occasionally in the past, these build-ups were associated with exceptional circumstances (usually wars) and they were reverted when these circumstances were over. While the most recent debt build-up was sparked by the recession that followed the second oil crisis, debt remained high after the recession was over and rose further during the recession in the first half of the 1990s. In general, the observed pattern for public debt seems to be inconsistent with business cycle considerations.[4] Therefore, the literature has pointed to political economy explanations of this phenomenon (for example, see Roubini and Sachs, 1989b, who discuss a number of alternative political economy explanations and provide some empirical support for these).[5]

Since the mid-1990s EMU-wide averages of public debt and deficits have fallen. All of the current EMU members have reduced their deficits (Finland and Ireland even ran budgetary surpluses at the end of the 1990s), while most of them have also reduced their debt/GDP ratios. In particular, Italy and the smaller member states have been able to cut their public debt levels rather substantially. However, most of the larger states (in particular, France, Germany and Spain) show some (minor) increase in public debt since 1995.

It is hard to say to what extent these developments can be attributed to the fear of being excluded from participation in EMU. For example, Ireland's debt has been on a downward trend already since 1988. However, the fact that it is mostly the small countries (and thus the ones that could have been excluded from EMU easily) or those with extremely large debts (Italy and Belgium) that made serious reductions in public debt suggests that the Maastricht budgetary criteria have played a more than marginal role.

Suppose that there was no Stability Pact and that the EMU governments were completely free in their budgetary policies. Could one expect new excessive deficits and debt build-ups in the future? Because the threat of exclusion from EMU has disappeared, one disincentive for fiscal profligacy has disappeared. The largest threat to budgetary prudence are the costs associated with the ageing of the European populations.[6] These costs are mainly driven by the rise in the number of public pensions to be paid out and the increase in public health care costs. They also depend crucially on the way in which pension systems and health care systems are organised. In particular, countries with pensions largely financed on a pay-as-you-go basis can expect substantial difficulties in dealing with the ageing problem. Franco and Munzi (1999, Figure 9.16) project, under the assumption of *unchanged* policies, debt/GDP ratios over the period up to 2050 for Belgium, Denmark, Finland, Germany, Italy, the Netherlands, Spain and (non-EMU member) Sweden. Projections are made for a 'best' and a 'worst' scenario. They differ substantially over countries, with Belgium, the Netherlands and, especially, Germany in the danger zone.[7]

2.2.2   Do Fiscal Excesses Lead to Adverse International Spillovers?

In a monetary union, there are various (possible) ways in which fiscal expansions in one country can affect other countries. The first channel, and probably the one that the original drafters of the SGP had in mind, is that some country runs into budgetary trouble and that other countries or, more likely, the European Central Bank (ECB) will be forced to choose between a systemic collapse of the banking system (following a run on the country's debt) or a debt bail-out, with the ECB buying the country's debt (thereby supporting the price of the debt and protecting the banking system).[8] Such a fiscal bail-out is formally forbidden under the Maastricht Treaty, but *ex post*, when faced with this dilemma, everybody may agree that this is the least costly response to a debt crisis. The costs of the debt bail-out would then be shared by all EMU members. However, this leads to moral hazard because, knowing that they will be rescued by a bail-out, countries have less incentive to restrain debt accumulation. An alternative to a fiscal bail-out would be a monetary bail-out, in which the real value of the troubled country's outstanding debt would be eroded through an increase in inflation.

A second, more direct channel of international spillovers from fiscal policy is the upward effect (in the absence of Ricardian equivalence) of an increase in a country's public debt on the world real interest rate because the total demand for capital on the world market rises (see, for example, the models of Chang, 1990, and Canzoneri and Diba, 1991). Empirically, it is not clear how important the response of the real interest rate is, but it is unlikely that the policies of a small country or even a middle-sized country can have a substantial influence on the world real interest rate. However, it is precisely the weak link between a more expansionary fiscal policy and the level of the interest paid on the public debt that may give rise to fiscal profligacy.

The enhanced access to the world capital markets in the 1980s and the 1990s weakened this link and changed the cost–benefit trade-off of issuing an additional euro of debt. The cost in terms of higher interest payments has fallen and, hence, the incentive to issue additional debt has increased. For this reason, in an uncoordinated equilibrium, average debt and the real interest rate can be expected to rise further.[9]

The previous argument is not connected to EMU *per se*, because monetary unification in Europe has hardly affected its members' access to world capital markets. If the public debt from the various sources in the world is perfectly substitutable in the perception of private investors, then EMU as such would be irrelevant for the effect of fiscal expansions on interest rates. However, to the extent that investors are not risk-neutral, EMU is likely to strengthen intra-European interest-rate spillovers because the substitutability of the public debt of its members increases (for example, through the elimination of exchange rate risk or because of economic shocks becoming more similar). In response to an increase in an individual member's debt, investors would only be willing to keep the other euro members' debt in their portfolios (and thus forgo diversification gains) if they are compensated by a sufficient increase in the average European interest rate. This spillover effect caused by monetary unification would provide an argument for fiscal restrictions on euro area governments.

A third type of international spillovers is based on the standard Mundell–Fleming argument that fiscal policy is more effective under fixed than under floating exchange rates (see also Chapter 12). Under EMU, the effects of a unilateral fiscal expansion on employment are no longer offset by exchange rate appreciations *vis-à-vis* the other union participants. Hence, the stimulus to employment from a unilateral fiscal expansion is larger and, therefore, more tempting for governments, especially prior to elections. Fiscal expansions put upward pressure on prices and force the ECB to tighten monetary policy. This has a contractionary effect on the other economies in the union.

2.3 THEORETICAL MODELS OF FISCAL LIMITS

2.3.1 Existing Models

A fully fledged theoretical analysis of the SGP would be complicated, because of the large number of specific features of the Pact. These

include the rather lengthy process (which involves voting and negotiations by EU member countries) that takes place between observing an excessive deficit and actually imposing sanctions if a country
persists in running excessive deficits. They also include the specific
sanctions menu and the Stability and Convergence Programmes that
EMU members are supposed to adhere to. Therefore, it is not
surprising that existing papers focus only on specific aspects of the
Pact. In fact, many papers focus on fiscal limits in general and try
to use their results to say something about the desirability of the
actual SGP. This section will discuss some of the relevant theoretical
models.

An early attempt to model the SGP is provided by Beetsma and
Uhlig (1999). They present a two-period model of monetary union
with myopic governments in the first period. Governments are myopic
because at the start of the second period they may be replaced by
another government with different preferences regarding public
spending.[10] Such myopia induces the first-period government to
issue more debt than a social planner would choose. Nevertheless,
because an increase in debt has adverse repercussions for the future
monetary policy, first-period governments are at least to some extent
restrained in their fiscal profligacy. However, if countries with myopic
governments form a monetary union, the adverse effect of a unilateral
debt increase on the common future monetary policy is diluted.
Therefore, the incentive to restrain debt accumulation is diminished
in a monetary union and, hence, the excessiveness of debt will be
exacerbated.[11] Thus, the spillover effect is that an individual increase
in public debt leads to a looser common monetary policy which affects
all the union participants.

The stability pact in Beetsma and Uhlig (1999) is modelled as a
fixed fine ψ for each additional unit of debt that is issued. Hence, the
stability pact raises the price of current public consumption relative to
the price of future public consumption. By setting an appropriate
value of ψ, individual governments are induced to properly internalise
the externalities of their individual debt policies. This way debt policies under monetary union will be the same as under national monetary policy-making. Actually, if one sets ψ even higher, one can
reproduce the social planner's outcomes.

Closely related to Beetsma and Uhlig (1999) is the work by Chari
and Kehoe (1998) who explore the need for debt restrictions in a two-
country model of monetary union. Restrictions on public debt are
needed in the absence of commitment by the union's central bank,

because union members do not fully internalise the welfare effects of an increase in nominal debt on the common union-wide inflation rate. In contrast to Beetsma and Uhlig (1999), Chari and Kehoe (1998) focus on rigid debt ceilings rather than gradually increasing fines for running higher debts. Moreover, the externality via the common inflation rate of a change in individual debt levels does not rely on political short-sightedness which is exacerbated in a monetary union. Giovannetti, Marimon and Teles (1997) extend the model of Chari and Kehoe (1998) into various directions. In particular, they allow for differences in initial debt levels and, therefore, differences in the most preferred monetary policy across countries.

All the papers mentioned so far have in common that the union's central bank is not only concerned with low inflation, but with other objectives as well. If the central bank was only concerned with maintaining low inflation in these models, then there would be no cross-country spillovers and, hence, there would be no reason to have a stability pact. Debrun (2000), in contrast, provides a rationale for short-run (deficit-based) fiscal constraints, in spite of the assumption that the ECB is totally committed to its inflation objective (as it should be according to the letter of the Maastricht Treaty). Crucial for this result is that countries' fiscal policies affect aggregate demand and supply and, hence, the equilibrium price level in the monetary union. The policy game is as follows. First, a 'fiscal principle' decides on a set of fiscal rules (that is, it offers governments a performance contract, with a pay-off dependent on the realised deficit).[12] Then, each government appoints a delegate to the ECB. This is followed by nominal wage contracting. After this, supply shocks occur. Finally, governments and the fiscal authorities simultaneously select their policy stances. In particular, monetary policy is set by a majority vote among the delegates.

The model features a lack of commitment both in monetary policy and in fiscal policy. A public deficit *bias* arises for two reasons.[13] First, governments try to stimulate aggregate demand by expanding fiscal policy. However, *ex post* these attempts are fruitless, because the ECB reacts by tightening its monetary policy. Second, they use deficits to move the common inflation rate into the direction they individually prefer: if they perceive the ECB's inflation target to be too tight, they manipulate fiscal policy to boost aggregate demand further, which in turn boosts inflation. In equilibrium these attempts will be fruitless too, because they are anticipated. To reduce the welfare loss associated with the second source of deficit bias, the delegates that the governments select for the ECB are 'liberal' (that is, they are less hawkish on inflation). As a result, the inflation rate ultimately selected by the ECB will be more in line with the governments' preferences. Hence, by appointing the appropriate delegates to the ECB's board, one source of deficit bias is eliminated or at least reduced. The remaining distortions in the model can then be addressed by means of a complete fiscal contract imposed at the start of the game. The optimal contract needs to be country-specific in order to take account of differences in preferences (about inflation and the trade-offs between inflation and output or deficits) across governments, differences in the effects of fiscal expansions on the economies, differences in labour market distortions and the different relative weights of countries' delegates in monetary policy decisions. Even aside from these cross-country differences, the optimal contract is rather complicated.

2.3.2   What Is Missing in Existing Models?

Existing models have so far failed to address some important aspects of the SGP. First, many models contain only two periods, which means that it is not really possible to make a meaningful distinction between deficits and debt. A longer modelling horizon would enable us to investigate in a systematic way the relative merits of sanctions based on debts versus sanctions based on dèficits (see below).

Second, the potential enforcement problems, which many observers deem to be important, have not been addressed in existing models. Unlike the original German proposal for a stability pact (see Chapter 4), sanctions will not be automatically imposed when an excessive deficit is observed, but can only be imposed after a rather lengthy procedure involving the discretion of the ECOFIN Council.[14] A careful analysis of the potential problems associated with enforcement should therefore take into account the specifics of this procedure together with its political economy aspects.

Third, and related to the previous point, the existing literature only partly takes into account the costs of violating the rules of the Pact. In particular, not-directly-measurable costs, such as the possible loss of political prestige in the case of a breach of the Pact's rules, have not been explicitly taken into account in existing models. Potential reactions of financial markets, who may lose confidence and, hence, charge higher interest rates, are also neglected.

2.4 EMPIRICAL SUPPORT FOR EXISTING FISCAL RULES

While the formal models reviewed in the previous section are generally fairly supportive of the SGP, this conclusion may well emerge from the fact that formal models find it hard to include all the relevant aspects of the SGP. To shed some more light on the potential usefulness of the SGP, it would be helpful to assess the empirical evidence on the effects of comparable existing rules. One source of evidence comes from the US states, which, except for Vermont, all have some type of balanced-budget requirement. The requirements can be divided into three groups, depending on the stage in the budget process at which balance is required (for a detailed description, see Poterba, 1996). Ranked in terms of increasing stringency, the first group of rules requires the governor to submit a balanced budget (44 states), the second group requires the legislature to enact a balanced budget (37 states), while the last group prohibits deficit carry-forward (24 out of the previous group's 37 states) if expectations and realisations differ from each other. The general fund, or state operating budget, is almost always subject to a balanced-budget rule, while this is less frequently the case for special funds that receive earmarked tax revenue or that are used to fund specific programmes. As a result, there is substantial variation across states in the fraction of spending affected by balanced-budget rules.

There is some empirical evidence that these subnational balanced-budget rules are more effective the more stringent they are. In particular, deficits tend to be lower and the reaction to adverse shocks tends to be faster when the fiscal constraints are tighter. Alt and Lowry (1994), for the period 1986–97, explore how fiscal policy reacts in the case of a deficit (which under a balanced-budget rule happens when realisations of expenditures or taxes do not match their planned levels). The response to a one-dollar deficit in Republican-controlled states drops from 77 cents (either through a spending cut or a tax increase) for states with a prohibition on deficit carry-overs to 31 cents for states without such a prohibition. For Democratic-controlled states, the figures are 34 cents and 40 cents, respectively. Bohn and Inman (1995), using a panel data set covering almost all states and a sample period of more than twenty years, find that rules that restrict end-of-year budget deficits lead to a statistically significant reduction in state general-fund deficits. Poterba (1994) compares reactions to fiscal shocks of states with weak anti-deficit rules and states with strong anti-deficit rules. While a one-dollar deficit overrun triggers a 17-cent spending cut in the former group, it triggers a 44-cent spending cut by the latter group. Tax changes in response to deficit overruns do not seem to differ for the two groups.

What does the evidence on the effectiveness of the US subnational budgetary rules say about the effectiveness of the SGP? On the one hand, the EMU members have much larger tax-raising powers and better access to world capital markets than the US states. Therefore, EMU governments may be less worried about running high deficits. In addition, the public support for the state-level budgetary rules in the USA is probably stronger than the public support in Europe for the SGP. Therefore, violation of the SGP criteria may be politically less harmful. On the other hand, while there is no external enforcement for state-level rules in the USA, the SGP can in principle count on supranational enforcement. Even abstracting from the possibility of pecuniary sanctions, peer pressure from other EMU countries may act as an enforcement mechanism.

As far as the effect on fiscal flexibility is concerned, the US evidence shows that the fiscal restrictions come at the cost of restraining anti-cyclical policies (for example, Bayoumi and Eichengreen, 1995). However, as shown by Alesina and Bayoumi (1996), the reduced budget flexibility has hardly any effect on output variability. They offer two possible explanations for this result. First, the stabilising role of fiscal policy at the state level may simply not be important, in which case it is hard to draw any inference from the US experience for the effect of the SGP on national output variability in Europe. The other possibility is that fiscal restrictions not only limit the positive effects of anti-cyclical policies, but that they also restrict politically motivated and biased policies which may have a destabilising effect on output. If this is indeed the case, then this provides support for imposing such rules also in the EMU context.

2.5   AN EVALUATION OF THE PACT

As argued above, if there is a danger of fiscal excesses, the first-best strategy is to solve the problem at its origin and reform the procedures governing the budget process. Given that this may be difficult to accomplish, the alternative is to impose some kind of fiscal rule. This step requires that two conditions be fulfilled. First, the problem that the rule is supposed to target is first-order. Second, given that the problem is first-order, the rule should do more good than harm. In section 2, I have argued that, in the absence of fiscal restrictions, one cannot exclude the possibility of future high deficits or debt levels. The danger of being excluded from EMU has vanished, while most of the participants or candidates for participation in the future face steeply increasing costs associated with the ageing of their populations. Given the uncertainty about future economic performances and the uncertainty inherent in current demographic projections, it is hard to predict whether fiscal rules will indeed be needed to contain fiscal profligacy. In principle, however, they can play a useful role in ruling out unfortunate eventualities. Moreover, experiences in various countries, for example Germany and Italy, show how hard it is to reach consensus on pension reform. Supranationally imposed fiscal rules combined with peer pressure from other governments may provide a government with useful external pressure to reform its pension systems.

Whether monetary unification *per se* enhances the need for fiscal rules is hard to answer. Section 2 discussed a number of fiscal policy spillovers that could potentially become stronger after monetary unification. Whether these are important is ultimately an empirical question. Nevertheless, the consequences of a debt bail-out or, probably much worse, a refusal to bail out, seem too serious to be ignored, even though this is an unlikely event.

Given the need for a fiscal rule, the question is whether the SGP, as it is currently designed, would be the appropriate rule to address the problem of possible fiscal excesses. The theoretical models reviewed in section 4 generally conclude in favour of having a Pact. However, they are at most very stylised representations of the actual SGP and (as already pointed out) they often lack the features of the actual Pact that so many people worry about. At present, the theoretical literature cannot pass any clear verdict on the SGP. Neither can the empirical literature reviewed in section 4. Therefore, the pros and cons of the SGP need to be assessed using qualitative arguments.

2.5.1 Strong Features of the Pact's Design

Probably, the natural starting point of any discussion about fiscal rules is that there is no 'perfect' rule (that is, one that has no disadvantages) and certainly not one that is also politically acceptable. However, although the 3 per cent deficit norm appears rather arbitrary, it has some major advantages. It is simple and precise (see also Willett, 1999), so that it is easy to establish, both by the general public and by other governments or supranational authorities, whether it has been violated. In reality, the disciplining effect of such a rule is not so much the threat of having to pay a fine (many commentators view the enforcement as uncertain and the amount of time that elapses between observing an excessive deficit and imposing a fine is in any case quite long), rather than a loss of prestige for the government. It is the pressure from the public and the peer pressure from other countries that makes the SGP most effective. Hence, the mechanism by which the SGP (should) acquire its credibility is quite similar to the mechanism that gives a central bank its credibility. Although some central banks have explicit performance contracts (for example, with the government in the case of the United Kingdom), their credibility largely depends on their prestige with the financial markets and the general public. Important examples are the Bundesbank in the period before EMU and the Federal Reserve Bank in the USA.

The credibility of the SGP is strengthened by the requirement that EU member states set medium-term budgetary targets that are close to balance or in surplus (see Chapter 6). EMU member states have to annually and publicly present Stability Programmes, while non-EMU member states have to submit Convergence Programmes. Their implementation is monitored by the European Council, which may give recommendations for corrections (that can be made public). As pointed out in Chapter 7 below, these programmes can serve as an early-warning signal if there is a danger of excessively rising deficits. Corrections can be taken early on and should be less difficult to implement than when the Excessive Deficit Procedure has already been set in motion.

2.5.2 Potential Weaknesses in the Pact's Design

The main objection commonly made against the SGP is that it reduces fiscal flexibility. In particular, the SGP may prevent automatic stabilisers from doing their job. Although this is a potentially serious disadvantage, it is mitigated by a number of factors. First, sanctions will be waived when GDP falls by at least 2 per cent and they may or may not be waived if GDP falls by between 0.75 and 2 per cent, depending on whether convincing evidence can be presented about the exceptionality of the economic downturn. Second, the time that elapses from the observation of an excessive deficit until the payment of a fine is at least two years, which should be enough to overcome a normal recession. Third, going from the detection of an excessive deficit to the actual pecuniary sanctions involves a number of steps at which the whole procedure may actually be stopped or, more likely, some political compromise is reached (in which case the country agrees to do some of the necessary adjustment, but does not have to do all of it). Finally, and most important, governments are supposed to run budgets that are in balance or in surplus in the medium run. A structural deficit that is around zero thus allows a cyclical deficit of 3 per cent before the SGP starts to bite.

Eichengreen and Wyplosz (1998) show that cyclical deficits of more than 3 per cent have been rare in the past. Moreover, the historical evidence for the EU countries presented in Buti, Franco and Ongena (1998) suggests that the undisciplined (that is, high-debt) countries did not have more budgetary flexibility in responding to output gaps than the more disciplined countries. On the contrary, high-debt countries have failed to pursue counter-cyclical policies when output gaps were positive. Hence, a stability pact which induces countries to run structural deficits close to zero may actually buy more fiscal flexibility.

Of course, the question is how to make the transition from a situation of structural deficits to a medium-term budget that is close to balance or in surplus, without in the meantime violating the excessive deficit criterion. Indeed, Canzoneri and Diba (Chapter 3) present this as an important objection against the SGP. According to them, the problem is not so much that there would not be any need for *some* type of fiscal rule. Their scepticism primarily concerns the specific design of the SGP. Its restrictions on deficits would be especially harmful in the short run, when governments are still trying to reduce their structural deficits. Violation of the reference deficit level would induce them to put pressure on the ECB to relax its policies. This would undermine its credibility, which is the opposite of what the SGP is supposed to achieve.[15] One solution is to interpret the formal sanctions prescribed by the Pact less strictly in the shorter run, but to pay more attention to the Stability Programmes and, hence, to the plans to achieve the appropriate budgetary targets in the medium run.[16]

The potential uncertainty about the enforcement of the SGP and the length of its procedure may create problems of its own. First, it enhances the chance that truly undisciplined countries escape sanctions. Second, as a consequence of the length of the procedure, sanctions may actually hit the successor of the misbehaving government.[17] Third, countries that try to push the implementation of the Excessive Deficit Procedure on some other country may become a target for retaliation in other areas of European Union policy-making. Fourth, there may be bias in the sense that, *ceteris paribus*, enforcement of the Pact on small countries is more likely than enforcement on large countries. Finally, the fact that sanctions only materialise after substantial bargaining may induce governments to forgo budgetary reform if they perceive that through bargaining they can escape part of the sanctions. Moreover, as Buiter and Sibert (1997) argue, if a less restrained fiscal policy has relatively large negative international spillovers, a country's bargaining power increases by not making any reforms, because a breakdown of the bargaining process would lead to greater damage for the other countries. While all these objections sound reasonable, the Excessive Deficit Procedure should be viewed as a rather unlikely event if the Stability Programmes of the Pact are sufficiently closely monitored.

The final set of objections concern the 'bluntness' of the SGP, because it only puts a limit on the public deficits, while leaving governments free to choose how to stay below the limit. This could affect the behaviour of governments. In particular, they may be tempted to respond to an excessive deficit by raising taxes rather than cutting spending,[18] or cutting spending on public investment instead of spending on public consumption. In addition, they can resort to 'creative accounting', as some of them did extensively in the run-up to EMU.

Let us address these worries one by one. Figure 2.2 (based on data from the Economist Intelligence Unit) displays the (unweighted)

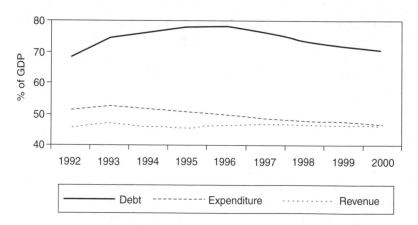

Figure 2.2   Debt, expenditures and revenues after Maastricht

averages of public debt, cyclically adjusted public spending and cyclically adjusted revenues for the EMU participants (excluding Ireland
and Luxemburg) since 1992. This is roughly the transition period
between Maastricht and EMU. While debt rose during the first couple
of years since Maastricht, it stabilised around 1995 and has been on a
downward trend since then. As far as the choice between lower
spending and higher revenues is concerned, the figures from 1995
onwards show that by far most of the adjustment burden has been on
the former. Revenues have hardly increased over the period, while
expenditures have fallen by around 3 percentage points.

Next, consider the composition of public spending. Tables 2.1–2.4
give both total public spending as well as public spending separated
into public consumption, non-consumption spending and interest
expenditure over the period 1995–99, that is, the period during
which countries became most serious in trying to fulfil the entry
criteria for EMU. Again, total spending has been cyclically corrected.
Under the assumption that all the cyclical fluctuations in public
spending are concentrated in non-consumption spending (which
includes transfers, for example to the unemployed), the latter has
also been corrected for the business cycle, while the other spending
categories are left unadjusted. Of course, this assumption is only an

Table 2.1   Total public spending in the euro area (% of GDP;
cyclically corrected)

	1995	*1996*	*1997*	*1998*	*1999*
Belgium	53.6	53.5	52.2	51.3	51.1
Germany	55.3	49.5	48.5	47.9	47.9
Spain	45.3	44.1	42.7	42.4	41.3
France	53.9	54.0	53.4	52.5	52.4
Ireland	40.5	38.7	37.2	35.1	35.4
Italy	53.3	53.0	50.9	49.4	48.9
Luxembourg	N.A.	N.A.	N.A.	N.A.	N.A.
Netherlands	55.3	48.4	47.2	46.5	46.3
Austria	54.5	54.0	51.3	51.8	51.5
Portugal	43.9	44.7	44.0	43.9	45.1
Finland	56.2	56.2	54.0	51.0	49.9
Euro area	53.5	50.8	49.5	48.7	48.4

Note: Euro area is the weighted average over all countries. N.A. stands for
not available.
Source: European Commission Services.

Table 2.2   Public consumption in the euro area (% of GDP)

	1995	1996	1997	1998	1999
Belgium	21.5	21.8	21.3	21.2	21.4
Germany	19.8	19.9	19.5	19.1	19.0
Spain	18.1	18.0	17.6	17.6	17.5
France	23.9	24.2	24.2	23.5	23.7
Ireland	16.4	15.8	15.2	14.5	14.0
Italy	17.9	18.1	18.2	18.0	18.1
Luxembourg	18.2	18.8	17.8	17.2	17.5
Netherlands	24.0	23.1	22.9	22.9	23.1
Austria	20.3	20.1	19.5	19.6	19.9
Portugal	18.6	18.9	19.2	19.3	20.1
Finland	22.8	23.2	22.4	21.6	21.5
Euro area	20.6	20.7	20.4	20.1	20.1

Note: Euro area is the weighted average over all countries.
Source: European Commission Services.

Table 2.3   Non-consumption public spending in the euro area (% of GDP)

	1995	1996	1997	1998	1999
Belgium	22.8	22.8	22.8	22.4	22.5
Germany	31.8	25.9	25.4	25.2	25.3
Spain	22.0	20.8	20.3	20.4	20.3
France	26.3	25.8	25.5	25.3	25.4
Ireland	18.6	18.4	17.8	17.1	19.0
Italy	23.9	23.4	23.4	23.3	23.9
Luxembourg	N.A.	N.A.	N.A.	N.A.	N.A.
Netherlands	25.4	19.7	19.1	18.7	18.7
Austria	30.0	29.7	27.9	28.4	28.0
Portugal	19.0	20.4	20.6	21.1	21.8
Finland	29.3	28.7	27.3	25.7	25.0
Euro area	27.4	24.5	24.0	23.9	24.0

Note: Euro area is the weighted average over all countries. N.A. stands for not available.
Source: European Commission Services.

approximation (for example, consumption spending includes public sector wage payments, which may be cyclically sensitive). Total public spending for the euro area as a whole fell by 5.1 percentage points from 53.5 per cent of GDP in 1995 to 48.4 per cent of GDP in 1999. Most of this fall is accounted for by the 3.4 percentage-point reduc-

Table 2.4   Interest spending in the euro area (% of GDP)

	1995	1996	1997	1998	1999
Belgium	9.3	8.9	8.1	7.7	7.2
Germany	3.7	3.7	3.6	3.6	3.5
Spain	5.2	5.4	4.8	4.3	3.6
France	3.8	3.9	3.7	3.6	3.4
Ireland	5.4	4.6	4.2	3.4	2.5
Italy	11.5	11.5	9.4	8.1	6.9
Luxembourg	0.4	0.4	0.3	0.4	0.3
Netherlands	5.9	5.6	5.2	4.9	4.5
Austria	4.3	4.2	3.9	3.8	3.6
Portugal	6.2	5.3	4.2	3.5	3.2
Finland	4.0	4.3	4.3	3.7	3.5
Euro area	5.5	5.6	5.1	4.7	4.3

Note: Euro area is the weighted average over all countries.
Source: European Commission Services.

tion in non-consumption spending. Interest spending accounts for 1.2 percentage points of the fall and consumption spending for 0.5 percentage points.[19]

A commonly voiced fear is that forced reductions in public spending mainly take place at the cost of the spending categories that are least politically sensitive, in particular public investment. The question thus is how much of the fall in non-consumption spending can be attributed to a reduction in public investment. Table 2.5 reports the public investment figures. For the euro area as a whole, public investment has only fallen marginally over the period 1995–99. Hence, the potential fear that budgetary adjustment would be achieved by squeezing out public investments is not confirmed by the data for the euro area as a whole.[20]

It is interesting to consider Belgium and Italy in isolation. These were (and are) the countries with the highest public debt levels and probably the ones most in need of budgetary tightening. In Belgium public spending fell by 2.5 percentage points over the period 1995–99, while in Italy it fell by 4.4 percentage points. However, public consumption and non-consumption spending hardly (for Belgium) or not all (for Italy) contributed to the reduction in total spending. Instead, rather than through deliberate policies by their governments, the fall in spending in Belgium and Italy was driven by reduced interest spending (caused by the fall in interest rates during the years preceding

EMU). This suggests that fiscal norms such as those included in the Maastricht Treaty and in the SGP are less effective for severely indebted countries.

How serious is the argument that the SGP may lead to 'creative accounting'? It is well-known that many countries have resorted to 'fiddles' to achieve the Maastricht budgetary criteria. Even so, the SGP is supposed to remain in existence as long as EMU lasts. Because there are limits to the amount of creative accounting that can be done (for example, there is a natural limit to the amount of revenues that can be generated from privatising state industries), it seems unlikely that countries can systematically resort to creative accounting in order to avoid excessive deficits.

2.6   ALTERNATIVES FOR THE EXISTING PACT

The previous section has argued that there may be a useful role for a stability pact and that the objections that have been put forward can probably be dealt with in a satisfactory way. Nevertheless, from a purely economic perspective, a better design of the SGP could have been possible. This is the issue addressed in this section. In addition, I will discuss some alternatives to the SGP.

2.6.1   Potential Improvements of the SGP

One possibility would have been to make the reference deficit levels contingent on the state of the economy. A simple contingency rule would have been easy to design. For example, instead of a reference deficit level of 3 per cent under (almost) all circumstances, the reference deficit level $\bar{d}_t$ in any period t could be set at:

$$\bar{d}_t = \bar{d}^n + \beta(\bar{y}_t - y_t), \quad \text{if } y_t < \bar{y}_t, \tag{2.1}$$

and $\bar{d}_t = \bar{d}^n$ if $y_t \geq \bar{y}_t$, where $\bar{y}_t$ is the (log of the) natural output level in period t, y_t is the (log of the) output level and $\bar{d}^n$ is the reference deficit level under economically neutral circumstances (that is, when $y_t = \bar{y}_t$). Parameter β could be set at the cross-country average sensitivity of the budget to the output gap. For a given year, the Excessive Deficit Procedure would only be activated when the actual deficit exceeds $\bar{d}_t$. Therefore, the reference deficit level under neutral circumstances could actually be set below the 3 per cent level. Given that governments are supposed to have their budget in balance or close to balance in the medium run, after an initial transition period of some years, $\bar{d}^n$ could be set at 1 per cent of GDP, say.

The adoption of a contingent rule like (2.1) faces several problems, however. One is that $\bar{y}_t$ is not directly observable. Therefore, it would be hard to agree what the relevant natural output level and, thus, the relevant output gap would be. Second, the rule may lead to moral hazard: governments have less incentive to conduct structural reforms, in particular those that make labour markets more flexible. Such reforms reduce the difference between $\bar{y}_t$ and y_t in an economic downturn, but they are often politically costly and under (2.1) they raise the likelihood that a given deficit will be considered excessive (see also Beetsma and Jensen, 2000).

An alternative way to address the 'flexibility problem' of fiscal policy would have been to formulate the fiscal limits in terms of debt/GDP ratio, rather than deficit/GDP ratio. Several arguments can be advanced in favour of either of the two approaches. Deficit-based sanctions act as an immediate check on governments' behaviour and help to avoid current governments being punished for bad policies conducted by their predecessors (at least if the lag between observing an excessive deficit and imposing a sanction is not too long). Moreover, as Perotti *et al.* (1998) argue, (changes in) deficits have stronger predictive power about future budgetary developments than debt has and are thus more relevant for assessing the risk that public finances become unsustainable.[21]

As is often argued, a debt-based pact rewards policies that are on average prudent, but allows for temporary increases in deficits if economic conditions are exceptionally problematic. This may be quite important for countries with a large government sector. Although the deficits of these countries are not necessarily higher on average than those of other countries, they are more volatile and therefore run a higher risk of falling in the range where they are considered excessive according to the SGP.[22] Of course, this problem has been recognised, by allowing the 3 per cent deficit limit to be temporarily exceeded if a country experiences a large fall in output. In addition, within the SGP framework countries with large government sectors, such as Sweden and Finland, have adopted more ambitious medium-term targets (instead of setting a close-to-balance target they target on significant budget surpluses; for example, see OECD (2000, Table I.7), which reports the projected budget targets for the coming years).[23]

A second argument in favour of a debt-based pact is that public indebtedness provides a better measure for the existing stock of credibility problems and, hence, for the potential pressure on the central bank to relax its monetary policy. This is especially true if the main concern is the potential political pressure on the ECB to lower interest rates (see Chapter 3). Such pressures are not unlikely, given that a small reduction in the interest rate can make a lot of difference to the budget of a heavily indebted government. A final argument in support of a debt-based pact is that deficit-based sanctions become effective only after some time and are lifted as soon as the excessive deficit has been corrected. A sequence of temporarily high and temporarily moderate deficits might go unchecked by any sanctions while still giving rise to an upward trend in the public debt.

Of course, countries have entered EMU with very different debt/GDP ratios. The obvious way to deal with this problem would have been to set time paths of debt limits that depend on the initial indebtedness. The path could be made conditional on GDP growth as well. It would be downward-sloping (although not too steep) for highly indebted countries, until it reaches some level that would remain the upper bound from then onwards. If the sanctions for breaching the limit path are credible, governments are induced to drive their debt sufficiently far below the limit path. This would provide them with sufficient leeway to run deficits larger than 3 per cent in economic downturns without the fear of incurring sanctions.

2.6.2 Alternative Fiscal Rules

So far, this chapter has discussed possible modifications to the Pact that would leave unaffected the feature that restrictions are imposed on the overall budgetary situation. An excessive deficit may be eliminated through spending cuts or through tax increases. Arguably, countries with a large government sector should resort to spending cuts. However, especially for these countries, the share of the population benefiting from high spending may be relatively large and, therefore, such measures would be politically hard to push through. Hence, the need to adhere to the Pact may actually result in higher taxes, thereby exacerbating the distortions that already exist in the economy. As discussed earlier, a possible weakness of the Pact perceived by some people is that it fails to distinguish among the various ways in which an excessive deficit can be avoided.

Milesi-Ferretti (1998) analyses a model in which unrestricted policy-making may result in a deficit bias because the government in the model is myopic. He compares budget rules to spending rules and argues that, *a priori*, it is not clear which one dominates the other in terms of social welfare. The disadvantage of a limit on spending is that, with a myopic government, it still leads to a deficit bias and, therefore, to a suboptimal *inter*temporal distribution of tax distortions (current tax rates are reduced at the expense of higher tax rates in the future). Moreover, the *intra*temporally optimal trade-off between spending and revenue decisions in response to economic shocks is distorted.

Even if there is a consensus about the necessity to cut public spending, there may still be disagreement about the composition of the spending cuts. As discussed earlier, from the perspective of political feasibility, it is generally easier to reduce public investment than public consumption or government transfers. Those who benefit from the last two spending categories can be more clearly identified, while, moreover, the benefits from maintaining a given level of public investment only materialise in the future. Although the data for the years in the run-up to EMU do not reveal a tendency to squeeze out public investment to meet the Maastricht criteria (see Table 2.5), one can

Table 2.5   Public investment spending in the euro area (% of GDP)

	1995	1996	1997	1998	1999
Belgium	1.75	1.61	1.59	1.54	1.80
Germany	2.29	2.13	1.89	1.81	1.85
Spain	3.72	3.12	3.09	3.35	3.30
France	3.26	3.21	2.96	2.90	2.90
Ireland	2.31	2.38	2.46	2.69	2.64
Italy	2.13	2.21	2.25	2.41	2.55
Luxembourg	4.56	4.67	4.25	4.59	4.51
Netherlands	2.96	3.13	2.90	3.04	3.05
Austria	3.04	2.82	1.95	1.86	1.86
Portugal	3.73	4.15	4.38	4.03	4.17
Finland	2.77	2.87	3.17	2.87	2.77
Euro area	2.68	2.58	2.42	2.43	2.48

Note: Euro area is the weighted average over all countries.
Source: European Commission Services.

never rule out the prospect of short-sighted governments that care very little about public investment.

A *capital budgeting rule* is designed to address this problem. It says that an additional euro of deficit has to be met by an additional euro of public investment. Dur (2000) and Pelletier, Dur and Swank (1999) compare the performance of a deficit rule and a capital-budgeting rule in a model that yields a deficit bias in the absence of fiscal restrictions. The deficit bias arises because the current government knows that in the future it may be replaced by another government with different preferences regarding the composition of public spending.[24] Hence, the incumbent government will increase current spending at the expense of future spending. One way to shift resources from the future to the present is by running a high deficit (or issuing a large amount of debt, which is the same, given that their analysis is conducted in the context of a two-period model). A budget restriction eliminates this channel. As a result, the incumbent government tries to find alternative channels to shift resources intertemporally. In particular, to increase current public consumption, the government reduces public investment, the benefits of which only materialise in the future, when they may be appropriated by a government of a different type. Hence, budget restrictions can be counterproductive in this sense. This leads the authors to argue in favour of a capital-budgeting rule which restricts deficits to the amount of public investment. Presumably, this was also what the drafters of the Maastricht Treaty had in mind. At the time that it was negotiated, public investment in Europe was approximately 3 per cent of GDP, the reference level for deficits.

Unfortunately, a capital-budgeting rule has at least two disadvantages. First, it does not allow the government to shift (part of) the returns on public investment to the present. Obviously, this could violate the smoothing of public consumption over time. Second, the distinction between public consumption and public investment is often not clear.[25] Hence, a fiscally profligate government would have an incentive to disguise public consumption as public investment.

2.6.3 Tradable Deficit Permits

Casella (see Chapter 16) proposes a market-based system of tradable deficit permits to induce fiscal discipline. The idea is inspired by the experience with tradable pollution permits in the United States. In each year a ceiling is set for the overall deficit of the monetary union.

This determines the total supply of deficit permits. Then each country gets a initial number of deficit permits which can be freely traded with other countries. Hence, if the ceiling on the overall deficit in the euro area is set at 3 per cent, a country could exceed the 3 per cent level by buying additional deficit permits from other countries.

As Casella argues, such a system has several advantages. First, unlike the current SGP, it is able to deal with differences between countries because additional deficit permits will be bought by the countries that need them most. Second, countries also have the possibility to save permits for future use. Third, the system is transparent. Fourth, it rewards good behaviour, because countries that manage to keep their finances under control can sell their permits to other countries. Finally, the total supply of permits can be changed over time. For example, the total number of permits would be increased in the case of a euro area-wide economic downturn. Casella emphasises, though, that the total supply of permits should be determined by some automatic (and transparent) rule.

Although the scheme has a number of advantages, it suffers also from some complications. First, it may be difficult to have countries agree on a supply rule for permits. Second, and most important, the question is what happens when a country exceeds the reference deficit level without having the required number of deficit permits. In that case, the country is supposed to incur an automatic and large fine. However, there is a danger that this could again lead to negotiations and the political exceptions that the system is supposed to avoid.[26]

2.6.4 Reform of the Budget Process

Reform of the budget process has the advantage that it can directly target the distortions that are the source of fiscal excesses, while a fiscal rule can only be an indirect way of addressing fiscal profligacy. As outlined in Chapter 7, the Maastricht Treaty also recognises the importance of budget processes that enable countries to keep their public finances sustainable (Article 3 of the Protocol on the Excessive Deficit Procedure). However, reform of the budget process is politically much harder to accomplish than the adoption of a fiscal rule. This is in particular the case if these measures are based on international agreements. Supranational enforcement of budget process reform can easily be seen as an intrusion into national affairs. Therefore, a fiscal rule like the SGP seems to be the maximum that can be achieved in a supranational arrangement. Nevertheless, once such an arrangement is in place, it may stimulate budget process reform at the national level.

Perotti *et al.* (1998) point out that the two most important distortions leading to fiscal excesses are 'fragmentation' of the budget process and the 'spreading of non-decisions'. Fragmentation arises when representatives of special interest groups in society can make spending decisions without having to take their full cost into account. While spending only benefits the constituency of the representative, the cost is spread out over all the taxpayers. This is an example of a standard common-pool resource problem. The obvious remedy is to centralise the budget, so that the externalities just described are internalised. One possibility is to delegate significant decision-maker powers to the finance minister, whose constituency is the general taxpayer and who thus internalises the externalities inherent in fragmented policy-making. Examples of this approach are France, Britain and Germany. Another possibility is the 'contract approach'. Here, the budget process is started by negotiating a set of spending targets for the individual spending departments. The bargaining process ensures that the participants internalise the externalities of their individual spending behaviour. Using an index of centralisation, von Hagen (1992a) and von Hagen and Harden (1996) show a strong negative correlation between centralisation of the budget process and average deficits and debt levels.

'Non-decisions' occur when government expenditures are largely determined by factors outside the budget process. Examples are the indexation of government wages and benefit payments to developments in the market sector. The government's budget then depends on institutions outside the budget process, such as private sector wage-setting arrangements and labour market regulations. Hence, achieving sustainability of the public finances, if necessary, would require the reform of institutions that are not involved in the budget process.

Bayoumi, Eichengreen and von Hagen (1997) discuss approaches that are even more ambitious than the reform of budgetary procedures. One possibility would be to set up independent agencies at the national level that monitor the budget and that prevent 'creative accounting'. Another more drastic possibility is that countries install National Debt Boards that set binding ceilings on the change in public debt. To ensure that these boards are independent from the governments, their members should be appointed for long terms in office.

2.7 CONCLUSION

This chapter has assessed the need for a stability pact under EMU. It has argued that excessive deficits or large debt build-ups in the future cannot be ruled out if the governments' hands are not in some way bound, for example, by means of a fiscal rule. The threat of exclusion from EMU has disappeared and many countries can expect steep increases in public spending as a result of population ageing. The first-best solution to fiscal profligacy is to eliminate the distortions in the budget process. Budgetary reform is often politically difficult to achieve. Outside pressure, such as agreements at the European level on how to reform national budget processes, is easily seen as Europe dictating what countries should do. At the supranational level, fiscal rules such as the SGP seem to be the maximum that is achievable. Nevertheless, they may stimulate national governments to reform their budget process, if necessary.

Existing empirical work on state-level balanced-budget rules in the USA suggests that such rules can be effective in limiting fiscal profligacy. Of course, one needs to be careful in translating the US results to the SGP. Strong features of the SGP are the simplicity of its 3 per cent deficit norm and the visibility of the governments' performances relative to this norm. These enhance its credibility, which is crucial for its effectiveness. The careful and regular monitoring of the Stability Programmes should further enhance the credibility of the SGP. These programmes provide early-warning signals, so that timely adjustments can be made, if necessary. The enforcement of the provisions of the Pact should rely more on the peer pressure from other countries than on pecuniary sanctions. The interest in exerting such peer pressure may be larger than is often conjectured. The reason is that a failure to enforce the Pact now will erode its credibility in the future. There would certainly be countries worried about this reputation effect. Credibility is a dynamic phenomenon and changes as a function of the actions taken at any moment.

The most serious objection against the SGP is its effect on fiscal flexibility. However, as pointed out by Artis and Buti in Chapter 8, if countries adhere to their commitment to achieve a structurally balanced budget,[27] then there is enough room to exploit the automatic fiscal stabilisers, as historical evidence suggests (Eichengreen and Wyplosz, 1998; and Buti, Franco and Ongena, 1998). The risk of violating the 3 per cent deficit norm as a result of an economic recession seems most serious in the very near future, because the room for using the automatic stabilisers is still small. Nevertheless, the budgetary targets projected for the years 2000 and 2001 are close to balance or even in surplus for most countries and, hence, provide some scope for optimism in this respect.

Notes

1. Stark (see Chapter 4) discusses in detail the original proposal by Waigel.
2. Similar objections have been raised earlier in the context of the Maastricht Treaty (for example, see Bean, 1992, 1998; and Buiter, Corsetti and Roubini, 1993).
3. This point is emphasised by Willett (1999). Of course, in the absence of international spillovers, the basis for *external* enforcement will be much weaker, because countries have no intrinsic interest in the enforcement of the Pact on other countries. Nevertheless, countries may still be prepared to enforce adherence to the Pact. The argument is a standard reputational argument often encountered in the monetary policy literature (see, for example, Barro and Gordon, 1983; Backus and Driffill, 1985; and Persson and Tabellini, 1990): even though countries have no intrinsic interest (if spillovers are absent) to do so, they may still want to enforce the Pact on another country, if this creates the expectation that there will be enforcement in the future again. This way they are able to bind themselves to low deficits.
4. The evidence in Eichengreen and Wyplosz (1998) reveals that the percentage of historical cases (for the OECD countries) in which a deficit of over 3 per cent would have been considered excessive by the criteria of the SGP (GDP does not fall by 0.75 per cent or more) is at least 85 per cent.
5. See also, for example, Alesina and Tabellini (1990), Tabellini and Alesina (1990) and Cukierman, Edwards and Tabellini (1992).
6. The contributions in de Beer and van Wissen (1999) contain detailed projections of population ageing for 33 European countries. While all these countries will face ageing populations, this demographic development is strongest for the Southern European and the Eastern European countries.
7. However, as Franco and Munzi (1999) note, the projections are highly dependent on the primary balance in the base year. This may explain the relatively optimistic projections for Italy, which starts the projection period with a large primary surplus.
8. This injects liquidity into the euro economies, which could be mopped up by selling other ECB assets. However, the ECB would be left with debt worth less than the price at which it was bought. Eventually, the costs will be spread out over the European taxpayers.
9. I have discussed this effect in isolation from other effects. The incentive to issue more debt depends on many factors of which this is only one.
10. This part of the modelling set-up in Beetsma and Uhlig (1999) follows Alesina and Tabellini (1990).

11.   It should be emphasised that excessive debt accumulation in the Beetsma–Uhlig model docs *not* rely on a failure of markets to properly raise funding rates in response to an enhanced chance of default (for such an analysis, see Restoy, 1996). There is no debt default in their analysis and the nominal interest rate adjusts one-for-one with expected inflation, so that the *ex post* real interest rate is unaffected.

12.   This idea is much in the spirit of Walsh's (1995) contracts for central bankers. See also Catenaro and Tirelli (2000), who consider a contract with a linear penalty in public spending.

13.   The incentive to stimulate the supply of goods is a third source of public deficit in the model. However, the deficit arising for this reason is not excessive.

14.   The details can be found in Chapter 6 and the legal text in Appendix A in Artis and Winkler (1997) or Appendix 2 in Buti and Sapir (1998).

15.   Canzoneri and Diba (Chapter 3) argue that the only possible rationale for its current design is that the SGP, if it is credible, puts the euro area in a 'monetary dominant regime' (although, according to them, there are better ways to achieve this). In such a regime, it is the fiscal authorities who adjust their policies to ensure that the intertemporal government budget is met. It may be helpful to contrast this view of the SGP with that in Beetsma and Uhlig (1999). Their rationale for the SGP is not that in its absence governments do not adjust their policies to ensure that the intertemporal government budget constraint is fulfilled. Instead, the role of the Pact is to induce governments to internalise the adverse externalities of national debt policies. While debt default is excluded in their model, debt will still be too high from a social planner's point of view.

16.   On the need to introduce the issue of long-run sustainability of public finances in the Programmes see Chapter 7.

17.   The SGP would probably become a stronger deterrent to fiscal excesses if sanctions were only actually imposed if the current, misbehaving government remained in power.

18.   Alesina and Perotti (1995) present empirical evidence that successful fiscal adjustments in the past have generally relied on spending cuts rather than tax increases.

19.   The data reported in Tables 2.1–2.4 are from the European Commission and may differ somewhat from the data used for Figure 2.2.

20.   However, Chapter 15 provides a somewhat different assessment of the share of the adjustment falling on public investment.

21.   For example, a higher deficit may arise from enhanced entitlements to (certain forms of) public spending, which persist into the future.

22.   Hence, a debt-based pact might motivate countries to constrain the use of debt so as to build up a 'buffer' against unexpectedly bad shocks.

23.   Average government debt of these countries in the 1980s and 1990s has been relatively small, which suggests that they indeed perceive a need for more room to let automatic stabilisers do their work.

24.   This set-up follows Tabellini and Alesina (1990).

25.   Educational expenses are an example. In principle, public education should be seen as a public investment. However, a large share of

expenses on education are grants and income transfers to students which are spent on consumption goods (such as beer and mobile telephones). See also Chapter 15 below.

26.   However, well-performing countries have a stronger incentive to enforce these fines than under the current SGP. No enforcement means that the value of the permits that they want to sell drops to zero.

27.   Artis and Buti (2000) show that the preferred medium-term target consistent with the 3 per cent deficit norm depends on the source of a shock, public finance variables (for example, the stock of debt and the cyclical sensitivity of the budget) and the size of the country.

3 The SGP: Delicate Balance or Albatross?*

Matthew B. Canzoneri and Behzad T. Diba

The Stability and Growth Pact tried to strike a delicate balance. On the one hand, it imposed constraints on national fiscal policy that were deemed necessary to protect the new European Central Bank (ECB) from outside pressures, especially during the period in which it tried to establish credibility.[1] At the same time, the Pact allowed some flexibility for a counter-cyclical fiscal policy. This too was deemed necessary in European Monetary Union (EMU): a stable ECB policy might be expected to create stable macroeconomic conditions for the euro zone as a whole, but it could not be expected to iron out regional cyclical imbalances. Did the Pact strike a workable balance? Or is the Pact an unnecessary albatross that could seriously hamper the whole EMU project?

To answer these questions, one needs to analyse the flexibility that is embedded in the Pact, and one needs a well-articulated explanation of the credibility problem that the Pact is supposed to address. Official institutions – the EU Commission, the OECD and the IMF – have done the former, but the official community has not really provided the latter. The academic literature provides a number of possible explanations, but it is not clear which, if any, of the explanations capture the concerns of the official community.

In section 3.1, we outline the key elements of the Pact, compare them with the convergence criteria in the Maastricht Treaty, and ask which fiscal criteria should be the focus of attention. In section 3.2, we

* The original version of this chapter was prepared for the Austrian National Bank's Workshop on 'Challenges for Economic Policy Coordination within EMU'; it was published with other workshop papers in a special issue of *Empirica* (vol. 6, no. 3, 1999). The current version of the chapter has been updated to reflect more recent studies and events; it also draws sharper conclusions. We would like to thank, without implicating, Marco Buti, Vitor Gaspar, Eduard Hochreiter and workshop participants for their helpful comments.

review official institutions' studies of the flexibility embedded in the Pact. Our review finds a strong consensus: the Pact's Excessive Deficit Procedure seems likely to constrain counter-cyclical fiscal efforts in the years ahead, or at least until EU governments make one last fiscal retrenchment to bring their structural deficits into balance. In sections 3.3, 3.4 and 3.5, we review conventional academic arguments that suggest a new central bank might need to be protected from external pressures,[2] and we ask if the constraints that were actually written into the Pact are likely to be helpful in this regard. In section 3.6, we present our conclusions. We may as well give our bottom line at the top: if the Excessive Deficit Procedure continues to be the main focus of the Pact, then we think that the Pact will be an albatross, and not a delicately balanced package of necessary fiscal constraints; if, on the other hand, the level of debt and the (implied) commitment to structural balance become the focus of the Pact, then our assessment would be more positive. We make three recommendations on how to proceed.

3.1   THE STABILITY AND GROWTH PACT

As explained in several chapters in this volume the Stability and Growth Pact has several elements:[3]

1. EU countries have committed themselves to 'medium-term' budgets that are 'close to balance or in surplus'; we will interpret this as an implied promise to balance structural (or cyclically adjusted) budgets.
2. EU countries have to submit annual programmes specifying medium-term budgetary objectives; so, there will be a track record for the Council or the public to examine when assessing a country's compliance with the terms in the Pact (or the 'convergence criteria' in the case of those who are not in the euro zone).[4]
3. Countries in the euro zone that run excessive deficits will be subject to financial penalties and public approbation; we think that the punishment for excessive deficits will be sufficient to affect government behaviour.[5]
4. Deficits are 'excessive' if they exceed 3 per cent of GDP, unless they occur under 'exceptional' circumstances. An annual decline in real output of more than 2 per cent of GDP would be considered exceptional; a decline of 0.75 per cent of GDP might be deemed exceptional if there is additional supporting evidence.

It is interesting to compare the provisions in the Pact with the fiscal convergence criteria in the Maastricht Treaty.[6] The convergence criteria set reference values for both the deficit/GDP ratio (3 per cent) and the debt/GDP ratio (60 per cent); there were no reference values for structural deficits. The Pact added a commitment to structural balance, but the Excessive Deficit Procedure is the only explicit enforcement mechanism in the Pact. Thus, actual deficits are the focus of the Pact; they seem to take primacy over both structural deficits and debt levels.

The ECOFIN Council has to approve each country's annual Stability Programme, and the Council will determine whether an individual country has an excessive deficit. It is not clear how strictly the Council will interpret the provisions in the Pact. The EU has a history of exerting its discretion in such decisions. For example, the Maastricht Treaty's reference value for debt played virtually no role in the final decision on which countries were qualified to participate in EMU; all attention was focused on the deficit criterion. As noted above, this primacy of actual deficits seems to have lived on in the Pact's Excessive Deficits Procedure. On the other hand, debt levels continue to play a role in the annual Stability Programmes, and debt levels may affect how strictly the Council interprets the provisions that are in the Pact. Similarly, structural balance may be taken into account. It is interesting to note, for example, that the European Commission (2000a) focuses heavily on structural deficits.

In this chapter, we ask which of the three criteria – actual deficits, structural deficits, or debt levels – should be the focus of attention. In implementing the Pact, should the Council focus on actual deficits as suggested by the Excessive Deficits Procedure, or should it focus on structural deficits and/or debt levels? More generally, should the Council take the Pact seriously, or should it interpret all of its provisions quite liberally?

3.2   IS THE PACT FLEXIBLE ENOUGH FOR STABILISATION?

Research coming from the European Commission, the OECD and the IMF suggests that the Pact will be flexible enough to accommodate the automatic counter-cyclical component of national fiscal policies *if member states bring their structural deficits close to balance* (see Chapters 8 to 10 below). The basic line of reasoning is as follows. In a typical EU country, the deficit rises by about 0.5 per cent of GDP when output falls by 1 per cent, and the output gap (the amount by which actual GDP falls short of potential) in a typical recession is about 3 per cent. Suppose the structural deficit of the same typical EU country is reduced to, say, 1.5 per cent of GDP. If the deficit/GDP ratio is 1.5 per cent when the gap is zero, then it will only rise to 3 per cent ($= 1.5 + 0.5 \times 3$) during a typical recession; the constraint on excessive deficits will not be binding. There are, in addition, two reasons why our typical EU country might wish to lower its structural deficit below 1.5 per cent: (1) the country may wish to pursue a more active counter-cyclical policy after EMU, when national monetary policies are no longer an option, than it did before EMU; and (2) the country may be risk-averse and wish to plan for recessions that are worse than average or unexpected developments in revenues and expenditures. In either case, the country should aim for a lower structural deficit, perhaps something 'close to balance or in surplus' as suggested by the Pact.

IMF, OECD and EC estimates of structural deficits in the EU have been decreasing, but for 1999 they were still rather large (1–2 per cent) in a number of countries (see European Commission, 2000a, Table III.5). Until this final investment in fiscal austerity is made, the Pact's Excessive Deficit Procedure is likely to be an ongoing constraint on national counter-cyclical fiscal policies.

Will the final investment be made? EU deficits have already come down dramatically, and Eichengreen and Wyplosz (1998) suggest that 'electorates lack the appetite for further spending cuts'. The European Commission's (2000a) assessment of medium-term prospects (based on updated Stability and Convergence Programmes) confirms their pessimism: 'On the expenditure side, most of the reduction comes from lower interest payments... [and on the revenue side] most Member States are generally pursuing a budgetary strategy involving reductions in the overall tax burden. Overall, the updated programs provide for only small improvement in the underlying budget position, with the cyclically adjusted primary surplus showing no improvement between 2000 and 2003.' EU countries came out of recession with the turn of the century, but there is little indication that they will use the opportunity to make a final investment in fiscal austerity.

In summary, the consensus seems to be that the Excessive Deficit Procedure could become a serious impediment to counter-cyclical fiscal policy if and when the EU falls back into recession. Refocusing attention on the promise of structural balance would avoid these problems. Would this make the Pact weaker? What would be the consequences for the credibility of monetary policy? What kind of fiscal constraint (if any) is necessary at the beginning of EMU. Having identified the costs of various fiscal constraints, we now turn to their potential benefits.

3.3 INTEREST RATE PRESSURES ON A CENTRAL BANK

It is extremely rare for a government to pressure its central bank directly to inflate. A sound currency is an unquestioned icon of national pride. Instead, the pressures to inflate generally take the form of complaints about interest rates. Both the Reagan administration and the Clinton administration complained about what they regarded as high interest rates coming from the Federal Reserve; both administrations claimed that the high interest rates were a drag on the 'pro growth' policies that they had an electoral mandate to institute. Paul Volcker, Chairman of the Federal Reserve Board, responded that the high interest rates were caused by the Reagan administration's borrowing to finance its deficits.[7] In Europe, much of the political concern in the 1990s has been that heavy refinance costs in high-debt countries would prohibit them from achieving the 3 per cent deficit/GDP ratio required for participation in EMU. As the discussion in the last section indicates, this concern is likely to live on in the Stability and Growth Pact until EU countries lower their structural deficits another 1 per cent of GDP.

Moreover, political concerns about labour market conditions have led some politicians in France and Germany to focus attention on the level of the euro–dollar exchange rate, and of course an argument for a 'competitive' exchange rate is a thinly disguised argument for a low interest rate. The Maastricht Treaty forbids national governments from putting direct pressure on the ECB to lower its interest rate, but the Treaty does give ECOFIN some say about the general orientation of exchange rate policy. Thus, we may well see political pressures for lower interest rates and 'competitive' exchange rates framed as proposals for formal agreements with the USA and Japan about exchange rate target zones.

Strong political pressures to keep interest rates low may undermine the credibility of any central bank's mandate for price stability. Following Barro and Gordon (1983), a vast literature argues that these pressures are even more perverse than they might at first seem.[8] The essential insight of this literature is that farsighted actors in the private sector will anticipate the inflationary consequences of such pressures, and they will demand higher nominal interest rates and higher nominal wage rates to compensate for the expected inflation. The central bank will then be faced with the unhappy choice of accommodating these inflationary expectations or ending up with real interest rates and real wage rates that are abnormally high (or higher than what they would be in an equilibrium with full information). If the central bank sticks to its mandated inflation objectives, then the high real interest rates and the high real wages will have unintended implications for employment and output growth; moreover, the government's fiscal situation may worsen, leading to even more pressure to decrease interest rates in the future. The literature argues that the central bank will compromise in such a situation between its inflation goals and its fear of the consequences of not accommodating the private sector's inflationary expectations, and inflation rate will be higher than desired. As long as the pressure for lower interest rates persists, so the argument goes, there will be a credibility problem and an inflation bias.

Suppose this reasoning captures the concerns that led to the fiscal criteria in the Maastricht Treaty and live on in the Stability and Growth Pact. We can now ask how effective the provisions in the Pact will be at easing the pressures, what the consequences would be of relaxing some of the provisions, and more generally whether other measures would be more effective.

First and perhaps foremost, it should be noted that much if not most of the political pressure for low interest rates may have nothing to do with government debt or deficits. New and more liberal governments have come to power in France and Germany, and unemployment seems to have replaced inflation as the major focus of political attention throughout most of the EU. It is difficult for us to see how the Pact will do anything to alleviate concerns for unemployment and growth; indeed, the Pact is more likely to aggravate them, as governments are required to curb their spending levels even further. Here again, the Pact may have perverse effects. It may actually increase pressure for low interest rates and make the ECB appear to be an institution still fighting the battles of the 1990s.[9]

What about political pressures that do come from difficulties in financing the debt? We have little doubt that these pressures exist. However, the point to be made here is that this is an argument for debt limits, not deficit limits. A country with little or no debt to finance (like Luxembourg) could be running rather large deficits, but its government would not have much incentive to pressure its central bank until the debt grew to a significant level. On the other hand, a country with a lot of debt (like Italy) can only limit its deficit to, say, 2.9 per cent of GDP by running huge primary surpluses. Its government may well have an incentive to lobby for a lower interest rate; even a modest drop in the interest rate would allow it to run much smaller primary surpluses and still stay under the 3 per cent cap specified in the Pact. The Pact does give a high-debt country an incentive to lower its debt level over time; so, the Pact would seem to have some bite. However, the Pact's total focus on deficits, to the exclusion of the level of the debt, does seem misplaced, especially if interest rate pressures are thought to be the main concern.[10]

What is the cost of loosening the parameters of the Pact, or giving the Pact a rather loose interpretation? As discussed in the last section, this might be particularly appealing in the years just ahead, as EU countries look for an opportune moment to lower their structural deficits another 1 per cent of GDP. To the extent that the Pact is actually limiting the political pressure for lower interest rates, any loosening of the constraints would presumably increase those pressures, and the theory suggests that this would intensify the credibility problem and increase the associated inflation bias. That bias increases in proportion with the political pressure.[11] Increasing political pressures at the same time as the new ECB is trying to establish its credibility would not seem to make sense. Those who think the Pact is necessary, and have in mind the reasoning outlined in this section, would probably be inclined to take a hard line on the Pact's interpretation in the next few years.

The discussion so far could apply equally well to the United States; and indeed, we have already made several references to US experience. The Federal Reserve seems to have managed its interactions with the US government rather well, and without the help of anything like a Stability and Growth Pact (or for that matter anything like the degree of legal and political independence that has been granted to the ECB). Does US history obviate the need for a Stability and Growth Pact in Europe? Before jumping to such a conclusion, we should note that there are at least two ways in which the situation in Europe is different from that in the USA. First, the Federal Reserve has a track record that many would argue has established its credibility; the ECB is a new institution with no track record. One might question the necessity of something permanent, like the Pact, to address what is presumably a transitional issue, but we do agree that the lack of any track record may be a genuine concern. Second, and perhaps more important in the long run, the EU is characterised by a weak federal government and a minuscule federal budget. For the most part, fiscal decisions are being made at the national level, and this situation is unlikely to change in the foreseeable future. Does the fact that the ECB will have to interact with several fiscal authorities make its situation fundamentally different from that of the Federal Reserve? We turn to this issue next.

3.4   MULTIPLE FISCAL AUTHORITIES

A large literature on policy coordination suggests that the multiplicity of governments – or more precisely the multiplicity of fiscal authorities – adds two strategic dimensions to our discussion. First, increasing the number of fiscal authorities erodes the strategic position of any one authority *vis-à-vis* the central bank; each authority's incentive to manipulate the central bank is reduced. This suggests that the ECB may have less need of protection than, say, the Federal Reserve. Second, each individual authority may fail to internalise the adverse effects of its policies on the other fiscal authorities; as we will see, this may create a bias towards excessive government expenditure and/or borrowing, and this may in turn put pressure on the central bank to provide inflationary finance. This suggests that the ECB may have more need of protection than the Federal Reserve.

We begin with the issue of the number of players.

Beetsma and Bovenberg (1998) extend the Barro–Gordon analysis to demonstrate the erosion of strategic positions as the number of fiscal authorities increases; in particular, they show that the inflation bias described in the last section decreases as new, equally important, countries are added to a monetary union. The euro zone, however, consists of three big countries (four, if the UK joins) and a periphery. Adding more countries to the periphery would not seem to diminish the influence of the big three significantly. However, the very fact that there are three large fiscal authorities instead of one does seem to make the ECB's situation different from that of the Federal Reserve:[12] the ECB may need less protection from fiscal authorities.

Institutional considerations also suggest that the decentralised political structure of the EU makes the ECB less susceptible to political pressure than the Federal Reserve. The Federal Reserve System is the creation of the US Congress, and Congress can change the way in which the Federal Reserve operates simply by passing a bill.[13] The European System of Central Banks (ESCB) is a creation of the EU, and its operation can only be changed by an amendment to the Maastricht Treaty. This is clearly a much more cumbersome process than passing a bill in Congress, and it gives the ECB more leeway to act in ways that might be deemed politically incorrect.

We turn next to the question of whether individual fiscal authorities pay enough attention to the adverse effects their policies may have on other members of the Union, and how a common central bank may interact with this fiscal coordination problem. The policy coordination literature suggests that a coordination failure may lead to an expenditure bias through the effect of national fiscal policy on real interest rates, and the expenditure bias may in turn lead to pressure on the central bank to inflate.[14]

In Canzoneri and Diba (1991), we present a model in which government purchases in any one country raise real interest rates and crowd out investment community-wide. The national fiscal authorities are assumed to care only about the welfare of their own citizens. Each fiscal authority weighs the costs and benefits for its own citizens of an increase in spending, and it ultimately decides to spend too much, since it ignores the adverse effects of higher interest rates and crowding-out on welfare in the rest of the community. So, there is a government spending bias, due essentially to the fact that fiscal authorities have access to community-wide capital markets.

Once this excessive government spending is set in place, it may induce a well-meaning central bank to produce an inflation bias. Our model assumes that the common central bank cares about community-wide welfare. Excessive spending ultimately means excessive taxation (which in our model is costly), but the central bank can decrease the tax burden by providing seigniorage. The central bank ends up setting inflation too high, relative to an equilibrium in which government spending is optimally coordinated across countries.

In fact, in our stylised model, the common central bank ends up choosing the same inflation rate that the fiscal authorities would have selected had they controlled monetary policy directly. This fact is not really surprising because once the level of government purchases is set, the inflation rate chosen by any welfare-maximising entity (the central bank or the fiscal authorities) is the solution to a standard Ramsey–Phelps public finance problem. The bottom line is that, in our model anyway, an independent central bank, charged only with maximising community-wide welfare, will not do anything to curb the excesses of the national fiscal authorities. Only a community-wide constraint on national government spending would do that.

Does this line of reasoning provide a cogent argument for the Stability and Growth Pact? Its focus on community interest rates and access to community-wide savings is reminiscent of discussions we have heard in the policy community. However, the characterisation of these concerns given by our model, and others like it, seems somewhat dubious in Europe today. The logic of these models may be impeccable, but empirical questions can be raised about its importance in practice.

The first, and perhaps most important, problem with this line of reasoning is that seigniorage revenues are a small fraction of total tax revenues in Europe. Will fiscal authorities bother to try to manipulate the ECB if the best they can expect is seigniorage revenues on the order of half a per cent of GDP? Will the ECB bother to take account of how its transfers may reduce the welfare loss from distortionary direct taxes? We strongly suspect that the answer to both questions is no, at least in normal times. In certain abnormal circumstances, however, seigniorage revenues of even this magnitude may become a relevant political consideration. We have already noted that the Stability and Growth Pact incorporates a rather unfortunate feature: a deficit that is 2.9 per cent of GDP goes unnoticed, while a deficit that is 3.1 per cent of GDP may trigger major political difficulties. For a fiscal authority whose deficit is hovering around the magical 3 per cent mark, transfers from the ECB may make the difference between meeting or exceeding the 3 per cent limit. Moreover, a slight easing of monetary policy may be expected to lower the deficit by decreasing debt payments (in high-debt countries anyway) or stimulating growth. These are clearly not arguments in favour of the Pact; indeed, they suggest the Pact may create political pressures on the ECB where none existed before.

There may be a second problem with this line of reasoning that was outlined above. Given the global nature of today's capital markets, and the financial deregulation that has occurred within the EU in the 1990s, Eichengreen and Wyplosz (1998) reject the notion that the actions of national fiscal authorities affect community real interest rates, and they present empirical evidence in support of that view. We think this is still an open empirical question deserving serious investigation. However, the basic notion that the actions of multiple fiscal authorities can pressure a common central bank to inflate does not require an interest rate channel to work through; indeed, it does not require any direct channel by which the actions of one fiscal authority affect welfare in another country.

Chari and Kehoe (1998) describe a fiscal externality that arises even though the monetary and fiscal policies of the countries involved have no effect on world real interest rates. The externality they highlight is clearly illustrated in a simple two-period model.[15] In period 1, fiscal authorities undertake expenditures and borrow from the residents of other countries outside the euro zone. The real interest rate on these loans is fixed at a world equilibrium level, but the nominal interest rate depends on expected inflation. In period 2, the ECB selects an inflation rate that maximises the welfare of countries within the euro zone. The ECB's choice trades off the welfare loss from inflation (modelled here as a reduction in output) against the welfare gain from higher consumption (as inflation erodes the real value of the nominal debt issued to foreigners). When each fiscal authority decides on the amount of debt to issue, it takes into account the fact that the central bank will inflate away part of that debt in period 2, and it also understands that inflation will be higher the more debt that it issues, lowering home output; however, the fiscal authority has no interest in the fact that higher inflation will also lower output in other euro zone countries. Therefore, each fiscal authority issues too much debt in period 1, and the ECB ends up setting the inflation rate too high in period 2. In equilibrium, world lenders rationally anticipate the high rate of inflation and demand a commensurately high nominal interest rate on bonds denominated in euro.

Does the Chari–Kehoe reasoning provide a more compelling rational for the Stability and Growth Pact? We doubt it. The externality they describe, unlike the one considered by Canzoneri and Diba (1991), does not hinge on fiscal authorities being able to affect real interest rates. It does, however, hinge on the assumption that government bonds are held by investors living outside the euro zone, investors whose welfare is of no consequence to the ECB. To the extent that the bonds are held within the euro zone, the ECB would not be tempted to impose this inflation tax. This fact may limit the practical importance of the Chari–Kehoe argument.

Moreover, the Pact's constraint on deficits seems to miss the mark. In the Chari–Kehoe argument, the inflation bias is created by the central bank's temptation to tax foreign lenders; so, the appropriate remedy would be a constraint on the holding of government debt by investors who live outside the euro zone. (This kind of targeted capital control would probably be difficult to implement in practice.) A constraint that restricts all government borrowing seems inefficient; it would, for example, preclude consumption smoothing between euro zone countries, which would lower welfare in (extensions of) the Chari–Kehoe model. A better – and probably more workable – remedy may be to require high-debt countries to issue inflation indexed bonds.[16]

Finally, we might note that the arguments in this section and the last have at least one thing in common. Whatever the relevant constraint might be, all of the arguments suggest that relaxing the constraint will lead directly to an increase in the pressures on the central bank to inflate, or in what we have called the inflation bias. If the Council decides to interpret the provisions in the Pact more leniently in the initial phase, then we would expect a proportionate increase in the pressures on the ECB. The arguments we turn to next do not have this property; if they are the true source of concern, then the constraints in the Pact might be loosened considerably without detracting from their effect.

3.5   FUNCTIONAL INDEPENDENCE: WHO ACTUALLY SETS PRICES? WHO PAYS THE BILLS?

Michael Woodford and Christopher Sims have popularised a new theory that emphasises fiscal aspects of price determination.[17] This fiscal theory of price determination (FTPD) suggests a different way of thinking about central bank independence; we call it a 'functional' notion of independence. While we know that the policy community did not have this theory in mind when it drafted the Stability and Growth Pact, we think that this theory may provide a better rationale for constraints on deficits than the arguments that were given in the last two sections.

The FTPD has its roots in a much earlier literature associated with Thomas Sargent and Neil Wallace.[18] Sargent and Wallace emphasised the fact that a present-value budget constraint must hold if the government is to be solvent. This constraint states that the real value of existing government debt must equal the expected present value of future primary surpluses inclusive of seigniorage revenues. Sargent and Wallace treated the real value of existing debt as given and focused on how the primary surpluses generated by the fiscal authority and the seigniorage revenues of the monetary authority must be expected to add up over time, to satisfy the present-value budget constraint.

This adding-up requirement raises the possibility that either the fiscal authority or the central bank may have to yield and allow their policies to be governed by the needs of fiscal solvency. Suppose the government's fiscal policy is firmly set in place, in the sense that the present value of primary surpluses is some fixed number. Then, the central bank has no choice but to deliver the seigniorage required to satisfy the budget constraint. In this case, Sargent and Wallace argued that the options open to the central bank are rather limited. It can keep inflation and seigniorage low for a while, but eventually it has to provide the seigniorage necessary to satisfy the budget constraint. Alternatively, suppose instead that the central bank's policy is firmly set in place, in the sense that the present value of seigniorage is a fixed number. Then, fiscal policy has no choice but to conform.

Absent from the Sargent and Wallace literature is much of any discussion about how either the central bank or the fiscal authority go about setting their policies firmly in place.[19] Nor does this literature address the question of what happens if neither the central bank nor the fiscal authority are willing to yield to the requirements of fiscal solvency. An important contribution of the new FTPD is to answer this question for the realistic case where the government issues nominal debt. In this case, if fiscal and monetary policy do not actively establish fiscal solvency, the government's budget constraint gets satisfied through changes in the price level, which adjust the real value of outstanding debt.[20]

More precisely, the present value budget constraint for year t is:

$$\frac{M_t + B_t}{p_t} = E_t \sum_{j=t}^{+\infty} d_j \left(\frac{T_j - G_j}{p_j} \right) + E_t \sum_{j=t}^{+\infty} d_j \left(\frac{M_{j+1}}{p_j} \right) i_j \tag{3.1}$$

where M_t is the money base at the beginning of year t, B_t is the face value of the debt that was inherited from past government borrowing, p_t is the price level, d_j is a discount factor (involving real interest rates), $T_j - G_j$ is the primary surplus in year j, and $M_{j+1}i_j$ is the central bank's transfer to the government (or seigniorage) in year j.[21] So, (3.1) says that the real value of total government liabilities must be equal to the present discounted value of present and future real primary surpluses plus the present discounted value of present and future real seigniorage; the expectation symbol, E_t, indicates that the right-hand side of (3.1) is really the market's perception of these present values.

Suppose now that the fiscal authority and the central bank ignore the needs of solvency and have their policies firmly set in place, so that the right-hand side of (3.1) adds up to some fixed number.[22] The budget constraint can still be satisfied if the price level, p_t, moves in equilibrium to make the real value of debt come in line. One way of understanding this point is to use the following analogy with a standard asset valuation equation.

The left-hand side of (3.1) is the real value of total government liabilities, and the right-hand side is the present value of expected payments on these liabilities. The two sides must be equal in equilibrium. If, for example, expected primary surpluses suddenly fall at date t, expected payments go down and the equilibrium value of liabilities is reduced via an increase in the price level. Although this way of thinking about the price level may be unfamiliar, it is not hard to grasp once we observe that the inverse of the price of goods represents the price of nominal liabilities in terms of goods.

For our discussion below, it will be convenient to rewrite (3.1) slightly to express liabilities, revenues and expenditures in terms of their ratios to GDP (since the provisions in the Pact are expressed in those terms). The budget constraint for year t can be expressed as:[23]

$$\frac{M_t + B_t}{p_t y_t} = E_t \sum_{j=t}^{+\infty} \delta_j \left(\frac{T_j - G_j}{p_j y_i} \right) + E_t \sum_{j=t}^{+\infty} \delta_j \left(\frac{M_{j+1}}{p_j y_j} \right) i_j \qquad (3.2)$$

where $p_j y_j$ is nominal GDP, and the discount factor δ_j now involves ratios of output growth to real interest rates. The interpretation of (3.2) is the same as the interpretation of (3.1), except that real liabilities, primary surpluses and seigniorage are measured per unit of output.

Once again we can think of a fiscal–monetary regime in which the fiscal authority and the central bank do not actively pursue fiscal solvency, and thus the ratios of the primary surplus and seigniorage to GDP evolve exogenously over time. In such a regime, nominal GDP ($p_t y_t$) must move in equilibrium to satisfy (3.2). And we have a fiscal theory of nominal income determination: nominal income moves in equilibrium to assure fiscal solvency.[24] We will refer to a policy regime with exogenous primary surpluses (inclusive of seigniorage) as a fiscal dominant (FD) regime.

We can also think of a regime in which fiscal policy actively pursues solvency. In this case, given the left-hand side of (3.2), the fiscal authority is expected to adjust the ratio of its primary surpluses to GDP over time, to satisfy (3.2). In this case, the needs of fiscal solvency do not pin down nominal GDP. Thus, nominal GDP can be determined in a more conventional way by monetary policy. We call such a regime money dominant (MD).

The possibility of an FD regime motivates our notion of the 'functional independence' of a central bank. In this regime, even if the central bank enjoys legal and political independence in setting monetary policy, it can still lose control of nominal GDP and the price level. For the central bank to be functionally independent of the fiscal authorities, it must be the case that fiscal policy actively pursues solvency and puts the economy in the MD regime.

Either one of the fiscal criteria written into the Maastricht Treaty would suffice, in theory, to guarantee that the euro zone is in an MD regime and to make the ECB functionally independent of fiscal policy. A cap on the debt/GDP ratio would make the fiscal authority responsible for solvency, and put the euro zone in an MD regime. But, it also turns out that a cap on the deficit/GDP ratio is a sufficient condition for an MD regime.

To see the latter point, consider any fiscal reaction function that makes the ratio of the primary surplus to GDP depend positively on the debt/GDP ratio:

$$\frac{T_j - G_j}{p_j y_j} = \alpha_j \left[\frac{B_j}{p_j y_j} \right] + x_j, \quad \alpha_j > 0, \tag{3.3}$$

where x_j is a bounded random variable. Equation (3.3) says that the ratio of the primary surplus to GDP may fluctuate over time due to changes in cyclical, political and other conditions reflected in x_j, but it also has a systematic tendency to rise with the debt/GDP ratio (because the coefficients α_j are assumed to be positive). Such a reaction function implies that as the debt/GDP ratio grows, the fiscal authority has to run larger and larger primary surpluses (relative to GDP). The larger surpluses will eventually curb the growth of debt and assure fiscal solvency.[25]

The Maastricht Treaty's 3 per cent cap on the ratio of the deficit inclusive of interest payments to GDP requires that

$$\left[\frac{G_j - T_j}{p_j y_j} \right] + i_j \left[\frac{B_j}{p_j y_j} \right] \leq 0.03, \tag{3.4}$$

where i_j is the nominal interest rate on debt. Since the nominal interest rate is positive, it serves as the coefficient α_j in (3.3).[26] That is, as the debt/GDP ratio increases so does the interest obligation on debt. Thus, the primary surplus must rise to satisfy the 3 per cent target for the deficit/GDP ratio. And this fiscal reaction (assuming that it occurs frequently enough) assures an MD regime.

Although the fiscal criteria of the Maastricht treaty are sufficient to assure the functional independence of the ECB, much weaker fiscal restrictions would also suffice, at least in theory, for (3.3) to hold. The cap on the deficit/GDP ratio could be (say) 5 per cent instead of 3 per cent. Or, the fiscal rule could require the sum of the primary surplus and (say) half the interest payments on debt to remain below (say) 3 per cent.[27] Either of these options would assure the functional independence of the ECB and at the same time loosen the fiscal restriction on countries that currently have high debt/GDP ratios. More generally, the restriction could also be stated in terms of structural deficits, instead of actual deficits.[28]

Our statement that looser fiscal constraints would work in theory is subject to the important qualification that such constraints must also be credible in practice. The right-hand side of (3.2) involves the private sector's expectations of how fiscal and monetary policy will behave in the future. So, putting a 10 per cent cap on the deficit/GDP ratio would not assure an MD regime if the private sector does not expect the cap to be enforced once the deficit/GDP ratios of some countries have risen to the 10 per cent level. From this perspective, the fact that some countries had to make a genuine and painful effort to meet the 3 per cent target set by the Maastricht Treaty was probably a useful investment in making the target credible.

Note that the relevant notion of credibility here is not the credibility of the ECB but the credibility of fiscal rules. From this perspective the best fiscal rules would be ones that are manageable (not too stringent), transparent (easily verified) and irrevocable (thus, fully credible). How does the Stability Pact's treatment of fiscal constraints score along these dimensions?

First, the fact that the Pact emphasises deficit caps and not debt limits is not problematic. Either type of constraint would suffice by itself to establish an MD regime. Second, the deficit constraint could have been modified by the Pact to a constraint on the structural (that is, full employment) deficit. For example, the Pact could have said that the structural deficit should not exceed (say) 2 per cent of GDP. Such a constraint would have the advantage of alleviating the concerns (discussed in section 1 above) about what the cyclical elasticity of deficits or the severity of future recessions may turn out to be. But to be transparent and credible, such a restriction would probably have to pin down how structural deficits are measured, and to make sure that the measurements are not subject to accounting gimmicks or manipulation by national fiscal authorities.

3.6 WHAT CONCLUSIONS DO WE REACH?

So, what do we finally conclude? Does the Stability and Growth Pact strike a workable balance between the fiscal discipline needed to protect the ECB from outside interference and the flexibility required for counter-cyclical stabilisation? Or is the Pact an unnecessary albatross that could hamper the entire EMU effort? When we began our assessment of this issue, we had some sympathy for the Pact; perhaps our view was coloured by our previous work in the area.[29] However, after reviewing all aspects of the question, we have moved considerably in the direction of thinking that the Pact will become an albatross. This assessment would change considerably if the focus of the Pact were shifted away from constraints on actual deficits and towards constraints on structural deficits or, better yet, constraints on debt levels.

In section 2, we reviewed studies done at official institutions – the Commission, the OECD and the IMF – on the flexibility built into the Excessive Deficit Procedure. While the studies differ in detail, a general consensus does emerge: in the long run – after governments have reduced structural deficits by about another 1 per cent of GDP – the Excessive Deficit Procedure should not constrain normal counter-cyclical efforts. For the foreseeable future, however, the prospects for achieving structural balance are not good. In this environment, the current emphasis on the Excessive Deficit Procedure seems misplaced. The promise to achieve structural balance should become the focal point of the Pact.

What does the Stability and Growth Pact buy at this potential cost to macroeconomic stability? Does it give the ECB needed protection as it tries to achieve credibility? In sections 3, 4 and 5, we reviewed arguments that have been made in the academic literature. Some of the arguments based on seigniorage seemed unlikely to be of much practical importance, and in any case we generally found that, once the argument was made clear, deficit constraints were weak or inappropriate instruments to address the problem at hand. In several cases, the appropriate constraint was on the level of debt, but the

Pact focuses exclusively on deficits. And the main reasons why one might expect the recently elected governments of France and Germany to lobby for lower interest rates – high unemployment, low capital formation – have nothing to do with budget deficits; indeed, if the effect of the Pact is to constrain social spending, then the Pact might increase the pressures for a monetary expansion.

Perhaps the best argument for some kind of deficit constraint came in section 5, where a new theory of price determination suggested that national fiscal authorities have to take responsibility for paying their bills if the central bank is to have the 'functional' independence to control its price level. However, we also argued that the Pact's Excessive Deficit Procedure was probably stronger than necessary to achieve functional independence for the ECB. If this argument captures the main concern, then the provisions in the Pact can be interpreted rather liberally in the next few years; all that matters is that the private sector must be convinced that fiscal authorities will eventually pay their bills. Moreover, we showed that the constraint could be written in terms of structural deficits; once again, the Excessive Deficit Procedure can be replaced by the commitment to achieve structural balance.

Generally speaking, we found the case for the Pact to be weaker in the EU than it would be in the USA, where experience suggests that it is probably not necessary. Arguments in the literature suggest that a multiplicity of fiscal authorities, instead of one federal authority, dilutes the pressures on a central bank. Moreover, the legal independence of the ECB seems much stronger than the Federal Reserve's; for example, political tampering with the ESCB legislation would require an amendment to the Maastricht Treaty, while tampering with the Federal Reserve System legislation would only require an Act of Congress. One big difference remains: the Federal Reserve already has a proven track record, while the ECB is just starting out. But, establishing permanent constraints on fiscal policy seems a heavy-handed way of addressing what is presumably a transitional problem.

The Maastricht Treaty's debt and deficit constraints seem to have forced a number of high-debt countries to reform their fiscal policies, and many would argue that these reforms were needed for reasons that have nothing to do with monetary policy *per se*. Those same people may worry that the reforms will be short-lived, and they may be happy to see some of the constraints live on in the Stability and Growth Pact, whether or not they have anything to do with monetary stability.

In this chapter, we have only considered the merits of the Pact from the point of view of assuring price and output stability. From this narrow perspective, we would make the following recommendations:

1. Change the focus of the Pact away from actual deficits, and towards structural deficits and/or debt levels. This may be difficult to do when the only explicit enforcement mechanism in the Pact is the Excessive Deficit Procedure; ideally, some carrots (for good performance on structural deficits and/or debt levels) would be added to the stick (of the Excessive Deficit Procedure).
2. Until the focus of the Pact has been changed, the Council should interpret its provisions liberally.
3. The need for the Pact should be reviewed by the Council periodically. It should probably be viewed as a temporary constraint on national autonomy, only needed while the ECB is gaining credibility. In the longer run, the Pact should not be needed for monetary stability, as long as fiscal policy has the discipline to guarantee fiscal solvency.

Notes

1. There is a tension – some might call it a logical inconsistency – in both the Delors Report and the Maastricht Treaty. If it were actually possible, and desirable, to create a completely independent central bank, dedicated solely to price stability, then why were constraints on fiscal policy thought to be necessary? Our interpretation is that the central bankers who wrote the Delors Report knew that it was impossible to make the ECB totally immune from external pressures (no matter what their official documents might have asserted), and that they therefore insisted upon the constraints. This chapter is written from that perspective.
2. There is a vast literature, and we have made no attempt to provide a comprehensive survey. We focus on a few articles that clearly articulate arguments we want to investigate. Our choice will be viewed as self-serving by some, in that it may (incorrectly) suggest that we have been the major contributors to this literature.
3. See Buti, Franco and Ongena (1998) and Part III of European Commission (2000a).
4. Part V of European Commission (2000a) describes recent developments in member states and their Stability Programmes.
5. This is of course debatable. To avoid financial penalties altogether, the member state would have to bring its deficit back to within 3 per cent of GDP one year after the excessive deficit is detected, or in other words, two years after it first occurs. If this does not happen, the member state

has to make an interest-free deposit of 0.2 per cent of GDP, plus 0.1 per cent of the amount by which its deficit/GDP ratio exceeded 3 per cent; the maximum deposit would be capped at 0.5 per cent of GDP. The deposit is forfeited after two years if the excessive deficit persists. We estimate that the forgone interest in the first year of sanctions would be in the range of 250–500 million euro for one of the larger member states. Forfeiture of the deposit would of course be much more costly, but it would only occur if the excessive deficit persisted for five years. We doubt that the financial penalties alone would be sufficient to deter excessive deficits; however, we suspect that the public approbation that goes along with them will be politically embarrassing enough to get the attention of governments.

6. The convergence criteria are the economic basis for the determination of eligibility to participate in EMU.

7. If fact, some speculate that Volcker's switch to monetarism (which deemphasised the direct setting of short-term interest rates by the Federal Reserve) was designed to allow him to make this claim, and assert that interest rates were set by the market and not the Federal Reserve.

8. Most of this literature is concerned with a central bank's incentives to keep unemployment below its natural rate. However, the general logic can easily be applied to political pressure for a real interest rate below its natural (or flexible price equilibrium) rate; see Canzoneri, Nolan and Yates (1997).

9. Eichengreen and Wyplosz (1998) carry this argument further. They note that governments have a finite amount of political capital to spend on institutional reform, and they worry that if governments expend the capital necessary to lower structural deficits further (as required by the Pact), there will not be enough capital left for the product and labour market reform that would address the unemployment and growth issues.

10. A more sophisticated argument for deficit limits might be constructed along the following lines. Large deficits might raise the natural (or full information equilibrium) real rate of interest. This could in turn increase the gap between the rate of interest desired by politicians and the equilibrium rate. In Canzoneri, Nolan and Yates's (1997) modelling of the problem, this would increase the inflation bias.

11. See Canzoneri, Nolan and Yates (1997).

12. The USA does have a large number of state fiscal authorities, and indeed about half of the total public spending is decided at the state or local level. However, Elmendorf and Mankiw (1998) note that 'Most state governments hold positive net assets, because they are prohibited from running deficits in their operating budgets, and because the assets they accumulate to fund employee pensions exceed the debt they issue to finance capital projects.'

13. An example of the political leverage this affords occurred at the beginning of the Clinton administration. Much of the independence the Federal Reserve System enjoys comes from its depoliticised selection process for the District Bank presidents, who have a vote on the policy-

making Federal Open Market Committee (FOMC). Congress held hearings on proposals to either politicise the appointment of District Bank presidents or take away their vote on the FOMC. In the end, these proposals were put on hold, but a prominent Democrat suggested that the issues might be revisited in six months' time, and he reminded the assembled District Bank presidents that the new administration had a pro-growth agenda that required low interest rates.

14. Coordination failures need not imply that government spending is too high. Chari and Kehoe (1990) model externalities involving the terms of trade effects of government purchases. These externalities may lead to government expenditures that are suboptimally large *or* small, depending on whether the country is a net exporter or a net importer of the good whose relative price increases with government purchases. Similarly, in stabilisation models, government expenditures can be suboptimally low, in the sense that they do not do enough to help neighbouring countries out of their recessions.

15. Chari and Kehoe also present a dynamic general equilibrium model of this externality.

16. This alternative may not be cost-free. It has been argued, for example, that nominal debt provides investors with a hedge against fluctuations in aggregate income. The constraint on government lending to foreigners appears to be the first-best solution.

17. Canzoneri and Diba (1998) present a policy-oriented introduction to this theory, and explain the notion of 'functional independence' in more detail. There has been an explosion of papers on this topic in the last few years. Recent papers that have a European focus include Woodford (1996), Sims (1998), and Bergin (1998).

18. This literature often goes under the heading of 'Unpleasant Monetarist Arithmetic'. See Sargent and Wallace (1981).

19. Wallace argued at the time that Paul Volcker and Ronald Reagan set policies in place that were mutually inconsistent with the budget constraint. He noted that in such a situation something has to give, but he did not speculate whether the government or the central bank would give in. He would presumably argue today, almost twenty years later, that US fiscal policy finally came into line with the low inflation policy set by the Federal Reserve. See Sargent (1987).

20. There is of course a large empirical literature that asks *whether* the budget constraint is satisfied, or whether the current policy of a particular government is sustainable. By contrast, the new theory of price determination argues that the constraint is implied by the optimising behaviour of the private sector. As such, the constraint will always be satisfied in equilibrium; the only question is *how* it gets satisfied.

21. In the simple accounting framework used here, the central bank issues money in exchange for government debt; so, M_{j+1} is equal to the central bank's bond holdings at the end of year j. At the end of each year, the central bank's profits (that is, the interest it collects on its bond holdings) are transferred back to the government's treasury; this is usually referred to as 'seigniorage'.

22.   Real money demand (M/P) depends on interest rates and output. So, once the path of i_j has been specified, the present value of seigniorage is determined.

23.   See Canzoneri and Diba (1998) or Canzoneri, Cumby and Diba (1998) for a more detailed discussion of the budget accounting framework.

24.   A further advantage of focusing on (3.2) instead of (3.1) is that we can discuss nominal GDP movements without taking a stand on how they are split into real GDP and price movements in the short run.

25.   See Canzoneri, Cumby and Diba (1998) for a formal proof.

26.   The variable x_j in (3.3) captures the numerical 3 per cent cap and the fluctuations of the actual deficit/GDP ratio, on the left-hand side of (3.4), below the cap.

27.   That is, the constraint could be on the primary surplus plus any fixed fraction of interest payments. Note, however, that a constraint on the primary surplus alone would not establish the positive linkage between debt and surpluses, and would therefore not guarantee that (3.3) holds.

28.   To see this, rewrite (3.4) in terms of structural deficits by replacing $p_j y_j$ with $p_j y f_j$, where yf represents potential output. Then, multiply the resulting inequality by $p_j y f_j / p_j y_j$. Equation (3.4) reemerges with 0.03 replaced by 0.03 ($p_j y f_j / p_j y_j$). The latter term corresponds to x_j in (3.3).

29.   See Canzoneri and Diba (1991 and 1998) and Canzoneri, Nolan and Yates (1997).

Part II
Where Does the Pact Come From?

4 Genesis of a Pact*

Juergen Stark

4.1 STARTING POINT

Economic and monetary union represents a decisive step forward in the forty-year-long drive towards political unification in Europe. When viewed from the standpoint of historical experience, traditional affinities and common interests – and, even more importantly, from the standpoint of comparable values and shared objectives – the process of integration which the European states have been undergoing appears at once logical and inevitable. The states are bound to each other, however, not just by historical and sociocultural ties but by economic relationships as well. Similar economic starting conditions and business cycles have brought economic policy across Europe much closer to uniformity than would have been possible between other industrialised nations. The rapid transformation of underlying economic conditions which has taken place since the early 1980s doubtless strengthened the resolve to achieve economic and monetary union. Economic and monetary union may thus be construed as a response to the challenges posed by the increasing intertwinement of industrial economies and by global competition.

The decisive step towards achieving a closer integration of Europe was embodied in the treaty which the finance and foreign ministers of the European Union signed on 7 February 1992 in the Dutch city of Maastricht. It reflects the results of an inter governmental conference on economic and monetary union. This conference, in turn, originated in a suggestion made in the context of a 1989 report issued by a

* I am indebted to several colleagues at the Deutsche Bundesbank and at the Federal Ministry of Finance (Bundesministerium der Finanzen) for the assistance given in connection with talks concerning the Stability Pact. I am especially indebted to Dr Uwe Bernhardt for granting me extensive access to files and enabling the perusal of documents, which helped me in the preparation of this chapter. I owe a particular debt of thanks to Klaus Regling, the former Ministerial Director in the Federal Ministry of Finance, now Director General for Economic and Financial Affairs at the EU Commission, for his share of support in our joint efforts at persuading our partners in the EU and for valuable comments made in the course of refreshing my memory on certain points.

working group consisting of EU central bank governors. This document, which was prepared under the chairmanship of the then President of the European Commission, Jacques Delors, outlined the necessary institutional arrangements and portrayed the path towards economic and monetary union in terms of a three-stage process. The purpose of the first stage would be to enable greater convergence among key economic data by arranging for a closer coordination of economic and monetary policy within the existing institutional framework. Any amendments to the Treaty that were considered necessary at the institutional level were also to be worked out and ratified before the start of the following stage. Stage 2 was conceived as a transitional period to precede the final stage and even more so as a 'learning process'. Within its confines, the basic institutions and structures of economic and monetary union were to be established and new means of coordinating macroeconomic policy tried out and extended.

The Maastricht Treaty is based on a strict stability orientation. Thus Article 2 of the Maastricht Treaty affirms as two of the European Union's basic values the promotion of sustainable, non-inflationary economic growth and a high level of employment. The 'fathers of European Union' were aware that only a monetary union based on growth and price stability could be successful and that for this it would be necessary to acquire the unqualified confidence of citizens and markets alike in the single European currency. In fulfilment of entry requirements, EU member states have had to, and must still, prove their eligibility with reference to contractually fixed, economically unambiguous reference values.

Adoption of the stability philosophy was certainly rewarded with success. A stability consciousness has taken root in Europe, given decisive impetus in many countries not only by the European Monetary System but also by the convergence criteria set down in the Maastricht Treaty. Up until the summer of 1995, however, actual implementation was not yet satisfactory in every respect. The degree of convergence attained suggested a mixed picture. Whereas eleven of the fifteen EU countries were within acceptable distance from the price stability and interest rate differential criteria, the fiscal positions of the public sector told a completely different story. Here only two countries fulfilled the relevant convergence criteria for accession to monetary union: Germany and Luxembourg. This is the reason why additional assiduous effort had to be made to accelerate the Europe-wide consolidation of public finances even more or – as sometimes proved to be the case – to at least begin with budget consolidation of government finance.

Widening general government deficits and a corresponding rise in government debt could be observed in many countries up to and including the early 1990s. Most of the reasons for this trend in public finance were 'home-made': lax spending habits even during long periods of sustained economic weakness, misguided employment policies based on the Keynesian paradigm, and the burden placed on social security systems by demographic trends. This hardening of financial structures was reflected in structural deficits that were difficult to reduce.

This occurred although it is indisputable that unsound fiscal policy practices have adverse effects on price stability, growth and employment:

- Large deficits and a large public debt place constraints on the ability of a country's economic policy-makers to act during different stages of the business cycle; also, high structural deficits entail a loss in the degree of automatic stabilisation.
- The state's absorption of resources which would otherwise have found their way into private investments results in higher long-term interest rates. This effect may be accentuated by market participants who expect greater fluctuations in business activity on account of weakened automatic stabilisers and who therefore demand higher risk premia.
- Unsound public finance policy or a stifling government spending/debt ratio impairs the overall efficiency of an economy and creates risks to price stability, which might provoke a restrictive response from the central bank.
- Unsound fiscal policy can threaten the external value of the currency by undermining the credibility of policy-makers.
- These problems are especially pronounced in monetary union since the danger posed by negative external effects increases with ongoing economic integration and with the formation of a single monetary policy. The policy of a single country might have adverse consequences for all the other participating countries. The inflationary fiscal policy of a single country would thus incur costs that would have to be shared by all member states.

4.2 PRECAUTIONS TAKEN BY THE MAASTRICHT TREATY TO ENSURE BUDGETARY DISCIPLINE

Continuing economic integration of European national economies presupposed not only the removal of obstacles to the free exchange of goods and services and common underlying economic conditions but also required that the member states had a shared economic policy orientation. Article 99 (formerly Article 103) of the Maastricht Treaty therefore stipulates that member states regard their economic policies as a matter of common concern and coordinate them within the ECOFIN Council. As already indicated, such coordination efforts are certainly in the interest of all participants since they make it possible to avoid negative external effects and undesirable free-rider behaviour. This type of coordination also contributes to the consistent formulation of policy objectives and to the efficient implementation of policy instruments at the national and European levels. The Maastricht Treaty considerably extended the provisions regarding coordination and surveillance that had previously been in effect and made them more specific. The Broad Economic Policy Guidelines, which are to be decided annually by the Council in keeping with Article 99 of the EC Treaty, and the procedure for monitoring budgetary policy laid down in Article 104 (formerly Article 104c) of the EC Treaty are now of central importance.

The Maastricht Treaty also includes different provisions ranging from Articles 101 to 104 (formerly 104 to 104c) intended to keep public deficits down and to ensure budgetary discipline on the part of the member states:

- prohibition of financing government deficits with the aid of the European Central Bank or the national central banks;
- prohibition of privileged access on the part of the public sector to financial institutions;
- exemption of the Community from liability for the commitments of member states;
- and, finally, the requirement for Stage 3 that member states avoid excessive deficits.

In this way, the Treaty attempts to ensure that the stability framework that has been established is not abandoned in Stage 3. In particular, Article 104 of the EC Treaty represents the 'ceiling' below which national fiscal policy must remain. However, it was not clear that this stability framework could withstand external pressures as well and that the participants in monetary union would be capable of fulfilling their treaty obligations at all times.

According to Article 104 of the Maastricht Treaty on determination of the fact that a country has incurred an excessive deficit, the Treaty does not specify the duration of individual stages or of the process as a whole. What is notably lacking is an automatic mechanism for rapidly correcting the public policy flaws of a member state. At every level of decision the Council and the Commission retain significant discretionary latitude, which could render the final result hostage to purely political decisions and, in so doing, perhaps undermine confidence in convergence as a lasting accomplishment and move the ECB to act.

4.2.1 Prerequisites for Deciding on the Existence of an Excessive Deficit: Recommendation of the Commission and Decision of the Council

In accordance with Article 104 of the Maastricht Treaty, the deficit of a country is assessed with regard to the development of the budgetary situation and to the ratio of government debt to gross domestic product. The reference values of 3 per cent and 60 per cent of GDP, respectively, are specified in a supplementary protocol. However, a figure above these values does not automatically denote an excessive deficit. This must be decided by a corresponding Council resolution, which must necessarily be preceded, in turn, by an assessment and recommendation of the Commission to that effect. The Commission and the Council, however, are not obliged to submit either an assessment or a recommendation. Thus an excessive deficit is not an objectively determinable figure and non-compliance with deficit criteria has no consequences as long as the Council refrains from issuing a finding to that effect.

4.2.2 Discretionary Options in Assessing a Deficit

Consistent with Article 104 of the EC Treaty, the Commission monitors compliance with the reference values mentioned in Protocol No. 11. It is especially concerned to monitor whether the ratio of the planned or actual government deficit to GDP exceeds the reference value of 3 per cent. The article allows, however, for certain exceptions; thus a deficit is not deemed excessive if either the ratio has declined substantially and continuously and reached a level approaching the reference value or, alternatively, the excess over the reference value is only exceptional and temporary and the ratio remains close to the reference value. The criterion which places the ceiling on public debt at 60 per cent of GDP may be violated if the ratio is sufficiently diminishing and approaching the reference value at a satisfactory pace. These exceptions leave the Commission with relatively broad discretionary powers.

If on review the Commission determines that the member state fails to fulfil at least one of the criteria, the Commission prepares a report in which it takes into account other relevant factors such as its medium-term economic and budgetary position or the ratio of government deficit to investment expenditure. The Commission may, however, already prepare a report regardless, if it is of the opinion that there is in future a risk of an excessive deficit.

Once the Economic and Financial Committee has delivered its opinion on the Commission Report, the Commission can recommend its corresponding findings to the Council, if it now considers that an excessive deficit or the risk that such may occur exists. The Council, acting by a qualified majority after having examined the entire situation and considered any observations the member state concerned may wish to make, then decides whether an excessive deficit exists. Although the recommendation of the Commission provides the basis for the Council's decision, the Council need not follow the recommendation. It can, contrary to the recommendation, deny that an excessive deficit exists but it cannot act without the Commission's recommendation.

4.2.3 Inadequate Sanctions: Article 104 Punishes Not the 'Sin' But Only the 'Failure to Repent'

In keeping with Article 116(3), (4) of the EC Treaty (formerly, 109e(3), (4)) the member states were only required during Stage 2 of economic and monetary union to strive to avoid excessive deficits. If an excessive deficit in a member state existed, the Council made a recommendation to the member state concerned, making it a condition that the situation be brought to an end within a given period. If there had been no effective action on the part of the member state within the period laid down, the strongest sanction available to the Council consisted in making its recommendation public.

Only in the final stage of economic and monetary union are the participants obliged to avoid excessive deficits, and other more stringent sanctions have been envisaged to encourage deficit reduction, if a member state persists in failing to put into practice the recommendations of the Council. The most stringent sanction available for a 'failure to repent' consists in the Council's requiring the member state concerned to make a non-interest-bearing deposit and, if necessary, in the Council's imposing fines 'of an appropriate size'. Both the type of measure and – in the case of financial sanctions – the size of the penalty are to be specified, in conformity with Article 104 of the EC Treaty, at the Council's discretion.

4.3 INITIAL ATTEMPT TO GAUGE THE RESPONSE TO GERMAN SUPPORT FOR AN ADDITIONAL AGREEMENT

At the start of Stage 2 of economic and monetary union on 1 January 1994, it seemed as if the start of Stage 3 might be decided as early as 1996 and monetary union initiated in the following year, if at all possible. The German public now became more conscious of the impending monetary union. Its sensibilities having been decisively formed by the experience of two hyperinflations in one century, it could not suppress a certain widespread scepticism with regard to the imminent exchange of the D-Mark, whose internal and external value had proven so durable, for a currency whose stability could not be foreseen with certainty. Making acceptance more difficult was the fact that the D-Mark was regarded by the German public as a symbol of economic recovery after the war and of newly restored international esteem.

At the same time, the responsible political authorities in Germany, having had time to learn from their initial experiences with the procedures envisaged in the Maastricht Treaty, now entertained more far-reaching considerations as to how these new regulations might be supplemented, if at all. The rationale behind these considerations was to prevent the monetary policy of the future European Central Bank from being undermined by the unsound fiscal policy practices of participating countries and to prevent the ECB from having to assume the burden of guaranteeing price stability alone. It was also intended to send a convincing signal that all member states would maintain sustained and lasting budgetary discipline even after the decision on eligibility rendered in Stage 3 and that budgetary discipline was not simply a one-off accession criterion to be met at the start of Stage 3 of monetary union. The confidence of the public and the market in the stability orientation of economic and monetary union was to be strengthened.

Thus the Federal Ministry of Finance expressed its interest in additional government budget provisions for states participating in Stage 3 of monetary union for the first time in London at a conference held by the US investment bank Goldman Sachs in May 1995. A lasting stability community would have to be established – so the argument ran – if the German public was to be won over to the idea of monetary union and a new currency. It was argued that mere reliance on positive economic prospects and larger tax proceeds would not suffice to fulfil the fiscal convergence criteria. The participating states in monetary union should agree among themselves to establish additional commitments and regulations that would ensure the adoption of sound fiscal policy practices in Stage 3 of monetary union as well. At the same time it was emphasised even then that the underlying intention was neither to postpone the start of monetary union nor to add another criterion for entry into monetary union.

The Deutsche Bundesbank endorsed this position. It had already pointed early on to the need to supplement monetary union with a political union in order to ease the potential conflict between a single monetary policy and decentralised fiscal policies. Only the introduction of additional regulations could defuse this incendiary situation, in which national jurisdiction over government budgets would have been left untouched. The main concern here was that countries after accession to monetary union might fall back into their old routines in the absence of genuinely binding budget rules and sanctions with teeth.

While, in late summer 1995, the Federal Ministry of Finance was giving preliminary expression to its thoughts on a supplementary treaty arrangement, attempts were made – at first on a bilateral basis – to gauge major EU partner countries' responses to German wishes regarding such an agreement, familiar at the time under the name 'fiscal policy Schengen agreement'. As events proved, a widespread consensus existed, in principle, that sound fiscal policy is the prerequisite for a stability-oriented monetary policy. The difficulty of getting both Parliament and the executive branch to agree on the national level, as required, to a modification of national budget law and of the budget implementation process in keeping with the consolidation requirements of the Maastricht Treaty was perceived as being the main problem. It was conceded that the consequences of the Maastricht Treaty for budget policy had up to that point not been given sufficient attention. The response of many of the partner countries to the proposals for more far-reaching regulations to ensure fiscal discipline was by comparison more circumspect. The need to act was downplayed; the existing treaty regulations were thought to be either sufficiently effective or still untested, in which case experience would first have to be gathered.

German thoughts on a supplementary agreement were first presented to a larger audience during a meeting of the ECOFIN Council
in Brussels on 18 September 1995. The most important requirements
were only sketched there:

- more restrictive budgetary targets were intended to ensure that
  the deficit ceiling of 3 per cent of GDP was not violated during any
  stage of the business cycle;
- more stringent, automatic sanctions were intended to add 'teeth'
  to the agreement in the event the rules had been violated.

The initial reactions to the German proposals were characterised by a
certain reserve, especially in the case of the larger member states. The
position taken was one already familiar from the bilateral exploratory
talks, namely, that the precautions taken by the Maastricht Treaty
were sufficient to ensure budgetary discipline. Again, they argued that
the status of the existing convergence criteria as barriers to entry
should not be modified. The Commission also showed signs of a
certain unease and warned, in particular, against unravelling the
Treaty by reopening specific issues. This would be tantamount to
opening a veritable 'Pandora's box' of desired amendments. It could
safely be assumed that the negotiations would again be subject to a
variety of new demands for treaty revisions.

Still the main reason for this negative attitude was probably the
apprehension on the part of certain countries that additional barriers
to entry into Stage 3 of monetary union were being erected at a time
when it still appeared doubtful that they could meet the existing criteria.
Another factor might have been the reluctance to accept additional
constraints on national sovereignty in the form of budgetary policy
restrictions when, at the same time, unfavourable economic conditions
made recourse to fiscal policy instruments appear desirable.

The German Federal Minister of Finance, Mr Waigel, attempted to
ease the situation by emphasising that a raising of the entry threshold
for monetary union had not been intended; nor, he added, was it
Germany's intention to reopen the negotiations on monetary union
that had resulted in the corresponding sections of the Maastricht
Treaty. Nevertheless there was interest in reaching an ancillary agreement. The Federal Government, he went on, was also bound by a
ruling of the Federal Constitutional Court, which stipulated that
monetary union take the form of a stability community. Finance
Minister Waigel again pointed out how important a sustained

consolidation policy and the fulfilment of convergence criteria were for the future acceptance of the single currency.

The European partner countries reversed their thinking on this matter within a few days of the meeting. During the informal ECOFIN meeting in Valencia at the end of September 1995, the participants acknowledged the need to establish regulations that would guarantee price stability for the following 'generations of finance ministers'.

4.4 THE FEDERAL MINISTRY OF FINANCE'S DRAFT OF THE STABILITY PACT

Up to that point the Federal Ministry of Finance had no extensively formulated text of the desired ancillary agreement. The Federal Ministry of Finance was now commissioned on very short notice to elaborate on what had hitherto been only a sketchy proposal for a 'stability pact' with a view to providing a basis for agreement between the heads of state and government that would require no amendments to the Maastricht Treaty.

The ten-page document which the Federal Ministry of Finance prepared in response emphasised that it was neither necessary nor desirable that fiscal policy be placed under the responsibility of the Community; the principle of subsidiarity applied as a matter of policy. Only if, however, the fiscal policies of member states were fundamentally sound could the advantages of monetary union be fully exploited and unnecessary tensions with lasting and adverse consequences for growth and employment be avoided. Consequently, the paper demanded that European economic and monetary union be protected against the unsound fiscal policies of individual member states. For this reason accession criteria and institutional safeguards built into the EC Treaty had to be made more precise and operationalised. Countries participating in Stage 3 had to sign a 'Stability Pact for Europe', which, in so far as they willingly imposed this restraint upon themselves, would be interpreted by the markets and residents as additional and unambiguous proof of their commitment to sound fiscal policy. The member states had to declare their interest in actively and sustainedly pursuing sound fiscal policies to promote growth and employment – albeit without denying national sovereignty in fiscal policy matters. The cornerstones of a common approach to national fiscal policy, to be pursued in the sense outlined, were to be:

- sustained support for ECB monetary policy through spending discipline and consistency in public sector policy;
- sparing use of financial markets;
- a ceiling on the government share in order to provide the public and private sectors with room to manoeuvre;
- greater preponderance in public expenditure of general government investments operating under near-market conditions and the promotion of private investments.

In the interests of achieving these goals, the paper drafted by the Federal Ministry of Finance set up the following rules, which the countries participating in Stage 3 of economic and monetary union were expected to embrace.

4.4.1 Budgetary Discipline

- Europe's stability requirements are to be taken into account when framing financial and economic policy measures, especially when drawing up budgetary and financial plans.
- The growth rates for government expenditure are – to the extent possible – to be held below the increase in nominal GDP over the medium term.
- The 3 per cent ceiling on deficits is not to be exceeded – not even during economically less prosperous times. This implies a medium-term deficit ceiling of 1 per cent of GDP during normal economic periods, if a safety margin is to be established that would allow the states to observe the 3 per cent deficit ceiling even in economically difficult times. Countries entering monetary union with a large amount of government debt (over 50 per cent) (note: this is the value actually mentioned in the Federal Ministry of Finance document) are committed to undershooting this target variable, if possible.
- Exceptions to the 3 per cent ceiling rule can only be made with the approval of a qualified majority of the states participating in monetary union and only in extreme cases.
- Even if the stock of government debt falls below the 60 per cent ceiling set by the Maastricht Treaty, it is to be consistently reduced in order to set a positive consolidation cycle in motion, to reduce the share of public expenditure comprised by interest payments, to gain greater latitude in fiscal policy and to limit budgetary risks.

4.4.2 Establishment of an Early-Warning System

Compliance with the ceiling specified above is monitored using data reported by the Commission in the spring and autumn of every year.

4.4.3 Mechanism for the Automatic Imposition of Sanctions

If it emerges that a country participating in monetary union has, either in its budgetary planning or in the implementation of its budget, exceeded the deficit ceiling of 3 per cent of GDP, the following mechanism for imposing sanctions is automatically activated:

- The member state concerned is required to make a non-interest-bearing deposit (a 'stability deposit'). The size of this deposit is equivalent to 0.25 per cent of the GDP of the member state concerned for each whole percentage point in excess of the deficit ceiling.
- The 'stability deposit' will be repaid as soon as the deficit incurred by the member state concerned ceases to exceed the reference value for government deficits.
- If, after two years, the deficit ceiling is still being exceeded, the 'stability deposit' is converted into a fine.

4.4.4 Stability Council

The member states form a European Stability Council within the ECOFIN Council, which decides on whether these self-imposed restraints have been violated and, if necessary, enforces them. It meets at least biannually, either on presentation of the deficit figures by the Commission or at the request of a member state. The European Stability Council examines fiscal policy with a view to its compatibility with the cornerstones and objectives of the Stability Pact, hears reports on the discharge of this self-imposed obligation, and, in extreme cases, decides on whether an exemption from the deficit ceiling rule is to be granted. Any discrepancies are explained there and a specific convergence plan is presented to remedy the situation. The European Stability Council is also permitted to issue general fiscal policy guidelines and to offer public recommendations for national fiscal policy as long as they are related to the attainment of the agreed objectives.

4.5 WORK IS DELEGATED TO THE COMMITTEES

On 7 November 1995, at the second reading of the Federal budget bill for the coming year, Finance Minister Waigel gave the Bundestag the first indication of his intention to propose a European stability pact. The stability pact, he said, would send another positive signal to the markets, which would contribute to the greater soundness and credibility of monetary union. The pact required no amendment to the Maastricht Treaty and no follow-up negotiations. In September, he went on to explain, he had already arranged for such an ancillary stability pact for Europe to be drafted in the form of a binding, self-imposed commitment on the part of the states participating in Stage 3 of monetary union.

Three days later, on 10 November 1995, the detailed proposals of the Federal Ministry of Finance were finally sent to the ECOFIN members. On the same day, while Finance Minister Waigel, on the occasion of the third reading of the 1996 Federal budget bill, spoke extensively before the Bundestag on the subject of the planned stability pact, media representatives were informed for the first time of the details of the project in a separate conference.

Finance Minister Waigel's proposals were exceptionally well-received in Paris. As the press reported shortly afterwards, the French minister of finance, Mr Arthuis, had spoken in favour of financial sanctions as a means of ensuring that the countries participating in Stage 3 of economic and monetary union exercise budgetary discipline. With his requirement that the budgetary positions of the members states be in balance – announced during a press conference – Arthuis went beyond even the German proposals. Stability pact negotiations must begin right away, he demanded.

The EU Monetary Committee considered the concrete proposals laid down by the Germans for the first time on 20 and 21 November 1995. Whereas in summer the comments which the exploratory talks had elicited from European partner countries had been largely sceptical, the response to the detailed German proposals for a stability pact was now mostly positive. After the ECOFIN meeting of 27 November 1995, which included a luncheon during which the plans were presented in detail, Finance Minister Waigel was able to report that the Stability Pact had met with broad consent on fundamentals. Again, it emerged that the positions of the major member states were not that far apart. France, in particular, described the proposals as being correct in substance and as being implementable without modification of the Maastricht Treaty. At the meeting, Germany received special support from small countries; they had recognised that the planned Stability Pact did not tighten the Maastricht criteria but rather protected small countries, in particular, from the consequences of unsound fiscal policies practised by the larger ones. The Scandinavian member states even went so far as to indicate that they would have to show budget surpluses over the medium term if they were to reduce their large government debt and come to terms with the ageing of their population. The mechanism for the automatic imposition of sanctions was also praised for its circumvention of political decision-making; this represented a substantial improvement in so far as the clarity and directness of the process was concerned. Every country knew in advance what it was getting itself into. This was a just, fair and clever solution, as Finance Minister Waigel described the German proposal to the press on a later occasion.

There were, however, also critical comments. Thus it was pointed out that the Mediterranean countries suffered from structural problems peculiar to them, which an undifferentiated approach to deficit figures could not adequately take into account. On the grounds that they still had to catch up in respect of investments, these countries suggested that the quality of public expenditure also be taken into account when assessing deficit size and that capital formation expenditure, in particular, not be counted when calculating the level of the deficit.

The European Council meeting in Madrid, on 15 and 16 December 1995, paved the way for the Stability Pact for it was here that the heads of state and government approved the project. In the Presidency Conclusions, the chairman highlighted the significance of budgetary discipline for the future success of economic and monetary union and for the future acceptance of the single currency by the general public. It must be ensured, it argued, that after the transition to Stage 3 financial positions continue to develop soundly and in keeping with the obligations imposed by the Maastricht Treaty. The ECOFIN Council was commissioned to issue a report on the problem of ensuring budgetary discipline as soon as possible.

The actual work involved in implementing the planned Stability Pact began during a meeting of the Monetary Committee on 17 January 1996; this work was subsequently supported by the Alternate Members of the Monetary Committee and by the Commission, with the assistance of the Council's legal service. The committee work schedule at first envisaged the compilation of an intermediate

ECOFIN report for the European Council meeting in Florence in the summer of that year. A 'substantial' statement of results was then to be presented at a meeting of the European Council in Dublin in December 1996.

While the general objectives of the German proposal found widespread support, a number of specific issues and problems had been raised at the start of the committee meetings, which could be resolved in the following months only through sometimes long and difficult deliberations. Among the economic problems raised were the questions of whether a more stringent absolute government deficit ceiling below 3 per cent of GDP was to be introduced and whether it would be advisable to define the medium-term government deficit target in a stricter fashion. A number of countries insisted on a more stringent ceiling than the German maximum requirement of 1 per cent of GDP. Other alternatives under consideration included differentiating medium-term target specifications according to country, establishing a medium-term target variable for the entire European Union, and possibly introducing a target value for the stock of government debt. Finally, discussions focused on whether the Excessive Deficit Procedure could be initiated on the basis of budget plans alone and whether government resolutions should be recognised as constituting, in themselves, effective actions to combat deficits. The criteria for determining what constituted exceptional circumstances proved particularly difficult to pin down, especially the question of what was to be understood by a 'severe recession', as did the criteria for determining the size of 'pecuniary sanctions'.

Among the legal issues still to be clarified, the most important concerned the basis for the Stability Pact, especially the basis for the mechanism for automatically imposing sanctions which Germany was seeking. Since there was general agreement that the EC Treaty itself was not to be reopened, the approach to be pursued consisted in 'moulding' the corresponding regulations wherever possible to fit into a supplementary body of secondary law relating to the Maastricht Treaty. Where this, however, proved infeasible, the German party to the debate entertained the possibility of an ancillary treaty, binding under international law and to be signed only by countries participating in Stage 3 of monetary union. The debate concerning the German demand for automatic sanctions, which was conducted parallel to the discussion of this problem, was more concerned with fundamental political issues. Controversy had arisen as to whether the individual stages of the procedure could be made to fall completely under the statutory commitment, in keeping with German preferences, or whether the discretionary powers, as defined in Article 104 of the EC Treaty, must be retained.

Meanwhile, as had already been announced at the European summit in Madrid, the Commission had presented a document entitled 'Towards a Stability Pact'. In so doing, the Commission was exercising its right to initiate legislation. The document listed the positive effects which sound fiscal policy practices would have for the entire economy without neglecting to mention at the same time that the budgetary discipline requirement was rooted in the Broad Economic Policy Guidelines for 1995 and that the Commission had insisted on a deficit target of substantially less than 3 per cent. The Commission came to the conclusion that a virtually balanced budget was better suited as a medium-term target than a budgetary imbalance of 1 per cent of GDP to ensure compliance with the deficit ceiling at all times. Given the differences in starting conditions, it was urged that the medium-term target values for deficits, the debt/GDP ratio and real convergence be flexible and tailored to the specific fiscal situations of different countries; the 1 per cent target should apply primarily to the member states as a whole. These requirements were supported by sensitivity analyses in which the responsiveness of government deficits to cyclical changes was examined. As for the question of legal implementation, the Commission noted that most of the points included in the planned Stability Pact could be put into practice on the basis of Articles 99 and 104 of the EC Treaty, including the provisions made there for secondary regulations. As it currently stood, however, the Maastricht Treaty provided no means of implementing the German requirement of automatic sanctions. Finally, the Commission pointed out that the Stability Pact required not only closer coordination of objectives and measures at the national and European Union levels but also improvements in the monitoring procedure. Consequently, the member states should design 'stability programmes' with medium-term budgetary targets instead of the convergence programmes envisaged by the Treaty. These programmes were to be discussed and modified at the European Union level before they could ultimately be approved by the Council.

The Commission document was praised by all sides, if not on all points. From the German point of view, it represented a positive development in the sense that the document as a whole provided yet another solid basis for the pending discussion. The document acknowledged the need for fiscal policy discipline but, more than that, its basic attitude towards the German proposals was clearly positive. Indeed, its insistence on a balanced budget went beyond German proposals. The German side, however, found itself unable to accept the proposals for a EU-wide deficit target or for a differentiation of target values according to country since this would have resulted in a corresponding loss of clarity, a blurring of responsibility and, in the final analysis, a loss of discipline. In addition, it was necessary that the legal issues associated with the Stability Pact continue to be examined with care. In this connection the German delegation had continually called attention to the fact that the most important component of an effective and credible stability pact – apart from enforced compliance with the deficit ceiling of 3 per cent throughout the entire business cycle and well-defined criteria for identifying exceptions – was the mechanism for the automatic imposition of sanctions.

One of the problem areas, in which a common position was found relatively quickly in the course of subsequent sessions, involved the call for a more stringent ceiling on the stock of government debt. Already as early as April 1996, participants in the informal ECOFIN meeting at Verona were unanimous in agreeing that the Maastricht Treaty restrictions need not be tightened. The reason was that compliance with the restrictive requirements concerning fiscal deficits would inevitably have required a considerable reduction in debt. The differentiation of deficit targets by country, which had been proposed, notably by the Commission, was also dropped later – for reasons already mentioned.

4.6   SCORE AT HALF-TIME: THE EUROPEAN COUNCIL IN FLORENCE

Another rapprochement had been achieved before the European heads of state and government met in Florence on 21 and 22 June 1996. ECOFIN's interim report to the European Council had come out in favour of regarding the reference value of 3 per cent of GDP cited in the Maastricht Treaty as placing an absolute ceiling on the budget deficit of a country, a ceiling whose transgression would be tolerated only in exceptional cases and provisionally, provided the deficit ratio remained close to the reference value. Each member state should strive towards budgetary positions close to balance or in surplus over the medium term so that the automatic stabilisers could remain effective throughout the entire business cycle without pushing the budget deficit beyond the reference value of 3 per cent of GDP.

As for the implementation of the Stability Pact, the ECOFIN Council's interim report, presented in Florence, announced that a plan for monitoring the medium-term budgetary position of the member states was being developed on the basis of a Commission proposal and in keeping with Article 99 of the EC Treaty. It was intended to ensure that excessive deficits could be detected early on and so avoided. ECOFIN also approved the structure of the Excessive Deficit Procedure, as outlined in Article 104 of the EC Treaty. A Commission proposal was being used here as well to find means, consistent with the Treaty, of accelerating the Excessive Deficit Procedure, the most prominent of these being short time-periods for each stage of the procedure. It was generally agreed to work on the assumption that the Council would, in fact, impose a fixed set of sanctions if it were determined that an excessive deficit continues to exist. Finally, ECOFIN considered extending the planned Stability Pact to cover member states with a derogation; certain regulations were not, however, to apply to these countries.

All in all, the meeting of the European Council did not fail to produce certain results; it left, however, other important issues associated with the Stability Pact proposal unresolved. Although the desire to shorten the general timing of the process was widely shared – despite the variety of proposals entertained – no agreement could be reached concerning the mechanism for automatically imposing sanctions, the criteria for identifying exceptional circumstances and the size of sanctions. On the contrary, the deliberations only raised new questions. Thus it proved to be unclear whether sanctions were to be imposed in the case of an already existing deficit or only in the event of a persistent one. The discussion also took a controversial turn when it entered on legal issues. The attempt to shorten the duration of the deficit procedure in a manner consistent with Article 104(14) of the EC Treaty raised the question of whether the existing Protocol for the implementation of the procedure would have to be replaced by a new regulation – which would have required a unanimous resolution – or whether a resolution passed by a qualified majority would suffice to amend the Protocol. In the end, the Commission announced that it would be presenting proposals on a legal instrument for implementing the Stability Pact after the informal ECOFIN meeting in Dublin from 20 to 22 September 1996.

4.7 THE PATH TO 'MARATHON'

After the summer break of 1996, the Federal Ministry of Finance launched a new initiative. Through bilateral talks conducted with all the finance ministries of the European Union it sought to enlist support for the objectives of the Stability Pact. It also looked into ways of resolving the still unsettled issues before the European Council in Dublin. Although the meeting of the informal ECOFIN in Dublin in September also failed to make progress on the main unresolved issues involving the Stability Pact, it was at least possible to work out problems in 'marginal areas'. Thus it was agreed, as part of the surveillance process specified in Article 99 of the EC Treaty, to require the 'ins' of monetary union to present Stability Programmes and the 'outs' to present Convergence Programmes, the programmes to be precisely specified in each case. The Commission's proposal for establishing an early-warning system, which is likewise based on Article 99, was also approved. The 'Protocol question', which had arisen in connection with the desire to shorten the excessive deficit procedure insofar permitted by Article 104(14) of the EC Treaty, was to be resolved by abandoning the existing Protocol but retaining the old reference values.[1]

In the course of the debate on the Excessive Deficit Procedure, an extensive treatment of the topics 'severe recession' and 'exceptional circumstances' had hitherto been dismissed as being premature. Another reason for this attitude was the prevailing conviction that such terms need not be quantified precisely and that a purely verbal description would suffice. In so far, however, as the German views had in the meantime met with general approval, more precise definitions were now indispensable if the credibility of the procedure was to be reinforced. Accurate definitions were to be inserted in the appropriate legal passages. At the same time the Commission, together with some countries, felt that the Council should be left a certain degree of discretion. The Council, at the instigation of the German party, then addressed a request to the Monetary Committee and to the Commission, inquiring whether it might not be possible in the interests of bolstering the decision-making procedure to reverse the burden of proof. This was the Deutsche Bundesbank's idea; the 'sinner' himself would have been responsible for showing that no excessive deficit exists.

Attempts to streamline the Excessive Deficit Procedure along the lines laid down in Article 104 of the EC Treaty resulted in a compromise which amounted to shortening the total duration of the procedure – from the first Commission report to the imposition of sanctions – to a maximum of twelve months. Alternatively, the six to seven months demanded by some large countries and by the Commission as well amounted to considerably less than what the other member states had envisaged. The decision in favour of a relatively narrow time limit also affected the decision as to what was to be recognised as an 'effective action for the deficit reduction'. Now even government resolutions were to be counted; still, if the system is politically stable, this does not seem inappropriate but rather logical. If, contrary to normal expectations, the government resolution is not confirmed by Parliament, the rating 'effective action' can be withdrawn.

Up to the beginning of December 1996 it had not been possible to reach a consensus in three important areas: the question of a mechanism for the automatic imposition of sanctions (that is, the self-imposed commitment of Commission and Council), the definition of what constitutes a 'severe recession' (that is, criteria for identifying exceptional cases) and, finally, the size of pecuniary sanctions. The likelihood that these problems might be resolved soon, that is, before the European Council met in Dublin in mid-December, had also decreased markedly, the main reason being that the economic climate had worsened in a number of European states. This fuelled fears on the part of vulnerable countries that the new 'austerity' measures and the loss of national sovereignty might act as a monetary and financial strait jacket. These fears manifested themselves in an increasingly rigid and critical attitude towards the German call for automatic sanctions, which would have left the Council no room for discretion in the event of an excessive deficit. Moreover, in some countries, the highest authorities were only informed of the Stability Pact at a very late stage. Some of the heads of state and government were concerned that they might have to consign political decision-making to some 'technocratic legal construction'.

At the ECOFIN meeting at the beginning of December 1996 the ministers were able to agree only on the size of sanctions and on the time limits for their imposition. The German position had originally envisaged fines amounting to 0.25 per cent of GDP for every whole percentage point in excess of the deficit ceiling and categorically rejected absolute ceilings. Other countries had dismissed this requirement as too extreme and declared themselves willing to accept at most an initial fine of 0.1 per cent of GDP. The compromise finally reached was in keeping with the Commission's proposal: a set fine of 0.2 per cent for every percentage point in excess of the deficit ceiling and a maximum sanction size of 0.5 per cent of GDP. A failure to meet the criterion for stock of government debt was not to be punished. The maximum time limit for the imposition of sanctions was set at ten months after determination that an excessive deficit exists; the final decision regarding the imposition of sanctions was to be taken, however, by the Council.

The Monetary Committee, which met two days before the European Council convened in Dublin, succeeded in mediating between the different standpoints on automatic sanctions; its main purpose was to prepare an ECOFIN report for the heads of state and government. The Commission now professed itself willing – on submission of a corresponding report as stipulated in Article 104(3) of the EC Treaty – to initiate the sanctions process any time when the planned or existing deficit of a country exceeded the 3 per cent mark. The report, however, did not oblige it to conclude that an excessive deficit existed. The Commission's report was to be forwarded to the Economic and Financial Committee which, in the final stage of monetary union, would be the Monetary Committee's successor. In keeping with Article 104(4) this Committee would formulate an opinion on the Commission's report within two weeks. Finally, the Commission addresses a written opinion to the Council, assessing whether an excessive deficit exists.

The Commission's self-imposed obligation, which was to be incorporated in Dublin in the European Council's envisaged resolution concerning the Stability Pact, was a very important step towards implementing automatic sanctions since only the Commission was legally authorised by the Treaty to initiate the Excessive Deficit Procedure. Strong differences of opinion continued to be expressed in the Monetary Committee concerning the Council's self-imposed obligation to decide according to Article 104(6) of the EC Treaty whether an excessive deficit exists. A number of countries resolutely insisted that the discretionary powers which the Treaty had envisaged for the Council in policy matters be left intact while the German position, which was supported by several other countries, defended prior constraints on the Council's decision. The decision as to whether the Council would subject itself in advance to this constraint was passed on to ECOFIN, the German position being captured in the sentence, 'the expectation is that the Council will respect the Commission's decision'.

In attempting to define the exceptional circumstances under which a violation of the 3 per cent ceiling could be justified, the Monetary

Committee agreed to acknowledge circumstances that lay outside a country's control such as natural catastrophes. In Dublin the following alternative definitions of a 'severe recession' were presented to ECOFIN for its consideration:

- A decline in real GDP of at least 2 per cent, either on an annual average or over four consecutive quarters, is to be deemed an exceptional circumstance. This was in keeping with the German position.
- An annual decline in real GDP of at least 1.5 per cent or 2 per cent (note: exact figures were not specified) is to be deemed an exceptional circumstance. A smaller annual decline in GDP, which must amount, however, to at least 1 per cent or 0.5 per cent (note: exact figures were not specified), is only to be deemed an exceptional circumstance, if other reasons can be given for doing so. This proposal was based on the so-called 'Box model', which originated with the chairman of the Monetary Committee, Sir Nigel Wicks, and which, in fact, came close to realising the Bundesbank's demand that the burden of proof be reversed.
- A severe recession is to be described purely verbally without any attempt at quantitative definition.

4.8   THE 'DUBLIN MARATHON'

The meeting of finance ministers and then of EU heads of state and government in the Irish capital on 12 and 13 December 1996 has gone down in the history of Council meetings as the 'Dublin Marathon'. It began at 4 p.m. on the first day and ended twenty-four hours later – and even then the Council of Finance Ministers was first able to reach a compromise on the report to be submitted to the European Council in the early morning hours of the second day. As had been expected, the main point of contention had been the automatic imposition of sanctions in the case of countries which had violated the ceiling placed on government budget deficits of 3 per cent of GDP: the German call for a clear definition of, and restriction on, extenuating circumstances – which, incidentally, was supported by a large number of other countries – was countered by an insistence on the Council's discretionary powers. The German arguments that as unequivocal a commitment as possible to a lasting and credible stability culture in Europe was indispensable were met with the objection that national sovereignty should not be curtailed further.

The talks were interrupted several times, not only to give the Irish ECOFIN Chairman, Mr Quinn, an opportunity to work out a compromise proposal but also to attempt to reconcile opposing standpoints through additional bilateral talks – in particular, between the French and German finance ministers. Finance Minister Waigel made a stirring appeal to his colleagues, saying it was no longer possible to turn away from the resolutions of Verona and Florence without sacrificing credibility. Indeed, had the expectation not been voiced at those Council meetings that the Council would under certain circumstances always impose sanctions?

At first the finance ministers concentrated their efforts on producing a document on the implementation and acceleration of the Excessive Deficit Procedure. The chairman proposed that, as a matter of principle, the Commission treat a deficit ceiling violation as exceptional in its mandatory report only if it were accompanied by a decline in real GDP of at least 1.5 per cent. If the decline in GDP lay between 0.75 per cent and 1.5 per cent the Council was to decide whether it was possible to justify the deficit in terms of exceptional circumstances.

This proposal amounted to revoking the discretionary powers of Council and Commission in cases where a country's deficit ceiling violation was accompanied by a slowdown in economic activity of less than 0.75 per cent in the period under review. This proposal, however, continued to meet with the opposition of countries which insisted on the Council's having absolute discretionary power irrespective of the size of the decline in GDP. In the end, Mr Juncker, the Prime Minister and Finance Minister of Luxembourg, succeeded in reviving the faltering talks. Recognising that agreement was possible on the text, he suggested that the figures be omitted for the time being. The consensus reached with respect to the deficit procedure was that in cases involving grey areas the Council should consider the defence entered by the country concerned and that a resolution would be passed by a qualified majority.

The German views had been incorporated in the draft which was finally agreed only in diluted form and as a quasi-automatic mechanism since the decisions which they had called upon Commission and Council to take were to follow only – as the corresponding clause indicated – 'as a rule'. Above all, this formula helped to preserve the discretionary power granted to the Council by the EC Treaty. To have revoked it, however, would have meant revising the corresponding Article of the Maastricht Treaty. Any attempt to reformulate this passage of the Treaty would have proved counterproductive since it would immediately have been greeted with demands that the accession criteria for the third stage of monetary union also be renegotiated and, if possible, relaxed. For this reason the German delegation at no time considered reopening treaty negotiations.

At the start of the European Council meeting of 12 December Chancellor Kohl, President Chirac, Commission President Santer and Council Chairman Bruton agreed to commission a small group of finance ministers (and their deputies) headed by Prime Minister Juncker to resolve still unsettled issues. During the second round of talks, which lasted several hours, the criteria for identifying exceptional circumstances were specified. Here the German negotiating team succeeded in gaining support for their requirement that a deficit be regarded as exceptional only if it is accompanied by a decline in real GDP in annual terms of 2 per cent – leaving aside events that are beyond a country's control. A decline in GDP of between 0.75 per cent and 2 per cent should be treated by the Council as a 'grey area' when rendering its decision, and room should be left for interpretation. In a gesture aimed at pleasing those countries which had insisted on unlimited discretionary power for the Council, it was agreed that the decision on whether exceptional circumstances exist should take the form of a resolution, in which the Council imposes its own constraints, rather than being issued via a regulation. This solution also signalled a breakthrough in the final problem area.

In its summary report presented to the European Council, dealing with the preservation of budgetary discipline during Stage 3 of economic and monetary union, the ECOFIN Council again emphasised how crucial sound public finance practices are for maintaining stable economic conditions in the member states and in the Community. They lessened the burden on monetary policy and nurtured expectations of lower and stable inflation rates, with the result that low interest rates could also be expected. Thus budgetary discipline was an essential prerequisite for sustained inflation-free growth and high employment. It was the wish of the Council that the agreement known from then on as the 'Stability and Growth Pact' consist of two Regulations – one on the 'Strengthening of surveillance and budgetary discipline',[2] the other on 'Speeding up and clarifying the implementation of the excessive deficit procedure' – and a European Council resolution. Except for those sanctions which could not be imposed on non-participating countries, the surveillance procedure and the Excessive Deficit Procedure were to apply to all EU member states.

The Council also sketched in its report the different elements of the Stability and Growth Pact. The requirement that the government budget be in balance or in surplus over the medium term and that convergence programmes be presented may be found in a chapter on 'reinforced surveillance'. The section on the 'early warning system' arranges for the routine surveillance of Stability and Convergence Programmes by Commission and Council, the section on the 'excessive deficit procedure' lays down the agreed position on the Commission's self-imposed obligation to submit a report and the schedules for the different committees. The 'structure and scale of sanctions' is also described. The resolution was to include an official political commitment on the part of the Commission, the Council and the member states to strict and timely application of the Pact.

The European Council in Dublin welcomed the consensus reached on the Stability and Growth Pact and enjoined ECOFIN to subject the Commission's proposals for the two Regulations to careful scrutiny. It also enjoined the Council to work out a draft resolution for the Stability and Growth Pact, which the European Council was to accept in June 1997. The European Council declared that the Council would, on acceptance of the resolution by the European Council, approve the corresponding Regulations.

4.9 THE IMPLEMENTATION OF THE STABILITY AND GROWTH PACT

The implementation of the Stability and Growth Pact in the form of two Regulations and a Council Resolution, which the European Council in Dublin had commissioned, occurred in the first few months of 1997. Two drafts which had already been submitted earlier but which were fundamentally revised after Dublin provided the basis for the Council working group's deliberations. The documents still contained a number of criticisms that would have to be addressed by April before a definitive version of the drafts could be presented to the finance ministers.

A major weakness affecting the Commission's documents was the use of the mitigating clause 'as a rule', which had been inserted in numerous passages, even in those places where the Dublin text, in implementing a policy preference of the European Council, had called for clarity. In the case of the draft regulations, the Council's legal service has justified this on the grounds that Articles 99(5) and 104(2),

(3) and (8) to (11) of the Maastricht Treaty granted the Commission and the Council a certain amount of discretionary leeway. A commitment on the part of Council and Commission to the quasi-automatic performance of certain actions that was made via ordinances amounted to an amendment to the Treaty, which could not be regarded as falling under secondary law. Even in the past, however, this argument had failed to persuade. The German delegation was certain that Commission and Council, in the future exercise of their discretionary powers, would be able to commit themselves in a broad sense. Binding the exercise of such powers to specific criteria and standards did not contradict the notion of discretionary powers but served instead to round out these powers and to make them more concrete. This is all the more true as the proposed constraint on discretionary powers is especially important in helping to attain the objective of the EC Treaty, that is, to establish a stability community. Numerous mitigating clauses also appeared in the draft resolution, which Dublin had intended to convey a strong political commitment (see item 37 of annex 1 to the Presidency Conclusions: 'Strong political guidance'). After lengthy discussions, the Monetary Committee headed by Sir Nigel Wicks and ECOFIN under Dutch chairmanship succeeded in deleting all but two of the eighteen 'as a rule' clauses (to be found in Articles 6 and 11 of the regulation according to Article 104 of the EC Treaty) which the legal service had inserted to preserve a certain discretionary leeway and which the German delegation had accepted with reservations.

An additional problem was posed by the budgetary surveillance requirement in Article 11 of the Commission draft, which called for an assessment of the adequacy of euro area budgetary policy and of budgetary policy throughout the Community as a whole. Germany as well as a number of other countries had categorically rejected this requirement. It was feared that this might lead to difficulties in determining individual responsibility for the aggregate deficit and that in isolated cases a less restrictive budgetary policy might be pursued: the surpluses of one country do not justify the deficit of another. It would also be unfair to insist that, in the event that fiscal policy should be perceived as being too lax, all member states adopt the same economising measures. In the case of Article 11 as well, it was possible to make the text clearer by excising the problematic expressions.

Finally, the question of sanction size and the related question, whether it is possible to accumulate sanctions (Article 12 of the

Regulation according to Article 104 of the EC Treaty), had to be clarified. The finance minister's report to the European Council in Dublin (item 35) was, in fact, ambiguous both with respect to the possibility of having several concurrent deposit requirements and with respect to the maximum size of deposits. The consensus reached envisaged an upper limit of 0.5 per cent of GDP for each deposit but no corresponding limit on the accumulation of deposits. The reason for keeping the latter open was that several deposits could be required for deficit ceiling violations in different years.

In the end it proved possible to adhere to the timetable for approving the Stability and Growth Pact, although at the beginning of June 1997 the new French government had again pointed to problems. These problems led the European Council to pass another resolution in Amsterdam on 16 and 17 June 1997, this time concerning growth and employment.

In Amsterdam, the European Council accepted the resolution which documented a commitment on the part of the member states, the Commission and the Council to implement the Stability and Growth Pact. At the same time it documented the prevailing consensus on both regulations, which represented that part of the Stability and Growth Pact concerned with the maintenance of budgetary discipline in EMU, and urged the Council to accept both regulations without delay. This step was taken at the next meeting of ECOFIN in Brussels on 7 July 1997.

The Stability and Growth Pact had a considerable role to play in the run-up to the European Council's decision. Mindful of the fact that the Stability Pact had provided an additional guarantee that sound fiscal policies would be continued, some politicians presumably found it less difficult to reach a decision at the special meeting of the European Council in Brussels from 1 to 3 May 1998. In the midst of the preparations for this conference, ECOFIN – again at the German Finance Minister Waigel's insistence – had arrived at an understanding of budget consolidation, which was welcomed by the heads of state and government at the European Council meeting in Cardiff on 15 and 16 June 1998. In this stability declaration, which dates back to 1 May 1998, the finance ministers had committed themselves, *inter alia*:

- to attaining nothing less than the prescribed budgetary goals;
- to examining the envisaged draft budgets for 1999 early on, that is, to submitting stability programmes early on;

- to accelerating budget consolidation in the case of favourable economic developments with a view to fulfilling the Stability Pact requirements as quickly as possible;
- to engaging in greater consolidation efforts in those countries in which the stock of government debt is the largest;
- to reducing the vulnerability of public sector budgets to interest rate movements.

4.10 WHAT THE PACT HAS ACCOMPLISHED

The resulting pact, with its requirement that the EU member states endeavour to attain a balanced budget or even a surplus over the medium term, went far beyond the original German proposal, which had simply called for a medium-term deficit ceiling amounting to 1 per cent of GDP. The result was a significantly shorter and more well-defined deficit procedure. The definition of a 'severe recession', which, in addition to being unambiguous, only allows for discretionary leeway with a decline in real GDP of at least 0.75 per cent, and the self-imposed obligation on the part of the member states, the Commission and the Council basically amounts to a quasi-automatic mechanism for imposing sanctions. Germany did not insist on a truly automatic mechanism, which could only have been achieved through an amendment to the Treaty. What was important, however, was that the final version of the Stability and Growth Pact did not end up being a non-committal statement of political purpose but has become part of EU law and is thus triable before the European Court.

Evidently, the political authorities in many member states were unaware – or only vaguely aware – that the signing of the Maastricht Treaty with its requirement that excessive deficits be avoided has limited national sovereignty in the area of fiscal policy. The discussion of the Stability Pact and its implementation have doubtless had the effect of highlighting this requirement once again and of increasing the political decision-makers' and the general public's understanding of the importance of sound fiscal policy.

Notes

1. As it turned out, subsequent implementation of the Stability Pact no longer required that the Protocol be either eliminated or amended.
2. The title of the Regulation was later formulated as follows (in accordance with the Commission proposal): 'On the strengthening of the surveillance of budgetary positions and the surveillance and coordination of economic policies'.

5 The SGP: How Did We Get There?*

Declan Costello

5.1 THE WAIGEL PROPOSAL

Political agreement on the Stability and Growth Pact (SGP)[1] was reached at the Dublin European Council of December 1996, and was a defining moment in the decision to proceed with the launch of the single currency. Despite its complexity and sensitivity, the SGP (two Council Regulations and two political Resolutions[2]) was on the statute books in some eighteen months, a relatively short period for the adoption of secondary legislation at EU level.

This speed reflected the political importance attached to the SGP, and required an intensive negotiation process. The arguments and considerations used during the negotiations are reviewed in this chapter from the perspective of the European Commission services, which hopefully complements Chapter 4 in this volume by Stark.

The initial call for a 'Stability Pact for Europe' was made by the then German Finance Minister, Theo Waigel, in a letter dated 10 November 1995, to fellow ECOFIN ministers. Essentially, it was all sticks and no carrots, comprising only dissuasive measures to ensure budgetary discipline in Stage 3 of European Monetary Union (EMU). It sought to convert the 3 per cent of GDP reference value from its then perceived status as a 'target' into an 'upper ceiling' which could only be breached in extreme exceptional cases. It also sought to introduce automatic decision-making by leaving no scope for discretionary judgement on the part of the Commission and Council. Finally, it called for a new Stability Council comprising only member

* The views expressed in this chapter are personal and do not represent the position of the European Commission. The author would like to thank Marco Buti, Anne Brunila, Mervyn Jones and Ulrich Wölker for assistance in preparing the chapter. The usual disclaimer applies.

states participating in the euro area that would meet twice a year to review and implement the Pact.

At first sight, the timing of the Waigel proposal may appear surprising given that most countries were then struggling to get deficits below the 3 per cent reference value, let alone meeting the suggested medium-term target of 1 per cent of GDP. Only three member states (Luxembourg, Germany and Ireland) did not have excessive deficits in 1995, and Germany was on course for a return to an excessive deficit position in 1996, right in the middle of the SGP negotiations. In retrospect, however, the deterioration in public finances since the entry into force of the Maastricht Treaty made a reexamination of the provisions to ensure fiscal discipline almost inevitable.[3]

The idea of a stability pact had already been informally floated by the German authorities in autumn 1995, and receipt of a formal proposal came as no surprise. However, the severity of what was proposed (automatic decisions with large and immediate financial sanctions) was not wholly expected. Although many had misgivings about the initiative, member states, in public at least, welcomed the proposal. Late 1995 was a period when the future of the EMU project depended on the German government being able to convince a sceptical public that the euro would be as stable as the D-Mark. There was little choice but to support an initiative coming from the largest economy of the future euro area. Consequently, the European Council of Madrid in December 1995 acknowledged the importance of sustaining budget discipline in Stage 3 of EMU and noted 'with interest the Commission's intention to present in 1996 its conclusions on ways to ensure budgetary discipline and co-ordination in the monetary union in accordance with procedures and principles of the Treaty'.

5.2 THE NEGOTIATION PROCESS

5.2.1 The Role of the Commission

As regards the organisation of the negotiations, the Commission (represented by the Directorate General for Economic and Financial Affairs) prepared all the main proposals and background documents.[4] A first reaction to the Waigel proposal was sent to national authorities in January 1996, and the first concrete outline for a pact was ready by March 1996. Not surprisingly, the Commission emphasised the need to find solutions within the existing treaty framework. This meant that any pact could not impose additional entry requirements for entry into EMU, and that the rights and obligations of countries not participating in the euro area would have to be fully respected.

From the outset, the Commission identified serious problems with the Waigel proposal. It questioned the economic desirability of a uniform medium-term target applying to all member states, and called for a balanced pact having both preventative as well as dissuasive elements. Serious doubts were cast on the possibility of automatic decision-making by the Commission and the Council, or the creation of a Stability Council outside the Maastricht Treaty framework.

At the same time, the Commission explored the scope for secondary legislation under Article 99 (formerly Article 103) and Article 104 (formerly Article 104c) of the Treaty that would encompass as many of the traits of the Waigel proposal as possible, for example, financial sanctions, binding deadlines, different obligations in the Excessive Deficit Procedure (EDP) between participating and non-participating member states. The Commission also mooted the idea of political commitments going beyond the Maastricht Treaty being encapsulated in a political resolution. By March 1996, the broad format and main elements of the final SGP had been identified: what remained was to agree upon the details.

Formal proposals for Council Regulations were proposed by the Commission in October 1996,[5] by which time the issue had been discussed at length with national authorities and a considerable degree of agreement had been reached.[6]

5.2.2   The Other Main Players

The ideas and suggestions of the Commission services were examined by the Monetary Committee[7] under the chairmanship of Sir Nigel Wicks.[8] A more detailed examination then took place in the Alternates of the Monetary Committee chaired by Vitor Gaspar.[9] The Alternates did not take decisions, but clarified the positions of member states and enumerated possible solutions which were then put to the parent Monetary Committee. In many ways, the role of the Alternates was a pedagogic one. Articles 99 and especially Article 104 are amongst the most complex in the Treaty.[10] There are eleven steps in the Excessive Deficit Procedure, and it was necessary to consider how each step would work under a variety of economic scenarios. This took a great deal of time, even for officials that had been heavily involved in EMU for many years.

On a regular basis, the Monetary Committee informed the ECOFIN Council of the negotiations under way and sought political guidance on key issues. A six-monthly cycle developed. The Monetary Committee supported by the Commission made a submission to the informal ECOFIN Councils[11] that are normally held in the first half of the Presidency. The political guidance of the informal ECOFIN Council provided a work programme leading to the European Council held at the end of each Presidency. It was successive European Councils which took the final decisions on the SGP, underlining the fact that the decisions affecting national budgetary rules have to be endorsed at the highest political level.

The informal ECOFIN Councils (Verona in April 1996, Dublin in September 1996, Noordwijk in March 1997) proved to be key staging posts. The informal setting allowed for a more open debate, and the practice for informal Councils to issue short Presidency statements (and not formal Council conclusions) was helpful, in that it provided some scope to all countries to draw their own conclusions on sensitive topics.

At an early stage in the negotiations, the European Monetary Institute (forerunner to the European Central Bank) announced that they would not formally participate in the negotiations. However, officials from national central banks, especially the Bundesbank, actively participated in the negotiations, and were amongst the vociferous in calling for strict budgetary rules.

The European Parliament was consulted[12] on both Regulations following the formal proposal of the Commission in October 1996. However, their input to the debate was constrained by the Maastricht Treaty which limits the Parliament's involvement in secondary legislation dealing with EMU. The Council eventually took on board a small number of drafting suggestions proposed by the Parliament.

Finally, it should be noted that while political agreement was reached at the Dublin European Council in December 1996, a great deal of detailed work had to be completed in a Council Working Group under the Dutch Presidency. The task of this group was to convert the Commission's proposal, the amendments proposed by the European Parliament and the political agreement reached in Dublin into a final legislative text. This led to some of the most intensive negotiations of the entire SGP negotiations.

5.2.3 The View from Outside

One possible downside to the negotiation method was a lack of information available to outside parties throughout 1996. Apart from the original Waigel proposal of November 1995, and some rather vague statements in ECOFIN and European Council conclusions in the first half of 1996 (which tended to stress the need for fiscal discipline), concrete details only became public with the publication of the Commission proposals for two Council Regulations in October 1996.

This lack of information fuelled the perception that the Pact would be similar to the original Waigel proposal, that is, only consisting of dissuasive measures. The preventative elements of the SGP are often overlooked or downplayed, while the dissuasive elements are frequently mentioned (even though they have never been used, and are far more nuanced than commonly perceived). To some extent, member states have nurtured this perception, with a view to reassuring a sceptical public on the commitment to fiscal discipline in EMU. However, this misperception continues to prevail in both press and academic circles.

5.3 THE LEGAL BASIS

5.3.1 The Basic Legal Framework

One of the first questions to be tackled was the scope for legislative action within the Maastricht Treaty. The work was largely carried out by the legal services of the Commission and the Council. It is unusual for the Council legal service to be actively involved in the early stages of the legislative process, that is, prior to a formal Commission proposal. Early involvement of the Council's legal service provided reassurance to some member states that the Commission services had indeed exhausted all legal options within the treaty framework (and was not jealously guarding its prerogatives). Their involvement also helped ensure that guidelines for good legislative drafting were respected.[13]

The Waigel proposal gave little idea of the legal nature of a 'Stability Pact for Europe', save that commitments should be legally binding but without altering the conditions for entry into EMU. With the Commission emphasising the need for a pact containing preventative as well as dissuasive elements, the obvious starting place was Article 99 on multilateral surveillance and Article 104 on the Excessive Deficit Procedure. It was also clear from the outset that secondary legislation should take the form of Council Regulations as these are binding and directly applicable in all member states, and unlike directives do not need to be transposed (with scope for differentiation) into national law.

5.3.2 The Legal Base for Preventative Elements

Prior to the SGP, the Broad Economic Policy Guidelines and the multilateral surveillance procedure already provided a framework for the monitoring of member states' economic performance, including budgetary developments. An obvious legal base for strengthening multilateral surveillance is found in Article 99(5) which states that 'The Council...may adopt detailed rules for the multilateral surveillance procedure'. The Commission considered that this Article provided a legal base to define an appropriate medium-term objective for budgetary positions, to require the submission of Stability and Convergence Programmes, and to establish an early-warning system whereby the Council could adopt a recommendation under Article 99(4) that the economic policies of a member state 'risk jeopardising the proper functioning of economic and monetary union'.

However, the Commission noted that secondary legislation under Article 99(5) could not accommodate the Waigel proposal in full. Legislation would apply to both participating and non-participating countries, including the UK and Denmark. Moreover, automatic decision-making could not be imposed on the Commission and Council, and in particular the decision to issue a recommendation under Article 99(4).

Several member states, in particular those with opt-outs, queried whether Article 99(5) provided a sufficient legal base for establishing a binding medium-term budgetary objective or the obligation to submit Stability/Convergence Programmes.[14] The Commission, support by the Council's legal service, reasoned that such obligations could be enshrined in secondary legislation to the extent that they are necessary for an efficient functioning of the multilateral surveillance process. In the end, this was a debate over legal form, as all member states recognised the need for an early-warning system based on Stability/Convergence Programmes.

5.3.3 The Legal Base for Dissuasive Elements

An International Agreement Outside Maastricht?

Reaching agreement on the legal base for the dissuasive elements of the SGP proved far more contentious. In its early submissions to member states, the Commission argued that legislation under Article 104 could significantly strengthen the Excessive Deficit Procedure (EDP); the interpretation of key provisions could be clarified; binding deadlines for each step of the procedure could be specified; guidelines could be fixed for the type and scale of sanctions.[15] However, the automatic features of the Waigel proposal were not feasible, that is, legislation would have to leave a margin for discretionary decision-making on the part of the Commission and Council. Moreover, the Treaty established a clear sequence of steps in the EDP which must be respected: it would be impossible to jump immediately from a decision on the existence of an excessive deficit to a decision to impose sanctions.

Not fully satisfied with the Commission's response, the German authorities came forward with more detailed ideas in February 1996. They suggested that a pact could be adopted partly under EU secondary legislation and partly via a legally binding international agreement (a budgetary 'Schengen' agreement). In particular, they favoured adopting a Regulation under Article 104(14) 2nd sub-paragraph, that would define the medium-term budgetary target, specify the criteria in Article 104(2a and 2b) permitting a breach of the reference value, fix the size of sanctions, and establish fixed time limits for each step of the EDP. They recognised that full automaticity in decision-making could not be accommodated in the Maastricht Treaty. A new international agreement outside the Maastricht framework could therefore be negotiated in which member states would pre-commit their votes, for example, always to vote in favour of imposing pecuniary sanctions. The German authorities reasoned that as member states retain competence in these fields, then they equally have the right to commit themselves to a future line of action.

The Commission refuted the German arguments in favour of a new international agreement.[6] The Maastricht Treaty not only contains an obligation to avoid excessive deficits, but also detailed rules and procedures for their identification and correction. Hence, there is no scope for a supplementary international agreement that *de facto* transfers Community competences to an inter governmental forum. Moreover, if it only consisted of 'ins', then countries would have to join the proposed Stability Council once they participate in the euro area: this would *de facto* be an unacceptable additional entry condition for membership of the euro area.

No member state displayed any enthusiasm for a separate international agreement, the focus of attention shifted to Article 104(14).

This Article presented two potential legal bases, namely replacement of the Protocol[17] on the EDP (2nd sub-paragraph) and laying down the detailed rules for the application of the provisions of the Protocol (3rd sub-paragraph).

Problems with the Protocol

Many member states maintained deep reservations throughout the negotiations about using the 2nd sub-paragraph as a legal base, and there was a clear preference for using the 3rd sub-paragraph. This is because the former potentially opened the door for the renegotiation of the convergence criteria on public finances. This concern was not unfounded: since the Maastricht negotiations, academics and some MEPs had expressed dissatisfaction with the convergence criteria and had called for the Protocol to be amended. ECOFIN Ministers had no desire to do so as the whole timetable for EMU would have been put in doubt. Moreover, they had recently ensured that the treaty provisions on EMU would not be modified as part of the Treaty of Amsterdam, negotiations for which were in full swing in 1996.

The Commission maintained strong doubts about using the 3rd sub-paragraph, arguing that secondary legislation was limited to ancillary and technical rules to implement existing provisions of the Protocol:[18] this would not allow for the inclusion of provisions in secondary legislation to clarify the interpretation of provisions found in the treaty Articles or to fix deadlines. In contrast, the 2nd sub-paragraph provided scope for a wide range of provisions.

A further, perhaps surprising, argument in favour of using the 2nd sub-paragraph is that legislation would be adopted by unanimity. The Commission stated that legislation designed to create a pillar of policy framework for EMU merited being adopted by unanimity: using a rather technical and obscure legal base with a qualified majority voting rule would have diminished the status of the SGP.

To overcome member states' concern, it was suggested that the existing provisions of the Protocol be left intact, and that the SGP only contain new supplementary provisions. There was immediate agreement on this point. At one stage, it was envisaged that the existing Protocol, without alteration, could be copied into the new Regulation. However, this still raised fears about reopening the debate on the convergence criteria: after all, the draft Regulation would have to be forwarded to the European Parliament for an opinion. In the end, the legal services confirmed that it would be unnecessary to copy the existing Protocol into the Regulation. The Regulation would only contain new provisions, which together with the existing Protocol, form an integrated set of rules for the application of the EDP.

5.4   STRENGTHENING MULTILATERAL SURVEILLANCE

5.4.1   The Medium-Term Target for Budget Positions

This section reviews the negotiations surrounding Council Regulation (EC) 1466/97 on the strengthening of the surveillance of budgetary positions and the surveillance and coordination of economic policies. It does not attempt to provide an exhaustive account of the debate on every provision.[19]

Targets for Expenditure and Debt?

The requirement for 'government budgets in the medium term of close to balance or in surplus' has perhaps been the most influential provision of the SGP. As argued in accompanying chapters of this volume, it has contributed to shifting the 3 per cent reference value from being a target into a hard upper ceiling. However, before turning to this issue, it is worth noting that the original Waigel proposal also called on the SGP to include provisions on public debt and public expenditure developments. They were not taken on board in the final agreement for the following reasons:

- Waigel called for 'keeping down the ratio of public sector expenditure, the deficits and tax and cost burdens in line with national priorities in order to gain room for action for both the public and private sectors to improve growth and stability'. However, the Treaty ensures that decisions on levels and types of public expenditures and taxes are a national responsibility. Many member states, not least the Nordic countries, strongly objected to provisions that might set limits on the size of the public sector or impose constraints on the rate of public expenditure growth. Consequently, such references were dropped at a very early stage in the negotiations.

- The Waigel proposal called for provisions requiring public debt to be reduced to below the 60 per cent reference value. The Commission and other member states questioned whether an additional provision on debt was necessary, as the trajectory of public debt would automatically be downwards provided member states meet a medium-term objective of 'close to balance or in surplus'.[20] Although the SGP contains no provisions on debt developments, the treaty obligation for *public debt to be below 60 per cent or on a continuous downward path* remains valid. Member states which fail to adhere to this rule risk being placed in an excessive deficit position.

The Quantitative versus Qualitative Debate

The main focus of attention in the negotiations surrounded the appropriate medium-term budget target. Waigel proposed a uniform medium-term deficit target of 1 per cent of GDP, arguing that it was clear, transparent and easily verifiable.

However, the Commission queried the economic rationale of having a uniform rule for all member states expressed in nominal terms. Calculations showed large differences between countries as regards their susceptibility to negative economic shocks, and the elasticity of budget positions to cyclical economic developments: a medium-term deficit of 1 per cent of GDP would not provide an adequate cyclical safety margin in all countries.

Nearly all member states favoured the approach of the Commission. Several cohesion countries stated that a higher deficit may be appropriate in a catching-up environment to finance higher investment needs. The most vociferous reactions came from Nordic countries, who argued that the recession of the early 1990s demonstrated that even a 'close to balance' target would not provide them with a sufficient cyclical safety margin, and that consequently they were aiming at budget surpluses over the medium term.

Agreement quickly followed on a medium-term target of 'close to balance or in surplus' which appeared in the Commission proposal of October 1996 and eventually Regulation (EC) 1466/97. In fact, this wording was already contained in the Broad Economic Policy Guidelines. Compared with the initial German proposal, the agreed medium-term target is both stricter and at the same time better reflects the differing budgetary and economic circumstances facing member states.

Actual versus Cyclically Adjusted Budget Balances

Three other important elements formed part of the debate on the medium-term target. First, there was the issue as to whether the medium-term target should be expressed in actual or cyclically adjusted terms. The Commission underlined the need to focus on cyclically adjusted budget positions, given that the underlying aim of the SGP was to ensure that member states have the budgetary capacity to deal with negative economic shocks. However, member states refused to go along with this, arguing that actual budget positions are readily observable and easily understood, whereas there is no consensus on how to measure balances cyclically.

A Transition Period to Reach the Medium-Term Target

A second issue was whether to specify a transition period by which time member states would be expected to reach the medium-term target. It was evident in 1996 that most member states adopting the euro would do so with deficits close to the 3 per cent reference value: that is, there would be little room for the automatic stabilisers in the event of an economic downturn. Eventually it was agreed not to define a specific transition period as this could encourage member states to delay budgetary adjustment, and more importantly would send a signal of a lesser commitment to budget discipline in the early years of EMU, precisely the time when it was most needed. An understanding was later reached that the medium-term target was to be reached within the time horizon of stability programmes, that is, three years.

A Medium-Term Target for the Euro Area

A third and controversial issue was the Commission's suggestion that the medium-term targets for member states be accompanied **by a budgetary target for** the Council 'to assess the overall actual and forecast budgetary positions for the EMU area as a whole implied by national stability and updated programmes'. What the Commission had in mind was to encourage member states to recognise the constraints on national fiscal policies in monetary union. Also, the submission of annual programmes would provide an ideal opportunity for ministers to assess the aggregate fiscal stance for the euro area in light of monetary conditions.

The majority of member states reacted negatively to this proposal. It was argued that a provision on the aggregate impact of the programmes for the euro area was unnecessary, as there is an implicit aggregate of budget balance provided all countries meet the medium-term objective. More importantly, the proposal stoked suspicion that the Commission was intent on centralising budgetary authority in EMU, by attempting to define a target deficit/surplus for the euro area as a whole.[21] Member states argued that a surplus in one member state provides no justification for a deficit elsewhere, and that member states could not be expected to adjust their budgetary position so as to 'contribute' their share to an aggregate target for the euro area. In the end Article 5.1 of Regulation (EC) 1466/97 only contains a rather general provision to the effect that 'The Council shall furthermore examine whether the contents of the stability/convergence programme facilitate the closer co-ordination of economic policies'.

It is interesting that some member states are now calling for measures along the lines of the initial Commission proposal.

5.4.2 The Early-Warning System

Rapid Agreement on the Content of Programmes

Stability and Convergence Programmes are the cornerstones of the early-warning system. The Commission was acutely aware of the need to substantially upgrade the coordination, commitment and monitoring procedures at EU level compared with the system of convergence programmes in Stage 2 of EMU.

To this end, the Commission proposed that programmes include a medium-term objective for the general government surplus/deficit, an adjustment path towards this target, the expected path of the general government debt ratio, a description of the measures to reach this target and a description of the key economic assumptions. They should have a time horizon of at least three years.[22] Most issues surrounding the content of programmes were agreed without much difficulty. However, member states did not agree with the Commission suggestion that annual updates be provided no later than two months after the presentation of annual budget proposals by a government to the national parliament. This debate touched on a broader theme on the extent to which national budgetary procedures have to fit in with EU obligations. The Council Regulation (EC) 1466/97 only requires member states to submit programmes no later than 1 March each year, although most do make an effort to submit them by the end of the year.

No Pre-Specification of Corrective Measures

Member states did, however, object to one suggestion, namely that the Stability/Convergence Programmes pre-specify measures to be taken in the event of significant divergence from the medium-term target or the adjustment path.[23] They maintained that pre-specification would interfere with the sovereignty of national parliaments in budgetary matters, and could result in inappropriate policy responses depending on the reasons behind any slippage. Moreover, it was argued that pre-specification would lead to tax increases rather than expenditure cuts. In its proposal for a Council Regulation, the Commission sought to introduce a general commitment 'to take additional measures when necessary to prevent slippage from targets'. However, even this proved too ambitious, and a general commitment was relegated to the Council Resolution on the SGP.

The Ins and the Outs

Throughout the negotiations, it was agreed that the SGP should cover both participating and non-participating countries in the euro area. Although the Commission proposal of October 1996 only referred to Stability Programmes, the informal ECOFIN Council of Dublin in September 1996 reached an understanding that non-participating countries should be required to submit Convergence Programmes which would be similar in content. Apart from the additional requirement to include information on monetary policy objectives, the provisions in Regulation (EC) 1466/97 on Convergence Programmes are identical to those pertaining to Stability Programmes.

Some discussion did take place on the reporting requirements as regards exchange rate policy. Several countries considered that countries not participating in the ERM-II should indicate in their programmes how they intend to fulfil their obligations under Article 124 (formerly Article 109m – the requirement to treat exchange rate policy as a matter of common interest). This argument was rejected, as it could result in unwarranted market reactions, and on the grounds that the exchange rate is an endogenous variable used as an indicator rather than an instrument of economic policy.

Feedback on Stability and Convergence Programmes

One aspect of multilateral surveillance which the Commission was determined to improve was the capacity to influence the contents of Stability/Convergence Programmes. The Commission was anxious to move away from the existing practice of 'welcoming' Convergence Programmes, towards a system that would require member states to strengthen elements of the programme deemed unsatisfactory by the Commission and Council. In other words, programmes when submitted should not be set in stone.

Most member states had difficulties with putting in place a procedure that would require them having to modify a 'flawed' programme. This, it was claimed, would interfere with sovereignty of their national parliaments. It was pointed out that the Commission and Council could, however, express dissatisfaction with a programme in a recommendation under Article 99(4). Member states also disagreed with the Commission's suggestion that Council could 'endorse' a stability programme as this would 'commit' the Council to a specific budgetary strategy even if it failed to deliver a satisfactory outcome.

Linking the Early-Warning System to the Excessive Deficit Procedure

A final issue in the negotiations was how to link the early-warning system of Article 99 with the Excessive Deficit Procedure of Article 104. No formal link is found in the Treaty: however, a substantive link clearly exists between an Article 99(4) recommendation on the risk of jeopardising the proper functioning of EMU, and a Commission opinion under Article 104(5) on the risk of an excessive deficit. At one stage, the Commission considered including a provision in the draft Regulation (EC) 1467/97 to the effect that it would 'take account of a recommendation against a Member State under Article 99(4) when assessing the risk of an excessive deficit'. Eventually, such a provision was considered redundant, since the Commission and Council would in any event have full knowledge that the member state concerned had received an early warning. The link between the early-warning system and the EDP is now found in the recitals of both Regulations and in the Resolution of the European Council.

5.5   REINFORCING THE EXCESSIVE DEFICIT PROCEDURE

5.5.1   Limiting Conditions Allowing a Breach of the 3 per cent Reference Value

This section reviews the negotiations surrounding Council Regulation (EC) 1467/97 on speeding up and clarifying the implementation of the

Excessive Deficit Procedure. As in the previous section, it does not attempt to provide an exhaustive account of the debate but only focuses on key issues.

The Make or Break Clause

Clarifying the interpretation of Article 104(2a) was to prove the make or break issue of the SGP negotiations. This Article outlines the conditions under which a breach of the reference value (on deficits) may take place without a member state being placed in an excessive deficit position. It is easy to see why this provision acquired such political significance. By virtue of offering a potential 'escape route' to member states, it became the litmus test for a strong commitment to fiscal discipline in EMU.

However, the political importance attached to this provision greatly outweighs its operational significance in the EDP. This is because to benefit from Article 104c(2), a deficit must be exceptional, temporary and close to the 3 per cent reference value. These conditions are cumulative, a point often overlooked. In practice, it is unusual for any breach of the reference values to fulfil all three conditions simultaneously.[24] Consequently, nearly all breaches will *de facto* lead to a decision on the existence of an excessive deficit as the Commission and Council have no grounds to decide otherwise.

Defining 'Severe Economic Downturn'[25]

The debate on this issue was a struggle between those who favoured a numerical definition (on the grounds that it could provide a clear and transparent rule) and those who favoured a qualitative definition (who argued that a sufficient degree of flexibility was required to cope with different economic circumstances of member states and different types of economic shocks).

The German authorities offered a two-part operational definition in April 1996 of 'exceptional' situations. It would first consist of unusual events that the relevant member state cannot control and that have a major impact on public finances. This would include natural disasters, and all member states agreed to this provision being incorporated into Regulation (EC) 1467/97.

In addition, the German authorities offered a definition of exceptional circumstances of an economic nature: it would consist of a severe economic downturn as measured by 'negative real growth rates after seasonal adjustment of the gross domestic product in more than four consecutive past quarters compared with the respective preceding quarters' or 'negative real growth rate of GDP in a calendar fiscal year exceeding 2%'. They maintained that the cyclical sensitivity of the budget in most member states is between 0.5 and 0.6, that is, a 1 per cent fall in GDP would lead to an increased deficit of between 0.5 and 0.6 per cent of GDP. Even with negative real growth of 2 per cent of GDP, the automatic stabilisers should only lead to a deficit below the reference value of 2 to 3 per cent of GDP provided the member state concerned meets the medium-term position of 'close to balance'.

The Commission (supported by several member states) did not agree with having a quantified definition of severe economic downturns and suggested a qualitative definition of 'clearly negative annual real growth'. It was argued that a uniform rule would result in unequal treatment between member states having different growth profiles. Moreover data could be subject to significant time lags, and in some member states quarterly data were not available. It was also argued that member states would not have sufficient room for manoeuvre to cope with negative real growth of 2 per cent of GDP: what is important is not the annual drop in growth but the accumulated output gap, that is, two years of zero growth would lead to an output gap of 4 per cent of GDP.

However, German pressure for a quantitative definition was intense. Despite the danger of extrapolating on the basis of past data (especially with the major regime change of EMU), the Commission services assessed the implications of various quantitative rules.[26] Applying the German definition of severe economic downturns to the EU-15 over the 1960–96 period, the exceptionality condition would have been met in only 13 out of 540 possible cases, a frequency of 2.6 per cent. This compared with a frequency of 8.6 per cent for the Commission's proposed definition of negative annual real growth.

Different suggestions were made in the final weeks running up the Dublin European Council. The formula which eventually achieved success was brokered by the chairman of the Monetary Committee, Sir Nigel Wicks. He proposed a 'box' solution whereby a fall of more than 2 per cent in annual GDP *would* be considered a severe economic downturn: a fall of between *X* per cent and 2 per cent in annual GDP *could* be considered a severe economic downturn depending on supporting evidence provided by the member state concerned on the abruptness of the fall and its path relative to past trends.

The key to agreement at the Dublin European Council was getting agreement on X per cent Suggestions ranged from -0.5 per cent to -1 per cent. Eventually agreement was reached defining X as an annual fall in GDP of -0.75 per cent. By any standard, this is an extremely restrictive definition of a severe economic downturn, and was only acceptable to member states once they grasped that in most cases it plays a very limited role in influencing the decision as to whether an excessive deficit exists.

Defining 'Temporary'

Again it was the German delegation that came forward with the first operational definition. Temporary situations would arise if the planned deficit of the current year shows a fall below the reference value when reported pursuant to Council Regulation (EC) 3605/93.[27] The Commission's early thinking followed similar lines, that is, that a breach would be considered temporary if planned data showed the deficit moving back below the reference value within one year.

However, it became evident that such an approach might be overly simplistic, and fails to reflect the fact that economic shocks do not respect calendar years. In the draft Council Regulation, the Commission proposed a rather convoluted wording:

> If the unusual event or the severe economic downturn has come to an end or if it is forecast that it will come to an end in the calendar year following the year in which the deficit exceeds the reference value, budget forecasts provided by the Commission must indicate that the deficit would fall below the reference value in the same following year.

Member states raised two difficulties. First, they pointed out that it can be difficult to pinpoint a precise end-point for some economic shocks, for example German unification. Second, the suggested definition would require the excessive deficit to be corrected in the same year as the exceptional recession occurs. This was considered too restrictive given the lagged effects of recession on budgetary positions. The text finally agreed in Regulation (EC) 1467/97 contains a more straightforward definition of temporary: 'if forecasts as provided by the Commission indicate that the deficit will fall below the reference value following the end of the unusual event or the severe economic downturn'.

5.5.2 Planned versus Actual Data

One of the key debates in the SGP was whether the decision on the existence of an excessive deficit position could be taken using planned data[28] alone without having to await actual data confirming a breach of the reference value. The German authorities, supported by some member states, argued that planned data would suffice to place a country in an excessive deficit position under Article 104(6). They reasoned that it would be politically unacceptable for the Council to be constrained from taking action against a country that flagrantly plans a breach of the reference value.

Most member states and the Commission did not agree and stated that actual data would be needed, that is, definitive proof and not a presumption of guilt. The potentially serious consequences of being placed in an excessive deficit position in Stage 3 of EMU (negative reaction of markets, possibility of sanctions) argued in favour of such a prudent approach. This view was shaped by the distinction made in the Treaty between the risk of an excessive deficit (Article 104(3)) and the existence of an excessive deficit (Article 104(6)).

The Commission's view was motivated by the fact that allowing decisions to be taken using planned data alone would involve a break with existing practice. The Treaty uses similar language for a Council decision on the existence of an excessive deficit position (Article 104(6)) and the decision to abrogate (Article 104(12)). A symmetric interpretation of these Articles is therefore needed. If, as suggested by Germany, countries could be placed in excessive deficit using only planned data, then a decision to abrogate could equally be taken using planned data. An agreement to this effect would have been viewed by markets as a significant relaxation of the entry conditions into EMU (and was totally unacceptable to Germany).

The Commission acknowledged that a decision could in certain circumstances be taken using only planned data if supported by additional robust information providing clear evidence that the reference value is being breached by a considerable margin. In practice, this would only apply in extreme situations, but at least it avoided a dogmatic insistence that actual data must be available. Further reassurance came from the fact that several of the early steps of the EDP can be taken using planned data, in particular the Commission opinion under Article 104(5) on the risk of an excessive deficit. Apart from raising the political pressure on the member state, completing these early steps of the EDP would lead to an accelerated timetable such that sanctions (if needed) could be imposed in less than the normal ten month period.

5.5.3 Accelerating the Timetable

Getting a Closed-Ended Procedure

A key German objective was to achieve a closed-ended EDP, and so prevent a decision on sanctions from being perpetually postponed. The Waigel proposal did not explicitly outline deadlines, as sanctions would be immediately imposed on breach of the reference value.

From the start, the Commission accepted the case for fixing binding deadlines for each step of the EDP in secondary legislation. However, a balance was needed: too slow a procedure and political momentum would be lost; too fast would lack credibility and risk antagonising national parliaments. Moreover, the Commission argued that the Treaty implies that adequate time must be left between each step: the deadlines could not be telescoped together nor could they be set so short as to be unfeasible.[29]

The debate ebbed and flowed between those who favoured short deadlines and those who favoured longer deadlines. In April 1996, the German authorities suggested a timetable that would provide for sanctions to be imposed within three months of the reporting of data on the existence of an excessive deficit. Around that time, the Commission proposed a more realistic timetable that could lead to sanctions within ten months.[30] This proposal involved progressively tighter deadlines for each step of EDP, thereby reflecting the growing seriousness of the situation of a member state failing to take corrective measures. Its main attraction was political, namely that sanctions could be imposed within the same calendar year.[31] With small modifications, this timetable was incorporated into Regulation (EC) 1467/97.

Although agreement was reached at an early stage in the negotiations on the overall length of the EDP, getting a final accord was far from easy. It required reaching agreement on three other issues, namely: what constitutes 'effective action' on the part of a member state to correct an excessive deficit; whether the errant member state is obliged to take actions or achieve results; and the rules on placing the EDP in abeyance. These are examined in turn below.

What Constitutes Effective Action

On being placed in an excessive deficit position, the Council under Article 104(7) issues 'a recommendation to the Member State concerned with a view to bringing that situation to an end within a given period'. It is the definition of what constitutes 'effective action', and consequently the length of time a member state has to take it, which is the key to completing the EDP within the calendar year. There is a trade-off between speed and certainty.

The Commission suggested that member states have four months from the decision on the existence of an excessive deficit position to take effective action, and that the Council 'may base its decision on official public decisions by the Government of the Member State'. Awaiting the adoption of legislation by national parliaments would have greatly extended the timetable. This proposal received broad agreement.[32]

An Obligation to Take Measures or Achieve Results?

The debate on 'effective action' underlined the importance of the Council recommendations under Article 104(7) for the smooth implementation of subsequent steps in the EDP. Moreover, it touched upon an issue that lies at the core of SGP, namely: are member states with an excessive deficit under an obligation to take action or to achieve results?

After long debate, it was agreed that both obligations apply, and that the Council recommendation must specify two deadlines. A first deadline would fix an obligation to take corrective actions.[33] Member states made clear, however, that the recommendation should not specify concrete actions to be taken as this would infringe upon national sovereignty and could make the Council co-responsible for measures that might fail to deliver the desired results. A second deadline would require the excessive deficit position to be corrected within a given period. Regulation (EC) 1467/97 specifies a presumption that excessive deficits should be corrected within one year unless there are exceptional circumstances.

A final issue concerned placing the EDP in abeyance. Basically this means putting the EDP on hold during the period when the member state is taking action to correct the excessive deficit. If at any time these actions are reversed, then the EDP immediately proceeds to the next step (usually a Council recommendation under Article 104(9)). In other words, the EDP starts up where it left off without any loss of time.

5.5.4   Sanctions

An Unprecedented Step

Like the debate on defining 'severe economic downturns', sanctions acquired a political importance in the negotiations that is somewhat disproportionate to its operational significance in the SGP. Although sanctions are a last resort and may never be used, their very possibility signifies that the SGP is an enforcement mechanism with real teeth and not just a political commitment.

Provisions on sanctions of this nature are unprecedented in international relations. No matter how unlikely the scenario, it is unprecedented for sovereign countries to sign agreements (which are binding and directly applicable under their own national law) that could result in financial sanctions of up to 0.5 per cent of GDP. In 2001, that is equivalent to €110 million for Luxembourg and €11 billion for Germany!

Getting Agreement on Workable Parameters

In fact, the sanctions proposed by Waigel were even tougher. He suggested that countries automatically pay a non-interest-bearing deposit which would be converted to a fine if the deficit did not fall below the reference value within two years. Sanctions would amount to 0.25 per cent of GDP of the member state concerned for each full or partial percentage point by which the reference value is breached, and there would be no upper limit.

Many considered the Waigel proposal to be so severe as to be unworkable. The Commission argued that sanctions need to be (1) designed in a way to have a preemptive deterrent impact, (2) easy to compute, (3) credible so that the Council could be expected to impose them, (4) timely so that member states have a strong incentive to take prompt corrective action, and (5) designed such that they contribute to the adjustment process and do not risk unduly aggravating the economic and budgetary situation.

To this end, a formula was proposed consisting of a fixed amount and a variable component based on the difference between the actual budget deficit and the 3 per cent reference value: there would also be an upper limit of 0.5 per cent of GDP. This fixed amount would clearly demonstrate that there is a tangible difference between having and not having an excessive deficit position; it would also provide an incentive to member states that are close to the reference value to make an additional effort to avoid the risk of sanctions. Finally, the variable component would penalise budgetary misbehaviour in a continuous fashion, but would avoid discrete jumps in sanctions.[34]

Member states quickly agreed that a fixed component was desirable and that the proportional approach of the Commission was better than the step-wise approach of the German authorities. Agreement was reached at the Dublin European Council on a fixed component of 0.2 per cent of GDP and a variable component equal to one-tenth of the difference between the deficit and the reference value as a percentage of GDP.

Sharing Proceeds of Sanctions Amongst the 'Virtuous Ins'

The sanctions issue proved so complex and delicate that it was not fully resolved at the Dublin European Council. A further six months of negotiations, some of the most extensive of the entire SGP, were required under the Dutch Presidency to resolve all outstanding issues. Most of this time was spent devising rules on the use of any proceeds from sanctions. The time and effort dedicated to resolving this matter is due to the difficulty in resolving questions about the Community budget. Moreover, there was an awareness amongst negotiators that it was essential to resolve the provisions on sanctions once and for all. A future Council decision to impose sanctions will be politically difficult, possibly one of the most difficult ever to be taken at EU level. However, it would be exponentially more difficult to take if at the same time ministers have to grapple with how to share the spoils.

The Commission proposal of October 1996 argued that any proceeds would result from the implementation of Articles enshrined in the Treaty, and should therefore accrue to the Community budget under the heading of 'miscellaneous revenues'. However, the Dublin European Council was not convinced and specified that the proceeds of financial sanctions should not lead to an increase in Community spending.[35] In fact the main concern was to devise a distribution system whereby the proceeds would only go to the 'virtuous ins'. Under the Commission's original proposal, all member states would benefit from contributions to the EU budget, including the errant member state and countries not participating in the euro (even though financial sanctions could not be imposed upon them).

In early 1997, the parties examined the scope, within the existing EU budgetary framework, to achieve such a result. However, it would have required introducing cumbersome changes to the Financial Regulation. In the end, a solution was found whereby proceeds will be lodged with the Commission and shared amongst the virtuous ins.

Clearing Up the Final Loose Ends

The Dutch Presidency was also responsible for tidying up three loose ends on sanctions. First, in addition to non-interest-bearing deposits and fines, Article 104(11) provides for other 'mild' sanctions, that is, requiring member states to publish additional information and inviting the European Investment Bank to reconsider its lending policy towards the member state concerned. There was general consensus that these sanctions on their own provide no deterrence. Agreement was reached that as a general rule, the Council would always impose pecuniary sanctions which could be accompanied with the 'mild' sanctions. Moreover, it was also agreed that deposits could not be returned to the member state until the excessive deficit is abrogated. The only sanctions which the Council can relax in response to progress being made to correct an excessive deficit (Article 104(12)) are the mild sanctions.

A second issue to resolve was the cumulation of sanctions over several years, that is should they be applied every year during which the reference value is being breached? Many member states felt that this would be unreasonable. Agreement was reached that the first sanction to be applied would consist of the fixed and variable component: an additional sanction would only consist of the variable component. A non-interest-bearing deposit would be converted to a fine after two years if the country is still in an excessive deficit position, at which time a new deposit (fixed plus variable component) must be made.

5.5.5 Automaticity

No Automatic Outcomes

The Waigel proposal involved automatic outcomes to decisions, with the Commission and Council surrendering all room to exercise judgement. From the outset, the Commission (supported by the Council legal services) was adamant that this was impossible. The Treaty provides scope for the Community institutions to exercise discretionary judgement, and this could not be done away with in either secondary legislation or a new international Treaty.

The challenge was to exploit the treaty framework fully to achieve fiscal rules in EMU that are as binding as possible. To this end, a number of imaginative legislative solutions were found as follows:

- As described above, clear definitions of key provisions in the EDP severely limit the scope for interpretation by the Commission and Council.
- Although it was impossible to fully pre-commit the Commission or Council, the SGP includes a strong presumption of expected actions on the part of the Commission (to issue a recommendation on the existence of an excessive deficit) and the Council (to vote in favour of imposing sanctions on countries in an excessive deficit position). Phrases such as 'shall be considered', 'as a rule', 'should be completed' are littered throughout the Regulations. Ultimately, the Commission and Council could opt not to follow the policy course outlined in the Regulations[5]. Nonetheless, these provisions shift the political balance: the Council no longer has to find reasons why sanctions should be imposed, but instead why not to impose sanctions.
- Article 2.3 of Regulation (EC) 1467/97 introduces an interesting 'reversal of the burden of proof' as regards the decision as to whether an economic downturn is exceptional or not. This provision tilts the balance from a presumption of innocence to a presumption of guilt. It is up to the errant member state to provide additional evidence (not the Commission or the Council) as to why a breach of the reference value is justified.

Automatic Obligation for the Commission and Council to Take Decisions

Some automaticity is in the SGP, but not the type of automaticity which most people expect. Regulation (EC) 1467/97 has binding deadlines for key steps in the EDP. Once the EDP is launched (and it is extremely difficult not to once the reference value is breached), automatic and legally binding deadlines are imposed upon the Commission or the Council to take decisions. The SGP legislation cannot wholly prescribe what decision the Council or Commission should take, but the decision must be taken. Ministers are usually loath to sanction a fellow minister, and would often find it politically convenient to postpone the day of budgetary judgement: this is no longer possible.

Additional Commitments in a Resolution of the European Council

Additional political commitments were enshrined in a political resolution on the SGP adopted by the European Council of Amsterdam. These go beyond the Maastricht Treaty, but clearly do not contradict it, and involve all three parties to the SGP – the Commission, Council and member states. While political resolutions are not legally binding, they do carry a significant weight. Three particular elements of the resolution were particularly important:

- the member states committed themselves not to invoke the 'escape route' of Article 2.3 of Regulation (EC) 1467/97 unless annual real GDP has fallen by more than 0.75 per cent;
- the Commission committed itself to trigger the EDP by preparing a report under Article 104c(3) whenever there is a risk of an excessive deficit or whenever planned or actual data exceed the reference values;
- the Commission would, as a rule, issue a recommendation for a Council decision on whether an excessive deficit exists under Article 104(6) following a request from Article 115.

These latter two commitments were designed to prevent a reluctant Commission from frustrating the will of the Council (as the Commission has a right of initiative and the Council cannot act if the Commission decides not to trigger the EDP). The likelihood of the Commission refusing to launch the EDP is small: as described above, the 'escape clause' is extremely limited and the Commission would hardly refuse to submit a recommendation requested by a majority of member states. The motivation for these commitments probably stems from a difference of opinion between the Commission and certain member states in 1994 as regards whether Ireland should be placed in a excessive deficit position. At that time, Ireland's deficit was below the 3 per cent reference value, but its debt was above the 60 per cent reference value, albeit on a steep downward path. The Commission took the view that Ireland satisfied the debt criterion and did not forward a recommendation to the Council. This episode underlined the independent and powerful role of the Commission in implementing the SGP.

5.6 OVERALL ASSESSMENT

Did the EU get a good deal? Compared with the initial Waigel proposal the SGP that finally emerged is:

- more balanced, with equal if not more importance attached to prevention as to deterrence. Subsequent events have proved the merits of this approach, as to date only the preventative elements of the SGP have been used while the provisions on deterrence have yet to be activated;
- on a much sounder economic footing. In particular the medium-term objective caters for the specific needs and circumstances of the members states;
- more ambitious. The medium-term objective of the SGP of 'close to balance or in surplus' goes beyond the 1 per cent deficit target suggested in the Waigel proposal, and has succeeded in converting the 3 per cent reference value into an upper ceiling;
- better attuned to the political economy situation of EMU. Mechanical budgetary rules for fiscal policy in EMU and the automatic imposition of sanctions would have proved politically unworkable, and indeed would lack credibility in financial markets. Although the SGP has significantly narrowed the margin for interpretation by the Commission and the Council, it does in the final instance require both institutions to exercise judgement when taking decisions.

Of course, the SGP, as outlined in several chapters of this volume, is not perfect. It is not a symmetric agreement: the mechanisms to influence budgetary behaviour in economic downturns are not matched with provisions to encourage good behaviour during economic upturns. However, with most countries approaching or surpassing a position of budget balance, it has at least helped bring about a situation where such measures can now be discussed.

Moreover, several of the suggestions which did not find their way into the SGP are starting to reappear on the ECOFIN agenda, for example, the use of cyclically adjusted budget balances, the aggregate fiscal stance of the euro area, improving national budgetary rules and procedures, addressing the sustainability of public finances in the light of ageing populations. These issues were possibly too much for member states to contemplate in 1996/97 when the enormous regime change of EMU was looming. A more favourable economic and political climate to do so is now emerging.

The only real test of the robustness of the deterrent effect of the SGP, and the willingness of the Commission and Council to exercise tough political choices, will come when EMU is faced with a severe economic downturn and budget positions approach or breach the reference value. There are some grounds for believing that the institutions will not shy away from placing countries in an excessive deficit position.

First, the only 'near miss' to date was in early 1999 when Italian authorities announced a potential slippage of 0.4 percentage points of GDP (from 2 per cent to 2.4 per cent) compared with the target announced in the Stability Programme. This meant that the 3 per cent reference value was being approached. A strong reaction to this announcement ensued from other member states, and eventually Italy recorded a deficit of 1.8 per cent of GDP for 1999 (see Chapter 6 by Cabral for more details). Nonetheless, this episode highlights the effectiveness of peer pressure and the radical shift that had taken place in EU budgetary ambition. A possible slippage of 0.4 percentage points of GDP provoked strong political pressure being placed on a country that nine years earlier (1990) had a deficit of 11 per cent of GDP and three years prior (1996) of over 7 per cent of GDP.

Second, as explained previously, the escape route allowing a breach of the reference value is so restrictive as to be almost non-existent. It is unlikely that a deficit above the 3 per cent reference value is simultaneously exceptional, temporary and close to the reference value. The Commission and Council will in most cases have no choice but to decide that an excessive deficit exists.

Third, the Commission and Council will be acutely aware that the public spotlight will be on them when the 3 per cent reference value is breached for the first time in EMU. They will be under intense pressure to act decisively or risk devaluing the dissuasive provisions of the SGP for ever. The fact that most member states have now achieved the medium-term target should facilitate the Council's task, as there should be some time to issue an 'early warning' in advance to the member state concerned.

Finally, the SGP did achieve some automaticity. Once the EDP is launched, the Commission and Council face politically binding pressure points. They are not automatically obliged to decide that an excessive deficit exists or to impose sanctions, but they are obliged to reach a decision.

Notes

1. For clarity, we use the term 'SGP' in this chapter and not 'Stability Pact' which was the phrase employed throughout most of the negotiations. 'G' for growth was only introduced at the Dublin European Council at the request of France.

2. See Chapter 6 by Cabral for a full description of the SGP. The Resolution of the European Council on growth and employment was adopted (at the request of France) so as to send positive messages about EMU, and to balance the perceived negative overtones of 'stability' and 'discipline'. However, this Resolution plays no operational role in the SGP and is not reviewed in this chapter.

3. A motivating factor behind the initiative may have been a 1995 review by the Monetary Committee that drew attention to shortcomings with the existing process of multilateral surveillance, and especially the Convergence Programmes. Member states attached little prominence to Convergence Programmes and their content was unsatisfactory. Moreover, they lacked ambition as the medium-term budgetary objective and the Council had real difficulties in getting member states to adjust their programmes to address weak points.

4. Prior to the formal proposal of the Commission for two Council Regulations, a series of papers was sent to the Monetary Committee which were to form the basis of the negotiations: 'Towards a Stability Pact' (II/11/96-EN of 10 January 1996); 'A Stability Pact to Ensure Budgetary Discipline in EMU' (II/163/96-EN of 18 March 1996); 'The Strengthening of Budgetary Discipline Mechanisms to Implement a Stability Pact' (II/298/96-EN of 21 May 1996); and 'Ensuring Budgetary Discipline in Stage Three of EMU' (II/409/96-EN of 19 July 1996).

5. COM(96)496 of 18 October 1996.

6. The timing of the Commission proposal raised some debate. Some member states favoured continuing 'informal' discussions as long as possible with a view to reaching as much agreement as possible for inclusion in the Commission proposal. The Commission favoured making its formal proposals earlier than some member states would have preferred. This would help guard its right of initiative. Moreover, the Commission was anxious to open up the debate to the public which had very little information about the details of the proposals being discussed. Eventually, the Commission awaited the outcome of the informal ECOFIN Council held in Dublin in September 1996.

7. The Monetary Committee (MC) consisted of senior officials from national finance ministries, national central banks, the Commission and the European Monetary Institute. It was responsible for preparing the meetings of the ECOFIN Council. It was replaced in Stage 3 of EMU by the Economic and Financial Committee which has a broadly similar membership.

8. Former Second Permanent Secretary to HM Treasury.

9. Former Director of Research of the Banco do Portugal and currently Director General of the Research Department of the ECB.

10. For a detailed description of the Excessive Deficit Procedure and the negotiations surrounding its adoption see A. Italianer (1997), 'The

Excessive Deficit Procedure: A Legal Description', in M. Adenas, L. Gormley, C. Hadjiemmanuil and I. Harden (eds), *European Economic and Monetary Union: The Institutional Framework* (Kluwer Law International).

11.   Informal ECOFIN Councils are held once every six months in the country holding the Presidency of the EU. They aim at providing a more informal setting in which ministers and the governors of central banks can exchange views more freely. There is no formal agenda and Council conclusions are not adopted.

12.   OJ C 380 of 16.12.1996.

13.   For the most part, the SGP was negotiated by economists, the majority of whom do not have a legal background. Combined with the fact that the ECOFIN Council rarely adopts secondary legislation, there was a tendency for the drafting to reflect the economics/finance background of negotiators.

14.   The Maastricht Treaty only obliged member states to submit Convergence Programmes in Stage 1 of EMU which ended on 1 January 1994. The submission of Convergence Programmes in Stage 2 of EMU continued on a voluntary basis only.

15.   At the same time, both the legal services of the Commission and Council discounted the use of Article 308 (formerly Article 235) as a legal base for the SGP, as the Treaty already contains a more specific legal base on budgetary surveillance.

16.   An additional reason for sticking within the boundaries of EMU articles when choosing a legal base is that doing otherwise would require the involvement of the General Affairs Council which is responsible for institutional questions.

17.   The Protocol on the Excessive Deficit Procedure (EDP) is annexed to the Treaty and is part of Community primary law. It contains provisions on the implementation of the EDP, for example, definitions of general government deficits and debt. It also specifies the reference values for the convergence criteria on public finances that are to assess whether member states can adopt the euro, that is, 3 per cent for deficits and 60 per cent for debt.

18.   The 3rd sub-paragraph had already been used as the legal base for Council Regulation (EC) 3605/93 of 22 November 1993 on the application of the Protocol on the Excessive Deficit Procedure.

19.   The Commission made two suggestions to reinforce budget discipline in EMU which did not find their way into the SGP. A first idea was to reinforce national budgetary rules and procedures (public expenditure planning and control, coordination between the different levels of government, monitoring and correction mechanisms). The German authorities in 1996 announced that they were negotiating a national stability pact with the *Länder*. Although several other countries have since reformed fiscal relations with sub-central authorities, the proposal did not take root in the SGP negotiations. A second suggestion was to enhance the role of financial markets in reinforcing fiscal discipline to encourage financial institutions to smoothly adjust the creditworthiness of sovereign countries at an earlier stage of debt accumulation. A

possible option was to modify Council Directive 92/121/EEC that dictates rules for monitoring and controlling large exposure of credit institutions so that member states running unsound fiscal policies would suffer negative discrimination in the market. A further idea was to modify Council Directive 93/6/EEC on capital adequacy requirements so that the debt of member states in an excessive deficit position would not be treated in the same way as debts of other member states. Concerns were raised about the politicisation of prudential supervision and the need to ensure the consistency of changes with international rules such as the Basle agreements. The ideas were quickly dropped in early 1996.

20. The Commission presented an illustrative calculation showing that public debt would decline steadily under this policy rule. There are exceptional circumstances when public debt could rise even if budget positions are in balance, say due to exchange rate developments which affect public debt denominated in third currencies. However, such outcomes are likely to be infrequent.

21. In retrospect, the Commission could have provided a clearer rationale as to why such a provision was needed.

22. See Chapter 7 by Fischer and Giudice.

23. At that time, some of the existing Convergence Programmes had general commitments of this nature, and several member states had introduced 'corrective' provisions as part of their annual budgets or into their budget law.

24. For example, a deficit of 5 per cent of GDP, even if due to exceptional circumstances, such as the collapse of Finnish export markets to the former USSR or German unification, would be considered as excessive as it is not close to the reference value.

25. No attempt was made to define 'close to the reference value'.

26. Implications of a quantitative definition of 'severe recessions' of 1 October 1996.

27. This Regulation requires member states to submit actual and planned data on budgetary positions by 1 March and 1 September each year.

28. Estimates or forecasts of budgetary positions for the current year made before the year is ended.

29. Deadlines would also have to be flexible as excessive deficits can arise at any time of year and not just when member states report budgetary data on 1 March each year.

30. The timetable is adjusted for the UK where the budget is not based on a calendar year. The UK authorities successfully argued that they should have the same time from the end of their budgetary year to take corrective action and correct excessive deficits.

31. In an earlier note, the Commission outlined a slightly longer timetable, allowing one year for a decision to be made on sanctions. The reasoning behind this suggestion was that the Council could benefit from new data following the March reporting exercise. On reflection, the Commission concluded that a new data set would actually complicate decision-making rather than facilitate it. Moreover, the decision to impose sanctions is based on a failure to take corrective action and not achieve results.

32.   The German authorities maintained that errant member states should only be given one month to take effective action and not the four months finally agreed.

33.   The Regulation allows the Council to reverse its decision on effective action if these official public positions were not enacted within a specified time limit or if they were modified substantially during the adoption process.

34.   Under the Waigel formula, a country deficit of 3.9 per cent of GDP could face a sanction of 0.25 per cent of GDP, whereas a deficit of 4 per cent would lead to a sanction of 0.5 per cent of GDP.

35.   This fear was largely unfounded, as an upper limit on Community spending is set in pluri-annual financial perspectives. In the event of (windfall) proceeds from the SGP, EU spending would not increase: instead, the contributions of all member states under the so-called 4th resource would be reducing in accordance with the share of Community GDP. However, member states were able to cite an unlikely scenario (involving a large fall in Community GDP) that could result in SGP sanctions causing a small increase in EU spending.

Part III
How Does the Pact Work?

6 Main Aspects of the Working of the SGP*

António J. Cabral

6.1 INTRODUCTION

The Stability and Growth Pact (SGP) has attracted much attention since the idea was first floated by Finance Minister Waigel late in 1995. Naturally, as highlighted in Chapters 2 and 3 above, there is not an unanimous view on the Pact: for some it is not necessary; for others the Pact is necessary but the way it was built is not satisfactory; finally, there are also those who consider that the Pact is a *sinister* construction which will, necessarily, lead to ever-increasing unemployment in the EU. This chapter will not focus on these issues; indeed it is our firm conviction that the full benefits of the single currency can only be harvested if fiscal discipline, which remains under the responsibility of each individual member state, is secured. The author of this chapter therefore belongs to those who consider that the Pact is a positive, if not fundamental, complement to the Maastricht Treaty (Cabral, 1997). This does not mean that the implementation of the Pact is not without problems and difficulties.

The chapter is organised as follows. In section 6.2 we review the main aspects of the SGP. In section 6.3 we look at the first experience with the implementation of the Pact, including the issue of what is, and how to quantify, a medium-term budgetary position consistent with the Pact. Some final considerations are presented in section 6.4.

---

* The views expressed in this chapter are the author's only and do not involve the European Commission. I would like to thank Mervyn Jones and Marco Buti, colleagues of mine in DG ECFIN, for their valuable comments. Of course any error is mine.

6.2   THE MAIN ELEMENTS OF THE STABILITY AND GROWTH PACT

The SGP entered into force, as far as its surveillance part is concerned, on 1 July 1998, while the dissuasive part entered into force on 1 January 1999, thus making the SGP fully applicable. The Pact is constituted by two Council Regulations and a Resolution of the European Council which are largely based on the Commission's proposals.[1] The first Regulation, 'on the strengthening of surveillance of budgetary positions and the surveillance and co-ordination of economic policies',[2] deals with the preventive dimension of the Pact and has Article 99 (ex 103) of the Treaty as its legal base. The second Regulation, 'on speeding up and clarifying the implementation of the excessive deficit procedure',[3] deals with the dissuasive part of the Pact and its legal base is Article 104 (ex 104c). Finally, the Resolution of the European Council provides political guidance to the parties who will implement the Stability and Growth Pact.[4]

6.2.1   Prevention: The Regulation on Surveillance

The Regulation on surveillance lays down an early-warning system in order to prevent a government deficit from becoming excessive. The backbone of the system is the following:

- Member states have to submit Stability or Convergence Programmes. Those member states having adopted the euro will submit Stability Programmes; the others will submit Convergence Programmes.[5]
- Stability and Convergence Programmes are focused on public finances; in both cases they will include a 'medium-term objective of a budgetary position close to balance or in surplus and the adjustment path towards this objective'.
- The programmes will be examined by the Council within at most two months of the submission of the programme; in particular, the Council shall assess 'whether the medium-term budget objective in the stability/convergence programme provides for a safety margin to ensure the avoidance of an excessive deficit'. The result of the examination is a Council opinion on the programme (in which the Council may request the member state concerned to adjust its programme). Both the examination by the Council and the formulation of its opinion are based on a recommendation from the Commission.

- The implementation of the programmes will be monitored by the Council; if the Council identifies a 'significant divergence of the budgetary position from the medium-term budgetary objective, or the adjustment path towards it' then a recommendation can be addressed to the member state concerned to take the necessary adjustment measures. If the divergence persists or worsens, the Council will make another recommendation to the member state, to take prompt corrective measures, but this time making the recommendation public.
- The difference between the Stability and the Convergence Programmes concerns only content and *a fortiori* the monitoring of implementation; only the Convergence Programmes will have to include information on 'the medium-term monetary policy objectives and the relationship of these objectives to price and exchange rate stability', since these are matters which will no longer be relevant at national level for member states participating in the single currency.
- The early-warning system relates to each member state taken individually; however, the Regulation also provides for an overall assessment. Indeed, when assessing each programme the Council 'shall furthermore assess whether the contents of the stability/convergence programme facilitate the closer co-ordination of policies and whether the economic policies of the Member State concerned are consistent with the broad economic policy guidelines'. In addition the Regulation restates Article 99(3) of the Treaty which requires an overall assessment of economic policies.

This Regulation follows very closely the initial Commission proposal, presented in October 1996; the Commission's approach remained unchanged and was extended to the non-participating member states. However, the Commission's proposal was stronger as regards the overall budgetary position. In fact, the Commission proposed that the Council should also assess the 'budgetary position for the EMU area as a whole implied by the national stability programmes'.

6.2.2 Dissuasion: The Regulation on Excessive Deficits

The purpose of the early-warning system is to prevent a member state from incurring an excessive deficit situation; however, such a situation might occur, either because the early warning was not heeded or because the excessive deficit emerged unexpectedly. It was therefore necessary to deal with these cases and such is the purpose of the Regulation on the implementation of the Excessive Deficit Procedure, which is based on Article 104 of the Treaty. This Article establishes in a clear way the several steps which constitute the Excessive Deficit Procedure, that is, from its identification to its correction. According to this Article of the Treaty several opportunities are given by the Council to the member state concerned to correct its excessive deficit once its existence has been decided; in case a member state does not take effective action to correct the deficit the pressure put by the Council increases, eventually leading to the imposition of sanctions.[6]

The Pact Regulation provides clarification on how to implement Article 104; in addition it sets precise deadlines for the different steps of the procedure. The main aspects of the Regulation are the following:

Definition of 'excessive deficit'

According to Article 104 (and the Protocol on the Excessive Deficit Procedure) a government deficit above 3 per cent of GDP is not excessive if 'the excess over 3 per cent is only exceptional and temporary and the (government deficit) ratio remains close to the reference value'. However, no precise definitions of these concepts is provided by the Treaty. While the Pact Regulation clarifies the concepts of exceptional and temporary, it is silent on the notion of 'close to the reference value'. It should be borne in mind that the issue of 'exceptional' (and 'temporary') circumstances is relevant for the assessment of whether a deficit is excessive or not; if the excess over 3 per cent is considered as being exceptional (and the temporary and 'close to' conditions are also satisfied) then there is no excessive deficit (that is, the Council does not take a decision in accordance with paragraph 6 of Article 104) and the process stops here. Conversely, if the Council decides that an excessive deficit exists, the procedure continues but there is no following step where the exceptional conditions could be invoked, namely as regards the application of sanctions.

Figure 6.1 illustrates five stylised paths for the deficit during and after an unexpected severe shock, by indicating for each of them the occurrence or not of an excessive deficit position.

The Pact Regulation considers that the excess over 3 per cent can be considered exceptional if (i) 'it results from an unusual event outside the control of the Member State' (for example, a natural

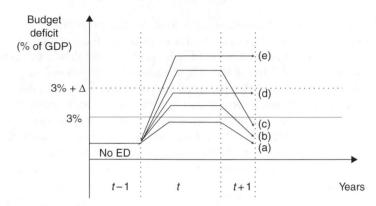

a: no excessive deficit
b: no excessive deficit
c: 'transient' excessive deficit (1 year)
d: excessive deficit
e: excessive deficit

$t-1$: pre-recession year
t: recession period
$t+1$: first year after recession period
Δ: allowed excess beyond 3%

Figure 6.1   Excessive deficit according to the Maastricht Treaty
Source: Buti *et al.* (1997).

disaster) or (ii) 'it results from a severe economic downturn'. What is a severe economic downturn? If there will be 'an annual fall of real GDP of at least 2 per cent' then this fact will be taken in consideration by the Commission when preparing the report under Article 104(3). This is the (factual) report that initialises the Excessive Deficit Procedure. According to the Regulation, the Commission will, even in this case, have to prepare a report. Moreover, in the European Council Resolution the Commission committed itself to always prepare a report when a deficit exceeds (or risks to exceed) 3 per cent of GDP. As a consequence, even if output falls by, say 2.5 per cent and the deficit widens to 3.5 per cent of GDP the Commission will have to prepare a report, thus triggering the procedure. The Commission's report is sent, for opinion, to the Economic and Financial Committee (EFC)[7] (ex-Monetary Committee from 1 January 1999 onwards). Based on this opinion the Commission has to make up its mind: if it considers that the deficit is indeed excessive, then it sends a recommendation for a Council decision in accordance with Article 104(6). When taking its decision, and according to the Pact Regulation, the member state concerned may present arguments justifying the deficit excess (over 3 per cent of GDP), namely as regards 'the abruptness of the downturn or the accumulated loss of output relative to past trends'. Such arguments, however, are to be presented by the member state concerned if the annual fall of real GDP was less than 2 per cent. This seems to imply that if the fall in output was at least 2 per cent then the Council would consider that the deficit was not excessive; in such a case one would expect that the EFC would, in its opinion on the Commission report, consider that the deficit was not excessive and the procedure would stop there (unless the Commission decided to pursue the procedure, which would not make much sense).

Let us return to the situation of a real GDP fall of less than 2 per cent in which the member state is presenting its arguments to the Council. There is a limit to such a presentation; indeed, in the European Council Resolution (point 7 under the heading 'The Member States') the member states have committed themselves to only present their defensive arguments if the annual fall in real GDP is at least 0.75 per cent. To sum up, the Pact rule concerning the use of 'exceptional' is the following: if real GDP falls by at least 2 per cent, then the excess (over 3 per cent of GDP) is exceptional and the Council does not decide that there is an excessive deficit; however, even in this case, the Commission will have to initiate the procedure. If the annual fall in real GDP is between 0.75 per cent and 2 per cent, the member state concerned can present to the Council arguments justifying the excess. Having listened to the arguments, the Council decides whether the deficit is excessive or not. If the fall in output is less than 0.75 per cent the issue of 'exceptional' should not be invoked.

In all these cases it is assumed that the Council, when deciding, has received from the Commission a recommendation as required by Article 104(13). In fact, this will necessarily happen. The only interesting case arises if the Commission and the EFC have different views on the issue. Suppose that in a member state real GDP falls by 1 per cent and the deficit reaches 3.25 per cent of GDP, and the Commission does not consider that the deficit is excessive but, following its commitment in the European Council Resolution, has prepared the (factual) report to the EFC. Suppose, however, that this committee gives an opinion according to which the deficit is indeed excessive. According to Article 104(5) the procedure will go on only if the Commission considers that an excessive deficit exists; if it does not, then the procedure stops. In this example the Commission would not initiate the procedure, not only because from the start it considered that the deficit was not excessive but also because it had not been convinced by the opinion of the EFC. However, in such an event of different views with the EFC the Commission, according to point 4 (under 'the Commission') of the European Council Resolution, will have 'to present in writing to the Council the reasons for its position'. If, in spite of the arguments presented by the Commission, the Council decides to activate Article 115 (ex 109d), then the Commission is committed (point 5 of the European Council Resolution) to make a recommendation for a Council decision on the existence of an excessive deficit. The Council will then most likely decide that an excessive deficit does exist because those had already been the views of the EFC.

The Time Span up to the Application of Sanctions

According to the Pact Regulation sanctions can be imposed ten months after data triggering the application of the procedure have been reported according to Regulation (EC) 3605/93, that is, by 1 March or 1 September. From this date up to the Council decision on the existence of an excessive deficit and the issuing of the Council recommendations under Article 104(7) a period of no more than three months can elapse. In case of data reported by 1 March of year $t + 1$ showing a deficit above 3 per cent of GDP in year t (the most likely case) then by 1 June of $t + 1$ the Council must have decided on the existence of an excessive deficit and made a recommendation to the member state concerned 'to bring that situation to an end within a given period' (Article 104(7)).

The recommendation under Article 104(7) gives four months for the member state concerned to take effective action to correct its deficit. In our example, the member state is expected to take action before the end of September of $t + 1$. If the Council considers that no effective action is taken then a notice under Article 104(9) is given to the member state within a month, that is, before the end of October in our example. If the member state fails to comply with the notice received from the Council, then within two months sanctions will be imposed. This means, in our example, that sanctions would be imposed before the end of year $t + 1$, that is before the end of the year following that in which the excessive deficit occurred.

The deadlines fixed by the Pact Regulation are a kind of baseline worst-case scenario: they address a situation in which the member state concerned does not take effective action in response to the Council recommendation/notice (see Figure 6.2). It is interesting to notice that the approach followed by the Treaty is, so to speak,

	Jan	Feb	Mar	Apr	May	Jun	July	Aug	Sept	Oct	Nov	Dec
Year N			Member states submit data[1]	Economic and Financial Committee formulates opinion	ECOFIN decides on excessive deficit and issues recommendations				ECOFIN assesses 'effective actions' and may decide to publish recommendations	ECOFIN gives notice of specific measures		ECOFIN decides to apply sanctions
			Commission prepares report	Commission prepares opinion					Member states submit data[1]			
N+1 and thereafter			Member states submit data[1]	ECOFIN decides to abrogate or intensify sanctions					Member states submit data[1]			

Figure 6.2 Timetable of the steps in the Regulation on excessive deficits
[1] According to Council Regulation (EC) 3605/93 member states must submit budgetary data twice a year: first until 1 March at the latest, afterwards until 1 September at the latest.

ad contrarium. In fact, the Council is never requested to decide formally that a member state has taken effective action but only the opposite: the Council acts if no effective action was taken by the member state concerned.

If the Council considers that effective action was taken, then the process is put in abeyance and the clock stops ticking. However, if the action taken by the member state is subsequently not being implemented or is considered inadequate then the clock starts ticking again: the procedure moves immediately to the step following the one at which it had stopped.

The Deadline for the Correction of the Excessive Deficit

Both the Pact Regulation and the European Council Resolution address this issue. The presumption is that the excessive deficit must be corrected promptly which means no later than the year following the identification of the excessive deficit; this is clearly stated in points 3 to 5 of the European Council Resolution (under 'The Council') and in paragraph 4 of Article 3 of the Pact Regulation. However, two comments are in order. First, there is the possibility of allowing a longer period for the correction of the excessive deficit, because the Pact states that the above mentioned rule holds 'unless there are special circumstances'. This suggests that the Council did not want to be very rigid in this area, recognising that there might be cases in which the correction of a deficit might require more time: the specific situation of each excessive deficit and the causes behind it should be examined by the Council. The second comment is on the ambiguity of the term 'identification'; it is difficult to accept any way of identifying an excessive deficit other than a Council decision for that purpose. Identification is not the same as occurrence: an excessive deficit may occur in year t but it is identified as such in March of year $t + 1$ and the Council decides accordingly no later than in June of $t + 1$. But then the member state has to correct the excess no later than $t + 2$, that is, two years after the excessive deficit has occurred.

Assessment of the Results of the Corrective Action Taken

The Council recommendation under Article 104(7) sets a deadline for the correction of the excessive deficit. The same is true as regards the Council notice under Article 104(9) although in this case the deadline is (much) shorter and stricter than in the previous case. As a consequence, after the member state concerned has taken the requested action and once the deadline has elapsed the Council must assess whether the expected results have been achieved, that is, whether the excessive deficit has indeed been corrected. The Pact Regulation takes a clear line on this issue: if data show that the excessive deficit has not been corrected then the procedure goes immediately to the next step. However, this move will have to be based on *actual* data, that is, data for a budgetary outcome of a year already elapsed. Suppose the Council decides in year $t + 1$ that an excessive deficit occurred in year t and makes a recommendation to the member state concerned to correct its deficit in year $t + 2$ (that is, the year after the identification of the excessive deficit); actual data on the deficit of year $t + 2$ will only be available in March of year $t + 3$. Only then can the Council give a notice under Article 104(9) to the member state concerned. It is also up to the Council, at that moment, to decide which time limit to give to the member state concerned. The Regulation says nothing about this, and rightly so. It belongs to the Council to assess the particular reasons why the excessive deficit was not corrected in year $t + 2$ and, in the light of this assessment, to set the time limit to be given in the notice. If the excessive deficit is not corrected within that time limit, than the Council immediately moves to the domain of the application of sanctions.

Application of Sanctions

This is the last step of the dissuasive part of the Stability and Growth Pact and, logically, is rather tough. Indeed, if the situation arrives at this stage the member state concerned cannot argue that it was not given enough opportunities to correct the excessive deficit. The imposition of sanctions is, in any case, a very serious decision for the Council to take. This must be the reason why the Treaty does not foresee, and as a consequence the Pact also does not, that sanctions can be imposed automatically. Each time the Council considers it necessary to impose or intensify a sanction then it has to formally decide accordingly. However, in the framework of the Stability and Growth Pact there is the presumption that if the conditions to impose sanctions are fulfilled then the Council will indeed impose sanctions. This seems to be the implication of points 3 to 5 (under the heading 'The Council') in the European Council Resolution (although the word 'invited' is used when it comes to the imposition of fines, rather than the word 'urged', which is used as regards the forms of the sanction).

The Amounts and the Mechanics of the Sanctions

If the Council decides to impose a sanction, then a non-interest-bearing deposit will be required from the member state concerned. The pecuniary cost of such a sanction is, naturally, the interest forgone. The deposit will remain constituted until one of the following two cases occurs: (i) if after two years since it was made the excessive deficit is not corrected, then the deposit is turned into a fine; (ii) if, before the two years have elapsed the Council considers that the excessive deficit has been corrected and abrogates its previous decision on the existence of an excessive deficit, then the deposit can be returned to the member state. Indeed, once a non-interest-bearing deposit has been made, the Council assesses, every year, whether the member state concerned has taken effective action to correct the excessive deficit. If the deficit has not been corrected then the Council intensifies the sanctions, namely through imposing the constitution of a new non-interest-bearing deposit. As a result, if a member state persists in not taking corrective action as considered necessary by the Council and the excessive deficit therefore remains, a non-interest-bearing deposit is constituted every year and is turned into a fine in (all of) the second year after its constitution. In such a system, there is always a non-interest-bearing deposit available to be turned into a fine. Suppose the case of an excessive deficit having occurred in year t, the Council having decided in $t + 1$ that an excessive deficit exists and decided to impose sanctions by December of that same year. The member state makes a non-interest-bearing deposit at the end of $t + 1$ or early in $t + 2$; by the end of $t + 2$ the Council assesses the situation: if everything remains as it is, a new deposit is required in year $t + 3$. By the end of $t + 3$ the Council makes a new assessment, and if the situation has not changed, then the deposit made in $t + 2$ is turned into a fine in $t + 4$ and a new deposit would be constituted also in $t + 4$. In the following year $(t + 5)$ the deposit made in $t + 3$ is converted into a fine and a new deposit is required, and so on and so forth, until the member state concerned takes effective action or the excessive deficit has been corrected.

The amount of the first deposit is calculated according to the rule *deposit in per cent of GDP* = $0.2 + 0.1 * (deficit - 3$ *per cent GDP*); this rule is presented in Figure 6.3. For instance, an excessive deficit of 4 per cent of GDP would lead to a deposit of 0.3 per cent of GDP. If an additional deposit(s) will be required only the variable part of the above formulae will then apply, that is, *new deposit in per cent*

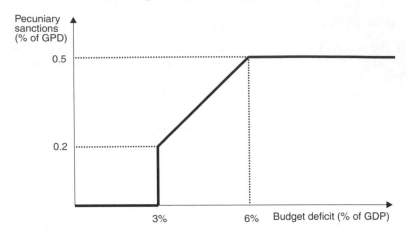

Figure 6.3   Sanctions under the SGP (non-interest-bearing deposits or fines in the first year)

of GDP = 0.1 ∗ (*deficit* − 3 *per cent GDP*). The application of these formulae is subject to a ceiling for each deposit: no single deposit can exceed 0.5 per cent of GDP. However, the amount for all the (successive) deposits is not capped. If a member state persists in running a deficit of 4 per cent of GDP, then after two years it will have made deposits amounting to 0.6 per cent of GDP.

It is curious to note that, according to the Pact Regulation, the amount of sanctions can be calculated only 'when the excessive deficit results from non-compliance with the deficit ratio criterion', which means that they cannot be calculated if an excessive deficit occurs due to non-compliance with the debt ratio criterion. In the case of an excessive deficit resulting from non-compliance with the debt ratio criterion there will be no pecuniary sanctions![8] This suggests that the Council does not seem concerned with debt developments in EMU. Non-compliance with the debt ratio criterion occurs if in those member states where the debt ratio is above 60 per cent of GDP there is an increase in the debt ratio. A slow (or even slightly negative) growth rate for the economy can lead to an increase in the debt ratio, in particular if accompanied by an accommodative government deficit, that is, a budgetary position which allowed the automatic stabilisers to make full use of the safety margin created in the framework of the Stability and Growth Pact. The debt ratio may also increase due to stock–flow operations, in particular those resulting from financial operations by the Treasury. One may argue that the likelihood of the events leading to an increase in the debt ratio is small, but one cannot deny that they are a possibility. In any case, in the terms of the Pact Regulation, if the Council decided that an excessive deficit exists only as a result of non-compliance with the debt ratio then no pecuniary sanctions can be applied according to the above-mentioned formulae.

The Use of the Proceeds of the Sanctions

The sanctions can be distributed only to those member states which have adopted the single currency and do not have an excessive deficit. The distribution between those member states will be proportional to their share in total GDP.

6.3 THE IMPLEMENTATION OF THE PACT: SOME CONSIDERATIONS ON THE FIRST TWO YEARS

The Stability and Growth Pact has been under full implementation since the beginning of 1999. The overall assessment on the implementation during the first two years of EMU is very positive: budgetary balances have in general improved and many member states will reach (or had already reached) a budgetary position of 'close to balance or in surplus' by 2001.

The developments displayed in Table 6.1 cannot but be considered as very positive. They show that fiscal consolidation did not come to a halt in 1997 once the fiscal convergence criteria had been met. This means that one of the main *raisons d'être* of the Pact, that is, securing the continuation of the convergence of fiscal positions, is thus being fulfilled.

6.3.1 The Stability and Convergence Programmes

Member states submitted (initial) Stability/Convergence Programmes by the end of 1998 and beginning of 1999.[9] All these programmes were, as foreseen in the Pact legislation, assessed by the European Commission and by the Council, which subsequently gave an opinion on each of them based on a Commission recommendation. While the Commission's assessments and recommendations for the Council opinions were not made public, all the Council opinions are published in the *Official Journal of the European Communities*.[10]

Table 6.1   Net lending (+) or net borrowing (−), general government
(as percentage of GDP)

	1997	1998	1999	2000[1]	2001[1]
Belgium	−2.0	−0.9	−0.7	0.0	0.5
Germany	−2.6	−2.1	−1.4	−1.0	−1.7
Greece	−4.6	−3.1	−1.8	−0.9	0.0
Spain	−3.2	−2.6	−1.2	−0.4	0.1
France	−3.0	−2.7	−1.6	−1.3	−1.1
Ireland	0.8	2.1	2.1	4.5	3.9
Italy	−2.7	−2.8	−1.8	−1.5	−1.3
Luxembourg	3.6	3.2	4.4	5.3	4.0
Netherlands	−1.2	−0.7	1.0	1.3	0.8
Austria	−1.9	−2.2	−2.1	−1.5	−0.7
Portugal	−2.6	−2.3	−2.1	−1.7	−1.5
Finland	−1.5	1.3	1.8	6.7	5.3
EURO Area	−2.6	−2.1	−1.2	−0.7	−0.8
Denmark	0.5	1.1	3.1	2.5	2.9
Sweden	−2.0	1.9	1.8	4.0	3.9
United Kingdom	−2.0	0.4	1.3	1.9	1.0
EU-15	−2.4	−1.6	−0.7	−0.1	0.0

[1] Net of the one-off revenues from the proceeds of UMTS licences.
Source: European Commission, spring 2001 forecast, *European Economy*,
Supplement A, no 3/4, Mar/Apr 2001.

In general, the Council considered that the programmes were in line with the requirements of the Stability and Growth Pact. No programme was rejected by the Council, but for some member states the Council regretted the lack of ambition of the proposed budgetary targets, for example Austria and Portugal.

What does being in conformity with the requirements of the Stability and Growth Pact mean? In other words, how do the Council and the Commission assess if a member state's medium-term budgetary objective is 'close to balance or in surplus'? With a view to giving an operational answer to this central question a methodology was developed by the Commission based on the concept of structural (or cyclically adjusted) budgetary balance. The starting point is that the budgetary position consistent with the Pact cannot be assessed by simply looking at actual deficits (or surpluses); the purpose of the Pact is to create, in each of the member state's public finances, enough leeway to accommodate the changes in the level of economic activity without leading the deficit to breach the 3 per cent of GDP threshold. This is clearly the view of the European Council which, in point 1 of its Resolution on the Stability and Growth Pact states that 'adherence to the objective of sound budgetary positions close to balance or in surplus will allow all Member States to deal with normal cyclical fluctuations while keeping the government deficit within the reference value of 3 % of GDP'. The conclusion is evident: the budgetary position consistent with the Pact has to be measured in terms which have been adjusted for the influence of the economic cycle, that is, in terms of what is usually called the structural balance or, when using the terminology of the European Commission, the cyclically adjusted balance.

The question is then how to quantify the cyclically adjusted balance which, for each member state, provides a sufficient safety margin to secure that the 3 % of GDP threshold for the government deficit is not breached in normal cyclical economic conditions. Such cyclically adjusted balances were designated by the Commission as 'minimal benchmarks'.

The method used by the Commission to calculate the minimal benchmarks takes into account the volatility of the economy of each member state (as evidenced by the evolution of the output gap) and the sensitivity of each budget balance to the cycle (see Chapter 8). *Ceteris paribus*, the higher the volatility of an economy and the higher the sensitivity of the budget to the cycle the more stringent will be the minimal benchmark. For example, the benchmark for Spain (a structural deficit of 0.4 per cent of GDP), as well as those for Sweden and Finland, mainly result from the high volatility of the economy. Conversely, for Austria, the relatively high benchmark mainly reflects the low volatility of the Austrian economy.

The judgment on the conformity of the programmes with the Stability and Growth Pact was largely based on the minimal benchmarks. It was agreed[11] that the medium-term objective of 'close to balance or in surplus' (and, *a fortiori*, the corresponding benchmarks) should be reached by 2002 at the latest, thus removing any uncertainty on what was considered the 'medium-term'. It must be stressed that, as their name indicates, the benchmarks are to be seen as minimum values. Indeed, there are other country-specific reasons that justify a wider safety margin, for example, a high stock of government debt, the need to make budgetary room for the consequences of ageing, and so on. Table 6.2 shows how the medium-term budgetary objectives set by each member state in its initial programme compared with the minimal benchmarks calculated by the Commission. Clearly, most member states were

Table 6.2   Cyclically adjusted budgetary objectives in the initial programmes[1] and minimal benchmarks (in percentage of GDP)

	1999	2000	2001	2002	Minimal benchmark
Belgium	−1.4	−1.1	−0.9	−0.5	−1.0
Germany	−1.7	−1.8	−1.4	−1.0	−1.1
Greece	−2.0	−1.7	−1.2	n.a.	−1.4
Spain	−1.7	−1.2	−0.6	−0.1	−0.4
France*	−2.0	−1.7	−1.4	−1.0	−1.5
Ireland**	0.6	0.3	0.8	n.a.	−0.9
Italy	−1.5	−1.3	−1.1	n.a.	−1.2
Luxembourg***	1.1	1.2	1.3	1.7	0.0
Netherlands	n.a.	n.a.	n.a.	n.a.	−0.1
Austria	−2.2	−1.9	−1.6	−1.4	−1.3
Portugal	−2.1	−1.6	−1.3	−0.9	−0.6
Finland	0.5	0.7	1.1	1.8	1.3
Denmark	1.9	2.5	2.5	3.5	−0.7
Sweden	0.3	1.3	2.0	n.a.	0.8
United Kingdom[a]	0.2	0.1	0.1	−0.1	−0.1

[1] Calculated with the method used by the European Commission services based on the GDP-real growth rates and budgetary targets included in the programmes.
* Favourable scenario.
** Figures calculated by the Irish authorities and included in the programme.
*** Figures for the actual surpluses, central scenario.
[a] Financial years.
Source: Commission services and national programmes.

expected to be *within* the benchmark in 2001, very few only in 2002 (Germany, Spain); Austria and Portugal are very close to the minimal benchmark in 2002, but remain above it.

The use of cyclically adjusted budgetary targets/outcomes is also relevant for the implementation of the 'significant divergence' clause, to which the SGP does not provide operational guidance. An important point in the application of this clause is that, once a member state has achieved the close-to-balance budgetary position, attention should be mainly concentrated on cyclically adjusted developments. While deviations from budgetary targets due to the operation of automatic stabilisers, measured in terms of actual balances, are allowed under the SGP, structural deterioration in the budget balance should be avoided. Indeed, a *small* divergence in actual balances can mask a *significant* divergence in cyclically adjusted terms. In such a case the member state concerned should be requested to take corrective action. This, would also be the case, of course, if the actual divergence would be threatening the 3 per cent of GDP reference value.[12]

6.4 FINAL REMARKS

This chapter has presented the main features of the working of the SGP and briefly assessed the experience of its implementation in the first two years. The main conclusion of the analysis is that the SGP appears a suitable framework for ensuring budgetary discipline in EMU.

Obviously, as any 'commitment technology' providing effective constraints on governments' behaviour, it may be accused of being 'too blunt'. For instance, is the use of the minimal benchmark a too mechanical/simplistic way of assessing how the programmes were in compliance with the Pact? In our view, the use of the benchmarks in the first years of the implementation of the Pact was not only appropriate but it was even perhaps the only way to go ahead. The point we want to make here is that in 1999 and 2000, but especially in 1999, the overriding concern was to ensure that fiscal positions would get closer to the benchmark. The issue was above all, one of credibility. If we look at the 1998 column of Table 6.1 (which largely corresponds to the information available when the programmes were being assessed), we see that in some member states, namely Germany, France and Italy, the government deficit was above 2 per cent of GDP, if not close to 3 per cent. In addition, the 1999 column in Table 6.2 shows that the budgetary targets for 1999, in cyclically adjusted terms, were still far from being in a position consistent with the Pact. In such a juncture, can one imagine what would have been the reaction of the financial markets if, in the first year of implementation of the SGP, the policy line was other than 'achieve in 1999 the fiscal targets of the stability/ convergence programmes'? This was the line taken by the Commission, and subsequently by the Council. In each of its opinions on the programmes one can find a recommendation of the type 'the Council recommends that the targets for 1999 are met'. This strategy proved to have been appropriate: budgetary targets in 1999 were met, even overachieved in some member states.

Those who argued against the policy line described above favoured an approach based on the functioning of the automatic stabilisers. One should recall that in the autumn of 1998 when all these issues were being debated, some were forecasting a significant deceleration of economic activity in 1999 as a result of the Asian cum Russia cum Latin America crisis. In that event, it was argued, one should let the automatic stabilisers work and, therefore, not stick to the budgetary targets of the programmes. The case of Italy provides a clear example of this line of thought: in spite of having in its programme a deficit target of 2.0 per cent of GDP for 1999, the Council, in the framework of the Broad Economic Policy Guidelines for 1999 and departing from the Commission's recommendation (European Commission, 1999) allowed Italy to slip up to 2.4 per cent on grounds of lower than expected economic growth. This was not well-received by the markets, although the Italian government reiterated its commitment on the target for 2000, thus meaning that the slippage in 1999 would be of a temporary nature. Indeed, with a deficit of 2.4 per cent of GDP Italy would remain very close to the 3 per cent threshold, hence close to triggering the dissuasive weaponry of the Stability and Growth Pact. At the end of the day Italy was able to achieve a deficit of 1.8 per cent of GDP in 1999.

The argument of allowing the automatic stabilisers to work is, in itself, very valid. Indeed, the Stability and Growth Pact intends, at the end of the day, to adjust the fiscal position of the member states in such a way that the automatic stabilisers are allowed to operate fully. But only once the fiscal position consistent with the Pact has been met!

Notes

1. Proposal for a Council Regulation (EC) 'on the strengthening of the surveillance and coordination of budgetary positions' and proposal for a Council Regulation (EC) 'on speeding up and clarifying the implementation of the excessive deficit procedure' (Com (96) 496 final, 16 October 1996).
2. Council Regulation (EC) 1466/97 of 7 July 1997.
3. Council Regulation (EC) 1467/97 of 7 July 1997.
4. Resolution of the European Council on the Stability and Growth Pact, Amsterdam 17 June 1997 (97/C 236/01).
5. Chapter 7 presents a thorough assessment of the role of the programmes in budgetary surveillance in EMU.
6. For a comprehensive analysis of Article 104, see Italianer (1997).
7. The Economic and Financial Committee is governed by the Council Decisions 'on detailed provisions concerning the composition of the

EFC' (no. 743/98 of 21 December 1998) and 'adopting the statutes of the EFC' (no. 8/99 of 31 December 1998).

8. This is in clear contrast with the draft Regulations proposed by the Commission.

9. For a complete description of the new Stability/Convergence Programmes, see European Commission (1999).

10. The Council opinions on the Stability and Convergence Programmes and the first updates are collected in European Commission (1999, 2000a).

11. See Monetary Committee opinion, October 1998.

12. For a thorough discussion of the interpretation of this clause, see European Commission (2000a).

7 The Stability and Convergence Programmes*

Jonas Fischer and Gabriele Giudice

7.1 INTRODUCTION

The core elements of the early-warning mechanism envisaged in the Stability and Growth Pact (SGP) are the national Stability and Convergence Programmes. In these programmes member states, according to the Pact, set out their medium-term budgetary plans in order to reach budgetary positions that should be 'close to balance or in surplus'.[1]

Since the launch of the Pact, budgetary developments have been favourable and budget deficits have been reduced sharply. The experience gathered with the completion of one round of programmes and one round of updates[2] has been positive until now, but it is also fair to say that the Pact has yet to prove its performance under more extreme conditions, that is, in significantly 'bad' or 'good' times, where pro-cyclical characteristics of public finances and/or severe economic developments could put the Pact under stress.[3]

Given the short experience[4] and the lack of conclusive empirical evidence, it is natural that the debate in economic policy and academic circles has focused mainly on the role of disincentives created by the dissuasive part of the Pact (namely the sanctions in the case of persistent 'excessive deficits') while the preventive arm (namely the programmes) has received much less attention. The purpose of this chapter, which tries to fill this gap, is therefore twofold: first, on the basis of the experience gained, to illustrate the practical aspects

* The opinions expressed in this chapter do not necessarily correspond to those of the European Commission. The authors acknowledge valuable comments from A. Brunila and M. Buti.

in the handling of the Stability Programmes and discuss some of the challenges involved and how these have been treated so far; second, to illustrate the implications of this procedure and how the programmes as such could be developed into an efficient tool for economic policy-making and coordination.

The chapter is organised as follows. Section 7.2 presents the main features of the programmes. Section 7.3 looks at the experience of moving into the practical aspects of handling, interpreting and assessing the Stability and Convergence Programmes. Sections 7.4 and 7.5 present the challenges ahead. Section 7.6 concludes.

7.2 HOW THE PREVENTIVE PART OF THE PACT WORKS

7.2.1 Content of the Programmes

The Stability and Convergence programmes are submitted annually at the same time as, or shortly after, the adoption of national budget proposals.[5] In this way, the programmes can include the main elements and targets of the forthcoming budget, as well as the medium-term objectives.[6] This contributes to the transparency of national fiscal policy and ensures constant peer pressure.

Yet, transparency and accountability of each member state's fiscal policy are only granted if the information in the programmes is complete and consistent across countries. To this end, but also to ensure comparability and equal treatment, a common framework has been designed to identify the content of the programmes and the methodology to be used when drafting them. This framework is defined by the SGP (in particular Council Regulation (EC) 1466/97) and by a Code of Conduct prepared by the Monetary Committee and approved by the ECOFIN Council[7] in 1998. The Pact lists the 'minimum requirements' for the information which must appear in each programme to allow for its proper assessment:[8] information needed to clarify the medium-term budgetary targets, the adjustment towards them, the expected path of the general government debt ratio, the main economic assumptions underlying the budgetary developments such as government investment expenditure, the expected sources of real GDP growth, and information on the cyclical position of the economy, employment, interest rates and the expected inflation rate, the implications of changes in growth and interest rates and the policy measures to be taken. The Code of Conduct makes this part of the Pact more operational, by defining in greater detail quantitative and qualitative information that should be provided in the programmes.

In addition to the quantitative requirements, the SGP attaches importance also to the policy intentions underlying the programmes, namely the planned and ongoing budgetary initiatives and reforms. Therefore, the adjustment path to the medium-term objective has to be identified, as well as the main features of next year's budget, major policy initiatives and budget measures which are taken or proposed to achieve the set objectives.

The information provided in the programmes has to satisfy common statistical framework according to European standards.[9] The budgetary data to be provided must be based on the European System of Accounts ESA-95 and cover the general government sector,[10] which comprises four subsectors: the central government, the state (or regional) governments, the local governments and the social security funds.

7.2.2   The Assessment of the Programmes

The Pact specifies in detail the handling of the programmes at EU level. These specifications cover procedures, deadlines, content of the Council examination and follow-up procedures, thus aiming at ensuring an equal treatment and a high degree of comparability.

The ECOFIN Council is responsible for the examination of each programme, where the final output is a 'Council opinion' on each programme. The ECOFIN Council does not assess the programmes alone: the European Commission and the Economic and Financial Committee (EFC) are formally involved. According to the Pact timetable, the Council should be ready with its examination at the latest two months after the submission of a programme.[11] Before the Council examination, there is a preparatory discussion in the EFC based on a Commission assessment of the programme and a Commission recommendation for a Council opinion. Updated programmes could be treated using a lighter procedure without the direct involvement of the Council. If deemed sufficient, the assessment can be based on the EFC examination only. Given the relative youth of the Pact and the need to build credibility around the overall framework, this 'lighter' procedure has not yet been implemented. All programmes and updates have been examined at the Council level with a formal Council opinion.[12]

The Pact stipulates the issues the Council has to examine (CR 1466/97, Art. 5). The assessment of quantitative targets is of course essential, as this is 'the core' of the Pact framework. To this end the Council must assess whether the medium-term budgetary objectives set in the programmes provide sufficient room for manoeuvre to ensure the avoidance of an excessive deficit. In this context the Council shall also examine whether the economic assumptions under-pinning the programme are realistic and whether the measures announced in the programmes will be effective in reaching the budget targets. The Council also has to examine whether the economic policies presented in the programme are consistent with the Broad Economic Policy Guidelines (BEPG); and how and whether the con-tent of the programme 'facilitates closer co-ordination of economic policies'.

The Council opinions cover formally all the areas as required by the legislation. Nevertheless, the experience so far indicates that qualita-tive aspects play a rather peripheral role and the focus is on the budgetary safety margins under the 3 per cent deficit ceiling. For example, in its assessments on the 1999 round of programmes, the Council found that the medium-term budgetary targets for all mem-ber states but Austria included a safety margin large enough to allow automatic stabilisers to operate fully in the event of a cyclical slow-down without the risk of breaching the 3 per cent deficit ceiling. Austria, being the exception, was urged to improve its targets in the next update. Other member states were also asked to increase their safety margins for different reasons. Germany and Portugal were asked to widen their safety margins quicker as they were on the limit and would only reach a safe position in 2002. France and the Netherlands were asked to use any additional room for manoeuvre to improve the deficit position further as they had used quite cautious assumptions. Also, highly indebted countries like Belgium and Italy were asked to make additional efforts to reduce more quickly their debt ratios. A similar recommendation was addressed to Austria whose debt ratio was set to increase over the 60 per cent of GDP reference value. All member states were judged to respect the BEPG except for Portugal where the increase in revenue and expenditure levels was questioned. Moreover, the need to use budgetary policy to reduce inflationary pressures was mentioned for Ireland and Greece. Overall, it can be said that the Council, although commenting on many topics such as ageing, the fiscal stance and the quality of public finances, has taken stronger positions only on issues directly linked to the appropriateness of the medium-term budgetary target, which has then become, *de facto*, the 'core of the Pact'.

7.3   THE PRACTICAL PROBLEMS: HOW TO MOVE FROM THEORY TO PRACTICE

The main challenge in the early years of the Pact has been to make the assessment and follow-up framework operational. To achieve this, it is necessary that the analytical framework be focused in order to be relevant, simple in order to be able to be based on the information available in the programmes and flexible enough to be applicable to all member states.

The fundamental element of the assessment is the evaluation of the medium-term objective for the budgetary position of close-to-balance or in surplus. The SGP indicates that such a position should allow to deal with normal cyclical fluctuations while keeping the government deficit within the reference value of 3 per cent.[13] Accordingly, the Code of Conduct clearly states that the assessment of the medium-term objectives has to take explicit account of the cyclical position and its effects on the budgets. Hence, the close-to-balance targets in the programmes are to be interpreted in cyclically adjusted terms. This represents an important improvement on the nominal requirement of the Maastricht Treaty.[14] In this context and given its implications, for example for the estimation of the 'minimal benchmarks',[15] the methodological issue of calculating cyclically adjusted balances comes to the fore.

7.3.1   Cyclical Adjustment of Budget Balances

When setting and monitoring targets, there is a need to take explicit account of the cyclical position of the economy and its effect on the budget. This is recognised in the provisions of the SGP according to which, in addition to fixing targets for actual budget balances, member states must provide enough detailed information on GDP developments in their Stability and Convergence Programmes to enable 'a proper analysis of the cyclical position of the economy'.[16] Hence, while there is no formal requirement to supply figures on cyclically adjusted budget balances, the distinction between actual and structural budgetary positions is implicitly recognised. Some member states actually provide cyclically adjusted figures. On the basis of information included in the programmes, the Commission applies statistical methods to single out fluctuations which are due to short-term cyclical developments from the underlying trend. However, since cyclical developments are unobservable, this type of calculation is always surrounded by a degree of uncertainty.

Different Approaches in Computing Cyclically Adjusted Variables

In an ideal world with sufficient information on all budgetary items and discretionary policy measures, it would be possible to adjust each budget item directly to reflect their 'true' structural position. In practice, information of such quality is not readily available. Consequently, indirect methods are used where the cyclical budgetary component is inferred from the covariation of government revenues and expenditures with output fluctuations.

The most common method is to apply marginal sensitivity of revenues and expenditures (ε_{rev} and ε_{exp}, respectively) to the output gap (OG) to determine the cyclical component of the budget balance (cc). The cyclically adjusted budget balance (CAB) is then obtained in (7.1) by subtracting the cyclical component from the actual budget balance (d):

$$CAB = d_t - cc = d_t - (\varepsilon_{rev} + \varepsilon_{exp})^* OG_t \qquad (7.1)$$

In view of the simplifying assumptions and usual estimation problems, the method can only produce an approximate decomposition of the budget balance into a cyclical and structural component.

Its results must therefore be interpreted with the necessary caution.[17] Whereas there is a broad agreement on the magnitude of the estimated budgetary sensitivities, there is less agreement on the best approach for estimating potential output and output gaps. To compute the output gap, an estimate of the potential or trend output is needed. Because these are not directly observable, a number of assumptions must be made to disentangle trend and cycle in actual GDP developments.

To estimate trend output and related output gaps one approach is to use a statistical filter. This has been the approach used by the Commission Services. Such a statistical method is simple to use and the results can be easily reproduced. It also minimises the need for judgemental interventions and so allows for a consistent treatment of member states. Moreover, the method is parsimonious on data requirements and the calculations can be made on the basis of information provided in the Stability and Convergence Programmes. The statistical filter has also the advantage that the estimated output gaps, and hence the cyclical components of the budget balance, cancel out over the cycle. A clear disadvantage of the filter, however, is its lack of economic foundations which makes its results and underlying assumptions difficult to interpret economically.

Another commonly used method to compute potential output and output gaps involves estimating a production function. Under the production function approach, potential output estimates, being based on theoretical grounds, can be interpreted from an economic standpoint. This allows the assessment of the underlying factors driving the results. On the other hand, the results depend strongly on assumptions on the functional form of the production technology, for example, returns to scale and the trend growth of technical progress, as well as on estimates of the structural unemployment rate. All these assumptions are subject to heated economic debate.

The differences in the results obtained with the two approaches depend, *inter alia*, on the variable that is looked at: the estimated *changes* in the output gap are quite similar, while in *level* terms the output gap estimates may still show considerable variation. These differences are particularly evident when calculating potential output during the disinflation period of the 1980s and the 1990s. A production function approach usually establishes a direct link between growth and inflation by incorporating a Phillips curve capturing the short-term trade-off between output and inflation. The output loss needed to bring down inflation is considered to have little effect on the production potential of the economy. Hence, large negative output gaps emerge. A statistical filter, instead, 'interprets' part of the subdued growth performance as a fall in potential output. Hence, the estimated output gaps are smaller.

This implies that unlike the filtering method, a method based on production function does not necessarily produce symmetrical output gaps. In the context of budgetary surveillance, the difficulty arises because of the uncertainty as to how much of these accumulated negative output gaps will in the end be retrieved. If the accumulated output loss is not going to be recovered, the corresponding revenue will actually never materialise. With a more stable macroeconomic environment the importance of this problem should be reduced in the future. The stability-oriented macroeconomic framework of EMU would itself contribute to smooth out these differences. Table 7.1 summarises in general terms the pros and cons of a statistical filter

Table 7.1   Synthesis table summarising the properties of different methods

Method	Methodological aspects					Results	
	Simplicity Transparency	Judgemental intervention	Data input requirement	Homogeneous application	Link to economic theory	Symmetry	Correlation trend and cycle
Filter	High	Low	Low	Yes	Low	Yes	Yes
Production function	Low	High	High	Difficult	High	No	Yes

technique versus a production function method to calculate output gaps.

The Commission Method in More Detail

To identify output gaps, the Commission estimates trend output by using the Hodrick–Prescott (HP) filter to the actual output series.[18] This produces a smooth trend, without phase shifts (that is, no leads or lags in turning points in the cycle) and results in symmetric output gaps over the cycle, that is, output gaps sum by construction to zero over the cycle. As such, the estimated trend GDP is merely a measure of the average GDP level, without ambition of any normative content.

Trend output based on the Hodrick–Prescott filter is obtained by minimising fluctuations in actual output around trend output subject to a constraint on the variation of the growth rate of trend output.[19] The setting of the smoothing parameter λ in the minimisation problem is arbitrary. Following what has become the norm in the literature and among practitioners, the Commission Services set λ at 100. In terms of the length of business cycles affecting the cyclical component, a λ at 100 means that cycles shorter than 15–16 years are retained while cycles above 20 years are fully filtered out.

The use of the statistical filter implies having to face the 'end point bias' problem, which relates to the fact that the otherwise symmetric Hodrick–Prescott filter becomes asymmetric towards the end of the series with unproportional emphasis put on the last few observations. 'End-point effects' are mainly noticeable for the last 3–4 observations in the series. One way of restoring symmetry is to extend the data series that is being analysed with projections, a line followed by the Commission Services. This solution has nevertheless the disadvantage of adding a forecast error problem. However, sensitivity calculations show that this seems to be limited in size and should not have a major qualitative impact.

The output gap is then calculated as the difference between the actual level of GDP and that of estimated trend GDP, expressed as a percentage of trend GDP.

To estimate the cyclical component of the budget, it is necessary to identify the value of the budget sensitivity of revenue and expenditure to the output gap. The overall revenue elasticity is a weighted average of four revenue elasticities (personal income taxes, corporate taxes, social security contributions and indirect taxes), whereby the different components are weighted by the relative share of each category in total revenue over the 1980–98 period. Elasticities for these specific tax categories, and also government unemployment expenditures, are those calculated and recently updated in OECD (1999a). A similar approach is followed in the case of government expenditure, although only government transfers to households (to cover costs related to unemployment) are assumed to react 'automatically' to cyclical fluctuations among all expenditure category.

The total budget sensitivity to the output gap, which is given by the sum of the revenue and expenditure sensitivities, is around 0.5 in the euro area and the EU as a whole (Table 7.2).[20] This implies that if the output gap changes by one percentage point, the budget balance changes by 0.5 per cent of GDP. In general, the major determinant of the size of the budget sensitivity is the overall size of the government sector in the economy (which is around 50 per cent of GDP in the EU). The revenue sensitivity is more important than the expenditure sensitivity because most tax revenues fluctuate with growth while only a small part of overall government expenditures (unemployment expenditure) is assumed to respond to cyclical fluctuations. This implies that automatic stabilisers predominantly work on the revenue side.

To obtain the cyclical component of the budget these sensitivities are multiplied by the estimated output gap. Deducting the cyclical component from the actual government budget balance gives the cyclically adjusted budget balance as a residual.

7.3.2 Assessing the Ambition of the Objectives Set Out in the Programmes

An important issue in the assessment of the programmes, especially for the calculation of the structural developments, is the observed tendency of member states to be overly cautious in their economic assumptions. While in the run-up to EMU member states may have had incentives to be overly optimistic showing quick progress in their consolidation efforts, now, once in EMU, the incentives have changed to the opposite, with cautious growth assumptions paying several forms of 'dividends' to governments. First, as growth is likely to be higher than assumed, the targets are very likely to be overachieved, giving the false impression that governments are overperforming. Second, an implicit 'room for manoeuvre' is built up which can be used for *ad hoc* discretionary budgetary measures without being restricted by the announced budget balance targets in actual terms.

Table 7.2 Budget sensitivities used by the Commission Services

	B	D	E	F	IR	I	NL	A	P	SF	EU 11	DK	EL	S	UK	EU 15
Expenditure	0.5	0.4	0.3	0.3	0.3	0.4	0.4	0.3	0.3	0.5	0.4	0.5	0.3	0.5	0.4	0.4
Revenue	0.1	0.1	0.0	0.1	0.1	0.0	0.3	0.0	0.0	0.2	0.1	0.3	0.0	0.2	0.1	0.1
Total	0.6	0.5	0.4	0.4	0.4	0.4	0.7	0.3	0.3	0.7	0.5	0.8	0.3	0.7	0.5	0.5

Finally, in the case of surplus countries, this caution helps avoiding domestic political pressure to give away the surpluses.

Another issue still open to interpretation makes the assessment of the programmes difficult: the question is whether the interpretation of the budgetary plans should be in actual or in structural terms. While the Commission strongly supports the view[21] that emphasis should be on underlying developments, not all member states agree mainly because of the uncertainties outlined above in the calculation of cyclically adjusted figures. Clearly, if 'peer pressure' were on cyclically adjusted targets, then the cautious attitude of member states would not create problems for the assessment. Indeed, as higher-than-assumed growth outcome would imply a smaller deficit/higher surplus in actual terms, member states would automatically be required, to respect their original commitment in the underlying terms, to attain better actual budget positions than envisaged in the programmes.

The simple calculation below illustrates how much member states should revise their actual targets in order to respect their original commitment in the underlying terms. Equation (7.2) identifies the change in the deficit level over the period covered by the programmes, where t and $t+3$ represent the first and the last year. $\Delta d_{t,t+3}$ represent the 'committed effort' in actual terms (but also considered as a commitment in structural terms) to reduce the deficit d over the lifetime of the programme.

$$\Delta d_{t,t+3} = d_{t+3} - d_t \tag{7.2}$$

To discount the degree of caution used by member states in their programmes, the given target figures should be revised to take into account changes in the 'starting position' and 'expected growth dividends'. RF in (7.3) is the sum of these revision factors. The first term in brackets on the right-hand side of the equation is the starting position factor which indicates how much better the actual deficit d^a in the year t was in comparison to the assumptions made in the programme. The expected growth dividend is calculated as the sum of the differences, over the rest of the period, between GDP growth assumed in the programmes, g_n, and the Commission forecasts, g_n^F, multiplied by ε, the budgetary sensitivity parameter.

$$RF = (d_t^a - d_t) + \varepsilon \left(\sum_{t+1}^{t+3} g_n - g_n^F \right) \tag{7.3}$$

In equation (7.4), $\Delta d^*_{t,t+3}$ shows what should be the effort in actual terms if the original effort $\Delta d_{t,t+3}$ were 'topped up' by the 'revision factors' RF, to maintain the same 'adjustment effort' announced in the programme, if that were interpreted in structural terms. Equation (7.5) then identifies the 'new' nominal target d^*_{t+3} which should be achieved if member states were committed to structural rather than actual objectives.

$$\Delta d^*_{t,t+3} = \Delta d_{t,t+3} + RF \tag{7.4}$$

$$d^*_{t+3} = d_t + \Delta d^*_{t,t+3} \tag{7.5}$$

Table 7.3 applies these calculations to the data provided by member states in the 1999 updates. In the table, the first two columns show the deficit targets for 1999 and 2002 as announced in the 1999/2000 updates. The change in the budget deficit from 1999 to 2002, in column 3, is the 'committed effort' over the period. Column 4 shows the starting position adjustment for 1999 while in columns 5–7 are indicated the expected growth dividends over the 2000–02 period. Column 9 shows the adjusted effort, given by the effort announced in the programme (column 3) adjusted by the revision factors (column 8). Column 10 indicates the 'new' targets in actual terms. From the table it is obvious that, if the 2002 targets are assessed only in actual terms (column 2), they are not very ambitious at all in comparison to the adjustments effort member states have (implicitly) committed to (column 10). In other words, an assessment only in actual terms can be very misleading.

7.3.3 The *ex post* Assessment of Budgetary Performance: Some Examples

The *ex post* evaluation of the budgetary performance of a member state relative to the announced targets is also not straightforward. There are some specific experiences that serve well to illustrate that both the reliability of macroeconomic assumptions and the lack of clarity as to the importance of the assessment of structural positions play a crucial role in the *ex post* evaluation.

The first experience concerns the actual budgetary developments in 1999 contrasted to what was assumed in the programmes. At the end of 1998 it became clear that growth in 1999 would not be as bright as previously perceived, the main reason being the expected negative

Table 7.3 Adjusted 2002 deficit targets from the 1999 updates, to take into account changes in the starting position and expected budgetary growth dividends

	SP/CP target 1999 d_t	SP/CP target 2002 d_{t+3}	SP/CP effort $\Delta d_{t,t+3}$	Starting position 1999 $(d_t^a - d_t)$	Growth dividend 2000 $\varepsilon(g_{t+1} - g_{t+1}^F)$	Growth dividend 2001 $\varepsilon(g_{t+2} - g_{t+2}^F)$	Growth dividend 2002 $\varepsilon(g_{t+3} - g_{t+3}^F)$	Starting and growth factors RF	Adjusted effort 99/02 $\Delta d_{t,t+3}^*$	Adjusted target 2002 d_{t+3}^*
	1	2	3 = 2 − 1	4	5	6	7	8 = 4 to 7	9 = 3 + 8	10 = 1 + 9
B	1.1	0.0	−1.1	−0.4	−0.8	−0.6	−0.5	−2.2	−3.4	−2.3
D	1.2	1.0	−0.2	0.2	−0.3	−0.2	0.0	−0.3	−0.5	0.7
EL	−1.5	−0.2	−1.7	0.3	−0.1	−0.1	−0.2	−0.1	−1.8	−0.3
E	1.3	−0.1	−1.4	−0.2	−0.2	0.0	0.0	−0.4	−1.8	−0.5
F	2.1	0.9	−1.2	−0.3	−0.2	−0.2	−0.1	−0.8	−2.0	0.1
IRL	−1.4	−2.6	−1.2	−0.5	−1.2	−0.7	−0.5	−3.1	−4.3	−5.7
IT	2.0	0.6	−1.4	−0.1	−0.3	−0.1	0.0	−0.5	−1.9	0.1
L	−2.3	−2.9	−0.6	−0.1	0.4	−0.4	−0.3	−1.2	−1.8	−4.1
NL	0.6	1.1	0.5	−1.6	−1.3	−0.8	−0.6	−4.3	−3.8	−3.2
A	2.0	1.4	−0.6	0.1	−0.2	0.0	−0.1	−0.2	−0.8	1.2
P	2.0	0.7	−1.3	0.1	−0.1	0.3	0.3	0.8	−0.5	1.5
FIN	−3.1	−4.6	−1.5	1.2	−0.7	−0.8	−0.8	−1.1	−2.6	−5.7
DK	−2.9	−2.3	−0.6	0.1	−0.7	−0.2	−0.1	−0.9	−0.3	−3.2
SW	−1.7	−2.0	−0.3	−0.2	−0.7	−1.1	−0.8	−2.8	−3.1	−4.8
UK	−0.4	0.0	0.4	−0.9	−0.5	−0.3	−0.3	−2.0	−1.6	−2.0

NB: A minus sign for the targets means a budget surplus.

impact from exports and higher interest rates consequent to the Asian financial crisis. Later on, however, the slowdown proved less sharp than expected. In these specific circumstances, difference in time of preparation and submission of the programmes among member states had diverse consequences. Specifically, the growth assumptions for 1999 looked too optimistic for several countries which had prepared or submitted the programmes in early autumn 1998. This was especially true for the Italian programme. After realising this, the Italian authorities wanted to adjust their deficit projection for 1999 from 2 per cent of GDP to a maximum of 2.4 per cent of GDP, to take into account the worse-than-expected cyclical development. The ECOFIN Council, reluctantly, accepted the revision. The reluctance by ministers was justified by the fact that 1999 was the first year of the euro and that the EMU framework was not consolidated credibly yet. Over and above this, in view of its past budgetary history and level of public debt, there was a widespread feeling that Italy was closely watched by financial markets. Nevertheless, this episode shows how much weight was given to actual developments rather than structural changes.[22]

Another important example showing the difficulty in assessing the implementation of the programmes concerns the French 1999 updated programme. First, since France was among the last countries to submit the programme, and expecting by then a sharp downturn which eventually proved to be less serious than assumed, the assumptions were overly pessimistic. Both the 1998 budgetary outcome and the growth assumptions for 1999 and onwards were clearly on the low side. This was recognised in the Commission assessment and in the Council opinion where the French government was urged to go beyond the set targets (a deficit of 1.7 per cent of GDP in 2000) and use the expected growth dividends to improve the budget balance. Second, only a few days after the discussion in the Council, the French authorities announced additional tax cuts estimated to be worth about 0.5 per cent of GDP for 2000, which were not included in the programme. The French authorities announced that despite additional tax cuts (now taking the better starting position into account) the actual target of a 1.7 per cent of GDP deficit in the programme would be met and overachieved anyway. The uncertainty on the use of the concept of structural balance and on the estimated figures, and especially since targets given in actual terms were to be fulfilled, made it impossible for the Council to take action. Nevertheless, taking the starting position and higher growth into account, this implied a clear deterioration in the structural balance. A clearer commitment to underlying developments could potentially have triggered action by the EU on the basis of a 'significant divergence' from the programme.

A third example of the difficulty in evaluating the programmes concerns the Netherlands, in this case because of the budgetary framework based on very cautious assumptions. The Dutch budgetary framework is conducted within a government coalition medium-term agreement based on expenditure control. Expenditure growth is based on very cautious GDP growth assumptions with additional 'rules' on how to allocate the budgetary growth dividends between the budget balance and tax cuts. This very cautious approach, which seems useful for procedural and policy purposes, gives prudent figures which are difficult to evaluate and are criticised by the Council for being unambitious, even though they are very likely to be overachieved (almost automatically) *ex post*. Overall, this case is a problem about presentation rather than substance but nevertheless difficult to handle in the framework of the Pact, especially if its interpretation is mostly in actual terms.

7.4 CHALLENGES FOR THE PROGRAMMES: EU LEVEL MONITORING

One of the challenges ahead for the multilateral surveillance of budgetary positions and strategies in the context of the SGP is to successfully ensure the monitoring of the fiscal developments and the correct implementation of the programmes. To this end the Commission and Council need a consistent approach to remove uncertainty and scope for 'political bargaining'. Within the SGP, this would require developing an operational framework for identifying 'significant divergences' from budget targets agreed in Stability and Convergence Programmes. This would allow any budgetary slippage, including a pro-cyclical loosening, to be rapidly detected. In this case the Council, acting on the basis of a recommendation from the Commission, can issue a recommendation for the member state to take corrective action.[23]

So far, this formal signalling procedure has not been actively used. This is not surprising given the difficulty in finding, during the first years of the Pact, clear events when a 'significant divergence' could potentially have occurred.

The focus in the monitoring of the programmes should evolve together with the changing objectives of the budgetary strategies. As budget balances in member states approach a position of 'close to balance or in surplus', the policy focus is moving away from 'pure' budgetary retrenchment to the issue of the 'quality' and long-run 'sustainability' of public finances (European Commission, 2000b). 'Quality', meaning the revenue and expenditure composition of fiscal plans, matters as it (1) is important for the durability of the fiscal retrenchment; (2) affects the contribution of public finances to growth and employment.

The focus on 'quality' reflects the findings of a growing body of literature on what sort of budgetary retrenchment achieves a successful fiscal consolidation and triggers so-called non-Keynesian effects. While the size of budgetary adjustment matters (Giavazzi and Pagano, 1990, 1996; Giavazzi *et al.*, 1998; Perotti, 1999), there is growing evidence that its composition is the most important factor determining its success, both in terms of sustaining an improved budget balance and achieving a positive growth effect. Successful and lasting consolidations appear to occur when the bulk of the adjustment takes place on the expenditure side, and especially current transfers and public wage expenditures with limited or no increase in labour taxation. This is attributed to the supply-side impact of fiscal policy on labour costs, profitability, private investment and competitiveness (Alesina *et al.*, 1999). Greater focus on the composition of public expenditure is warranted as very specific budget items are usually responsible for sharp deteriorations in budgetary performance (Perotti *et al.*, 1998).

As regards the long-run 'sustainability' of public finances, it is essential to assess longer-term developments by carrying out projections that take into account the budgetary impact of ageing populations. This issue should also be addressed in the programmes[24] and consequently in the assessments.[25]

To take into account these indications, the assessment of member states' budgetary plans should then focus increasingly on the quality and sustainability of public finances. However, data availability (for example, the functional composition of public finances is not yet presented properly in the programmes) and uncertainty in long-term budgetary developments (for example, on the impact of ageing population on public finances) make this task difficult to accomplish.

As new and broader issues are coming to the fore, it becomes less clear what are the boundaries of the programmes. To illustrate the 'potential' scope of the programmes, Figure 7.1 gives a schematic presentation of what could be analysed on the basis of information delivered in the programmes. The right-hand figure shows how the

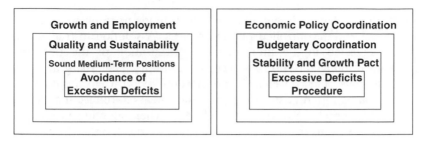

Figure 7.1   Objectives and procedures

SGP is positioned *vis-à-vis* the other tools used in EU-level policy coordination, while the left-hand figure shows the coverage of the analysis. Looking at the figure to the right, the Excessive Deficit Procedure (EDP), that is, a deterrent for avoiding excessive deficits, represents the core of the SGP which adds to it the obligation for member states to define a medium-term budgetary strategy and a medium-term target of close-to-balance. Going beyond the medium-term positions, the next step in the analysis covers the quality and sustainability of the outlined budgetary strategies. As these issues are more and more relevant in EMU for their cross-border budgetary implications, this analysis could serve as a basis for budgetary coordination across the EU.[26]

Furthermore, since the programmes contain at least some elements to assess the implications of public finances on growth and employment, they could be analysed in this broader setting and could serve as a basis for general economic policy coordination.

7.5   CHALLENGES FOR THE PROGRAMMES: NATIONAL MONITORING

7.5.1   Reinforcing the National Budgetary Process

The Maastricht Treaty (in Article 2 of the Protocol on the Excessive Deficit Procedure) includes a specific provision requiring the governments of member states to ensure that their national budgetary procedures and institutions enable them to fulfil their obligation to maintain sound and sustainable public finances.[27] The SGP adds to the pressure to establish 'discipline-friendly' budgetary procedures.[28] This requires dealing with the main weakness affecting budgeting institutions, namely fragmentation, which tends to result in excessive spending and uncontrolled public finances. A solution to fragmentation suggested in the literature is centralisation of the decision-making of budgetary process (see, for example, Hallerberg and von Hagen, 1999; and von Hagen and Harden, 1994). Centralisation, by coordinating different spending proposals, helps to reduce the 'deficit bias'. A comprehensive view of the budget where all budgetary implications of various measures are taken into account forces the participants to the process to recognise the real costs and benefits of each measure. In general, there are two ways of reaching a higher degree of centralisation: delegation and contracting (see von Hagen *et al.*, 2001). *Delegation* implies essentially a transfer of power from the parliament to the government and within the government from the various spending departments to one minister, normally the finance minister. The latter sets the constraints and has a strong monitoring role. Once the government has approved the budget, the parliament can make only limited amendments to it. Under the *contract* approach, the targets are negotiated among the different ministers at the beginning of the process, often on a multi-year horizon. Agreed targets become binding for all departments and are regularly reviewed to verify the compliance with them. The parliament has a strong position in this process as it can make important amendments on the budget proposal and monitors strictly its developments. Most member states have developed one or the other system to a different degree.[29]

In the course of the 1990s, several countries have strengthened their budgetary process, using the opportunity of the Maastricht process and the new obligations under the SGP to improve their national budgetary institutions, and reinforced the centralisation of the national budgetary process. The result is that the programmes have been integrated, at least partially, in the budget process. A majority of member states now use the Stability and Convergence Programmes as the main multi-annual reference document[30] and several tend to consider the targets of the programmes as direct policy objectives. In addition, there is feedback between the two procedures. Although not in a fully satisfactory way in all countries, the programme is in general a multi-annual extension of the budget just approved and its (multi-annual) targets are in some countries also used to draft the annual budget for the following year.

Regarding the involvement of parliament the evidence suggests that only rarely is the parliament actively involved in the preparation of the programmes, as generally governments draw and decide their programmes autonomously.[31]

The Pact foresees that in case of a new government taking office, a new programme should be submitted which illustrates its fiscal strategy. In principle, therefore, the new programme is not bound by the strategy set by the previous government. However, if the previous programme has been accepted by the Council, it means that the strategy in it is consistent with the main thrust of the Broad Economic Policy Guidelines, implying that the new government cannot radically change the strategy without risking a contradiction with the BEPG. The Austrian case, so far the only episode of a change in the government, seems to confirm this: although a large part of the programme has been revised, the main targets of the previous programme have been retained, suggesting that the medium-term commitment is considered binding for the domestic policy.

7.5.2 Coordination Between Central Government and Other Levels of Government

As the central government makes commitments on behalf of the whole general government sector, this has also implications on the coordination within the general government, involving also local and regional government and other subsectors of the government in this process.[32] Considering the financial relevance of regional and local institutions in the budget process[33] these entities are likely to demand closer (formal) involvement and coordination in the preparation of the programmes over time.

Coordination between national and decentralised governments can develop around four major axes: setting the targets in the programmes, ensuring their observance, identifying the responsibility for taking corrective action, and sharing possible pecuniary sanctions. To solve the coordination problem, several member states have already adopted special arrangements among government levels. The most evident example, as it is directly linked to the SGP process, is the introduction of an 'internal stability pact' by several member states, especially where subnational governments control a large part of the public finances or were in the past a source of concern.[34] A common characteristic in the internal stability pacts is the effort to clarify and share the responsibility for budget discipline among the different levels of government. In some cases, the pact consists of a joint declaration on the willingness to consolidate the budget balance, in others it also includes a set of rules according to which subnational governments are made responsible for a part of the deficit. Often these internal pacts also set up monitoring committees to follow up jointly the development of local public finances and even request local entities to submit annual and multi-annual plans for their debt.

Agreements like internal stability pacts are important as the observance of the targets by the subsectors can be warranted only if they internalise the commitments taken in the programmes. Indeed, in some member states, the lower levels of government have agreed to respect the targets, albeit that is often an informal agreement. This is, for example, the case in Germany, where the *Länder* have agreed that it is a common task of all levels of government to ensure respect of the deficit target. In Italy since 1999 the regions and the local authorities have been involved in the effort to respect the commitments under the Pact. In Austria subnational governments are made responsible for a part of the deficit, distributed mostly according to the share of the population living in the territory. Clearly, the more lower levels of government are involved in the definition of the targets, the stronger should be their commitment to respect them.

When corrective actions must be taken in order to respect EU commitments, agreements on shared responsibility within general government could also be desirable. The degree of responsibility of local authorities in making sure that the targets are respected at their level is different across countries. This factor seems to depend on the extent of financial assistance from the central government to regions and local communities, which can vary substantially.[35] In general, however, local and regional institutions are now under the supervision of some central authority which monitors the development of the finances while any intervention from the central government is conditional. In addition, the extreme case of unconditional grants or unrestricted borrowing seems to be disappearing from the European landscape, especially since the beginning of the 1990s. It could be argued that this is an effect of the top-down rule-based institutional development started with the obligations introduced with the Maastricht Treaty and reinforced with the Pact. Via the setting of clear ceilings and targets, often decided in agreement with the central government, financial accountability at regional and local level is increasing across EU countries.

The repartition of the responsibilities can go as far as defining the share of the sanctions to be paid. While the central government is responsible *vis-à-vis* its EU partners, the fines may be caused by irresponsible behaviour at local or regional government level. Given the growing distinctions between the budgets of different government levels, it becomes an issue to define which entity ultimately pays the fine. That is why, in some cases, this issue is dealt with in agreements between the actors. The Austrian internal stability pact, for example, specifies the procedure to be followed in case of a sanction following an excessive deficit: each government entity pays a proportion of the sanction corresponding to its share in the excessive deficit. The definition of such procedures will inevitable help secure the cooperation of all the levels of government in respect of the SGP targets.

7.6 CONCLUSIONS

This chapter has discussed a number of issues related to the Stability and Convergence Programmes. As they are the main instrument of the early-warning procedure of the SGP, the programmes are the most tangible element of the multilateral budgetary surveillance in the EU.

Thanks to the standardised format and content and their relatively coordinated presentation, the programmes should help foster the transparency and accountability of EU budgetary policies. The Commission and the Council can use them effectively to judge whether member states are in line with the core objectives of the Pact. Given the focus on the budgetary developments and the information which they include, the programmes are increasingly used as a communication instrument of national budgetary strategies.

As shown by the experience of the first two years of implementation, the early-warning system is working well. Member states submit their programmes regularly and the EU-level surveillance is effectively taking place. Being a new coordination process, clearly, there are also difficulties. There are methodological problems, as well as questions of interpretation. Therefore, more needs to be done to refine the analysis and to successfully ensure the monitoring of the fiscal developments. Furthermore, to make sure that the monitoring is effective and takes into account all the elements, the coverage of the programmes should be extended to cover more thoroughly 'quality' and 'sustainability' issues related to public finance developments.

In addition, beyond their justification as a communication instrument and a tool for budgetary discipline, the programmes have a role in promoting coordination of budgetary and economic policies between member states. By presenting their budgetary strategies and explaining their actions within a common framework, governments are submitted to external critique and face peer pressure with respect to the commonly agreed budgetary objectives. Stretching this function to new open land, the programmes could be used for budgetary assessment for the euro area as a whole. One idea floated in this direction is that the Euro Group could carry out coordination of national fiscal policies on the basis of the Commission analyses of the aggregate stance and the national strategies outlined in the programmes.

The programmes also give incentives for budgetary coordination within the member states. This relates mostly to the procedures used to prepare and approve the budget and the programmes, as well as those related to their implementation. A new or a more refined relationship between the national actors involved in these procedures seems to be developing. This applies particularly to the relationships between government and parliament, and between central and local government entities. In some cases it has taken the form of agreements, also called 'internal stability pacts', among the different institutions. Nevertheless, the transition to a fully integrated procedure involving the use of the programmes in the national framework is not yet completed.

Notes

1. See Chapters 6 and 8 of this book for a discussion of what is a budgetary position close to balance or in surplus.
2. The first round of programmes was presented in the autumn of 1998. The first set of updates was provided in autumn 1999 and the second round of updates was being prepared during autumn 2000.
3. This development cannot be excluded given the past European experience. See European Commission (2000a).
4. However, although the Stability Programmes have been submitted formally as of late 1998, they are not something completely new. They build on the successful experience of the Convergence Programmes prepared by the member states already since 1994.
5. The programmes submitted after the initial submission at the end of 1998 are referred to as 'updates'. See Chapter 6 for a detailed description of the timing of submission and handling of the programmes.
6. Many countries submit programmes up to the year $t + 4$.

7. Opinion of the Monetary Committee on the content and format of Stability and Convergence Programmes, document MC/482/98 of 15 September 1998. Note that the Monetary Committee was replaced by the Economic and Financial Committee on 1 January 1999.

8. The governments of those member states which are not part of EMU and therefore submit only Convergence Programmes should also indicate their assumptions on monetary policy objectives.

9. The SGP requires that governments apply the Council Regulation (EC) 3605/93 on the application of the Protocol on the Excessive Deficit Procedure (EDP) annexed to the Maastricht Treaty.

10. According to the European System of Accounts ESA-95 (1996), the data therefore include 'all institutional units which are non-market producers whose output is intended for individual or collective consumption, and mainly financed by compulsory payments made by units belonging to other sector, and/or all institutional units principally engaged in the redistribution of national income and wealth'.

11. See Chapter 6 of this book for a presentation of the detailed timetable.

12. The opinions are collected in European Commission (1999, 2000a).

13. Resolution of the European Council on the Stability and Growth Pact, 17 June 1997, OJ C 236, 2.8.1997.

14. For a discussion on why nominal targets have been used in the Maastricht Treaty, see Buti and Sapir (1998).

15. For a detailed discussion of the 'minimal benchmarks' see Chapters 6 and 8 of this book.

16. See note 7.

17. This presentation links the cyclical component to the overall output gap. While more complex, an alternative approach is to make the link to various GDP components, thus capturing also the effects of changes in the composition of growth.

18. It should however be noted that the Commission also calculates output gaps using a production function. Nevertheless, for the calculation of cyclically adjusted budget balances only the output gaps based on the HP filter have been used.

19. The HP filter calculates the trend as the solution to the following minimisation problem: $\underset{\{y_t^T\}}{\text{Min}} \sum_{t=1}^{T} \left[(y_t - y_t^T)^2 + \lambda[(y_{t+1}^T - y_t^T) - (y_t^T - y_{t-1}^T)]^2 \right]$

20. While this is an estimate generally accepted in policy circles, a number of studies find different results. For instance, Mélitz (1997, 2000) finds a much lower reaction of budget deficits to cyclical fluctuations.

21. Expressed by the Amsterdam European Council in its Resolution on the SGP.

22. However, it turned out *ex post* that this renegotiation was not necessary as the outcome was even better than the initial projection, with a deficit of 1.9 per cent of GDP. In fact, and this was a general feature in almost all programmes, the budgetary performance in 1999 was clearly better than expected in the programmes partly because of a 'tax-friendly' composition of growth.

23.   This procedure is based on Article 6 of Council Regulation (EC) 1466/
       97 and refers to Article 99(3) of the Treaty, that is, the framework of
       the general multilateral surveillance and the Broad Economic Policy
       Guidelines.

24.   In its report to the Helsinki European Council on the coordination of
       economic policies, the ECOFIN Council called for 'a broadening of the
       scope of public finance issues covered in the stability and convergence
       programmes and more emphasis on medium to longer-term sustain-
       ability issues'.

25.   For a comparative assessment of the long-term sustainability of public
       finances with respect to ageing populations, see European Commission
       (2000a) and Economic Policy Committee (2000).

26.   Buti and Martinot (2000) conclude that enlarging the scope and enhan-
       cing the credibility of the Stability and Convergence Programmes to
       become a true instrument of fiscal policy coordination in the euro area
       would be a first step in lifting the uncertainties surrounding the imple-
       mentation of the SGP.

27.   Article 3 of the Protocol on the Excessive Deficit Procedure.

28.   For a debate on the use of rules on government budget deficits to
       ensure discipline see Chapter 2. See also Buti and Sapir (1998) which
       includes a discussion on numerical versus procedural rules, and de
       Grauwe (2000a).

29.   Hallerberg and von Hagen (1999) show that the choice between these
       two approaches is influenced by the country's voting system.

30.   In some cases it is the only multi-annual document, in other cases it is
       very similar to the main internal document.

31.   The parliament is however informed, although it often debates on the
       programmes only after they are already decided upon by the govern-
       ment. In no member state does the parliament vote on the programme
       before it is submitted.

32.   Balassone and Franco (1999b) provide a game theory presentation of
       how the SGP alters the attitude of central and local governments
       towards fiscal discipline.

33.   Local government budgets are particularly important in federal states
       (Germany, Spain, Belgium, Austria) and strongly regionalised states
       (Italy).

34.   Balassone and Franco (1999b) and von Hagen *et al.* (2001) provide a
       description of 'internal stability pacts' and/or budgetary reforms in Italy,
       Austria, Belgium, Spain, Germany and Sweden.

35.   On the one hand, the local entities can be responsible in full for their
       own financial sustainability (that is, have no financial guarantees from
       central government); at the other extreme, they could receive large
       financial assistance from the central government in the form of uncon-
       ditional grants or unrestricted faculty to borrow.

Part IV
'Close to Balance or in Surplus': The Medium-Term Budgetary Targets

8 Setting Medium-Term Fiscal Targets in EMU*

Michael J. Artis and Marco Buti

8.1 INTRODUCTION

The Stability and Growth Pact, which is the backbone of fiscal policy in EMU, demands that the countries of the European Union (EU) aim for 'medium-term objectives of budgetary positions close to balance or in surplus'. The Pact can be seen as strengthening the procedures introduced by the Maastricht Treaty, at least in relation to the deficit criterion. Its objective is to ensure that fiscal prudence, as embodied in the fiscal criteria, applies not only in the run-up to the single currency, but becomes a permanent feature of the new EMU framework.

The aim of this chapter is to explore the meaning and provide a quantification of the 'close to balance' rule of the Pact. The EMU institutional framework is taken as given and we do not reevaluate the economic merits of numerical rules à la Maastricht or discuss the pros and cons of the set-up laid out in the Stability and Growth Pact. We ask how to set the medium-term fiscal targets having in mind the need to strengthen the credibility of EMU fiscal discipline and the objective of preserving sufficient room for cyclical stabilisation in EMU.

As pointed out in the debate[1] and recalled in Chapter 6, in setting the appropriate medium-term target, countries should take into account the influence of fluctuations in economic growth on the government's budget. As stated in the Resolution of the European Council on the Stability and Growth Pact, 'adherence to the objective of sound budgetary positions close to balance or in surplus will allow all Member States to deal with normal cyclical fluctuations while keeping the government deficit within the value of 3% of GDP'. A supplementary safety margin around the medium-term budgetary

---

* This chapter draws on a more comprehensive study on the same subject (Artis and Buti, 2000). A slightly different version was originally published in *Public Finance and Management*, vol. 1 (2001). The views expressed herein belong to the authors and should not be attributed to the European Commission.

positions may be required to cope with erratic movements in the budget balance arising from non-cyclical factors such as unexpected tax shortfalls, spending overruns, interest rate shocks, and so on.[2]

This chapter addresses these two issues. In doing so, the basic assumption is made that member countries will treat the prospect of infringing the 3 per cent deficit ratio as one to be strictly avoided. That is, we assume that the cost of risking the triggering of the sanctions procedure of the SGP is regarded by all countries as large. That cost includes not only the formal financial penalties envisaged in the sanctions procedure but also the additional penalties that the market might inflict and the loss of reputation that could be involved. As we do not consider situations where political horse-trading may imply delaying or not implementing the sanctions, our analysis can be treated as a 'full credibility' benchmark.

In the next section, we illustrate the economic mechanisms at work through a simple model which examines the interplay between national fiscal authorities and a supranational monetary authority. The third section presents the European Commission estimates of the cyclical safety margin. The fourth section provides a quantification of unforeseen fiscal developments which, if sizeable, may also be a source of risk. The final section concludes.

8.2 RESPECTING THE DEFICIT CEILING: AN ILLUSTRATIVE MODEL

The approach underlying the Pact is that EMU countries select an appropriate structural budgetary position and then let the automatic stabilisers work freely. This target should be sufficiently ambitious to withstand cyclical fluctuations without exceeding the 3 per cent deficit ceiling. The model developed in this section, in line with the Maastricht institutional framework, assumes that the overriding concern of fiscal authorities is to prevent the budget deficit from exceeding a given ceiling even in bad circumstances whilst allowing the built-in stabilisers to operate fully. As argued by, for example, Eichengreen and Wyplosz (1998), and confirmed by the concrete experience so far with the application of the Pact, this implies that the 3 per cent 'limit' is viewed as a 'hard' ceiling.

The safety room under the deficit ceiling depends on several factors. In order to explore the mechanisms at work, we lay out a simple model which illustrates various channels influencing the choice of the medium-term fiscal target.

We look at a country within a monetary union formed of two identical countries. The model encompasses a demand (IS) equation and a supply (Phillips curve) equation of standard type determining the value of the output gap, G, and inflation, π:

$$G^D = \phi_0 + \phi_1 d - \phi_2(i - \pi^e) - \phi_3(\pi - \pi_f) - \phi_4(G - G_f) + \varepsilon_1$$

(8.1)

$$G^S = \omega(\pi - \pi^e) + \varepsilon_2$$

(8.2)

where d is the budget deficit (per cent GDP), i is the nominal interest rate, ε_1 is a demand shock and ε_2 is a supply shock. The superscript ^{e} indicates expected variables, the subscript $_f$ the rest of the monetary union. The model is for a member country of a monetary union. The terms $(\pi - \pi_f)$ and $(G - G_f)$ in (8.1) capture, respectively, the competitiveness and the absorption effect within the currency area. The rest of the world is omitted. The coefficient ω in (8.2) can be interpreted as the degree of labour market flexibility: a high ω implies that an inflation surprise, by lowering real wages, entails a strong rise in supply; on the contrary, a low ω implies that real wages are rigid and supply responds little to unexpected inflation.

The policy rules specify the setting of d by fiscal authorities and i by the central bank.

According to the approach sketched out above, national fiscal authorities set a target for the cyclically adjusted balance, d_s, and then let automatic stabilisers work freely:

$$d = d_s - \alpha G + \varepsilon_3$$

(8.3)

where α is the cyclical sensitivity of the budget and ε_3 is a fiscal shock. The nominal deficit d should not exceed a deficit ceiling: $d \leq \bar{d}$. This formulation implies that, when interest rates move, there occurs an internal compensation between the interest burden and the primary balance so as to keep the structural balance constant. Therefore, even if there is no active Keynesian fiscal policy in the model, some discretionary adjustments within the budget do take place.

The medium-term budgetary target for the cyclically adjusted balance is computed on the basis of the 'worst possible' shocks affecting the economy. These shocks, by feeding through the economy and interacting with the monetary and fiscal behaviour, give rise to large, negative output gaps. The initial deficit position has to be sufficiently low to accommodate such adverse circumstances without exceeding the deficit ceiling. To be on the safe side we focus on the most binding cases across different types of shocks. Formally, the targeted structural budget balance is set so as to have $d = \hat{d}$ for *maximum* adverse shocks $(\hat{\varepsilon}_1, \hat{\varepsilon}_2, \hat{\varepsilon}_3)$.

The monetary authority minimises a loss function featuring the Union-wide average inflation and output gap. As supported by recent evidence, it is also assumed that the central bank likes to smooth interest rates:[3]

$$\operatorname{Min} L(CB) = \bar{\pi}^2 + \beta_1 \bar{G}^2 + \beta_2 (i - i_{-1})^2 \tag{8.4}$$

where i_{-1} is the interest rate holding in the previous period. If in $t - 1$, the system was in equilibrium, i_{-1} equals $(\phi_0 + \phi_1 d_s)/\phi_2$.

In equation (8.4), without loss of generality, the inflation target has been set to zero. $\bar{\pi}$ and $\bar{G}$ are the monetary union *average* inflation and output gap, respectively:

$$\bar{\pi} = \frac{\pi + \pi_f}{2} \text{ and } \bar{G} = \frac{G + G_f}{2}$$

Provided that the coefficient of the output gap is sufficiently low, this formulation appears to be consistent with the primary statutory duty of the ECB to ensure price stability. Moreover, as pointed out by Svensson (1999), a positive weight on the output gap may signal that the central bank is concerned about future inflationary pressures rather than explicitly caring about output stabilisation. Given the fact that the monetary authorities do not target an output level below the natural rate, the model does not exhibit the Barro–Gordon inflation bias.

Under rational expectations, the model can be solved for the output gap and inflation. However, in order to obtain a definite solution, we need to make assumptions about the type of shocks affecting the monetary union. The interactions within the monetary union arise via the behaviour of the central bank and trade linkages between the member countries (the currency union as a whole is assumed to be a closed economy). These two channels are influenced by the type of shocks hitting the countries. In order to simplify the analysis, two extreme categories of shocks are considered:

(a) *'pure symmetric'* shocks. Since we disregard the asymmetric responses to symmetric disturbances arising from different transmission mechanisms across currency area members (for example, industry structure, degree of labour market flexibility, size of automatic stabilisers, and so on), these shocks affect the member countries in an identical manner and the countries' external balance does not change. Hence, beside 'domestic' stabilisers, only the monetary smoothing channel is at work.

(b) *'pure asymmetric'* shocks. Under this assumption, a shock hitting the domestic country is fully offset by an identical shock of the opposite sign affecting the other member countries. As the average output gap and inflation of the currency area do not change, the interest rate does not move and only the balance of payments operates to smooth output.

Under the extreme cases of 'pure symmetric' and 'pure asymmetric' shocks, the solution is immediate because we do not need to model explicitly the behaviour of inflation and output gap in the rest of the monetary union.[4]

Under *pure symmetry* the solution for the output gap is the following:

$$G = \frac{\beta_2 \omega^2 (1 + \phi_1 \alpha)(\varepsilon_1 + \phi_1 \varepsilon_3) + \phi_2^2 \varepsilon_2}{\phi_2^2 (1 + \beta_1 \omega^2) + \beta_2 \omega^2 (1 + \phi_1 \alpha)^2} \tag{8.5}$$

Equation (8.5) shows the fundamental role played by interest rate smoothing. If, contrary to the assumption above, β_2 is set equal to zero, all demand-side parameters disappear from the output gap solution which depends only on the supply shock, the degree of labour market flexibility and the central bank preference over output and inflation. This implies that the central bank can offset perfectly any demand shock. The intuition is straightforward: as the output gap and inflation move in the same direction, the central bank faces no dilemma and, via a sufficiently strong response of interest rates, is able to close the output gap and preserve at the same time its inflation target.

By replacing G in equation (8.3) and setting the shocks at their maximum level, we obtain:

$$\hat{d}_s = \bar{d} + \alpha \frac{\beta_2 \omega^2 (1 + \phi_1 \alpha)\hat{\varepsilon}_1 + \phi_2^2 \hat{\varepsilon}_2 + \beta_2 \omega^2 (1 + \phi_1 \alpha)[\phi_1(1 - \alpha) - 1]\hat{\varepsilon}_3}{\phi_2^2 (1 + \beta_1 \omega^2) + \beta_2 \omega^2 (1 + \phi_1 \alpha)^2} \tag{8.6}$$

The interplay between monetary and fiscal behaviour is illustrated in Figures 8.1 and 8.2 which picture the policy response to a symmetric, negative demand shock and supply shock, respectively. Both reaction functions are positively sloped. It is easy to show that the slope of the fiscal authorities' reaction function (*FP*) is higher than that of the monetary authorities (*CB*).[5] The deficit does not have to exceed a ceiling, $\bar{d}$.

In the case of a demand shock, *FP* moves to the right and *CB* shifts down. The effect on d and i depends on the various parameters. In the case pictured in Figure 8.1, both automatic stabilisers and interest rate smoothing are strong. The result is a substantial rise in the budget deficit. Hence, the initial budget balance has to be sufficiently far from $\bar{d}$ to avoid an excessive deficit position such as that corresponding to E'. If the initial deficit is sufficiently low (as in the figure at $d = d_0$), in the case of a large, negative shock, the new equilibrium will be E'', that is, d will attain $\bar{d}$, but without exceeding it.

In the event of a supply shock, as shown in Figure 8.2, the likelihood of exceeding $\bar{d}$ is higher because, under a conservative central banker, the interest rate reaction accentuates the negative effects of the shock.

Under *pure asymmetry*, $\bar{\pi}$ and $\bar{G}$ do not change: the *CB* schedule is flat and i remains unchanged. The parameters of the central bank reaction function are irrelevant and, hence, the output gap solution becomes:

$$G = \frac{0.5\omega(\varepsilon_1 + \phi_1\varepsilon_3) + \phi_3\varepsilon_2[\phi_3 + 0.5\phi_4]}{\omega[0.5(1 + \phi_1\alpha) + \phi_4] + \phi_3} \tag{8.7}$$

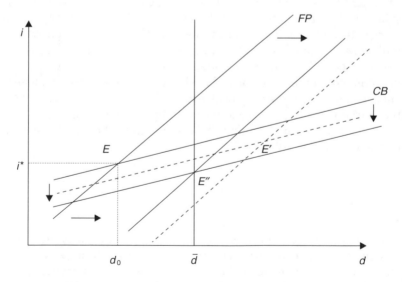

Figure 8.1   Policy reactions to a symmetric demand shock

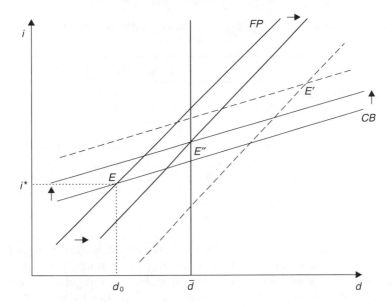

Figure 8.2 Policy reactions to a symmetric supply shock

Interestingly, if shocks are asymmetric, unlike in the previous case, demand disturbances have an impact on the domestic output gap, whatever the degree of interest rate smoothing and central bank preferences. This result substantiates the claim by, for example, de Grauwe (2000b) that, under monetary union, there exists an undersupply of monetary stabilisation from the standpoint of individual country members.

By replacing the expression of G in (8.3), the medium-term target becomes:

$$\hat{d}_s = \bar{d} + \frac{\alpha[0.5\omega\hat{\varepsilon}_1 + \phi_3\hat{\varepsilon}_2] - [0.5\omega + \phi_3 + \omega\phi_4]\hat{\varepsilon}_3}{\omega[0.5(1 + \phi_1\alpha) + \phi_4] + \phi_3} \qquad (8.8)$$

In sum, the fiscal target is influenced by the structural features of the model and the reaction function of the central bank. Crucially, the way in which these elements affect the fiscal target depends on the most binding shock and its synchronicity across frontiers.

The impact of structural parameters and policy preferences on the medium-term budgetary target under various configurations of shocks is summarised in Table 8.1.

Going beyond the 'extreme' assumptions made above, our analysis has relevant implications for setting 'SGP compatible' fiscal targets.

Table 8.1   Influence of structural parameters and policy preferences on the budgetary target

		ϕ_1	ϕ_2	ϕ_3	ϕ_4	α	ω	β_1	β_2
Symmetric shocks	$\hat{\varepsilon}_1, \hat{\varepsilon}_3$	+/−	+	0	0	−	−	+	−
	$\hat{\varepsilon}_{2+}$	+	−	0	0	−	+	+	+
Asymmetric shocks	$\hat{\varepsilon}_1, \hat{\varepsilon}_3$	+	0	+	+	−	−	0	0
	$\hat{\varepsilon}_2$	+	0	−	+	−	+	0	0

Note: The signs in the table are those of the partial derivatives of the solution for d_s in equations (8.6) and (8.8). A positive sign indicates that the medium-term deficit (surplus) target can be higher (lower), and vice versa. Recall that $\hat{\varepsilon}_1$ and $\hat{\varepsilon}_2$ are negative and $\hat{\varepsilon}_3$ is positive.

In the case of *demand shocks*, a country which is in tune with the rest of the currency area (hence is affected mainly by symmetric disturbances) can select a less (more) ambitious budgetary target if monetary smoothing is stronger (weaker) than the balance of payments smoothing. This is likely to be the case of a large country, which is less affected by the external balance and, by influencing the monetary union average, can more likely trigger a favourable monetary response. On the opposite side of the spectrum, a small country with a cycle 'out of sync' with the rest of the currency area will have to face the perverse effect of monetary policy whilst benefiting from the rise in net exports. Notice that a higher effectiveness of fiscal policy has an ambiguous impact on the budgetary target. This is due to the reaction of monetary policy to the fiscal boost. Since a higher stabilisation can be attained through fiscal policy, a lower change in the interest rate is required. This allows a reduction of the central bank's costs of departing from the existing level of the interest rate. In principle, a stronger fiscal impulse coupled with a smaller change in interest rates may imply a lower overall degree of cyclical stabilisation thereby requiring a more ambitious medium-term target.[6] Countries with a more flexible labour market (that is a higher coefficient of the inflation surprise in the Phillips curve) need to select a more ambitious budgetary target because the fall in inflation brings about a larger fall in the output gap. Again, this effect is higher in the case of asymmetric shocks. A high degree of interest rate smoothing, by reducing the monetary response to the output fall, requires a more ambitious fiscal target.

In the case of *supply shocks*, a rise in inflation goes hand in hand with a negative output gap. The fiscal target is influenced by the degree of conservatism of the central bank. If the shock is symmetric, a 'hard-nosed' central bank will react to the rise in inflation with a pro-cyclical rise in interest rates, which leads to an even larger negative output gap. Hence, in order to let automatic stabilisers work fully without breaching the deficit criterion, the fiscal target has to be more ambitious. If the shock is asymmetric, the net smoothing effect brought about by the external balance depends on the relative importance of the income effect (positive) and the competitiveness effect (negative).[7] All in all, a small country 'out of sync' with the average cycle of the currency area can choose a less ambitious budgetary target. Contrary to the case of demand shocks, countries with a more flexible labour market can select a less ambitious fiscal target. A high degree of interest rate smoothing, by limiting the rise in interest rates, prevents output from falling further, thereby allowing the selection of a less ambitious budgetary target.

Fiscal shocks cover essentially unexpected tax shortfalls or expenditure rises. These also include interest rate shocks to the extent that the change in the interest burden is not fully offset by an opposite within-year move in the structural primary balance. As discussed below, whilst demand or supply shocks are likely to be the 'binding' shocks, adverse fiscal shocks can play a role if the country wants to be on the safe side by creating an additional safety margin under the deficit ceiling.[8] In all cases, as expected, the higher the budgetary sensitivity to the cycle, the lower the deficit target will have to be.

The main conclusion of the above discussion is that the degree of ambition of the medium-term target is influenced by the type of 'most binding' shock (either supply or demand shock), the size of the country (which affects the degree of symmetry of the shocks) and the public finance variables (cyclical sensitivity of the budget, likelihood of 'pure' fiscal shocks). The behaviour of the central bank also has an important role. Given the reaction function of the central bank, under the assumption of a 'hard-nosed' central banker, large countries (affecting the monetary union average) should fear more negative supply shocks, whilst in the case of small, desynchronised countries negative demand shocks are more likely to bite.

8.3 ESTIMATES OF THE CYCLICAL SAFETY MARGIN

The simple model in the previous section indicates that many factors influence the choice of the medium-term target. In particular, the output gap responds to shocks differently according to the value of a number of structural parameters and policy preferences. Many of these elements are likely to change in the new EMU framework.

Size, origin and synchronicity of the shocks will affect the size and volatility of cyclical fluctuations in output. While EMU will entail changes it is not clear in what direction these will run. In the longer run, it might be expected that cyclical variations will become more synchronised between euro area members. Given the stability-oriented macroeconomic framework of EMU, country-specific, policy-induced shocks are likely to decrease in the euro area. Furthermore, trade integration may spread shocks more uniformly across frontiers and higher competition in product markets will reduce the risk of wage-setting shocks (Buti and Sapir, 1998). Sound macroeconomic conditions will also increase the smoothing effectiveness of fiscal policies.[9] The extent of these convergence-promoting effects is not known, however, and trade-induced patterns of industrial specialisation may change in a direction that promotes some divergence (Rose, 1999). However, in the shorter run, different economic structures as well as lack of full availability of stabilisation instruments may work in the opposite direction.[10] Furthermore, what is relevant for the present analysis is not the impact of the new EMU framework on the 'normal' cyclical profile of EMU members, but the exposure of these economies to important economic shocks giving rise to 'large' output gaps.

It is also unclear whether the sensitivity of budget balances to the cycle will change significantly once in EMU. OECD estimates (van den Noord, 2000) show that, in the second half of the 1990s budgetary sensitivity has remained stable or has fallen in most EU countries (the exceptions being Belgium, Denmark and the Netherlands).[11] Even in the event that the ongoing reforms of the tax system – in particular of corporate taxes and social security contributions – and of transfer payments to the unemployed lead to a further reduction of the budget's cyclical sensitivity, such an effect will not take place overnight. It can therefore be assumed that the sensitivity of the budget to the cycle will not change much in the coming years.

As discussed in the previous section, the nature of the ECB's monetary strategy is bound to play an important role. In relation to the pre-ERM era, of course, countries are giving up the possibility of using their own monetary policy actions to stabilise their economies; however, compared to the ERM period, (non-German) countries can expect a proportionate weight in ECB decisions which they did not have in the Bundesbank's policy.[12]

All in all, EMU is as yet 'too young' to allow us to identify the direction of change. Given these uncertainties, the safety margin recently computed by the European Commission relies on analysis of past cyclical behaviour of EU economies, specifically, by using the latest available estimates for the sensitivity of the budget to cycle, and an 'extreme' value of the negative output gap experienced in the past (European Commission, 2000a).

The basis for the estimates, which are detailed in Table 8.2, is conveyed in Figure 8.3. Here the level of output gap (G) is measured along the horizontal axis, the budget surplus (s) and deficit (d) ratios along the vertical. Each downward-sloping line represents a country's 'fiscal programme'. The slope of the schedule corresponds to the budget sensitivity to output gap changes. The policy rule implies that the 3 per cent ceiling is not exceeded in the event of adverse shocks leading to a large, negative output gap ($\hat{G}$ in the chart). The deficit target, d_s, is the structural deficit which satisfies this condition. Clearly, as shown in the figure, the higher the budget sensitivity, the more ambitious the target must be (B compared to A in Figure 8.3).

The budget sensitivity to the output gap is shown in the first column of Table 8.2. Clearly, the selection of the 'worst case' output gap is critically important to the calculation of the 'safe' structural deficit. In order to compute $\hat{G}$, three alternative assumptions about the output

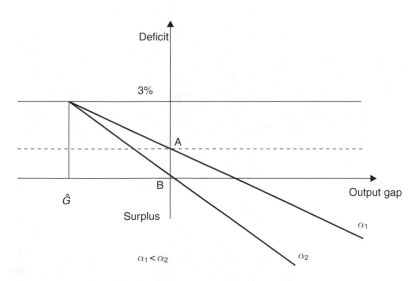

Figure 8.3   Building in a safety margin for cyclical fluctuations

Table 8.2.   Cyclical safety margin and budgetary targets

	Budgetary sensitivity	Max. negative Output gap (% GDP)	Cyclical safety margin (% GDP)
B	0.60	3.3	2.0
D	0.50	3.8	1.9
EL	0.40	4.0	1.6
E	0.65	4.0	2.6
F	0.55	2.7	1.5
IRL	0.55	3.8	2.1
I	0.50	3.6	1.8
L	0.60	5.0	3.0
NL	0.75	3.9	2.9
A	0.50	3.4	1.7
P	0.50	4.8	2.4
FIN	0.65	6.6	4.3
Euro-Area	**0.55**	**3.6**	**2.0**
DK	0.70	3.3	2.3
S	0.90	4.2	3.8
UK	0.70	4.1	2.9
EU-15	**0.60**	**3.7**	**2.2**

Source: European Commission (1999).

gap are considered. The first of these is the unweighted average of the largest negative output gaps in EU member states which, over the period 1960–98, was estimated to be 4 per cent of GDP. The second is the largest negative output gap that has been recorded in each member state since 1960. The third is the average volatility of the output gap in each member state, as measured by two times its standard deviation. The value of the output gaps which could have triggered the application of the 'exceptionality' clause under the Pact (that is, those corresponding to a fall in real GDP by more than 0.75 per cent) have been netted out. For each country, the two worst cases of these three alternatives have been retained. It is the average of those two values which is shown in the second column in Table 8.2. The cyclical safety margin, presented in the last column of the table,[13] is simply the product of the values in the first two columns and hence represents the deficit swing (in ratio to GDP) to be expected in the event of a worst case realisation. To avoid trigging the sanctions procedure, the structural deficit should be set at the value of 3 minus the cyclical safety margin value.

As shown in Table 8.2, and assuming that the cyclical behaviour of EU economies does not change with the advent of EMU, a number of countries would need a broadly balanced budget (between 0.5 and −0.5 per cent of GDP) to cover for the cyclical fluctuation risk. The rest of the countries, who need a lower safety margin, would have to set their structural deficit at around 1 per cent of GDP or slightly higher.

The application of the above approach leads to the identification of cyclical components that are much in line with those resulting from similar calculations made by other international organisations. The IMF (1998a) and the OECD (1997) find that a structural deficit in the range of 0.5 to 1.5 per cent of GDP and below 1.5 per cent of GDP, respectively, would be enough to allow the automatic stabilisers to operate without breaching the 3 per cent of GDP deficit threshold even in periods of pronounced cyclical slowdown.

Similar conclusions were obtained by Dalsgaard and de Serres (Chapter 9), in the context of an estimated structural VAR model. The results of this study also show that, for a majority of EU countries, a structural deficit between 1 per cent and 1.5 per cent of GDP would help to avoid breaching the 3 per cent of GDP threshold with a 90 per cent certainty over a three-year horizon. If governments aimed for a structural position between zero and 1 per cent of GDP, the confidence horizon was extended to between five and seven years.

On the basis of stochastic simulations on the NiGEM model of the National Institute for Economic and Social Research (NIESR), Barrell and Dury (Chapter 10)[14] indicate very low probabilities of collision with the sanctions procedures of the Pact if countries stick to the (cyclically adjusted) targets announced in the Stability and Convergence Programmes (European Commission, 1999), a result that is robust to variation in assumptions about the monetary strategy pursued by the ECB. Their study confirms that, if the countries adhere to their Stability and Convergence Programmes, the built-in stabilisers and the Stability and Growth Pact are broadly compatible.

8.4 QUANTIFYING ERRATIC BUDGETARY DEVELOPMENTS

The risk of exceeding the 3 per cent ceiling is not only related to the cyclical component of the budget, but also to unforeseen fiscal

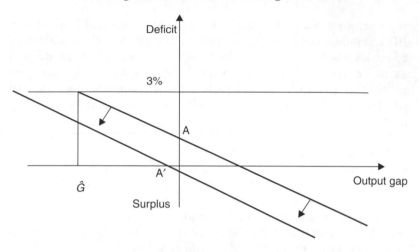

Figure 8.4   Accounting for cyclical and 'erratic' budgetary risks

developments not directly linked to the working of built-in stabilisers. Unexpected tax shortfalls or higher-than-projected spending commitments can push up the deficit and represent a further source of fiscal instability. Figure 8.4 illustrates the point. The Figure is identical to Figure 8.3 except in allowing that a fiscal shock might displace the fiscal schedule. As can be seen, the previously 'safe' structural deficit could result in an infringement of the SGP and a more ambitious target is required (A' instead of A).

Unforeseen budgetary developments include tax shortfalls and unexpected spending overruns. They may include also the budgetary impact of interest rate shocks. In the model above, it is assumed that there is a within-year fiscal rebalancing between the primary surplus and the interest burden whenever the latter changes following a change in monetary conditions. However, such behaviour may be both infeasible and undesirable as it would introduce excessive volatility in tax rates or spending plans. Interest rate shocks may be a serious problem especially for highly indebted countries whose budget is more vulnerable than that of the low-debt countries – this also depends, obviously, on the maturity structure of their debt.[15] The risk associated with interest rate shocks has been recognised by the Council which stressed this point repeatedly in its opinions on the Stability and Convergence Programmes of countries with a high debt ratio (European Commission, 1999).

In order to disentangle this erratic component from other budget-ary developments, Artis and Buti (2000) look at fiscal forecast accuracy, a strand of research recently developed by Artis and Marcellino (1998, 1999).

The forecasts for which the descriptive error statistics are quoted are those generated in the spring of year t for year t – so-called 'current year forecasts' – and are forecasts for the general government deficit in per cent of GDP. Clearly, a prime source of fiscal forecast error lies in mistaken output growth projections (see, for example, Artis and Marcellino, 1999). This source of error – which is already allowed for in the cyclical safety margin computed in the previous section – is netted out by using the values for the budget sensitivity to the cycle and the output forecast errors. The latter are tabulated in Keereman (1999) who examines the track record of Commission forecasts.

Formally, the expected and the actual budget deficits as a share of GDP can be written as follows:

$$d^e = d^e_s - \alpha G^e \tag{8.9}$$
$$d = (d^e_s + \varepsilon_3) - \alpha G \tag{8.10}$$

where the symbols are the same as in the second section. The total forecast error is given by the forecast error on the discretionary component, ε_3, and the error on the cyclical component of the budget. Under the assumption that trend growth does not change over the forecast period and that the forecast error on the output gap corresponds to the forecast error on real GDP growth, y, we can derive the expression of the erratic component in the budget:

$$\varepsilon_3 = d - d^e + \alpha(y - y^e) \tag{8.11}$$

As shown in equation (8.11), in order to gauge the size of the erratic component in the budget, the effect of the GDP growth forecast error has to be netted out. Estimates of the 'pure' erratic component in the deficit are set out in Table 8.3.

The data shown in Table 8.3 accordingly pertain to the period 1986–97. The first two columns show the overall mean and variance of the 'pure' fiscal shock component. As can be seen, for the most part these are relatively small. Our concern, however, is with upside risks on the deficit, since we try to quantify what allowance, if any, countries should make in setting their deficit target to prevent 'pure fiscal error' from triggering the onset of the sanctions procedure in the Pact. Accordingly, the 75 per cent quantile, which indicates the largest value of three-quarters of all observations, is presented. Some of the values are large and in two countries (Ireland and Luxembourg) are 2 percentage points of GDP or higher. In three other countries (Netherlands, Germany and Portugal) deviations are larger than 1 per cent of GDP. In all other countries the 75 per cent quantile lies between 0.3 and 1 per cent of GDP.

However, as stressed in Artis and Buti (2000), given the fact that some of these large deviations occurred in the early years of the sample, 'extreme' values may not be representative of 'bad' risks in the current situation. Accordingly, the last column of Table 8.3 shows the mean of positive deviations. With the exception of two countries (Ireland and Luxembourg), the average deviations lie in the 0.3 to 1 per cent range.[16]

Summing up, while further research is required to disentangle the various factors behind the results of the above analysis, and in line with European Commission (2000a), Artis and Buti (2000) conclude that the additional margin for fiscal shocks to be allowed for in the computation of 'safe' structural deficits would be of between 0.5 and 1 per cent broadly corresponding to the average range of positive fiscal shocks over the sample period.

Table 8.3.   Statistics on the 'fiscal shock' component

Country	Mean (% GDP)	Variance	75% Quantile (% GDP)	Mean of positive deviations (% GDP)
Belgium	0.1	0.58	0.5	0.3
Germany	0.4	1.45	1.4	0.7
Greece	−0.2	6.10	1.0	0.9
Spain	−0.1	2.75	0.9	0.6
France	−0.1	0.72	0.3	0.3
Ireland	1.6	3.16	2.6	1.9
Italy	0.1	0.46	0.6	0.4
Luxembourg	0.6	5.09	2.0	1.2
Netherlands	0.6	0.78	1.2	0.8
Portugal	0.6	2.00	1.6	1.0
Denmark	−0.3	0.74	0.3	0.3
United Kingdom	−0.0	1.30	0.5	0.4
EU	0.1	0.48	0.8	0.4

Source: Artis and Buti (2000).

8.5 CONCLUSIONS

This chapter has examined an important aspect in the implementation of fiscal policy in EMU, namely that of choosing a medium-term budgetary target consistent with the provisions of the Stability and Growth Pact. Via this choice, attention is shifting from the nominal, uniform 3 per cent deficit ceiling – two features of the EMU set-up often criticised in academic debate – to cyclically adjusted, country-specific targets.

As shown by European Commission (1999) and reported above, a number of countries would need a broadly balanced budget (between 0.5 and −0.5 per cent of GDP) to cover for the cyclical fluctuations risk. The rest of the countries would need to set their structural deficit at around 1 per cent of GDP or slightly higher. The risk of breaching the deficit ceiling pertains not only to the cyclical component, but also to unexpected budgetary variability due to tax shortfalls or spending overruns not linked to cyclical developments. The additional safety margin to cover for such risks is estimated to be of the order of 0.5 to 1 per cent of GDP. All in all, creating sufficient room for manoeuvre under the 3 per cent ceiling would bring most EU countries towards a balanced budget or a small surplus.

Stability and Convergence Programmes and recent updates show a continuation of the reduction in deficits in the years to come. According to the programmes, a large majority of member states aim at achieving broadly balanced budgets by 2002–03 (+/− 0.5 per cent of GDP), with some of them – namely Ireland, Luxembourg, Finland, Denmark and Sweden – aiming at a sizeable surplus (2 per cent of GDP or larger). The evidence reviewed in this chapter confirms that such targets seem to be by and large consistent with the 'close to balance' requirement of the Pact.

These conclusions have to be treated with caution. In particular, the simple model in this chapter indicates that the source of the 'most binding' shocks, the degree of symmetry of shocks, the structure of the economy and the behaviour of the central bank all affect the appropriate degree of ambition of the medium-term target. These aspects will be different in the new EMU framework from the pre-euro era, thereby affecting the size of the safety margin. Furthermore, the 'demand' for fiscal stabilisation may be higher in EMU to compensate for a monetary stance which may be less than optimal from an individual country's standpoint. However, a high degree of uncertainty remains on the direction and pace of these changes. Clearly, as evidence on these aspects emerges, the issue of adequate medium-term targets will need to be addressed again.

Notes

1. See Buti *et al.* (1998) and European Commission (1999).
2. It has been suggested that ambitious medium-term targets are also important to preempt, at least partly, the budgetary impact of ageing populations. For a discussion of the interplay between medium-term targets and long-term sustainability of public finances, with particular attention to the budgetary impact of ageing, see Artis and Buti (2000) and Buti (2000).
3. For a summary of the evidence, see Clarida *et al.* (1999).
4. In the case of purely asymmetric shocks, since the average output and inflation of the currency area do not change, the value of such variables in the foreign country can be derived immediately as a function of the same variables in the domestic economy.
5. The expressions of the slope of *FP* and *CB* are, respectively, $\frac{1+\phi_1\alpha}{\alpha\phi_2}$ and $\frac{\phi_1\phi_2(1+\beta_1\omega^2)}{\phi_2^2(1+\beta_1\omega^2)+\beta_2\omega^2(1+\phi_1\alpha)}$. In the case of purely asymmetric shocks, *CB* is flat as interest rates do not react to country-specific developments.
6. This is more likely to occur if ϕ_2 and β_1 are large.
7. An important aspect not captured in this simple framework is the persistence of the shock. If, for instance, a long-lasting negative supply shock reduces output potential, taxes and spending will have to be adjusted on a structural basis. However, cyclical stabilisers may ease the adjustment process.
8. If fiscal shocks encompass not only unforeseen budget variability, but also discretionary 'surprise' fiscal policies, governments with a taste for Keynesian fiscal policies will have to set tougher medium-term fiscal targets to create the room for active use of the budget.
9. For a discussion of the interplay between fiscal discipline and fiscal stabilisation, see Artis and Buti (2000).
10. For an account of the debate, see Buti and Suardi (2000).
11. See van den Noord (2000) and European Commission (2000a).
12. In the context of a simple IS-LM framework, Buti and Suardi (2000) argue that the move from a German-dominated ERM to EMU should improve the convergence of economic cycles in the euro area. If this is the case, the role of the ECB in responding to shocks will be enhanced.
13. This approach was first used by the Commission to estimate the so-called 'minimal benchmarks' which are given by the 3 per cent reference value minus the estimated cyclical safety margin (European Commission, 1999). The results are reproduced in Artis and Buti (2000). For a discussion of the differences between the results in Table 8.2 and other estimates, see European Commission (2000a).
14. See also Barrell and Pina (2000) and Dury and Pina (2000).

15. As shown by Missale (Chapter 14), public debt management can help deficit stabilisation under the Stability Pact.
16. An additional reason for not focusing on outliner values is the fact that large positive shocks do not seem likely to occur when the deficit is already large for cyclical reasons. Artis and Buti (2000) find a positive correlation between the actual growth rate of output and the pure fiscal shock suggesting that positive deficit shocks tend to coincide with periods of high growth. See that paper for a discussion of the possible reasons explaining this result.

9 Estimating Prudent Budgetary Margins[*]

Thomas Dalsgaard and Alain de Serres

9.1 INTRODUCTION

The Maastricht Treaty imposes a debt limit of 60 per cent of GDP and a deficit ceiling of 3 per cent of GDP for countries participating in Stage 3 of European Monetary Union (EMU). The Stability and Growth Pact goes further and specifies the circumstances under which a deficit can be regarded as excessive, speeds up the procedure and defines the sanctions in the event of excessive deficits.

The imposition of such debt and deficit ceilings does not necessarily impose a binding constraint on the use of counter-cyclical fiscal policy because countries can run a structural deficit that is well below 3 per cent of GDP. How far below 3 per cent is likely to be enough to allow the government deficit to play its role as a shock absorber in times of an economic slowdown or recession? The answer to this question depends on the size of economic shocks, the sensitivity of deficits to those shocks, and the extent to which the authorities might want to go beyond automatic stabilisation.

To shed some light on these issues a structural VAR model has been estimated for eleven of the fifteen EU countries, capturing the effects of economic shocks on the deficits that have historically prevailed in each country. Based on the estimated distributions of these shocks, stochastic simulations are performed to build up probabilities of breaching the 3 per cent ceiling in the future. Fiscal policy is assumed

---

[*] The authors would like to thank Professor Carlo Giannini and their colleagues Martine Durand, Jørgen Elmeskov, Robert Ford, Claude Giorno, Peter Hoeller, Vincent Koen, Paul Van den Noord, Ignazio Visco and Eckard Wurzel for comments and suggestions on previous versions of the chapter. They also thank Desney Erb, Chantal Nicq, Sandrine Phélipot and especially Jens Lundsgaard Jorgensen for technical support, and Jackie Gardel and Muriel Duluc for secretarial assistance. A previous version of this paper appeared in *OECD Economic Studies*, no. 30, 2000/1.

unchanged in the simulations in order to capture the pure movements in the deficit stemming from automatic stabilisation and other sources not originating from fiscal impulses (that is, movements due to supply shocks, real private demand shocks and monetary shocks). The likelihood of exceeding the ceiling increases with the initial budget deficit and with the time horizon considered, since over a longer period of time there is an increased probability of a sequence of unfavourable events hitting the economies.

The approach followed here should be seen as complementary to other studies (referred to below), in which measures of historical output gaps are combined with estimated budget elasticities to derive prudent budgetary margins. The main advantage relative to these studies is that estimates of output gaps are not required and it also considers a wider range of contingencies than looking at historical deficit episodes can reveal. Even though the probability distribution of each shock is based on past observations, the occurrence of shocks is drawn randomly in the stochastic simulation and non-zero probabilities may thus be attached to events that have never occurred simultaneously in history but may happen sometime in the future. More generally, by considering a wide range of time horizons and degrees of confidence, the method proposed provides an explicit meaning of the concept of prudent fiscal stance. The findings generally validate the 'close-to-balance' rule stipulated by the Stability and Growth Pact for the eight euro countries included in the study (Germany, France, Italy, Austria, Belgium, the Netherlands, Spain and Finland). With cyclically adjusted balanced budgets, these countries would face a reasonably high likelihood (that is, above 90 per cent) of not breaking the 3 per cent deficit limit over a horizon of three to five years without having to resort to discretionary fiscal tightening. The budgetary requirements appear to be somewhat higher for the non-euro countries included in the study (the United Kingdom, Sweden and Denmark).

The next section presents a review of other studies that provide estimates of prudent budget margins or which apply structural VAR techniques to examine fiscal policy issues. The two-step methodology used in the chapter is presented in section 9.3. The choice of variables and the results of the VAR estimates are discussed in section 9.4. Section 9.5 presents the estimates of prudent budget margins over different horizons and levels of confidence and discusses the cross-country differences. An analysis of sensitivity and conclusions appear in sections 9.6 and 9.7.

9.2   LITERATURE OVERVIEW

The Stability and Growth Pact (SGP) is designed both to limit the extent to which budgetary developments in individual countries impinge on their neighbours, particularly via their effects on interest rates, and to make future bail-out requests unlikely. Elaborating on the Maastricht Treaty's fiscal rules, the Pact sets a 3 per cent of GDP limit on budget deficits, though with an escape clause for modest temporary overshoots due to exceptional circumstances such as a severe recession. It compels governments (i) to bring budgets back towards sustainable trend positions, and (ii) to adopt a symmetric approach to let automatic stabilisers work over the cycle. The Pact is underpinned by the Excessive Deficit Procedure – which has been in force since the start of Stage 2 of EMU in January 1994 – involving surveillance and possible penalties. The most common criticism of these rules is that by focusing on actual rather than structural deficits, they could tie the hands of government with regard to fiscal stabilisation policy (see Chapter 3 above). To limit such risk, the SGP states that a 'close-to-balance' or surplus budgetary stance in the medium term would be required in order to provide sufficient scope for flexibility over the cycle.

As an empirical matter, the answer to what constitutes a prudent budgetary margin could be found in several ways. A simple approach consists in doing a retrospective application of the Excessive Deficit Procedure. This involves assessing past policy in terms of an institutional framework and incentive structure that did not exist at the time, which, in turn, probably leads to finding 'too many' retrospective excessive deficit episodes. Such an exercise was carried out by Buti *et al.* (1997) for the EU countries over the 1961–96 period. Based on movements in deficits and growth during 50 episodes of recession or abrupt slowdown in growth, they conclude that an excessive deficit would have occurred in eleven cases if the budget had initially been balanced, but in 28 cases if the starting point had been a deficit of 2 per cent of GDP – that is, more than a doubling of the risk of running into excessive deficits. They also conclude that the risk of incurring an excessive deficit is high in the case of protracted recessions, even if the starting point is a balanced budget. The same conclusion is drawn with respect to exceptionally severe recessions in which real GDP falls by more than 2 per cent.

An alternative approach consists of looking at the maximum negative output gap observed in the past for each country, and, on the basis of the average cyclical sensitivity of that country's budget, deriving the distance that would be needed from the deficit limit in order to be able to accommodate such a shock in the future. Table 9.1 summarises historical declines in output relative to potential output and applies elasticities of the response of deficits to output changes, as drawn from the OECD INTERLINK model.[1] For most euro area countries, a structural deficit below 1.5 per cent of GDP would be enough to avoid breaching the 3 per cent threshold for an output gap of 3 per cent, which roughly corresponds to the mean value of the maximum output gaps recorded in recessions in the major EU economies during 1975–97. Based on the largest negative output gap recorded in each country over the 1970–97 period, and applying roughly the

Table 9.1   Sensitivity of fiscal deficits to changes in output gaps

	Estimated effect of 1 per cent increase in output gap on the fiscal deficit (per cent of GDP)			Fiscal balance required to avoid a deficit higher than 3 per cent of GDP for an increase in output gap of 3 per cent	Mean value of the maximum output gap recorded in recessions
	OECD	*EC[1]*	*IMF[1]*		*1975–97*
Belgium	0.6	0.6	0.6	−1.3	−2.2
Germany	0.5	0.5	0.5	−1.6	−2.8
Greece	0.4	0.4	0.4	−1.7	−2.2
Spain	0.6	0.6	0.7	−1.2	−3.0
France	0.6	0.5	0.6	−1.3	−2.5
Ireland	0.4	0.5	0.5	−1.7	−4.7
Italy	0.3	0.5	0.4	−2.0	−2.9
Netherlands	0.6	0.8	0.7	−1.1	−1.8
Austria	0.5	0.5	0.6	−1.5	−1.8
Portugal	0.5	0.5	0.4	−1.5	−3.9
Finland	0.6	0.6	0.6	−1.3	−4.8
Denmark	0.6	0.7	0.8	−1.3	−3.0
Sweden	0.7	0.9	1.1	−0.8	−2.2
United Kingdom	0.5	0.6	0.6	−1.5	−2.7

[1] European Commission estimates shown are from Buti *et al.* (1997). The figures for the International Monetary Fund are based on OECD Secretariat calculations using data supplied by the IMF.
Source: OECD, *Economic Outlook 62*, December 1997.

same elasticities, the International Monetary Fund (1998a) notes that structural deficits in the range of 0.5 to 1.5 per cent of GDP (depending on the country) would allow the full operation of automatic stabilisers without exceeding the Treaty's reference value for most euro area countries.[2] Another study (Buti *et al.*, 1998) reckons – using the same methodology, but applied to the EU Commission's measure of output gaps – that structural deficits between 0 and 1 per cent of GDP would be appropriate for most EU countries. These results are interpreted as providing support to the 'close-to-balance' rule recommended in the Pact.

A third approach is based on time-series estimation techniques of which the structural VAR model used in the present chapter is an application. Roodenburg *et al.* (1998) use a univariate time-series analysis of GDP data to assess the order of magnitude of the necessary safety margin for the Netherlands. Their analysis indicates that under a scenario of 2 per cent trend growth per year, a cyclically adjusted budget deficit of 0.5 per cent of GDP would give the authorities about 90 per cent confidence of not breaching the 3 per cent threshold. The multivariate VAR methodology has been used recently by Becker (1997) to test the extent of Ricardian behaviour in private households, by Koren and Stiassny (1998) to look at the causality between taxation and expenditure, and by Bruneau and de Bandt (1997) to investigate the contribution of fiscal shocks to real output dynamics in Germany and France, as well as the correlation of fiscal policy shocks between these two countries.

To our knowledge, however, no study has so far focused on the issue of prudent budgetary margins using the methodology presented in this chapter, although a recent study has estimated budgetary safety margins for France using a two-variable VAR model and taking into account the possibility that a deficit above 3 per cent of GDP is 'allowed' by the Stability and Growth Pact if it occurs simultaneously with a severe economic downturn (IMF, 1998b). The study finds that, for France, a structural deficit of around 1 to 1.5 per cent of GDP would provide 90 per cent confidence that an excessive deficit will not occur. A balanced structural budget would provide 99 per cent confidence.

9.3   METHODOLOGY

The derivation of prudent budgetary margins is based on a two-step approach. In the first step, a four-variable VAR model is estimated to capture the effects on the public sector net lending ratio of economic shocks that have prevailed in the past in each EU country. In the second step, stochastic simulations of the estimated VAR equations are performed to build up probabilities of breaching the 3 per cent ceiling in the future.

9.3.1 Methodology of the Structural VAR Models[3]

The main purpose of the VAR model is to decompose the fluctuations in the general government deficit/GDP ratio into different sources of structural disturbances (that is, that can be given an economic interpretation). One of these disturbances can be interpreted as a change in discretionary fiscal policy. In addition to the fiscal policy shock, the VAR model identifies an aggregate supply shock, a real private demand shock and a nominal shock. Following an approach pioneered by Blanchard and Quah (1989), the identification is obtained by imposing a set of restrictions on the long-run effect of each disturbance on the level of the four variables included in the VAR model: the change in the ratio of government net lending to GDP ($\Delta n \lg q_t$), real output growth (Δq_t), the inflation rate (Δp_t) and a measure of private sector savings (Δpsq_t).[4]

Three of the restrictions imposed come from the assumption that neither fiscal policy nor the other demand shocks have permanent effects on output, so that in the long run its level is exclusively determined by supply shocks. Evidently, many theoretical frameworks would predict that aggregate demand shocks, such as a change in fiscal policy or a shock to private savings, could have some effect on output in the long run via relative price changes and their implications for capital accumulation, or if hysteresis effects are present. However, the same models generally predict that the long-run effects of demand-side shocks on production are fairly muted relative to the effects of productivity or labour supply shocks of comparable magnitude.

Two additional restrictions are based on the assumptions that real private demand shocks and nominal shocks only have temporary effects on the ratio of government net lending to GDP. While these shocks can have important short-run effects on government balances, mainly via the automatic stabilisers mechanism, the presumption is that in the long run, the government net lending/GDP ratio is unaffected by demand shocks other than those induced by fiscal policy. In contrast, no restriction is imposed *a priori* on the long-run effect of a permanent supply shock on the net lending ratio. The sixth and final restriction assumes that nominal shocks have a permanent effect on the aggregate price level (or the inflation rate) but leave all other variables of the system unchanged in the long run.[5]

9.3.2 Methodology to Derive Prudent Budgetary Margins

Once the VAR model is estimated and the identification of the structural shocks is achieved, techniques of stochastic simulations are used to assess the risk of breaching the 3 per cent deficit level over different time horizons and for given initial budget balances.[6] Each stochastic simulation generates a hypothetical path for the four variables of the model. These paths are based on the random drawing, at each time period, of values for each of the structural disturbances from their estimated distribution as well as on their propagation via the estimated lag structure of the VAR model. A different path for the level of the net lending ratio over a ten-year horizon is thus generated in each experiment based on a combination of supply, private demand and nominal shocks whose relative size is determined by their estimated variance. As noted above, fiscal policy shocks are turned off in the simulations in order to capture the pure effects from automatic stabilisation and other induced changes to the budget balance (for example, interest rate changes, changes to potential output, and so on). It should be stressed, however, that only the *unexpected* change in fiscal policy is treated as a fiscal shock and turned off in simulations. To the extent that fiscal policy has reacted in a systematic and predictable fashion to other economic disturbances in the past, such a fiscal reaction function is captured by the lag structure of the VAR system and therefore plays an active role in the simulations.

For illustrative purposes, Figure 9.1 shows three hypothetical simulated paths for semi-annual budget balances. For each simulation, the minimum value of the net lending ratio reached over the relevant time horizon is extracted. In the example of Figure 9.1, this implies that for an horizon of one year, the net lending ratios corresponding to points A, B and C would be selected. If the relevant horizon is extended to three years, then points B, D and E are extracted instead. Based on a thousand simulations, the minimum values of net lending ratios extracted are ranked in ascending order to form a distribution. Such a distribution of minimum net lending ratios can be drawn for each relevant horizon, up to ten years. As illustrated in Figure 9.2, the shorter the horizon, the closer to the initial balance will the distribution be. This is because shocks are assumed to be symmetrically and normally

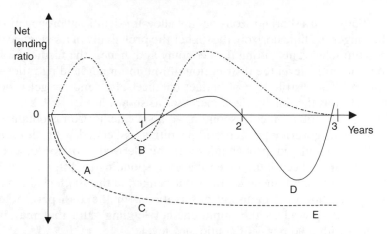

Figure 9.1 Three hypothetical simulated paths for the budget balance

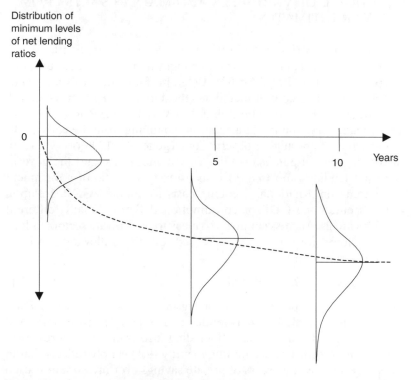

Figure 9.2 Hypothetical distribution of minimum budget balance levels

distributed and a short horizon does not allow for significant propagation. The longer the time horizon, the higher the probability of a sequence of unfavourable events hitting the economy and, hence, the further away from the initial level the distribution of minimum net lending ratios is centred.[7] The distribution of budget balances also tends to get wider and flatter as the time horizon increases as shown in Figure 9.2.

Once a distribution corresponding to a specific horizon is obtained, the level of government net lending ratios associated with different levels of cumulated probabilities can be derived. To do so, each distribution is sliced into percentiles corresponding to different levels of probabilities. For instance, the value ranked in the 100th position in the distribution of a thousand observations (or the 10th percentile) can be interpreted as the minimum net lending ratio that may be reached with a 90 per cent confidence level.

9.4   CHOICE OF VARIABLES AND MAIN RESULTS FROM THE VAR ESTIMATES

The methodology described in the above section is applied to eleven of the fifteen EU countries, including eight members of the euro area (Germany, France, Italy, Austria, Belgium, Finland, the Netherlands and Spain) and three non-members (the United Kingdom, Denmark and Sweden).[8] For each country, a four-variable VAR model is estimated using semi-annual data generally spanning from the early 1960s to most recently available observations (generally 1996 or 1997).[9] In each case, real output (q_t) is GDP in volume terms, and the government net lending ratio ($n \lg q_t$) is measured as a ratio of government net lending on a national accounts basis to nominal GDP. Inflation (Δp_t) is either the GDP or consumption deflator. Finally, different variables are used across countries to measure net private sector lending.

The choice for the latter is based on the following National Accounts flow identity:

$$S - I = (G - T) + (X - M) \tag{9.1}$$

where S and I are private sector savings and investment, G and T are public sector spending and revenues and X and M are exports and imports of goods and services (including also transfers, interest payments, and so on). The accounting identity (9.1) simply reflects that in an open economy the excess of private savings over investment is used to either finance a public sector deficit or to generate an external account surplus. Rewriting (9.1) in ratios of nominal GDP, and expressing the public sector deficit as net lending yields:

$$nlpq = cbq - n\lg q \tag{9.2}$$

where *nlpq* is the ratio of net private savings to nominal GDP and *cbq* is the current balance as a ratio of nominal GDP.

Based on the identity (9.2) the variable used in the VAR to capture real private sector demand shocks is generally either the private net lending ratio ($nlpq_t$) or the current account as a per cent of nominal GDP (cbq_t). However, in some cases, the gross saving ratio of households ($savq_t$) or private consumption (cpv_t) are used in order to obtain a longer sample period or better empirical results. As mentioned above, one additional restriction in choosing the real private demand variable is that any subset of variables in the VAR system should not be co-integrated since this would violate the assumptions of uncorrelated shocks as well as the long-term restrictions imposed on the system.

The set of variables chosen for each country is shown in column 2 of Table 9.2.[10] Since the VAR equations must be estimated with stationary variables, they are included in first-difference form.[11] In an economic sense, the inclusion of net lending ratios in first differences implies that the model does not rule out the possibility of ever-increasing debt ratios, which indeed has been a characteristic for most countries since the mid-1970s. Likewise, by including inflation in first differences for all countries (except for Germany and Austria where inflation is included in levels), the possibility of a permanent increase in the rate of inflation is not ruled out by assumption. The ranking of the variables in the second column of Table 9.2 corresponds to the ranking in the VAR system. In most countries, the ranking is consistent with the set of long-run restrictions described in the previous section.[12]

Since no restrictions are imposed on the short-run effect of the shocks, it is possible to verify whether the identified shocks behave in a way that is consistent with their economic interpretation. For instance, real output and inflation are expected to move in opposite directions following a supply shock and in the same direction following a demand shock. Moreover, the fiscal policy shock is expected to move the net lending ratio and output in opposite directions in the short term – or in other words, a tightening of fiscal policy is expected to temporarily lower the level of output.

Table 9.2 Model overview

Country (sample period)	Model	LAGS[1]	Exogenous variables	Main features/results
Germany (1961:1–1997:2)	Δq, $\Delta n \lg q$, Δcpv, $\Delta pgdp$	4	Constant	• Inflation rate is stationary: entered in level • A 1 percentage point discretionary increase in net lending ratio temporarily lowers output by about 1 per cent after three semesters (peak) • A permanent output (supply) shock has no significant long-run effect on the net lending ratio
France (1972:1–1997:2)	Δq, $\Delta n \lg q$, $\Delta nlpq$, $\Delta^2 pcp$	2	Constant	• A 1 percentage point discretionary increase in net lending ratio temporarily lowers output by about 0.25 per cent after one semester (peak) • A 1 per cent permanent positive output (supply) shock leads to a permanent increase in the net lending ratio of about 0.5 percentage points
Italy (1961:1–1996:2)	Δq, $\Delta n \lg q$, cbq, $\Delta^2 pcp$	4	Constant Linear trend	• Current account as a ratio of output is stationary: entered in level • A 1 percentage point discretionary increase in net lending ratio temporarily lowers output by about 0.5 per cent after two years (peak) • A 1 per cent permanent positive output (supply) shock leads to a permanent increase in the net lending ratio of about 0.4 percentage points

| United Kingdom (1965:2–1996:2) | $\Delta q, \Delta n \lg q, nlpq, \Delta^2 pgdp$ | 4 | Constant Linear trend | • Net private lending ratio stationary: entered in level
• A 1 percentage point discretionary increase in net lending ratio temporarily lowers output by about 0.7 per cent after three semesters (peak)
• A permanent output (supply) shock has no significant long-run effect on the net lending ratio |
| Austria (1966:1–1995:2) | $\Delta q, \Delta n \lg q, \Delta savq, \Delta pgdp$ | 3 | Constant Linear trend | • Inflation rate is stationary: entered in level
• A 1 percentage point discretionary increase in net lending ratio temporarily lowers output by about 0.8 per cent within one semester (peak)
• A 1 per cent permanent positive output (supply) shock leads to a permanent increase in the net lending ratio of about 0.2 percentage points |

Table 9.2 (continued)

Country (sample period)	Model	LAGS[1]	Exogenous variables	Main features/results
Belgium (1963:1–1996:2)	$\Delta^2 pgdp$, Δq, $\Delta n \lg q$, $\Delta nlpq$	4	Constant Linear trend	• Net private lending is defined excluding transfers to extend data availability • Inflation ranked first in the VAR • A 1 percentage point discretionary increase in net lending ratio temporarily lowers output by about 0.7 per cent after three semester (peak) • A 1 percentage point permanent inflation shock raises output by 1.5 per cent in the long run but has no significant long-run effect on the net lending ratio • A 1 per cent permanent positive ouput (supply) shock has no significant long-run effect on the net lending ratio
Denmark (1962:1–1996:2)	Δq, $\Delta n \lg q$, $\Delta nlpq$, $\Delta^2 pcp$	2	Constant Linear trend	• Net private lending is defined excluding transfers to extend data availability • Net government lending defined less capital transfers and other capital transactions to gain degrees of freedom • A 1 percentage point discretionary increase in net lending ratio temporarily lower output by about 0.3 per cent after one semester (peak) • A 1 per cent permanent positive output (supply) shock leads to a permanent increase in the net lending ratio of about 0.6 percentage points

Finland (1961:1–1997:2)	$\Delta q, \Delta n \lg q,$ $\Delta savq, \Delta^2 pcp$	2	Constant Dummy in 1989:2	• Dummy in 1989:2 to capture collapse in exports • Results strongly influenced by the large negative output shock of the early 1990s • A 1 percentage point discretionary increase in net lending ratio temporarily lowers output by about 0.3 per cent within one semester (peak) • A 1 per cent permanent positive output (supply) shock leads to a permanent increase in the net lending ratio of about 0.4 percentage points
Netherlands (1970:2–1996:2)	$\Delta q, \Delta n \lg q,$ $\Delta savq, \Delta^2 pgdp$	2	Constant Linear trend Dummy in 1975:1	• Dummy in 1975:1 to allow for change in trend growth rate of real GDP • A 1 percentage point discretionary increase in net lending ratio temporarily lowers output by about 0.5 per cent after one semester (peak) • A 1 per cent permanent positive output (supply) shock leads to a permanent increase in the net lending ratio of about 0.4 percentage points

Table 9.2 *(continued)*

Country (sample period)	Model	LAGS[1]	Exogenous variables	Main features/results
Spain (1964:1–1995:2)	$\Delta^2 pgdp$, Δq, $\Delta n \lg q$, cbq	2	Constant Linear trend	• Inflation ranked first in the VAR • Current account as a ratio of output is stationary: entered in level • A 1 percentage point discretionary increase in net lending ratio temporarily lowers output by about 0.5 per cent after one year (peak) • A 1 percentage point permanent inflation shock raises output by 0.6 per cent in the long run but has no significant long-run effect on the net lending ratio • A 1 per cent permanent positive output (supply) shock leads to a permanent increase in the net lending ratio of about 0.2 percentage points

| Sweden (1962:1–1997:1) | $\Delta^2 pcp, \Delta q, \Delta n \lg q, \Delta savq$ | 2 | Constant
Linear trend
Dummy in 1976:1 | • Net private lending is defined excluding transfers to extend data availability
• Dummy in 1976:1 to capture shift in behaviour of net lending ratio
• Inflation ranked first in the VAR
• A 1 percentage point discretionary increase in net lending ratio temporarily lowers output by about 0.3 per cent after one semester (peak)
• A 1 percentage point permanent inflation shock raises output by 0.6 per cent in the long run and leads to a permanent increase in the net lending ratio of about 0.9 percentage points
• A 1 per cent permanent positive output (supply) shock leads to a permanent increase in the net lending ratio of about 0.9 percentage points |

[1] The number of lags has been chosen on the basis of the likelihood ratio test (5 per cent critical value) over a span of one to six lags (see de Serres and Guay, 1995).

The main features of the key impulse responses are reported in the last column of Table 9.2.[13] Regarding first the *response of government net lending* as a ratio of GDP to each of the four shocks, the main characteristics across countries generally confirm the *a priori* assumptions:

- The net lending ratio (that is, the fiscal surplus) increases significantly (at the 90 per cent confidence level) in response to a contractionary fiscal shock, both in the short and long term.

- A positive supply shock raises the net lending ratio in all countries in the short term except for Germany, where output improves more than the fiscal balance, leading to a lower ratio. Long-run effects are significant in seven countries: France, Italy, Denmark, Finland, the Netherlands, Spain and Sweden. The long-run effect of supply shocks on the net lending ratio is one of the main factors driving the outcome of the stochastic simulations.

- The net lending ratio responds positively, but not always significantly, to an inflationary shock (exceptions are the United Kingdom and Spain). It responds mostly negatively to a negative real private demand shock, but again not always in a significant way. In Germany and Sweden, however, positive (negative) real private demand shocks deteriorate (improve) the net lending ratio in the short term, with the effect being significant in the latter country. For Germany this is due to the fact that nominal GDP increases more than government net lending, thus giving rise to a decreasing net lending ratio, while for Sweden the model suggest that output improves initially in the face of a domestic savings shock. This reaction could be due to favourable terms of trade effects and/or interest rate crowding in. Long-run effects from monetary shocks and real private demand shocks on the government's net lending ratio are ruled out by assumption.

Positive supply shocks raise output significantly in both the short and the long term. Contractionary fiscal shocks lowers output in the short run[14] in all countries, although not always in a significant way. In all cases, a change in the stance of fiscal policy towards consolidation leads to a temporary decline in activity (and vice versa) with an elasticity that varies from 0.25 to about 1 per cent. The response of inflation (price level in the case of Germany and Austria) to supply shocks and fiscal shocks shows the expected signs for most countries: a positive supply shock (raises output and) lowers inflation in the short term, and a contractionary fiscal shock lowers (output and) inflation.[15] These effects, however, are not significant in most countries. Finally, for most countries there is a clear tendency for private savings to decrease in the event of a restrictive fiscal shock (see Table 9.2). To an extent that differs across countries, this result suggests the presence of crowding-in effects and/or at least some income smoothing or partially Ricardian behaviour in the private sector.

9.5   RESULTS OF THE STOCHASTIC SIMULATIONS

The results of the simulations for each country are shown in Figure 9.3 for different time horizons and levels of confidence. The budgetary requirements to avoid breaking the 3 per cent ceiling rise in the desired level of confidence and the time horizon considered, since over longer time horizons the probability of a series of adverse events hitting the economies increases. For Germany, for example, the simulation results suggest that if the government was to aim for a *cyclically adjusted* deficit of 1 per cent of GDP, the *actual* deficit would, with a 90 per cent likelihood, remain within the 3 per cent limit over a horizon of three years without a need to adjust fiscal policy in a pro-cyclical fashion. This horizon would be extended to ten years if Germany instead opted for a cyclically adjusted balanced budget.

Another way to interpret the result is (as can be seen from Figure 9.3) that the likelihood of remaining within the 3 per cent threshold for a cyclically adjusted deficit of 1 per cent of GDP would drop from 90 per cent to only 50 per cent if the time horizon considered by policy-makers extends from three to ten years. The results also reveal that most countries face relatively similar trade-offs between budget deficits and levels of confidence. Cyclically adjusted budgetary positions around balance, or even small deficits, would thus provide most countries with a 90 per cent likelihood of keeping the deficit within the 3 per cent margin over a of three to five year horizon without having to resort to discretionary pro-cyclical fiscal tightening (Figure 9.4). However, for the three countries outside the euro area (the United Kingdom, Denmark and Sweden) the requirements are somewhat higher – that is, surpluses in the range of 0.7–2.4 per cent of GDP would be needed over a five-year horizon.

This suggests that assuming countries do achieve their budget deficit/surplus objectives set for 2003 and allow for the budget income to improve beyond target if aggregate demand were to exceed potential, then the risk of exceeding the deficit ceiling would in most cases likely

···◆··· 1 year —■— 3 years —✕— 5 years —▲— 10 years

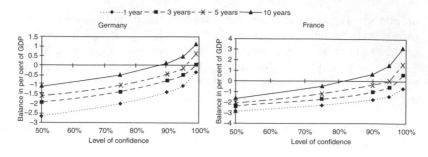

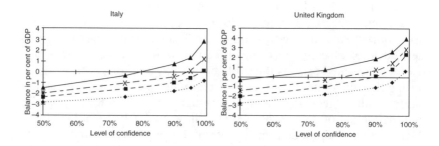

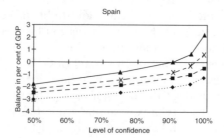

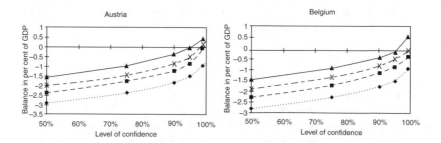

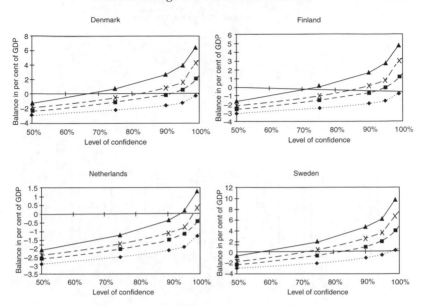

Figure 9.3   Cyclically adjusted balance required to avoid breaking 3 per cent deficit with different levels of confidence

remain within 5 per cent. On the other hand, more ambitious medium-term targets than those specified in the Stability Programmes may be desirable (in particular for France, Italy and Austria) if one considers additional factors such as the implications of population ageing on pension and health care costs.

It should be stressed that the study does not address the question of excessive deficits, that is, to what extent deficits above 3 per cent of GDP will coexist with severe recessions (fall in real GDP above at least 0.75 per cent) or by other means be exempted from the Excessive Deficit Procedure in the ECOFIN Council. This implies that the risk *de facto* of being forced to undertake pro-cyclical fiscal tightening during an economic downturn is slightly lower than indicated by the simulations. This caveat is likely to be of minor importance to the policy implications of the simulation results since historically only around 10 per cent of the episodes of deficits above 3 per cent of GDP (for EU-15) have occurred simultaneously with a drop in real GDP of more than 0.75 per cent (and only 2–3 per cent have occurred

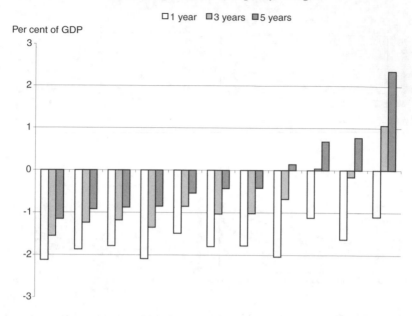

Figure 9.4   Government balances required to meet the 3 per cent of GDP deficit criterion with 90 per cent confidence over different time horizons

when real GDP was falling by more than 2 per cent). Another reason is that deficits sometimes lag behind real activity such that the provisions of the Stability and Growth Pact concerning severe economic downturns may not apply in the same years as when the deficit exceeds the 3 per cent limit. Finally, the results are obtained using semi-annual data. Since the Stability and Growth Pact is concerned solely with *annual* budget outcomes, the derived levels of confidence could be biased (even though the raw semi-annual data used are annualised). However, sensitivity analysis using the averages of two consecutive semi-annual observations to convert the results into calendar years does not display significant differences to the results obtained by semi-annual data (typically the cyclically adjusted net lending ratio for any given level of confidence and time horizon would deviate by a maximum of 0.1–0.2 percentage points of GDP).

It should also be emphasised that the estimated budgetary requirements do not, or only partly, capture more recent changes to political
and budgetary frameworks as well as to economic structures, and that
particular historical episodes may be dominating the results for some
countries. The most notable examples are Finland and Sweden, both
of which have been experiencing extreme changes in their budget
balances since 1990. These episodes imply that the VAR model identifies some excessive shocks for Finland and Sweden, which in turn
lead to results for prudent budgetary margins that are somewhat higher
than would be relevant when considering the current economic environment and policy framework in the two countries. In order to capture
better likely future shocks for these two economies, it was thus chosen
to base the results on an average of shocks experienced by the
four major EU economies rather than past shocks in the countries
themselves.[16]

The simulation results should be considered policy-relevant mainly
for time horizons of no longer than five years since beyond that the
cumulative effects of non-linearities in the economic variables which
may not be properly captured by the model could blur the results.[17]
Moreover, planning horizons of up to five years are quite common for
fiscal policy.

The differences in the results across countries can largely be
explained by three factors:

- the variance of the change in the deficit: higher variance implies
  higher budgetary requirements;
- the importance of fiscal policy shocks – relative to the other three
  types of shocks – in explaining movements in the deficit: the more
  important is the role of fiscal shocks, the lower the budgetary
  requirement;
- the quality of the VAR model, that is, how much of the volatility
  in the four variables is captured by the lag structure of the model
  and how much remains in the residuals. Intuitively, it may not
  matter as much whether the unconditional variance of the variables is captured ultimately by the variance of the residuals or by
  the lag structure. However, it may have some influence on the
  final results given that one of the shocks (that is, the fiscal shock)
  is turned off in the simulations.

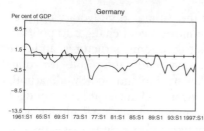

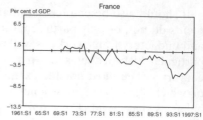

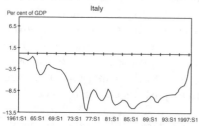

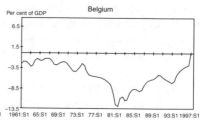

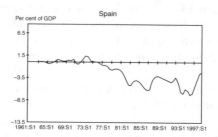

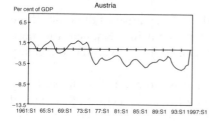

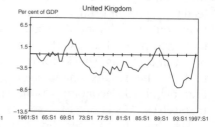

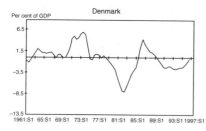

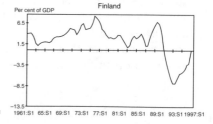

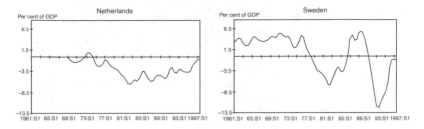

Figure 9.5   Government net lending in per cent of GDP
Source: OECD, *Economic Outlook 63*, databank.

Government net lending/GDP ratios for the eleven countries are shown in Figure 9.5. The least volatile deficits over the 1960–97 period have been found in Germany, France, Austria and the Netherlands, whereas deficits in Italy, Finland and Sweden have had the largest volatility. Based on movements in deficit levels, one might expect to find that more stringent budget requirements are necessary in the latter countries to provide an adequately prudent budgetary margin. However, for purposes of automatic stabilisation, it is important to distinguish between the cyclical change in the deficit and its long-term drift. A large variance of the deficit level reflects, in most cases, the presence of a unit root and should therefore not necessarily be interpreted as a meaningful indication of the sensitivity of the budget balance to business cycle developments. Indeed, since the deficit is included in the VAR in first differences, it is the variance of the *change* in the deficit level – rather than the variance of the level – that has a determining influence on the outcome (in the sense that the higher the variance, *ceteris paribus*, the more stringent the budget requirements will be for prudent budgetary margins).

The cases of the United Kingdom and Italy are illustrative in this respect. Italy has had much higher volatility in the government net lending/GDP ratio than the United Kingdom, but Italy's deficit has shown a long and relatively smooth downward trend followed by a long and smooth correction, whereas the UK deficit ratio has been dominated by two major cycles (Figure 9.5). The implication is that volatility of the first difference of the deficit ratio has been slightly lower in Italy than in the United Kingdom. This would tend to imply a lower budget requirement in Italy than in the United Kingdom. Figure 9.6 shows a relatively close link between the variance of the first difference of the deficit ratio and the budgetary requirement

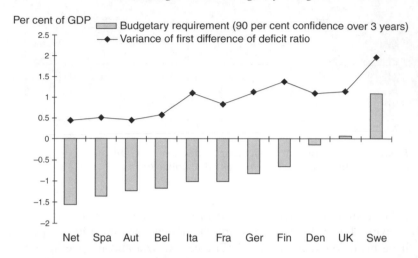

Figure 9.6   Cyclically adjusted budget balance requirements and volatility in deficits

(here illustrated by the case with 90 per cent confidence and a three-year horizon). The volatility of the change in the deficit would indicate that countries like Austria, Belgium, the Netherlands and Spain would face relatively low budgetary requirements, whereas Finland and, in particular, Sweden[18] would need significantly better budget positions to achieve the same safety margin. Germany, France, the United Kingdom, Italy and Denmark are in intermediate positions.

The relative importance of fiscal policy shocks in explaining the movements in the deficit also has an important influence on the cross-country differences. If a large part of the unpredicted movement in the deficit is accounted for by fiscal policy-induced shocks, then the budgetary requirement would be relatively low given that such shocks are turned off in the simulations. This partly explains the somewhat less stringent safety margin needed in Germany relative to France and Italy despite a comparable variance in the change in the deficit ratio. On the opposite side, the very stringent requirements obtained for Denmark and Sweden are partly attributable to the strong influence exerted by supply shocks on the deficit in the long run in these countries.

Finally, variations in the quality of the four estimated equations of the VAR model can also explain some of the cross-country differences in the results. Poorly estimated VAR equations mean that a larger portion of the fluctuations in the variables are accounted for by the model's residuals. In turn, this implies that larger shocks are drawn during the simulations. The effects are not unambiguous, however, since a poorly estimated model may display a lower propagation of the shock – and hence a lower budgetary requirement.

9.6 SENSITIVITY ANALYSIS

In order to asses the implication for the results of leaving out the fiscal shock, the simulations have also been carried out when including all four shocks (Figure 9.7). It turns out, as expected, that the inclusion of the fiscal shock raises the budgetary requirements (additional volatility requires higher margins). However, the relative ranking of countries remains fairly unchanged – and the stricter requirements for

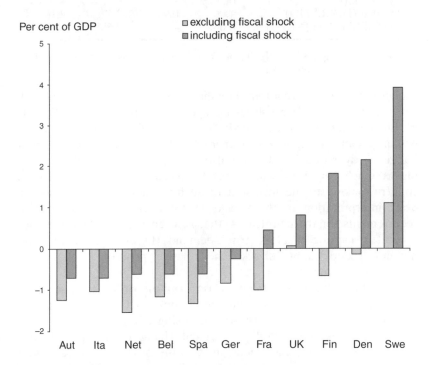

Figure 9.7   Cyclically adjusted government balances required to meet the 3 per cent of GDP deficit criterion with 90 per cent confidence over a 3 year horizon

Table 9.3   Sensitivity of the results to a change in variable measuring real private demand

	Three-year horizon (90 per cent confidence)		Five-year horizon (90 per cent confidence)	
	Base model	With D1NLPQ	Base model	With D1NLPQ
Belgium (D1NLPQ)	−1.18	−	−0.88	−
Germany (D1CPV)	−0.85	−0.74	−0.54	−0.43
Spain (CBQ)	−1.35	−1.43	−0.85	−0.88
France (D1NLPQ)	−1.02	−	−0.42	−
Italy (CBQ)	−1.03	−0.91	−0.43	−0.40
Netherlands (D1SRATIO)	−1.55	−1.52	−1.15	−1.13
Austria (D1SRATIO)	−1.25	−1.30	−0.92	−0.89
Finland (D1SRATIO)	−0.68	0.28	0.14	1.48
Denmark (D1NLPQ)	−0.16	−	0.77	−
Sweden (D1SRATIO)	1.06	0.90	2.37	2.16
United Kingdom (NLPQ)	0.04	−	0.68	−

Note: A − implies that NLPQ or D1NLPQ is used as the base model for the country concerned.

Finland, the United Kingdom, Denmark and Sweden are maintained. The inclusion of the fiscal shock changes the results most significantly in France and the three Nordic countries. This could capture a genuine relatively large effect from fiscal policy decisions on past budgetary dynamics, but it could also be a result of the model allocating too much weight to fiscal shocks. In any case, the robustness of the country ranking to the inclusion of all four shocks implies that the exact interpretation of the shocks is not decisive for the relative requirements for the countries – that is, even if the model does not accurately capture what is 'true' demand (fiscal, real private and monetary) and supply shocks the relative position of countries remains almost unaltered.

Simulations have also been carried out in order to assess the sensitivity of the results to changes in the variable measuring real private demand. Table 9.3 shows that using net private lending (in first differences) only implies marginal changes for the countries where other variables have been used in the base case model – that is, the budgetary requirement changes by less than 0.2 per cent of GDP in all cases except for Finland. Simulations have also been carried out to test the impact of ranking inflation last – instead of

Table 9.4. Sensitivity of the results to a change in the lag length
of the VAR model

	Three-year horizon (90 per cent confidence)			Five-year horizon (90 per cent confidence)		
	Optimal lag minus one	Optimal lag	Optimal lag plus one	Optimal lag minus one	Optimal lag	Optimal lag plus one
Belgium	−1.13	−1.18	−1.04	−0.73	−0.88	−0.57
Germany	−0.25	−0.85	−0.75	0.13	−0.54	−0.35
Spain	−0.97	−1.35	−1.24	−0.33	−0.85	−0.45
France	−1.04	−1.02	−1.12	−0.30	−0.42	−0.58
Italy	−0.80	−1.03	−1.36	0.10	−0.43	−0.83
Netherlands	−1.40	−1.55	−1.73	−0.82	−1.15	−1.40
Austria	−1.37	−1.25	−1.50	−1.00	−0.92	−1.22
Finland	−0.06	−0.68	−0.81	1.24	0.14	−0.05
Denmark	−0.38	−0.16	1.00	0.80	0.77	2.98
Sweden	2.41	1.06	2.01	5.00	2.37	3.95
United Kingdom	0.34	0.04	−0.20	1.20	0.68	0.42

first – for Spain, Belgium and Sweden. Once again, the budgetary requirements change only slightly, that is, less than 0.4 per cent of GDP for a five-year horizon and with 90 per cent confidence. Finally, the sensitivity of the results to a change in the lag length has been examined and found to be fairly low, although with the three Nordic countries exhibiting a non-negligible sensitivity (Table 9.4). Taken together these sensitivity results imply that the budgetary requirements found by using different country-specific models are fairly robust compared with applying exactly the same model for all countries (that is, same variables, ordering and lag length).

9.7 CONCLUSION

A two-step methodology has been used to estimate prudent budgetary margins, that is, that would allow automatic fiscal stabilisers to fully operate over the business cycle while preventing the general government deficit to breach the limit of 3 per cent of GDP set under the Stability and Growth Pact. A structural VAR model has first been estimated for eleven EU countries, capturing the effects on the deficits of economic shocks that have historically prevailed in each country. Based on the estimated distributions of these shocks, stochastic simulations have then been performed to build up probabilities of breaching the 3 per cent ceiling in the future. During each simulation, fiscal policy was assumed to be unchanged in order to purely capture the movements in the deficit stemming from automatic stabilisation and other sources not originating from fiscal impulses (that is, movements due to supply shocks, real private demand shocks and monetary shocks). Under this methodology, budget targets become more stringent as longer-term horizons are considered, because the probability of a sequence of unfavourable events hitting an economy increases over time.

The simulation results suggest that, for the majority of countries, if governments were to aim for a *cyclically adjusted* budget deficit between 1.0 and 1.5 per cent of GDP, the *actual* deficit would, with a 90 per cent likelihood, remain within the 3 per cent limit over a three-year horizon, without the need to adjust fiscal policy in a pro-cyclical fashion. This horizon would be extended to between five and seven years if governments opted for a 'close-to-balance' budget rule, defined as a cyclically adjusted deficit between zero and 1 per cent of GDP. Given that such a horizon encompasses the average length of a business cycle, these results largely endorse the recommendations of the SGP and the conclusions reached by Artis and Buti (Chapter 8) and Buti *et al.* (1998). For Finland, the United Kingdom and Denmark (in ascending order), moderate (cyclically adjusted) surpluses would be needed to minimise the risks of breaching the 3 per cent limit over a five-year horizon, whereas the requirement for Sweden is a more substantial surplus to achieve the same level of confidence.

The results indicate that the medium-term deficit targets – as set out in the individual countries' Stability Programmes (for euro area countries) and Convergence Programmes (for non-euro countries) – submitted to the European Council appear to be overall prudent, at least with respect to a horizon of three to five years.

Notes

1. Such elasticity estimates are, of course, subject to uncertainty, temporal instability, and, in particular, they could be affected by EMU participation. In any case, the OECD Secretariat estimates are similar to those used by the IMF and the European Commission.
2. Taking the variation in output gaps into consideration, the IMF shows how a structural budgetary position between balance and a deficit of 1 per cent of GDP would accommodate full automatic stabilisation within

the 3 per cent limit with 95 per cent confidence (assuming output gaps in all the euro area countries are drawn from the same normal distribution).

3. For a more detailed and technical exposition of the application of the structural VAR methodology to the issue addressed in this chapter, the reader is referred to the working paper version (Dalsgaard and de Serres, 1999, website www.oecd.org/eco/eco).

4. For a review of topics in structural VAR econometrics, see Amisano and Giannini (1997).

5. This set of restrictions assumes that all the variables in the system should be integrated of the same order but should not be co-integrated. As described below, the set of restrictions has been slightly modified for a few countries in order to obtain impulse responses that seemed more compatible with economic priors.

6. Interpreted as the cyclically adjusted level of government net lending.

7. Likewise, the distribution of maximum values would be centred around increasingly higher surpluses.

8. There are no government accounts for Luxembourg, and it has not been possible to obtain well-specified models for Portugal and Greece, partly due to problems with the government accounts data for these countries. Ireland has been excluded since government accounts data only go back to 1977, implying potential problems with too few degrees of freedom.

9. Semi-annual data were chosen in order to get sufficient degrees of freedom for the models. One problem with using semi-annual data for fiscal analysis is that budget balances follow yearly patterns and semi-annual data may thus be misleading in some cases. Moreover the other data – especially for some of the smaller countries – sometimes exhibit an apparently excessive erratic behaviour from one semester to another.

10. All the data are taken from the OECD Analytic Data Bank and are measured on a National Accounts basis.

11. Standard unit root tests have been used to determine the order of integration.

12. Exceptions are Spain, Belgium and Sweden where the change in inflation is ranked first in the VAR rather than last. In those cases, permanent inflation shocks (which are interpreted as monetary shocks) can have permanent effects on output and the net lending ratio. The reordering is justified in those cases by the finding that under the alternative ranking, the disturbances interpreted as supply shocks in fact behaved as demand shocks (that is, a positive shock raises both output and inflation). This can be interpreted as evidence of hysteresis. It turns out that the ranking of inflation has only marginal effects for the final outcomes of the stochastic simulations for these three countries (that is, the results are invariant to whether inflation is ranked first or last in the system).

13. Given space limitations, impulse response figures are not shown in this chapter but are available upon request from the authors or can be found in the working paper version (Dalsgaard and de Serres, 1999, website www.oecd.org/eco/eco).

14. Fiscal policy is restricted to have temporary effects on the level of output.
15. Exceptions to this are Belgium, Spain, the United Kingdom and Sweden where inflation rises at impact and then starts falling after two to four semesters.
16. Based on the country-specific shocks instead of the average of the big four country shocks, the budget requirement over a five-year horizon and 90 per cent confidence would be 3.7 per cent of GDP for Sweden (instead of 2.4) and 1.4 per cent of GDP for Finland (instead of 0.1).
17. This is particularly true for countries where the aggregate supply shock is found to have a permanent effect on the deficit ratio (in addition to the fiscal shock itself which is turned off during simulations).
18. Besides the volatility of the deficit, several studies have found a somewhat higher sensitivity of the budget to cyclical movements for Sweden than for other EU countries (see Table 9.1).

10 Will the SGP Ever Be Breached?*

Ray Barrell and Karen Dury

10.1 INTRODUCTION

The European Union economies have embarked on a programme of economic transformation that changes their mode of governance. Rules for monetary policy-making have been fundamentally altered for euro area members and all fifteen are variously bound by Treaty or Protocol to fiscal programmes that have significant implications for the flexibility with which they operate stabilisation policy. The Stability and Growth Pact (SGP) puts clear limits on the size of deficits that can be run, and has a rather loose system of fines associated with it. In this chapter we focus on the likelihood of member countries breaching this criteria and the extent to which changes in monetary policy affect this outcome. In particular we investigate what effects different types of simple monetary policy rules have on a country's ability to keep within the SGP criteria. One of the most common criticisms of the SGP is that it may be too binding in that governments will be unable to use fiscal stabilisation policies. This chapter throws light on the scope for fiscal activism in stabilising individual EMU economies.

The likelihood of breaching the fiscal criteria will depend on how effective policy rules are in stabilising economic variables, such as prices and output and the extent to which economic fluctuations feed through to fiscal balances. Evaluating monetary and fiscal policy by deterministic simulations is of great value to our understanding of the effects of particular shocks to the economy. However, the evaluation of options and risks in an uncertain world is important

* This work has been financed by ESRC awards R022250166 and L38251022.

and the ability of policy rules to deal with repeated shocks is the most effective way in which they can be evaluated. Hence, we use stochastic simulation techniques to evaluate the likely macroeconomic performance of EMU economies. This methodology also allows us to calculate event probabilities, in this case, the probability of breaching the SGP.[1]

The simple approach here reaches similar conclusions to those in Buti, Franco and Ongena (1997), for instance. They discuss the likelihood of a breach of the SGP using retrospective evidence, and show that if budgets were to follow similar response patterns to the past, starting from a position of close to balance, then even severe recessions would not cause deficits to breach the 3 per cent limit. We extend this literature by analysing the SGP using a model, NiGEM, that reflects the current and anticipated structure of European economies rather than looking at past outturns. The model also enables us to analyse the results under different monetary regimes for EMU. Studies using historical data cannot reflect the new single currency and interest rate regime we now have in place in EMU, nor do they reflect the recent changes in economic structuring that are included in NiGEM. This work is related to that described by Dury and Pina (2000) and Barrell and Pina (2000), but they include a more detailed formalisation of the operation of the SGP.

Recent analyses of the SGP by Allsopp, McKibbin and Vines (1999) have shown that fiscal consolidation by a single country within a monetary union is more costly, as compared to being outside, in terms of short-run output losses as an accompanying easing of monetary policy cannot be implemented. If all countries consolidate collectively then the matching easing of monetary policy union-wide can be induced. Hughes Hallet and McAdam (1999) also argue that the policy mix is crucial and if monetary or fiscal policy is constrained, the ability to reach desired outcomes is lost. They find that fiscal consolidation has to be done with all countries acting together and point out that the SGP lacks any incentive for countries to coordinate. However, our results indicate that fiscal policy will not be heavily constrained by the SGP.

The chapter starts with a brief discussion of the policy environment and then goes on to discuss some background to fiscal policy in Europe and assess the likelihood of individual EMU countries breaching the SGP. The conclusion is that different monetary policy rules have little effect on the probability of default and leave substantial room for fiscal activism. The potential link between the probability of default and the volatility of the government budget ratio is then examined. We find evidence of a correlation between increased variability of the budget ratio and higher probabilities of breaching the SGP. The chapter also examines how the policy rules affect economic variability and then analyse how this feeds through to the variability of the government budget ratio by decomposing it into its components, the primary deficit ratio and the government interest payment ratio. We find that whilst the main source of variability comes from the primary deficit ratio, the term structure of a country's debt may affect this conclusion. The final part of the chapter presents estimates of the 'safe' level for the target budget deficit.

10.2 FISCAL POLICY DEVELOPMENTS IN THE EURO AREA

Most of the euro area members have pursued fiscal consolidation in the 1990s. The reduction in government deficits has generally been successful with some countries running budget surpluses in 1999 and into 2000. However a number of countries still had deficits of around 2 per cent of GDP in 1999, as special measures that were designed to achieve targets in the run-up to monetary union were unwound. This poses the questions of whether current fiscal consolidation has been sufficient to remain below the reference value of 3 per cent of GDP if growth slows down more than expected, and whether the Stability Programmes are sufficient for all countries, or whether some governments may have to introduce additional measures.

The need to meet the strict fiscal guidelines laid out in the SGP is likely to continue to restrain the growth of expenditure. The EU countries outside EMU are also maintaining a fairly tight or neutral fiscal policy, in accordance with the Convergence Programme guidelines of the SGP.

The April 1999 baseline forecast for deficits (Table 10.1) is used in order to evaluate the first five years of EMU and the SGP.

Government budget ratios for Germany, France and Austria were forecast to be greater than 2 per cent for 1999. Spain, Italy, Netherlands and Portugal were forecast to be between 1 and 2 per cent and Belgium less than 1 per cent for 1999. Fiscal surpluses were expected in Finland and Ireland. Anticipated improvements in government finances are expected to lead to substantial reductions in the ratio of government debt to GDP over the next several years.

Table 10.1   Baseline government budget deficit/GDP ratios

	B	D	E	F	IRL	I	NL	A	P	FIN
1999	−0.93	−2.28	−1.48	−2.51	2.32	−1.93	−1.63	−2.51	−1.97	2.81
2000	−0.49	−1.85	−1.01	−1.74	2.28	−2.26	−1.31	−2.27	−1.80	2.67
2001	−0.56	−1.57	−0.18	−1.33	2.17	−2.05	−0.86	−1.04	−1.33	2.32
2002	−0.67	−1.22	0.05	−1.20	1.77	−1.67	−0.67	−0.71	−1.16	2.18
2003	−0.70	−0.84	−0.28	−1.10	1.13	−1.68	−0.64	−0.68	−1.22	1.45

Note: Figures for the budget deficit as a per cent of GDP are from the NIESR April 1999 baseline forecast. B = Belgium, D = Germany, E = Spain, F = France, IRL = Ireland, I = Italy, NL = Netherlands, A = Austria, P = Portugal, FIN = Finland.

10.3   THE POLICY ENVIRONMENT AND THE ANALYSIS OF POLICY

10.3.1   Monetary Policy

The analysis in this section uses simple policy rules, as is common on large macroeconomic models, because they are easy to understand and interpret. Advocates of simple policy rules argue that they are helpful in monitoring the performance of the authorities (see, for instance, Taylor, 1985 and 1999). Three possible feedback rules for the interest rate are compared: a standard monetary policy rule, where the central bank targets some monetary or nominal aggregate;[2] a combined nominal aggregate and inflation-targeting rule; and a pure inflation-targeting rule. In order to investigate the performance of these regimes, an explicit form to the policy rule that is to be followed is needed. The three interest rate rules investigated here are encompassed by:[3]

$$r_t = \gamma_1(Y_t - Y_t^*) + \gamma_2(\pi_t - \pi_t^*) \tag{10.1}$$

where r is the change in the short-term nominal interest rate from base values, $\pi = $ the annualised domestic inflation rate, Y is the log of nominal output and a star denotes target variables. Interest rates will change according to some proportion of the deviation of the targeted variable from its desired path. The policy rule that the ECB follows will depend on the aggregates for the euro zone and interest rates react to these.[4] For the combined rule γ_1 and γ_2 are both positive whereas for the pure inflation targeting rule the coefficient γ_1 is zero.

As stressed by Duisenberg (1998), the ECB has adopted a two-pillar strategy that can be described as a combination of money base targeting and inflation targeting. In what follows, it is assumed that the ECB has a combined nominal aggregate and inflation-targeting rule based on a reference value for detrended M3 (which will move in line with nominal GDP) and an inflation target. We also look at targeting inflation on its own. The target inflation rate in the rules is measured by the Consumer Price Index (CPI).[5] The rules target the current rate of inflation and the current level of a nominal magnitude. It is sometimes argued that a measure of forecast inflation is more appropriate due to the lag in monetary policy affecting the economy.[6] In a forward-looking model, current conditions are in part reflecting future outturns and, as Blake (2000) argues, policy-related expectations only embed current information and the model that is used. For these reasons, the monetary policy rules used here are formulated as current deviations from target.

10.3.2 Fiscal Policy

In the simulations it is assumed that budget deficits are kept within bounds in the longer term, and taxes rise to do this. Governments are assumed to adjust tax rates slowly to offset any changes in their deficits from their target trajectories, and hence the long-term solvency is guaranteed in the simulations (see Barrell and Sefton, 1997). The simple fiscal rule can be described as:

$$Tax = Tax(-1) + \phi[GBRT - GBR]$$

where *Tax* is the direct tax rate, and *GBR* and *GBRT* are the actual budget deficit ratio and the target budget deficit ratio respectively. The feedback parameter, ϕ, is designed to remove an excess deficit in less than five years. It is clear that the variability of output growth can be reduced when government spending is varied according to the economic cycle with spending rising when growth is slow and falling when growth is fast. Instead of this the focus here is on the scope for fiscal activism and the degree to which fiscal policy could be used, given the monetary policy feedback rule, without breaching the Stability Pact criteria. Examination of these issues allows us to throw light on the debate on the use of automatic stabilisers discussed in Buti and Martinot (2000).

10.3.3 Breaching the Criteria? Stochastic Simulations Results

The Pact puts clear limits on the size of deficits that can be run. A deficit of 3 per cent of GDP is set as a floor, and if sustained deficits above 3 per cent are maintained, then a system of fines becomes operative (see Chapter 6). Hence, it is relevant to look at the likelihood of individual countries breaching the SGP criteria and to make some assertions as to the potential for the individual member countries to use fiscal policy to offset shocks without breaking the Pact. Probability questions can be directly answered by using stochastic simulations. Once the stochastic simulation procedure has been set up and the event defined, estimating the probability of that event occurring is straightforward. For each trial a record is kept as to whether or not this event has occurred, and from this the event probabilities are calculated. The distribution of possible outcomes, and hence the target deficit that would ensure that there is little risk that the Pact would be breached, is also calculated.

The stochastic simulations are undertaken on the National Institute's Global Econometric Model, NiGEM, in order to examine the likelihood of EMU member countries defaulting on the SGP. NiGEM is a large econometric global model, with forward-looking behaviour in financial markets and labour markets and full working models of all OECD countries.[7] The model is subjected to a sequence of random shocks taken from the past. The shocks are drawn from the period 1993 to 1997 on the assumption that the near future will be similar to the near past. These unexplained events are then repeatedly applied to our forecast (which runs 24 years into the future).[8] The shocks are applied over a five-year period, running the model forward to calculate the expectations that would be a reasonable response to the news. All model equations, including the exchange rate where appropriate, are shocked.[9]

Table 10.2 shows the probability of individual member countries exceeding the 3 per cent deficit limit under each monetary policy rule for the whole shock period, 1999 to 2003. According to the results, there is a very low probability of breaching the SGP criteria for all countries, and this is true under all monetary policy rules, even though including an inflation component into the rule gives a modest rise in the probability of default. This indicates that there is substantial room for fiscal policy movements in response to shocks. This would enable the building of stronger automatic stabilisers in the fiscal structure to reduce output volatility. The countries showing the highest probabilities of breaching the Pact are Germany, Italy and Austria, at least based on the projected deficits in April 1999. The combination of data revision in Germany and stronger-than-anticipated revenues in Italy has meant that the outturns as of autumn 2000 have been better than

Table 10.2   Probability of government budget deficit ratio exceeding 3 per cent under the three monetary policy rules

Nominal targeting rule

	B	D	E	F	IRL	I	NL	A	P	FIN	EU-11
1999	0	11	0	2	0	2	0	14	0	0	0
2000	0	3	0	0	0	5	0	22	0	0	0
2001	0	1	0	0	0	2	0	1	0	0	0
2002	0	0	0	0	0	0	0	0	0	0	0
2003	0	0	0	0	0	0	0	0	0	0	0

Combined rule

	B	D	E	F	IRL	I	NL	A	P	FIN	EU-11
1999	0	15	0	9	0	3	0	16	0	0	0
2000	0	5	0	0	0	12	0	19	0	0	0
2001	1	2	0	0	0	5	0	1	0	0	0
2002	1	0	0	0	0	0	0	0	0	0	0
2003	1	0	0	0	0	1	0	0	0	0	0

Inflation targeting

	B	D	E	F	IRL	I	NL	A	P	FIN	EU-11
1999	1	13	0	6	0	8	0	25	0	0	0
2000	1	3	0	0	0	9	0	8	0	0	0
2001	2	1	0	0	0	3	0	1	0	0	0
2002	2	0	0	0	0	1	0	0	0	0	0
2003	2	0	0	0	0	1	0	0	0	0	0

Note: B = Belgium, D = Germany, E = Spain, F = France, IRL = Ireland, I = Italy, NL = Netherlands, A = Austria, P = Portugal, FIN = Finland.

anticipated in April 1999. Euroland as a whole appears never to breach the 3 per cent deficit limit on our April 1999 baseline.

10.4   MONETARY POLICY RULES AND THEIR EFFECT ON THE GOVERNMENT FISCAL POSITION

10.4.1   Variability of Government Budget Ratios

The probability of breaching the SGP is closely related to the variability of the government deficit ratio, which in turn will be affected by

the variability of economic variables such as income, prices and interest rates. In this section we present results for the variability of the
overall deficit ratio under each policy rule and explore the link between
this and the probability of default. Table 10.3 presents the results for
the overall government budget ratio for each country under the three
monetary policy rules. Following the analysis of Bryant, Hooper and
Mann (1993), the results from the stochastic simulations are reported
as root mean squared deviations (RMSDs) from their target path.[10]
This summary statistic gives a simple average of the deviations from
target over the whole time period considered. The table also contains
an index value for the variability of results under the combined rule
(CR) and the inflation-targeting rule (INF) compared to the nominal
targeting rule (NOM), to enable an easy comparison of the results.

The results show that for all countries (except Spain and Austria),
the variability of the deficit ratio is higher when an inflation target is
added to the nominal rule as compared to the nominal aggregate rule
on its own. This increase in variability of the deficit ratio is also
reflected in the increased probability of default for Germany, France
and Italy, as can be seen from a comparison of the results under
various monetary policy rules in Table 10.2. Other countries experi-

Table 10.3 RMSDs for government budget deficit ratios. Index value
for the combined rule and inflation targeting rule compared to the
nominal targeting rule (NOM = 100)

	RMSDs			NOM = 100	
	NOM	CR	INF	CR	INF
B	1.11	1.11	1.32	100	120
D	0.55	0.61	0.64	111	116
E	0.70	0.66	0.73	**96**	105
F	0.31	0.38	0.39	120	124
IRL	0.82	0.89	0.85	109	104
I	0.45	0.56	0.56	125	124
NL	0.50	0.55	0.61	110	122
A	0.69	0.68	0.74	**98**	107
P	0.30	0.33	0.33	108	108
FIN	0.78	0.83	0.77	106	**99**

Note: NOM = Nominal GDP targeting rule; CR = Combined rule; INF =
Inflation targeting rule. B = Belgium, D = Germany, E = Spain, F = France,
IRL = Ireland, I = Italy, NL = Netherlands, A = Austria, P = Portugal,
FIN = Finland.

ence increased variability in their government budget ratios but this is not reflected in higher default probabilities.

The countries that have a noticeable chance of default (Germany, France, Italy and Austria) under the simple nominal targeting rule have that chance increased when an inflation component is added to the rule. The chance of default is increased further when the nominal targeting rule is replaced by the inflation-targeting rule. In addition, Belgium moves to having a noticeable chance of breaching the Pact under the inflation-targeting rule. Under this rule short-term interest rate volatility rises and as the Belgium debt stock is large and heavily concentrated at the short end, the volatility of the government debt interest in Belgium increases. Countries with a negligible chance of a breach under the nominal rule maintain that position under the inflation-targeting rule, reflecting in part, the distance of the baseline deficit from the lower limit of 3 per cent as well as the size and composition of debt.

10.4.2   Variability of Output, Prices and Interest Rates

Table 10.4 below shows the variability of some of the main economic variables of interest, such as output, prices and interest rates, under the different monetary policy rules. An index value is included for the variability of results under the combined rule (CR) and the inflation-targeting rule (INF) compared to the nominal targeting rule (NOM).

Output Volatility

Including an inflation component in the rule either increases output volatility or leaves it unchanged for all but three economies, Germany, Austria and Spain. For the euro aggregate, output volatility increases slightly. However, as we remove the nominal aggregate from the combined rule and move to a pure inflation-targeting rule, output becomes much more volatile in all countries and for Euroland as a whole.

Price Level Volatility

The volatility of the price level falls considerably for the four largest economies in EMU and for Euroland for the combined rule compared to the nominal aggregate rule. However, moving to a pure inflation-targeting rule, price level volatility rises substantially in all countries and for the aggregate.

Table 10.4   RMSDs for output, prices and short- and long-term interest rates. Index value for the combined rule and inflation-targeting rule compared to the nominal targeting rule (*NOM* = 100)

	RMSDs			NOM = 100	
	NOM	*CR*	*INF*	*CR*	*INF*
Real output					
B	1.64	1.69	1.72	103	105
D	3.17	3.15	3.29	99	104
E	1.97	1.88	2.07	95	105
F	1.22	1.24	1.36	102	111
IRL	3.03	3.03	3.13	100	103
I	1.11	1.15	1.20	104	108
NL	2.16	2.18	2.25	101	104
A	3.08	3.06	3.15	99	102
P	2.35	2.35	2.41	100	103
FIN	1.10	1.14	1.22	104	111
EU-11	1.72	1.73	1.85	101	108
Price level					
B	0.81	0.83	0.98	102	121
D	1.40	1.32	1.63	94	116
E	1.92	1.81	1.97	94	103
F	0.79	0.70	0.90	89	114
IRL	1.28	1.28	1.47	100	115
I	1.03	0.92	1.30	89	126
NL	1.13	1.17	1.30	104	115
A	1.27	1.29	1.48	102	117
P	0.98	0.96	1.02	98	104
FIN	0.75	0.80	0.92	107	123
EU-11	0.98	0.90	1.26	92	129
Inflation					
B	1.89	1.88	1.91	99	101
D	1.09	1.12	1.16	103	106
E	0.98	0.97	1.04	99	106
F	0.62	0.58	0.66	94	106
IRL	0.99	1.00	1.05	101	106
I	1.03	1.00	1.06	97	103
NL	0.95	0.96	1.00	101	105
A	1.76	1.74	1.77	99	101
P	1.66	1.63	1.61	98	97
FIN	0.63	0.63	0.67	100	106
EU-11	0.60	0.59	0.68	99	114
Short rates					
EU-11	0.71	1.28	0.81	182	114

Long rates					
EU-11	0.09	0.11	0.08	119	95

Note: NOM = Nominal GDP targeting rule; CR = Combined rule; INF = Inflation-targeting rule. B = Belgium, D = Germany, E = Spain, F = France, IRL = Ireland, I = Italy, NL = Netherlands, A = Austria, P = Portugal, FIN = Finland, EU-11=Euroland.

Inflation Volatility

Including an inflation target in the monetary policy rule reduces the variability in the inflation rate for most EMU countries and for the euro aggregate. A pure inflation-targeting rule generally increases the variability of individual country inflation and the variability of euro aggregate inflation rate also rises.

Overall a combined nominal aggregate and inflation-targeting rule reduces price level and inflation variability for the euro area as a whole. However, the majority of countries see output variability either unchanged or increasing under the combined rule. A pure inflation-targeting rule gives higher output, price level and inflation variability for all individual countries (the only exception is Portuguese inflation), and for the aggregates as a whole.[11] These results suggest that inflation targeting may increase the variability of the primary deficit (PD) component of the budget deficit ratio, as we would expect this to move in line with the economic cycle.

Interest Rate Volatility

Both short- and long-term interest rates are considerably more volatile under the combined rule than with the nominal aggregate rule, and this may have a significant impact on the variability of the government interest payments (GIP) ratio. Moving from a combined rule to a pure inflation-targeting rule both short- and long-rate variability fall but the variability of the short rates is still higher than under the nominal aggregate rule whilst the variability of the long rates is lower. As long rates look forward 40 periods in the model, this implies that pure inflation targeting is having a stabilising effect beyond the end of the period of the application of shocks and this is affecting the variability in the long rates in the period we are considering.

From these results it would seem that inflation targeting is likely to give the highest variability in the primary deficit ratio. However, there may be an offsetting effect from reduced variability in the government interest payments ratio due to reduced variability of the interest rates compared to the combined rule. The covariance structure of the budget ratio will also have an impact and we explore this below.

The results highlight an important distinction between price-level targeting and inflation targeting. Under the combined rule (CR), where we are essentially targeting the euro area price level and inflation rate, we see a fall in euro area price-level variability. The inflation component in the rule has the effect of making the rule react quickly to any changes, helping to remove any inertia in the feedback rules. However, a pure inflation-targeting rule introduces a random walk component into the price level as it will, to an extent, treat past target misses as bygones. Therefore the price level is allowed to drift as time passes, implying increasing price-level variability. As we move to a pure inflation-targeting rule, the variability of the price level for the euro aggregate rises. If inflation is higher in one quarter, then targeting the price level will induce mean reversion in the price level whilst inflation targeting will not, and hence our results follow.

10.4.3 Variability of the Government Budget Deficit Components

To analyse the sources of volatility in the budget deficit, it is decomposed into its components, the primary deficit (*PD*) ratio and the government interest payments (*GIP*) ratio. The covariance between the components must also be taken into account, as can be seen if we write the variance of the budget deficit ratio at time t as:

$$\mathrm{Var}(GBR) = \mathrm{Var}(PD - GBR)$$

$$= \frac{1}{J}\sum_{1}^{J}[(PD - GIP) - (PD^* - GIP^*)]^2$$

where *GBR* is the government budget deficit ratio, *PD* is the primary deficit ratio, *GIP* is the government interest payment ratio and *J* is the number of stochastic simulations. This can be written as:

$$\mathrm{Var}(GBR) = \mathrm{Var}(PD) + \mathrm{Var}(GIP) - 2^*\mathrm{Cov}(PD, GIP)$$

Table 10.5 summarises the variability of the budget deficit and its components, so that for each country the source of volatility is shown. We can also assess how economic fluctuations affect the overall deficit. The first column presents the variance (as opposed to the RMSD) for the overall budget deficit ratio (these figures correspond

Table 10.5   Variances of government budget ratios and their components

		Var(*GBR*) = Var(*PD*) + Var(*GIP*) − 2*Cov(*PD*, *GIP*)			
		Var(*GBR*)	Var(*PD*)	Var(*GIP*)	2*Cov(*PD*, *GIP*)
		Col 1	*Col 2*	*Col 3*	*Col 4*
B	NOM	1.22	0.87	0.17	−0.18
	CR	1.23	0.95	0.31	0.03
	INF	1.75	0.99	0.31	−0.46
D	NOM	0.31	0.35	0.05	0.08
	CR	0.38	0.39	0.05	0.06
	INF	0.41	0.47	0.05	0.1
E	NOM	0.48	0.54	0.14	0.20
	CR	0.44	0.51	0.16	0.23
	INF	0.53	0.59	0.13	0.19
F	NOM	0.10	0.15	0.07	0.12
	CR	0.14	0.17	0.10	0.13
	INF	0.15	0.21	0.07	0.12
IRL	NOM	0.68	0.66	0.01	0
	CR	0.80	0.76	0.01	−0.02
	INF	0.73	0.69	0.01	−0.03
I	NOM	0.20	0.28	0.33	0.42
	CR	0.32	0.32	0.57	0.57
	INF	0.31	0.31	0.33	0.33
NL	NOM	0.25	0.15	0.03	−0.08
	CR	0.31	0.21	0.03	−0.07
	INF	0.38	0.25	0.03	−0.1
A	NOM	0.48	0.49	0.02	0.04
	CR	0.46	0.47	0.02	0.02
	INF	0.55	0.57	0.02	0.03
P	NOM	0.09	0.22	0.22	0.36
	CR	0.11	0.25	0.23	0.38
	INF	0.11	0.23	0.23	0.36
FIN	NOM	0.61	0.58	0.36	0.32
	CR	0.69	0.61	0.39	0.31
	INF	0.59	0.63	0.36	0.4

Note: NOM = Nominal GDP targeting rule; CR = Combined rule; INF = Inflation-targeting rule.

to the square of results shown in Table 10.3). The second column presents the variance of the primary deficit ratio, the third column gives the variance of the government interest payment ratios and the fourth column gives the covariance between the government interest payment and the primary deficit ratios.[12]

Comparing columns 2, 3 and 4 in Table 10.5 above, we see that the majority of the variability in the overall budget deficit ratio comes from the variability of the primary deficit. Italy, Portugal and to some extent France are the only exceptions. As shown in Table 10.3, moving from a nominal aggregate rule to a combined rule generally increases the variability of the budget deficit ratio. Table 10.5 above shows that the variability of the primary deficit also generally increases.[13] The variability of the primary deficit ratio will depend on fluctuations in the economy and the operation of the fiscal feedbacks. Output, price level and inflation variabilities are generally increased substantially for almost all countries under the pure inflation-targeting rule. Table 10.5 shows that all countries, with the exception of Italy, Portugal and Ireland, see a rise in output variability feeding through to higher variability in the primary deficit ratio as we move from a combined rule to a pure inflation-targeting rule.

The variability of the government interest payments/GDP ratio will be sensitive to the variability of the interest rate. Table 10.4 showed that the variability of the short- and long-term interest rate rose as an inflation component was included in the nominal aggregate targeting rule. For most countries the variability of interest payments/GDP ratio either remains unchanged or increases moderately suggesting that the ratio is not that sensitive to changes in the variability in the interest rate. However, for two countries, Italy and Belgium, the variability of this ratio increases. Both are high-debt countries with a large proportion of that debt held in short-term bonds and hence are highly sensitive to the substantially increased variability in the short-term interest rate. Other countries hold a much more long-term debt and so will be more sensitive to changes in the long rate.

Decomposing the variability of the government budget ratio indicates that variability in the primary deficit ratio is the main source of variability in the overall deficit ratio. There also appears to be some evidence of increased economic fluctuations feeding through to increased variability of the primary deficit ratio. The structure of government debt has important implications for the variability of the government interest payment ratio. However, the overall impact on the variability of the budget ratio will also be affected by the covariance structure of the primary deficit and government interest payment ratios. We would expect a positive covariance between the two as increased economic activity improves the government fiscal position, and interest rates rise and increase the interest payments on government debt. Of course, what happens to interest rates depends on what is happening to EMU as a whole. One individual country experiencing a rise in economic activity, and hence fiscal revenues, may not see a corresponding rise in interest rates if the rest of EMU is not affected by the same shocks. However, for most of the countries we see a positive relationship and this increases as we include some form of inflation component in the rule.

10.5 SETTING THE TARGET DEFICIT TO AVOID BREACHING THE CRITERIA

In order to assess the probability of a country breaching the fiscal guidelines, some estimates of the volatility of output and the effects of output on the deficit are needed. We also need some baseline estimates of the expected deficit in order to put bounds around it. The work reported in Buti and Sapir (1998) underlying the calculations of the so-called 'minimal benchmarks' (see Chapter 8), used Hodrick–Prescott filters to obtain estimates of trend output and hence of the volatility of output around trend. They use a relatively long time span, and they calculate that output is (was) most variable (as measured by its standard deviation as a per cent of GDP) in Finland (2.2), Sweden (1.7), Spain (1.5) and the UK (1.4) and least variable in Italy (0.7), Austria (0.7) and France (0.8). These depend on history, the nature of automatic stabilisers and the policy reaction functions in place over the period and they may not be good indicators for the future. For instance, politically induced devaluation cycles are at least part of the reason for volatile output in the first four countries mentioned, and this can explain why Finland and Spain have chosen to give up the exchange rate instrument and join EMU.

The effects of volatile incomes depend on the sensitivity of the budget deficit to the cycle, and these again depend upon automatic stabilisers. Buti, Franco and Ongena (1997) have calculated these for the European economies, and they suggest that a 1 per cent of GDP fall in output causes a 0.7 per cent worsening of the budget deficit in Sweden, 0.6 per cent in the Netherlands and 0.5 per cent in the UK, Finland and Belgium. Other countries are lower. If historical volatilities are applied to these coefficients it is clear that budget deficits would be most volatile in Sweden and Finland, much as they have been since the 1970s.

If we have the standard deviation output and the impact of changes in output on the budget, the probability that the deficit differs from baseline by any given amount can be calculated. It is possible to ask, given historical volatilities, what the target deficit would have to be to reduce to 1 per cent the probability of having a deficit in excess of 3 per cent of GDP. The information in Buti and Sapir (1998) suggests that the Finns and the Swedes would have to aim for surpluses of 2.5 per cent of GDP and 1.8 per cent of GDP respectively. The UK, the Netherlands (both −0.5 per cent), Spain (−0.6 per cent) and Denmark (−0.7 per cent) should heed the Commission's desire to keep within a target range of 0 to −1.0 per cent. However, the less volatile or responsive countries could aim for larger deficits than the Stability and Growth Pact suggests. Belgium (−1.4 per cent), Portugal (−1.5 per cent), Ireland (−1.6 per cent) and Germany (−1.7 per cent) could all run reasonable deficits, and the rest of the members of EMU could aim at −2.0 per cent.

Given these estimates the Pact appears to be rather tight given its initial aims. We should of course treat the estimates for the more historically volatile countries with caution, as they have all attempted to reduce uncertainties by either adopting an inflation-targeting regime (UK and Sweden) or they have joined EMU to ensure the same thing. Studies using historical data cannot reflect the new single currency and interest rate regime we now have in place in EMU. Using a model that reflects the current and anticipated structure of European economies rather than looking at past outturns can give a more realistic analysis. For instance, history would suggest that Spain and the Netherlands would have a chance of breaking the Pact, but our estimates do not, whilst we suggest that Austria is rather too near the border. The former two countries have undergone significant changes in their labour markets over the 1990s, as is well documented, and our model encompasses these changes. They have clearly made it easier for them to fit into the new framework. Our results on Austria reflect a more sceptical (and as of mid-2000) a more realistic view of potential budget outcomes.

The 'safe' budget target will depend on the regime in place for monetary policy as well as the structure of shocks that affect the economy. Table 10.6 gives a set of 'safe' budget targets that could be set given the variability from our stochastic simulations. They give a 1 per cent probability of the target being exceeded, which should leave a significant safety margin within the SGP. It is clear that they are more generous than those implied by the simple analysis of history.

Table 10.6   Target deficit required for a 1 per cent
chance of breaching the 3 per cent limit

	NOM	CR	INF
B	0.47	0.46	−0.03
D	1.73	1.59	1.53
E	1.41	1.48	1.33
F	2.28	2.14	2.11
IRL	1.12	0.96	1.05
I	1.97	1.71	1.72
NL	1.85	1.73	1.59
A	1.42	1.44	1.30
P	2.31	2.25	2.25
FIN	1.22	1.10	1.24
DK	1.07	0.82	0.81
S*	0.27	0.12	0.27
GR	1.37	1.26	1.37
UK	1.45	1.30	1.31

* With Sweden in Monetary Union the results show
that the deficit is allowed to rise slightly to 0.3.

Deficits in excess of 1.5 per cent of GDP are common for the large
countries in this table and target deficits are smallest in the very high-
debt countries such as Belgium, as stressed above, and in the more
volatile Nordic countries. Even here the target deficits are reasonable,
and do not indicate the large surpluses an analysis of history would
suggest. The stability of the Finnish economy has clearly improved as
it has converged to EMU, and its target deficit hardly needs to be any
different from the rest of the EMU countries. In our analysis the
Swedes are assumed to be outside EMU, but they are presumed to
effectively target inflation and hence they would not suffer from the
budgetary consequences of the pattern of devaluations they saw in the
past. Our results are 'Lucas Critique' protected in that they take
account of the effects of changes in policy regimes on the outcomes
for the economy. This is not possible when we use historical statistics
to evaluate targets.

Setting target deficits 'close to balance' can be seen as aiming for a
target range of 0 to 1 per cent of GDP, therefore the 'safe' budget
targets shown in Table 10.6 would suggest room for much stronger
automatic stabilisers than we have operating on our model. There are
three possible effects of the economic cycle on the budget, in that tax

revenues automatically rise with incomes and expenditures on items such as unemployment insurance automatically fall, and also as revenues improve there are political pressures to lean with the wind and cut taxes and raise spending. The first two are best described as automatic stabilisers. Our model has similar effects of the cycle on unemployment-related transfers and other spending to those in van den Noord (2000), but probably has smaller cycle-related tax elasticities. Barrell and Pina (2000) embed the 'industry standard' tax elasticities into the model and show that the volatility of the deficit increases somewhat, but not enough to make target deficits in the range 0 to 1 per cent of GDP induce more than the very occasional breach of the SGP. There is clear scope within the current arrangements for the unfettered operation of automatic stabilisers. However, there are good reasons to be cautious and set target deficits closer to zero than those in Table 10.6.

The 'close to balance' rule can also be seen as being designed to offset some of the potential bias introduced into the budgetary system by bureaucratic offsets discussed, for instance, in Mélitz (1997). There is clear evidence in Mélitz that expenditures exhibit a pro-cyclical pattern, as budgetary constraints become looser when revenues are strong. This should mean that the target balance has to be set to take account of the asymmetric nature of the outturns for the deficit, especially if financial market-based constraints on government behaviour have been released by the formation of EMU. We would presume, as in the 1980s and 1990s, that governments will find it difficult to run surpluses even when they are appropriate to the cyclical position. Hence a tighter target than that implied in Table 10.6 would be appropriate, and it would allow automatic stabilisers to work fully in recessions and allow some offset for bureaucratic laxity in upturns. We would conclude that deficits around 1 per cent of GDP would be suitable for almost all countries in EMU.

10.6   CONCLUSION

This chapter has investigated the likelihood of EMU member countries defaulting on the SGP. We have used stochastic simulations on the National Institutes Global Econometric Model, NiGEM, to examine potential fiscal instabilities and their source. We find that while different monetary policy regimes of the ECB can have a considerable impact on the stability of economies and this can feed through to the changes in the variability of the budget ratio, there is little evidence that the SGP will be breached under any policy rule. The ECB has adopted a 'two-pillar' strategy, and this gives the most room for fiscal manoeuvre amongst the class of rules we investigate.

We conclude that there is substantial room for fiscal activism in helping to reduce economic fluctuations. The world has changed, and historical outturns for budget deficits in the 1980s and 1990s tell us little about the prospects for budgets in the next decade. Many of the breaches of the 3 per cent guideline that we saw in the past were the result of discretionary policy by governments. Although a return to discretion and profligacy cannot be ruled out, the structure of fiscal policy-making in Europe has been changed, and deficits should be much easier to control. Our results suggest that most European countries could run deficits as large as 1.5 per cent of GDP over the cycle and still avoid breaches of the SGP guidelines and allow some automatic stabilisers to work. In order to strengthen stabilisers, which would be wise, it would be sensible to aim at a deficit target of around 1 per cent of GDP. Given that the political pressures on governments are asymmetric, with pressure to increase spending when there is a cyclical surplus being stronger than pressures to cut it when there is a matching cyclical deficit, it would seem wise to build in a degree of safety in the budget target. Deficits of 1 per cent or just below would be sufficient, and the current target of in balance or surplus over the cycle would be unnecessarily restrictive in the short term. This target would lead to some degree of turbulence in the long bond markets as the supply of government debt dried up.

The probability of breaching the SGP constraints depends on how the variability in the economy feeds through to variability in the budget deficit. We show that the main source of variability in the budget as a per cent of GDP comes from the variability of the primary deficit ratio. However, variability of the short-term interest rate and the size and structure of government debt can have important implications. We saw that this was particularly important for Italy and Belgium, two highly indebted countries that hold a large proportion of their debt in short-term bonds. With a high proportion of debt held in short-term bonds, a high variability of the short-term interest rate will have a greater affect on the variability of the government budget deficit ratio.

However, we should not be complacent about the SGP and its guidelines, as Buti and Martinot (2000) argue. Our results suggest that it may be more appropriate for the primary deficit ratio to be the target and not the overall budget ratio as this is in the control of the fiscal authorities. What happens to government interest payments can be reflected in the variability of short-term interest rates which is in the hands of the monetary authorities.

Notes

1. We undertake stochastic simulations on the National Institute's Global Econometric model (NiGEM) to investigate these issues. NiGEM is a large econometric global model, with forward-looking behaviour in financial markets and labour markets and full working models of all European countries.

2. These terms are used as substitutes for each other, as a velocity de-trended monetary aggregate will move in line with nominal GDP in the medium term, and as we are not assuming that the authorities wish to hit their target period by period, responses will be similar with either target.

3. For further details on policy rules that are encompassed within a general framework, see Barrell, Dury and Hurst (1999a).

4. Denmark is not in EMU but has declared that it will follow EMU monetary policy and Denmark is also used in calculating the EMU aggregates. Sweden and Greece are out of EMU and their individual policy rule is left unchanged across the stochastic simulations.

5. Issues arising from targeting the domestic inflation rate (where only inflation in the domestic component of the CPI, or GDP deflator, is targeted) are dealt with in Svensson (2000).

6. See Svensson (1997).

7. This includes South Korea. China is modelled seperately and there are country groupings for East Asia, Latin America, Africa, Miscellaneous Developing Countries, and Developing Europe. For a full description of the model and the stochastic simulation techniques applied, see Barrell, Dury and Hurst (1999b). Further details can be found in NIESR (2000), available in mimeo or HTML form from the Institute.

8. The model is run far enough into the future to ensure that the end of the run does not affect the beginning of the simulation. We run 200 stochastic simulations for each policy regime. As shown in Barrell, Dury and Hurst (1999b), after roughly 100 stochastic simulations the results settle down.

9. We use a synthetic set of shocks for the euro as it did not exist in the 'draw' period, 1993q1–1997q4. The issue of shocking the exchange rate is dealt with in Barrell, Dury and Pain (2000).

10. $RMSD = \sqrt{(1/N)\sum_{t=1}^{N}\left\{(1/J)\sum_{j=1}^{J}\left[\frac{(x_{it}^{j}-x_{it}^{B})}{x_{it}^{B}}\right]^{2}\right\}}$ where x_{it}^{j} is the value of variable i in period t from the jth trial, x_{it}^{B} is the value of the variable i on the base in period t, J is the number of trials taken. For variables such as interest rates and inflation rates, absolute deviations are measured.

11.   These results imply that the covariance structure of Euroland inflation matters and changes over the rules. This issue is discussed in Barrell, Dury and Hurst (1999a). The paper shows that slightly different parameterisations of the policy rules can shift the weight of evidence further in the direction of choosing the combined rule.
12.   Col 1 = Col 2 + Col 3 − Col 4. Errors due to rounding.
13.   With the exception of Spain and Austria, whose output and total deficit variability also falls.

Part V
Fiscal Policy Coordination Under the Pact

11 Fiscal Policy, Automatic Stabilisers and Coordination*

Matti Virén

11.1 INTRODUCTION

This chapter deals with the fiscal policy behaviour of EU/EMU countries. Fiscal policy has become increasingly important in economic policy in general and in the case of European Monetary Union in particular. As far as EMU is concerned, only fiscal policy can be used in offsetting country-specific shocks. On the other hand, fiscal policy is now subject to certain limits that reduce the room for policy manoeuvring. The excessive deficit criterion (laid down in the Maastricht Treaty and in the Stability and Growth Pact) may have far-reaching influence on policy behaviour because now the policy-makers have to consider very carefully what is the correct and feasible policy stance. Accordingly, there is less room for fiscal policy errors.

This change obviously has several implications for policy considerations. It means that we have to know much more about the cyclical situation, the role of automatic stabilisers and the effects of policy instruments. Also, the question of whether fiscal policy actions are coordinated across countries becomes much more important in assessing the performance of fiscal policy, and thus decision-makers in a single country have, at the very least, to find out what the other countries do and preferably also what is the effect of the other countries' policies on their country.

At the theoretical level, it is quite easy to demonstrate that policy coordination pays off and/or that decentralised policy-making is inefficient (see Canzoneri and Gray, 1985; Buiter and Marston, 1985; and Hamada, 1985; but see also Rogoff, 1985, for a counter-example[1]).[2]

---

* I am grateful to Ville Haukkamaa and Heli Tikkunen for research assistance and Anne Brunila, Erkki Koskela and David Mayes for useful comments. Financial support from the Yrjö Jahnsson Foundation is also gratefully acknowledged.

The problem is that it is a long way from the theoretical level to actual policy.[3] This can be seen simply by examining the structure of the theoretical models (see Oudiz and Sachs, 1984; and Kehoe, 1987). The fact that coordinated (fiscal) policy dominates the autarky solution does not, of course, tell very much of how the coordinated policy should be conducted. There are also problems with the empirical and practical implementation of policy coordination. Very little work has been done to demonstrate that policy coordination is actually possible and that the benefits are important (see, however, Canzoneri and Minford, 1988). This chapter is concerned specifically with the issue of practical implementation. We evaluate the problems that policy-makers face in pursuing coordinated fiscal policies in the EU/EMU countries. Although we focus on the EU countries, some comparative analyses cover all the OECD countries, which also represent an interesting challenge for policy coordination.

In order to find answers to these questions we scrutinise the differences between these countries in terms of the prerequisites for fiscal policy action and in terms of the cyclical behaviour of the whole economy and the public sector, in particular. We analyse the cyclical sensitiveness of government expenditures, revenues and deficits. We compare the effects of fiscal policy in different counties in the case of uncoordinated and coordinated fiscal policies. We also focus on measurement and forecasting problems, especially as regards the behaviour of automatic stabilisers.

In addition, we try to find out whether there is any evidence of fiscal policy coordination since the 1960s and whether there are any explanations for possible deficiencies in policy behaviour. With this aim in mind, we look at the fiscal policy reaction (reaction functions) in these countries.

In the analysis, we abstract from many important practical questions related to policy coordination. Thus, for instance, we do not discuss the questions of (a) how to coordinate policies, (b) which policies should be coordinated, (c) which instruments should be used and, finally, (d) which institutions/organisations should carry out coordination. As far as the first question is concerned, we can only point out that policy coordination can either be based on different rules (the above-mentioned deficit criterion is in fact such a rule) or it may simply apply to discretionary policy actions. It may also be the case that the only form of coordination is related to automatic stabilisers. Whether that can be called coordination or not is really a matter of semantics. It is rather hard to imagine that discretionary policy coordination could succeed in practice given the institutional system of the European Union. Our empirical analyses cannot shed much light on this issue because they do not draw any distinction between (the effects of) discretionary and rule-based policies.

The chapter is structured as follows. First, in section 11.2 we analyse the economic environment in which policy coordination is really possible. In section 11.3, we discuss how the Stability and Growth Pact affects the need and possibilities of policy coordination. In section 11.4 we try to identify the cyclical and discretionary components of fiscal policy using alternative measurement procedures. Then, in section 11.5, we carry out a comparative analysis of the policy effects in the case of coordinated versus uncoordinated policies, and in section 11.6 we examine the evidence on policy coordination. Finally, in section 11.7, we present some concluding remarks.

11.2 REQUIREMENTS FOR FISCAL POLICY COORDINATION

Fiscal policy coordination will not take place unless certain requirements are fulfilled. In particular, the following (partly overlapping) conditions can be considered to be essential:[4]

1. The cyclical behaviour of the economies and the nature of shocks must be similar.
2. Countries must have similar prerequisites for policy actions – thus, we must at least exclude different corner solutions.
3. The tax and transfer systems, as too the budgetary process, must be similar so as to provide reasonably similar automatic stabilisers.
4. Forecasts and the assessment of the current situations must be sufficiently accurate.
5. Effects of fiscal policy actions must be reasonably similar and predictable.
6. Coordinated policy actions must be much more effective than uncoordinated actions.
7. Different countries must share the same policy view (in terms of the instruments and objectives of policy).
8. Policy commitments must be enforceable (and, of course, credible) in different countries.

Some comments on these points merit note here.[5] If the cyclical movements (of a large set of countries) are completely unrelated, there is obviously no need for policy coordination. In other words, if the output shocks are entirely country-specific, policy measures must also be country-specific. By contrast, if the shocks are common to (a relevant set of) countries, it is easier to make out a case for policy coordination. The empirical magnitude of this problem is illustrated in Figure 11.1, on p. 266. In this figure, output shocks are classified as common (to the EU) and country-specific.

Clearly, the cyclical movements (output shocks) are far from being highly correlated. In some countries, like Finland, country-specific shocks dominate output fluctuations. Important changes have, however, taken place over time. It seems that the variability of output has decreased considerably over time for most of the sample countries. The EMU-11 countries seem to behave in a similar manner but even among them country-specific shocks represent about one-half of the total output variability.

The fact that output shocks are strongly correlated does not, of course, imply that fiscal policy coordination or fiscal policy in general pays off. As pointed out by, for example, Blanchard (2000), the outcome depends very much on the nature of shocks. In the case of demand shocks, there is no problem, but in the case of supply shocks, fiscal policies, or just automatic stabilisers, may do the wrong thing. While they stabilise (smooth) the output path they do not allow for the adjustment of output that would be desirable.[6] Thus, output gaps would, in fact, increase, not decrease. The problem is that the nature of shocks cannot be judged on the basis on pure output (growth) data and hence it is quite difficult to distinguish which countries have experienced demand and which supply shocks.

As far as policy prerequisites and constraints are concerned, we know that the EU countries differ a great deal, for instance, in terms of debt and the size of the public sector. Thus, some countries might face a corner solution in which only restrictive policies can be applied. We also know that countries differ in terms of the functioning of the labour market and the inflationary effects of aggregate demand changes. All of these differences obviously make it very difficult to pursue similar policy rules in different countries.[7]

In most empirical evaluations (and practical applications) of the gains from coordination, the sign and symmetry of inter-country spill-over effects of policy are crucial in determining the direction to take in coordinating macroeconomic policies. The nature of the spillover effects is obviously not the only thing which makes policy coordination so difficult. Coordination also requires very good estimates of the policy transmission mechanism. Therefore, we need to know reasonably well both the nature and magnitude of automatic stabilisers and the actual policy effects. In addition, we have to know the effects of coordinated (*vis-à-vis* uncoordinated) fiscal policy actions.

As for the automatic stabilisers, it is essential that the tax and transfer systems (progressivity of taxation, indexation of transfers and so on) are quite similar across countries and, of course, that the relevant parameters are known to policy-makers. For instance, if the cyclical behaviour of deficits differs very much across countries, all assessments of the state of government finances become very difficult and optimal policy (in the certainty equivalence sense) cannot be pursued (as already shown by Brainard, 1967).

Obviously, systematic fiscal policy also critically depends on the availability of accurate forecasts. Thus, if forecast values of the cyclical behaviour of output are completely unrelated to actual values and if the forecast errors are uncorrelated between countries, policy coordination may fail, although one could, of course, attempt to coordinate policy actions. The problem not only applies to forecasts of the cyclical situation (that is, the GDP growth rate) but also to assessment of the current and future fiscal situation. In practice, this means that we must be able to distinguish between the cyclical and structural components of expenditures, revenues and the deficit. It is well-known (see Brandner, Diabalek and Schuberth, 1998) that such assessment is very difficult and may produce a wide range of different results.

A traditional way of analysing the benefits of policy coordination makes use of a Keynesian-type model which highlights the importance of fiscal and foreign trade multipliers (see Fair, 1979).[8] Alternatively, the terms of trade could act as the main channel of transmission. Thus, for instance, the traditional Laursen and Metzler (1950) model predicts that domestic autonomous government expenditures, which raise domestic output, lower the level of output abroad, that is, domestic spending is transmitted negatively to the rest of the world. The Frenkel and Razin (1985) model produces a similar result. Macromodel simulations of Helliwell and Padmore (1985), Bryant *et al.* (1988) and Taylor (1993) provide somewhat different results. Thus, an increase in government expenditures increases both output and prices abroad. With the price effect, some ambiguity exists, however. All in all, one gets an impression that the gains from coordination are likely to be small and quite sensitive to models and basic assumptions (concerning, for example, flexibility of prices, wages and exchange rates).[9] One has, however, to be careful in interpreting the early findings. As pointed out by Frenkel and Razin (1992), most comparisons have not been made between optimal uncoordinated and coordinated policies but between some suboptimal policies. Moreover, some gains from coordination may be unobservable (showing up in other policies and structural changes). Finally, most comparisons have assumed that governments will adhere to agreements also in the light of changed circumstances and that coordination may not affect the incentives to stick to agreements to enhance reputation.

Policy coordination is obviously successful only if fiscal policy has desirable effects on aggregate demand (and other relevant variables). In addition, we have to assume that policy effects are similar. Thus, if, for instance, an increase in public expenditure by, say, 1 per cent of GDP increases GDP by 0.1 per cent in one country and 2 per cent in another country, it may become difficult to design the contents of the coordinated policy package. Clearly, the problem would be aggravated if some of the relevant relationships were non-linear. Then, we simply could not aggregate the EMU country numbers and design policy simply on the basis of average values of different macro variables.

Assuming that policy effects are of reasonable magnitude and reasonably similar (and that other coordination problems are not relevant), we have to demonstrate that policy coordination also pays off in practice. If the effect of coordinated actions is only marginally larger than uncoordinated actions we have to question the practical usefulness of coordination. Of course, this is really a question of the practical importance of spillover effects, and given the information that we have we would be surprised to find that the effects of coordinated and uncoordinated actions were the same. Obviously, the fact that coordination pays off for a set of countries may not be enough. One might also be interested in the distribution of the benefits of coordination between countries.

The question of policy goals is rather difficult because there is no agreement between economists and policy-makers on the desirability of policy activism and the direction and magnitude of 'the right policy'. The problem, in Europe at least, is that opinions as regards policy activism also seem to follow geographical lines to some extent.

Finally, policy coordination is subject to all possible problems of political economy. Commitments should both be accepted and effectively enforced at the national level. It is not hard to imagine the kind of political problems that could arise and in this light it seems that discretionary policy coordination can only succeed in very special cases.

11.3 FISCAL POLICY COORDINATION WITHIN THE STABILITY AND GROWTH PACT

As explained in several chapters in this volume the Stability and Growth Pact does two quite different things. It allows national fiscal policy but it imposes strong constraints on it. The fact that some flexibility in national fiscal policy is allowed has obvious reasons. Monetary policy cannot play any role in offsetting country-specific shocks and given the relatively large differences between member countries (shown in Figure 11.1) some country-specific policy instruments must be available.

At the same time as this need is acknowledged, the excessive deficits constraint is imposed to safeguard the European Central Bank's independence and credibility.[10] Basically the constraint does the right thing even if it can be thought that (large) highdebt countries may try to put pressure on ECB for lower interest rates to avoid the penalties and public discrediting.

The Stability and Growth Pact has some direct implications in terms of policy coordination. The most important point is related to the effectiveness of fiscal policy. Because it is obvious that national fiscal policy in a small open country setting is not very powerful because of (increased) imports, some coordination between member countries is required to enhance the effects of fiscal policy. The more effective is fiscal policy the smaller are the deficits, which are required to adjust negative output shocks (and vice versa). Except for imports, we might expect fiscal policy to be effective in individual countries that have fixed exchange rates (as suggested by the conventional Mundell–Fleming model). By contrast, in the whole EMU, which has flexible exchange rates, fiscal policy is ineffective (assuming that the EMU is still 'small' in the world perspective; see Marston (1985) for further details). Clearly, this gives individual countries greater incentive to activist fiscal policy and creates a (potential) conflict of interests between member countries and the Union. Obviously, this conflict of interest further motivates the Stability and Growth Pact. Notice also that there might be some difference in policy incentives between small and large member countries because small countries (as opposed to large countries) may safely assume that a deterioration of their financial balances does not show in the EMU-wide interest rates and exchange rates.

The Stability and Growth Pact also means that the consequences of policy uncertainty become crucial. Wrong estimates of the relevant

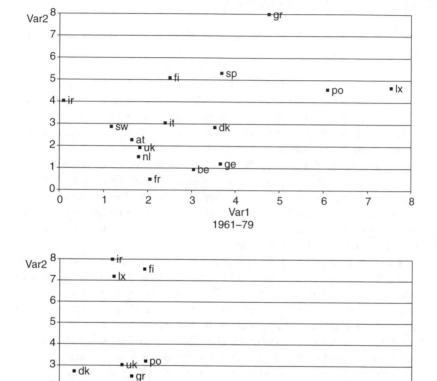

Figure 11.1   Common and country-specific variances of GDP for EU countries, 1960–98

Note: Var1 = common variance for the EU and Var2 = country-specific variance. The values are obtained by running a regression $\Delta y_{it} = \alpha + \beta \Delta y_{EU,t}$, where Δy_{it} is the GDP growth rate for country i while y_{EU} denotes the corresponding value for the EU aggregate. In this sence $\mathrm{Var}(u_t)$ and $(\mathrm{Var}(\Delta y_{it} - \mathrm{Var}(u_t))$ represent the common and country-specific variance components.

(fiscal policy) parameters may lead to the regime of excessive deficits which represents a new penalty for an excessively ambitious policy stance and which, *ceteris paribus*, leads to more cautious policy. The basic reason is the non-linearity that the Excessive Deficits Procedure produces: a 2.9 per cent deficit is completely different from a 3.1 per cent deficit. The possibility of a policy error obviously forces the member governments to closer coordination (a) to increase policy effectiveness by coordinated efforts, (b) to acquire more information of other member governments' policy aims and (c) to harmonise the propagation mechanisms of both policy and automatic stabilisers. In this respect the Stability and Growth Pact can be important because it inevitably increases fiscal policy dialogue, information exchange, peer pressure and monitoring fiscal policy in the EMU. If the tax and transfer systems in the member countries become more similar (due to various harmonisation plans), that might also alleviate the policy uncertainty problem.

However, policy coordination would not help much if the output shocks were country-specific. Then policy coordination would require a country to pursue a certain discretionary policy for another country's sake (say, Germany would have to pursue more expansionary policy to help Italy out of a recession). This would obviously be quite difficult (impossible) because of obvious *political economy* problems.

'Discretionary' policy coordination of the type just described probably makes sense only in the case of extreme economic crises. Otherwise, coordination has to rely on some accepted rules. However, in EMU's policy framework and with the exception of the Stability and Growth Pact (and, in a sense, automatic stabilisers), no such rules exist and it is not clear what kind of rules should be developed. Perhaps the most obvious candidates for such rules would be tying the degree of fiscal tightness to the relative sizes of the output gaps (that is, higher-than-average-growth countries would exercise some extra tightening in fiscal policy).

It is, of course, much easier to work with automatic stabilisers and, in fact, it is generally thought that fiscal policy in the EMU should be primarily based on automatic stabilisers. Although they have some convenient properties they also have some problems. First, there seem to be important differences between different member countries (as can be seen in the next section). Second, the automatic stabilisers often reflect the most distortionary elements of public finance. The most important element is typically progressive taxation. Another element is the unemployment compensation system. From the supply point of view, there is obviously no point in increasing the role of automatic stabilisers by making taxes more progressive and the replacement rate of the unemployment compensation closer to unity.

11.4 DISTINGUISHING BETWEEN CYCLICAL AND STRUCTURAL DEFICITS

Automatic stabilisers constitute an essential ingredient of fiscal policy. In order to be able to pursue correct cyclical policy, it is necessary to know what is the nature and magnitude of cyclical elements in both expenditures and revenues. In addition, one should know the type of shocks: whether they are demand or supply shocks and whether they are temporary or permanent shocks (see again Blanchard, 2000). If cyclical sensitiveness is very pronounced, discretionary policy measures may not be needed. Overly sensitive cyclical deficits may, however, create problems in satisfying the excessive deficits criterion. Thus, already in a modest recession the deficit may fall below the 3 per cent level (see Chapter 9 and Kiander and Virén (2000) for analysis on the importance of this problem for EU countries). The seriousness of the problem obviously depends on the initial state of deficits and debt. The main implication is that there is less scope for high debt.

Therefore, it is very important to be able to distinguish between the cyclical and structural components of expenditures, revenues and the deficit. Although the basic idea as regards distinction is quite simple, empirical applications are not that easy. Assume, for instance, that the government pursues systematic (counter) cyclical fiscal policies. How can the effect of such policies be distinguished from pure cyclical effects (automatic stabilisers) if we used only unrestricted time-series models in deriving the cyclical effects, as is customarily done? With current adjustment procedures (see Banca d'Italia, 1999) this seems impossible. If the policies were totally discretionary, the task would be a little easier but by no means trivial even then. Not surprisingly, there are several competing ways of making the structural corrections, and there is really no consensus on how to make the decompositions. International organisations like the IMF, OECD and European Union make their own adjustments and, in addition, several other (national) adjustment procedures are applied.

The most important differences are not, however, related to the cyclical adjustment methods, but the actual cyclical behaviour of government expenditures and revenues. The GDP elasticities are not only different in terms of magnitude but even different in terms of sign. It is therefore very difficult to forecast developments in government expenditures and revenues and it is clear that even if output increased (decreased) in a similar way in all countries, government deficits would behave in a completely different way. The differences in other policy environment variables (debt and unemployment) are, however, even larger. The most surprising fact, however, is that the GDP elasticities of government revenues and expenditures differ enormously between countries, suggesting that the systems are very different indeed (the elasticities are reported in some depth in Mäki and Virén, 1998).

In order to analyse the cyclical behaviour of budgets, three alternative model structures are used:

1. A single-equation model for the determination of deficits;
2. A four-variable VAR model;
3. A multi-country macromodel (NiGEM).

These three models are used to ensure the robustness of results in terms of (a) the simultaneity bias, (b) dynamic specification and (c) the type of output shocks.

11.4.1 Single-Equation Models

The analysis is mainly based on a simple reduced-form specification for the deficit/output ratio. This equation could be seen as some sort of data description equation rather than a strict behavioural equation (reaction function of the fiscal authority). Thus, the estimating equation is simply of the form:

$$\frac{def}{y^*} = \alpha_0 + \alpha_1 trend + \alpha_2 \left(\frac{def}{y^*}\right)_{-1} + \alpha_3 \Delta y + \alpha_4 r + \alpha_5 \left(\frac{debt}{y}\right)_{-1} + u,$$

$$(11.1)$$

where *def* denotes the general government deficit (positive values correspond to a surplus), *y* is output (GDP), y^* trend output, *trend* is the time trend, *r* is either the nominal or real (long-term) interest rate, *debt* is general government debt and u is the error term. In addition to this linear specification, we estimate a non-linear threshold model specification of the following form:

$$\frac{def}{y^*} = \alpha_0 + \alpha_1 trend + \alpha_2 \left(\frac{def}{y^*}\right)_{-1} + \alpha_{31}\Delta y | \Delta y < 0 + \alpha_{32}\Delta y | \Delta y > 0$$

$$+ \alpha_4 r + \alpha_5 \left(\frac{debt}{y}\right)_{-1} + u \tag{11.2}$$

where $\Delta y | \Delta y < 0(\Delta y | \Delta y > 0)$ denotes negative (positive) values of GDP growth.[11,12] The data, which cover the period 1960–99, are from the EUROSTAT data bank. Here we only report the coefficient estimates of Δy. The values of a linear specification ($\alpha_3 = \alpha_{31} = \alpha_{32}$) are reported in Table 11.1 while the non-linear output growth terms α_{31} and α_{32} are illustrated in Figure 11.2. As can be seen from Figure 11.2, empirical evidence does provide strong support for the hypothesis that the relationship between public sector deficits and output is non-linear. Thus, the sensitivity is much larger in recession than in growth periods. This is clearly due to the non-linearities in the determination of revenues and expenditures (see Virén, 2000b, for further details).

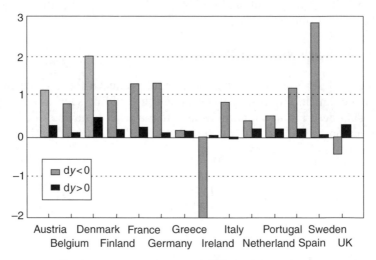

Figure 11.2   Non-linear effects of GDP on deficits in the EU countries
Note: The bars indicate the coefficient estimates α_{31} and α_{32} in (11.2). $\Delta y =$ change in GDP.

If the relationship between public expenditures and revenues, on the one hand, and output, on the other hand, is indeed non-linear, it is very difficult to predict the effects of output growth. From the policy coordination point of view, non-linearities are a difficult problem in other respects as well because it is essentially an aggregation problem. One can no longer assume that there is stable relationship between the average cyclical situation in the EU and the average fiscal position in the EU. On the basis of Figure 11.2, it can be argued that the EU-wide fiscal situation is crucially affected by the distribution of output growth rates and other cyclical indicators.[13]

11.4.2   VAR Models

The single-equation model (11.1) is obviously based on several restrictive assumptions (particularly in terms of the dynamic specification) which may crucially affect the estimation results. One may ask whether a more general, say a VAR-model-type, specification would produce similar results. To explore this possibility we carried out an analysis using the following unconstrained VAR model:

The set of endogenous variables: Δy, rr, def/y^* (where rr is the real long-term interest rate)

The set of exogenous variables: Δy^{OECD} (which is the growth rate of GDP in the OECD area)

The ordering of variables: Δy, rr, def/y

The number of lags: 4

Impulse responses: Computed for 40 lags using the Cholesky decomposition. Standard deviations are computed by Monte Carlo simulation with 500 replications.

In the analysis, we used individual country data so that the time series typically consist of 36 annual observations for 1964–99. For space reasons, we report here only a set of impulse responses of def/y^* to (standardised 1 per cent) shocks in the GDP growth rate Δy (cf. Table 11.1). For a full exposition, see Virén (2000b).

11.4.3   NiGEM Simulations

The final step in our analysis is to use the multi-country NiGEM model to derive the estimates of the cyclical deficit effect (see

NIESR, 1999). Basically, we examine how a 1 per cent increase in GDP affects the level of the deficit/GDP ratio. Although the basic idea of the analysis is quite simple, it is not easy to perform this kind of analysis because there are numerous ways of generating the GDP growth effect.[14]

Here we introduced a temporary 1 per cent shock in GDP so that the duration of the shock was four quarters. This was done by shocking GDP directly and controlling that the GDP growth effect was actually 1 per cent.[15] We also performed the simulation so that (exogenous) exports were shocked by 1 per cent of GDP. The results in terms of deficits were qualitatively very similar to the first simulation (and therefore they are not displayed here). A short summary of the simulation results is reported in Table 11.1. The reported values are differences between the alternative and base solutions of the deficit/GDP ratio.

11.4.4 Comparison of Results

When scrutinising the results in Table 11.1 one has to remember that the three models are quite different in terms of construction and their results have different interpretations. The coefficient α_3 (in 11.1) reflects the short-run effect of a permanent change in the output growth rate on deficits. In the case of the VAR model, the impulse response reflects the impact of a (temporary) GDP innovation on deficits while the NiGEM model results reflect the effect of an (temporary) increase in (the level of) GDP on deficits.

Against this background it is somewhat surprising that there are still similarities in the results (in Table 11.1) for different countries and different models (to the extent that the three models and their output can be compared). Thus, in the short run, acceleration in GDP growth by 1 per cent will reduce deficits (the deficit/GDP ratio) by one-third of a per cent. The medium-run (and long-run) effects are obviously much larger.[16] Altogether, the size of automatic stabilisers is clearly non-trivial and their impact should be known in evaluating the need for 'additional' fiscal policy actions.[17]

But how then can the cyclical and non-cyclical components be distinguished in practice? The answer is that there are several (quite different) ways of doing this. All of them are based in one way or another on the estimated elasticities but there are big differences in terms of the reference variables (output growth, or output gap, or unemployment rate and so on). Because there is no consensus on the correct way of distin-

Table 11.1   Comparison of cyclical behaviour of deficits

	Linear model	NiGEM (t–4Q)	VAR (t–2Y)
Belgium	.25	.15	.66
Germany	.19	.12	.31
Spain	.27	.41	.42
France	.28	.38	.26
Ireland	.05	.09	.18
Italy	.10	.32	.41
Netherlands	.28	.42	.36
Austria	.25	.42	.37
Portugal	.48	.20	.30
Finland	.25	.34	.35
Denmark	.36	.61	.33
Sweden	.78	1.21	.22
UK	.10	.02	.25
Average	.30	.36	.34

Note: The second column corresponds to the coefficients of the GDP growth rate in a linear model (11.1) estimated from EU data, the third column the NiGEM model effects of a 1 per cent GDP shock and, finally, the fourth column the impulse responses of *def/y** to a 1 per cent GDP growth rate shock from a four-variable VAR model (explained in the text).

guishing the cyclical and structural components, different procedures are followed, for example, by the EU, IMF and OECD.

The problem is that the uncertainty associated with choosing the proper measure is not the only difficulty we have to contend with in evaluating the fiscal situation. We also have the problem of knowing the correct way of updating and computing the corresponding indicator. The fact that the forecast values of cyclical/structural deficit vary a lot is no surprise – the problem is that the values computed for the current and past periods seem to be overly sensitive, reflecting both new data and new computational solutions (disaggregation, detrending methods, and so on).

In the case of the OECD, the 'updating' error seems to be of the magnitude of 2–4 per cent, which is obviously too much when we take into account the error that is related to different organisations' assessments. The OECD numbers are by no means extraordinary in the sense that other cyclical adjustments would produce clearly smaller errors. This becomes evident when we scrutinise the IMF values for the structural deficit (see Mäki and Virén, 1999). The difference between historical values is really striking: one does not always know whether the policy stance has been restrictive or expansionary. All in all, we can say that the Stability and Growth Pact can be useful by setting in motion the improvements and harmonisation of the indicators of automatic stabilisers and structural deficits.

11.5   A COMPARISON OF POLICY EFFECTS IN DIFFERENT COUNTRIES

This section tries to assess the importance of policy coordination for policy effectiveness. For that purpose, we use the multi-country NiGEM model to compare the effects of different fiscal policy actions in the single country setting and in the case of collective policy action.[18] The NiGEM model simulations were carried out by increasing either public consumption or direct taxes. Simulations were carried out so that in the first case public consumption was increased in all EU countries in an uncoordinated way (that is, the model simulations were carried out in a country-by-country manner). In the second case, public consumption was increased in all EMU countries at the same time and by the same amount (that is, 1 per cent).[19]

The results from these simulations are reported in Figures 11.3–11.4. Figure 11.3 contains a summary of the short-run effects and Figure 11.4 a summary of the maximum effects (which could, of course, also be short-run effects). Basically, the comparison is very easy. In all cases the coordinated fiscal expansion produces almost twice as much increase in output as an uncoordinated fiscal expansion.

The multiplier values reveal that in an uncoordinated case fiscal policy effects remain relatively small for the small countries, with many of the multiplier values of the magnitude of 0.5 only. The reason for these low values is simply (increased) imports. For large countries, the values exceed 1 but not by very much. The average value for all countries is 0.72 (with four lags) and 0.63 (with eight lags), 0.85 being the average maximum value. In the case of coordinated policies, there is not much difference between small and large countries. Thus, the average value is 1.25 (with four lags) and 1.17 (with eight lags), 1.46 being again the average maximum value. The multiplier values (in the coordination case) are, in fact, quite close to the values obtained by Cohen and Follette (1999) with the US FRB/US macroeconomic model.[20] On the other hand, they are a bit higher than the SVAR values obtained by Blanchard and Perotti (1999) which are about 1.

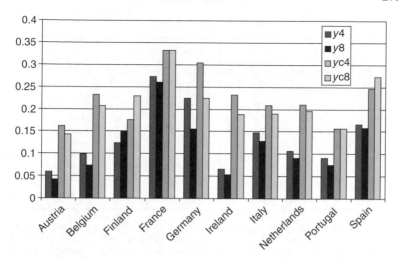

Figure 11.3   Short-run effects of a 1 per cent increase in public consumption on GDP with (yc) and without (y) policy coordination

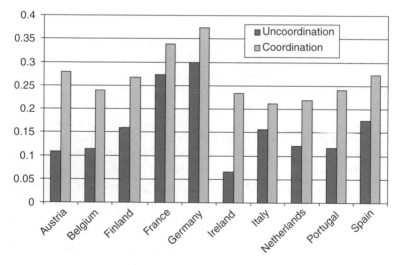

Figure 11.4   Maximum effects of a 1 per cent increase in public consumption on GDP with and without policy coordination

The multiplier values in the uncoordinated case are, of course very low (suggesting that the marginal propensity to spend out of income is very low and the income elasticity of imports is very high) but also in

Table 11.2   A summary of public consumption simulation

	y4	y8	yc4	yc8	ymax	ycmax	def	defc	ym	ymc
Belgium	0.099	0.074	0.233	0.208	0.113	0.239	−0.220	−0.107	0.536	1.131
Germany	0.224	0.156	0.304	0.224	0.299	0.374	−0.167	−0.130	1.574	1.967
Spain	0.166	0.159	0.246	0.274	0.175	0.274	−0.157	−0.109	1.109	1.732
France	0.273	0.261	0.333	0.332	0.274	0.339	−0.168	−0.144	1.130	1.398
Ireland	0.065	0.054	0.232	0.189	0.066	0.233	−0.127	−0.079	0.488	1.740
Italy	0.147	0.128	0.208	0.189	0.156	0.212	−0.146	−0.102	0.829	1.128
Netherlands	0.107	0.090	0.211	0.195	0.121	0.219	−0.230	−0.144	0.891	1.612
Austria	0.059	0.042	0.162	0.143	0.107	0.279	−0.154	−0.075	0.574	1.489
Portugal	0.092	0.076	0.156	0.157	0.116	0.241	−0.185	−0.144	0.574	1.193
Finland	0.124	0.151	0.175	0.228	0.159	0.268	−0.117	−0.050	0.741	1.251
Average	0.136	0.119	0.226	0.214	0.159	0.268	−0.167	−0.108	0.845	1.464

Note: $y4$ ($y8$) denotes the output effect of an uncoordinated increase in public consumption (by 1 per cent) after four (eight) quarters, $yc4$ and $yc8$ denote the corresponding values in a case where all countries increase public consumption by the same amount, $ymax$ and $ycmax$ denote the maximum values of y over twenty quarters and ym and ymc the corresponding multiplier values for an increase in public consumption by 1 per cent of GDP. def and $defc$ denote the deficit effects of an increase in public consumption computed after twenty quarters.

the case of coordinated fiscal policies the multipliers are not terribly high although they obviously still facilitate fiscal policies. Note also that in the case of uncoordinated policies, the output effect diminishes more rapidly than in the case of coordinated policies.

The effect of an increase in public consumption on government deficits is almost equally clear (see Figure 11.5). Deficits increase but because output also increases the effect on the deficit/GDP ratio differs from the pure deficit effect. The values for various countries are surprisingly different, reflecting the differences in the output effects. In other respects, it is rather difficult to say why the country results are so different (the size of the country and the size of the public sector do not seem to explain the size of the output and deficit effects).

When examining the long-run effects, we obviously have to pay attention to developments in government debt and the sustainability of fiscal expansion. With this aim in mind, we analysed developments in output and deficits (deficit/GDP) in the case of no solvency requirements (denoted by insolvency) and with solvency requirements (in the latter case, direct taxes were increased to offset increased indebtedness). The results for the whole EU area (in the case of a coordinated policy action) are presented in Figure 11.6.

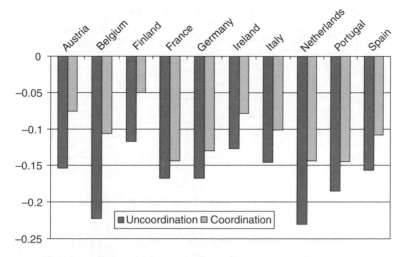

Figure 11.5   Long-run effect of a 1 per cent increase in public consumption on government surplus/GDP with and without policy coordination

Not surprisingly, imposing the solvency condition makes a lot of difference, particularly in the long run (when the additional taxes start to have an effect). Thus, the GDP effect almost completely vanishes and the effect on deficits is also quite marginal. If countries increase public consumption and balance the budget in the long run by raising taxes, the long-run output effect is simply zero or even negative. If the whole of the EU/EMU does the same and ignores the solvency condition, some output gains are achieved even in the long run.[21] As pointed out already earlier, gains from coordination seem too much larger for small countries while the impact of the solvency requirement depends mainly on the size and nature of the fiscal policy effect.

So far, we have considered public consumption only. The story as regards direct taxes is very similar. Coordination makes a lot of difference in terms of output effects but the results are less clear as regards the deficit/GDP ratio. The problem stems from the output effects. When taxes are increased, output and income decrease, which eliminates part of tax revenues and – *ceteris paribus* – increases the deficit/GDP ratio because of lower output.

The long-run effect of direct taxes (on output) is noticeably larger than the effect of public consumption. This mainly reflects the larger GDP share of taxes compared with public consumption. The dynamics

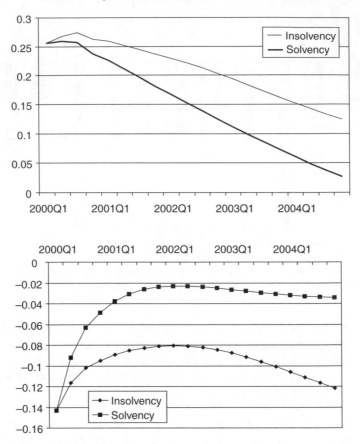

Figure 11.6   Effect of the solvency requirement on the impact of public consumption on GDP (upper panel) and government surplus/GDP (lower panel)

of the effects are, however, quite different, as can be seen from Figure 11.7, which illustrates the effects for the whole EMU area. The effect of public consumption diminishes over time while the tax effect shows no signs of a diminished impact.

When dealing with fiscal policy simulation, an obvious question is what happens to interest rates. As discussed in the chapter by Barrell and Dury, the answer provided by the NiGEM model is: not very much. Thus, imposing the inflation-targeting assumption for monetary policy produces only a 5-basis-point increase in long rates in the case

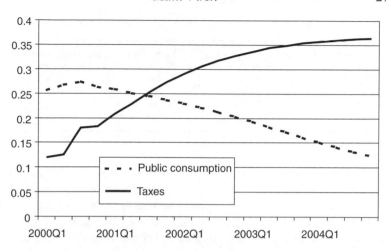

Figure 11.7   Comparison of expansive fiscal policy effects in the euro area

of coordinated policies. In the case of uncoordinated policies, the result is practically zero (for instance, in the case of Finland, just one-tenth of a basis point). The NiGEM model, like most other models, generates the somewhat odd result that interest rates have a strong impact on deficits while deficits have only a very marginal effect on interest rates. This latter result is obviously in sharp contrast with all theorising on credibility and peso effects (but not necessarily with empirical evidence; see, for example, Alesina *et al.*, 1992). The model result only reflects the direct crowding-out effect and does not account for direct expectations and portfolio effects (nor the possibility that monetary policy would directly react to deficits). That is clearly a weakness of the model (and of all similar models). The weakness may also be quite crucial with regard to the assessment of policy coordination effects within EU.

11.6   EVIDENCE ON POLICY COORDINATION

At this point, there is good reason to ask to what extent there has been coordination – albeit imperfect – in fiscal policy when policies have been so different. In trying to find out whether policy actions have actually been coordinated, we simply scrutinise the cross-country correlations between fiscal policy indicators (that is, structural

Table 11.3   Correlation coefficients between countries' structural deficits

Structural deficit	Average correlation	Observations	5 per cent critical value
EU	0.385	30	0.361
IMF	0.340	27	0.381
OECD	0.339	31	0.355
BFI	0.073	39	0.320

deficits). Some summary statistics of these correlations are presented in Table 11.3. We also used the variance decomposition procedure (which we applied above in the context of the output growth relationships reported in Figure 11.1). Thus, we run regressions between deficits in country i and EU aggregate deficits in the following way:

$$\frac{def_i}{y_i} = \beta_0 + \frac{\beta_1 def_{eu}}{y_{eu}} + u \tag{11.3}$$

Equation (11.3) is estimated for both actual deficits (deficits/GDP) and cyclically adjusted (structural) deficits (in relation to trend GDP) using the EU data for 1960–99. The results are presented below in Figure 11.8 (variances) and Table 11.3 (explanatory power).

Turn first to the correlation coefficients between different structural deficit measures. The coefficients have been computed between all countries (assuming zero lags and leads). Thus, for each measure, we have 91 (off-diagonal) coefficients (corresponding to fourteen countries). As can be seen from Table 11.3, the coefficients are not very high. For the EU, IMF and OECD measures, about half of the coefficients are different from zero (at the 5 per cent significance level). In the case of the Blanchard Fiscal Impulse (BFI) measure (see Blanchard, 1990), only a few coefficients exceed the conventional critical values. The low values of the BFI indicator are presumably due to the fact that this measure really focuses on the difference in primary deficit, not the level of deficit as do the other three measures.

On the basis of correlations one can conclude that fiscal policies have had some features in common but one cannot really speak about common policy or a common policy rule.

As for the variance decompositions, which are illustrated in Figure 11.4, it can be seen that the cross-country differences are considerable. Ireland, Greece and Finland represent some kind of

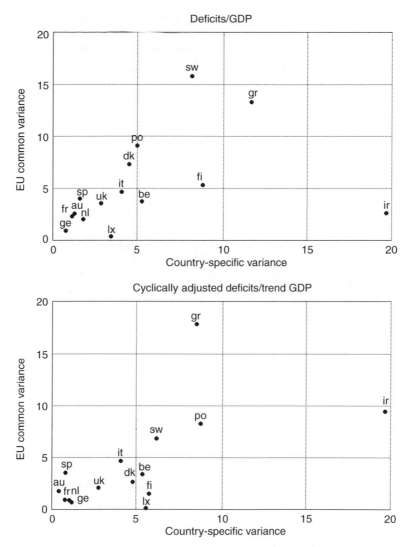

Figure 11.8   Common and country-specific variances of government deficits

outliers while Austria, Germany, France and the Netherlands seem to form a set of core countries also in terms of fiscal policy behaviour. One way of assessing the cross-country differences is to examine the explanatory power of equation (11.3). To do this we report the R_s^2 in Table 11.4.

Table 11.4   Multiple correlation coefficients of equation (11.3)

	Deficits/GDP	Cyclically adjusted deficits/trend GDP
Belgium	0.41	0.31
Germany	0.47	0.35
Greece	0.51	0.61
Spain	0.70	0.70
France	0.64	0.49
Ireland	0.08*	0.01*
Italy	0.51	0.53
Luxembourg	0.05*	0.00*
Netherlands	0.52	0.44
Austria	0.63	0.60
Portugal	0.63	0.47
Finland	0.33	0.15
Denmark	0.60	0.32
Sweden	0.62	0.51
UK	0.54	0.39
Average	0.48	0.39

* Not significant at the 5 per cent level.

Not surprisingly, the indicators for structural deficits are more loosely related suggesting that (discretionary?) policies have indeed been quite different. If we eliminate Ireland, Luxembourg and Finland from the sample, the situation looks a little different.

Correlation analysis is not, of course, a very powerful tool in analysing the performance of policy coordination. To obtain more affirmative results, one should try to identify the relevant policy reaction functions. The problem with this kind of analysis is the identification of the cross-country spillover effects, which would require at least a large amount of data. There have been some analyses in which the fiscal policy reaction functions have been estimated (see, for example, Virén, 1998) but very little success has been achieved in identifying and estimating the spillover effects.

Given the differences between EU countries, it would have been surprising to find that they have pursued similar policies in the past. As it turns out, the findings are not completely negative in terms of policy coordination. The 'core' countries have actually pursued quite similar policies and because these countries' economies seem to be becoming increasingly integrated over time (see Figure 11.1), one might expect that coherence of fiscal policies will also increase in the future.

11.7 CONCLUDING REMARKS

Policy coordination within EMU will be very much a new departure. Up till now, the EMU countries – like all the OECD countries – have pursued predominantly nationally oriented policies. Given the policy environment this is not surprising. Large differences between countries – both in terms of institutions and values of various macroeconomic indicators – create formidable obstacles to coordinated policy actions. The need for such policies also varies from country to country and time to time. Also, the effectiveness of various policy instruments appears to be different. To achieve better coordination it is necessary to harmonise the key elements of the fiscal policy process so that, at least, the basic prerequisites for policy actions and automatic stabilisers are reasonably similar. It is also necessary that the role of automatic stabilisers be better known than it is at present. Great uncertainty concerning key policy parameters hinders policies even if policies would otherwise pay off as it probably is in the case of coordinated fiscal policies. In this respect, the Stability and Growth Pact can make a major contribution in focusing on the problem, increasing dialogue and exchange of information. Whether or not it depends on the Pact, we have already now seen a huge increase in research on fiscal policy in Europe.

As for the pay-off from policy coordination, there seem to be quite marked differences between large and small countries regarding their position on (coordinated) fiscal policies. It is interesting to see whether these differences also show up in the decision-making process within the EU. This question may become more relevant given the fact that, to some extent at least, policy views also seem to follow country-size (and North–South) lines.

Notes

1. The models, which show that policy coordination may be an inferior solution typically, make use of the idea of dynamic inconsistency. Thus, in the case of Rogoff (1985), the basic idea is the following: as coordinated policies yield greater output expansions, this will increase the policy authorities' incentives to use policies and this, in turn, will exacerbate their credibility problems in terms of their private sectors. In the case of monetary policy, the outcome is a higher time-consistent rate of inflation (see also Obstfeld and Rogoff, 1996). See Canzoneri and Henderson

(1988) for a critique of Rogoff's analysis. See also Kehoe (1988) for an alternative explanation of why coordination may be undesirable. Kehoe demonstrates that with international policy coordination the joint policy must tax away all the return on savings. This would lead to zero investment which is clearly an inferior solution compared with the case of international tax competition (no coordination) that would lead to low taxes on income from savings and high investment. Canzoneri and Diba (1991), instead, consider the beneficial effects of coordination. They show that under financial integration a rise in government spending generates a smaller increase in the rate of interest compared with a financial autarkic situation. Clearly international policy coordination is beneficial since if an individual government makes its spending decisions it internalises the cost to other governments associated with debt servicing.

2. It seems even more obvious that fiscal policies in general (in a single country setting) can produce positive welfare gains. The problem is that this assumption can also be challenged (see Lucas and Stokey, 1983; and Chari, Christiano and Kehoe, 1993). We cannot really deal with this basic theoretical problem here.

3. The theoretical literature is bypassed here without going into any details about the models. The main reason for this is that that most policy cooperation models are quite old-fashioned ('obsolete Keynesian models', as Obstfeld and Rogoff (1996) call them in this connection) and static without any explicit micro foundations.

4. The set of requirements is in a sense too strong. Already within a single country (say, at the regional level) there are important differences in terms of shocks and policy effects, for instance, but still we take it granted that fiscal policy is coordinated.

5. See also Frenkel and Razin (1992) and Branson et al. (1990) for further discussion (and evaluation) on these conditions.

6. In the case of supply shocks, output variability could even increase. Take for instance oil shocks. Higher prices would push up nominal wages, which (with incomplete indexation of the tax system) would lead to higher real taxes and lower (too low) consumption. The simulations of Cohen and Follette (1999) with the FRB/US model suggest that this might not be the case but even so supply shocks constitute a difficult problem for both discretionary fiscal policy and automatic stabilisers.

7. See Oudiz and Sachs (1984) for a review of problems in specifying a model for policy coordination and evaluating the gains from coordination. See also Tanzi and Schuknecht (1997) for cross-country comparisons of the role and size of government.

8. A classical example of the consequences of policy coordination failures is the experience of Mitterrand's government when it attempted to pursue independent expansionary policies for France in 1981–83.

9. The benchmark reference in this respect is Oudiz and Sachs (1984) who investigated the quantitative gains from international policy coordination. They estimate that the gain from cooperation among the G3 countries would be about 0.5 per cent (compared with the best non-cooperative outcome).

10. If the SGP is interpreted from the viewpoint of the new fiscal theory of inflation, one could say that the Pact effectively guarantees (by imposing the solvency conditions) that the 'money dominant' regime dominates the 'fiscal' regime. See Canzoneri and Diba (Chapter 3) for more about this perspective of the Maastricht Treaty and the Stability and Growth Pact.

11. In both equations we have an obvious simultaneity problem as fiscal policy will affect output growth and causality does not run from output growth to deficits only. Thus, we face an identification problem, which seems particularly difficult because it is not all clear how the identification restrictions should be imposed. Typically (for instance, in setting the restrictions in a VAR model) it is assumed that deficits (policy) react to contemporaneous output whereas the fiscal policy effect shows up in output growth with a lag. In this panel data setting it is rather difficult to take this problem into account. However, we also estimated the system using the Instrumental Variable estimator (see Virén, 2000b). The results turned out to be quite similar to the OLS estimates. In fact, the GDP growth rate coefficients increased somewhat when the IV estimator was used. Thus, the results may not perhaps be affected so much by the simultaneity bias. We may also point out that in the three sets of models which we use here simultaneity bias is (probably) quite different but still the results are pretty similar which suggests that the problem is not absolutely crucial. See Schinasi and Lutz (1992) for a nice summary of the simultaneity problem.

12. Threshold models are perhaps the most widely used non-linear specification (see Granger and Teräsvirta, 1993). They are relatively easy to estimate and the results are also easy to interpret. Testing for the existence of the threshold is, however, rather tricky. It is also difficult to accept the crude nature of the regime shifts in models of this kind.

13. The importance of the aggregation problem stems from the relatively large differences which seem to persist between EU countries. In 1999, for instance, the maximum GDP growth rate was 8.3 per cent and the minimum 1.3 per cent. At the quarterly level, the differences are even more striking.

14. The reported simulations were made so that the nominal interest rates were fixed. All countries were assumed to be insolvent (that is, no automatic tax reaction to changed deficit and debt was allowed).

15. A 1 per cent shock in GDP did not produce exactly a 1 per cent change in GDP. Therefore, the simulated values were rescaled so that the GDP effect was indeed 1 per cent.

16. In the case of equation (11.2), the average estimate of α_1 is 0.81, which implies that the long-run effect of Δy on def/y^* is 1.4.

17. Ideally, of course, the size of automatic stabilisers should be estimated at the same time as the effectiveness of fiscal policy is evaluated. See Blanchard and Perotti (1999) for an attempt to do that in an SVAR framework.

18. In evaluating the effects of fiscal policy, an obvious analytical framework is provided by (structural) VAR models (see Blanchard and Perotti, 1999; Dalsgaard and de Serres (Chapter 9); and Virén, 2000a).

Because we concentrate here on the policy coordination problem, structural multi-country models are, however, more convenient.

19.   The share of public consumption in GDP differs somewhat across EU countries, and so the corresponding GDP effects also differ. The differences in the public consumption/GDP ratio are after all not so large as the following 1998 values indicate: Austria 18.7 per cent, Belgium 21.1 per cent, Denmark 25.5 per cent, Finland 21.4 per cent, France 24.2 per cent, Germany 19.0 per cent, Greece 14.8 per cent, Ireland 13.4 per cent, Italy 18.8 per cent, Luxembourg 14.0 per cent, Netherlands 13.6 per cent, Portugal 20.2 per cent, Spain 15.8 per cent, Sweden 25.9 per cent and the UK 18.2 per cent.

20.   The Cohen and Follette (1999) value with US data (with four lags) was 1.23 which may be compared with our average EMU-10 value of 1.25. When the tax rates were set to zero in the FRB/US model the multiplier increased to 1.35 which indicates how much (or, in fact, little) automatic stabilisers will affect the multiplier. An interesting thing is that the multiplier value of 1.25 implies a relatively low value of the marginal propensity to consume. Assuming the average tax rate to be 0.4 we end up with a marginal propensity to consume to be about 0.3 only (or 0.4 if we account for imports).

21.   The importance of the solvency condition obviously depends on the level of debt in the country concerned. Given the fact that indebtedness still varies a great deal among the EU countries, we again face an aggregation problem in pursuing EU fiscal policies (see Mayes and Virén, 2000, for more about this problem in terms of monetary policy).

12 Fiscal Policy Coordination in EMU: Should it Go Beyond the SGP?*

Sixten Korkman

12.1 INTRODUCTION

The fiscal policy requirements of EMU have attracted much attention in the Community.[1] Since the mid-1990s the discussion has focused almost exclusively on budget discipline in the context of the Stability and Growth Pact (SGP). The SGP stipulates rules which, if adhered to by member states, ensure that 'excessive' general government financial deficits are avoided. This should be helpful for the macroeconomic policy mix by containing upward pressure on interest rates, while at the same time creating room for the automatic fiscal stabilisers to operate. The SGP may also improve the functioning of the economy in more indirect ways: sound public finances, in combination with price stability, should reduce uncertainty of expectations, enhance confidence of market participants, and strengthen incentives for social partners and governments to tackle structural problems hampering the functioning of markets.

It is by now widely agreed that the SGP constitutes an appropriate framework for fiscal policy coordination, though its practical implementation may leave some room for improvement.[2] Fiscal policy coordination has come to be identified with the collective endeavour to ensure budget discipline. This was not always the case: in the 1970s it was thought that fiscal policy at the EU level should contribute more actively towards a favourable macroeconomic development, and in the 1980s schemes were invented for the sharing of macroeconomic risks within a currency area. The ambitions for fiscal policy coordination appear to have been declining at the same time that the single currency is finally becoming reality.

---

* The views expressed in this chapter are those of the author, not of any institution. Useful comments of the editors are acknowledged.

The focus of this chapter is not on the SGP as such, rather on some old but still relevant issues of fiscal policy coordination in EMU going beyond the requirements of the SGP. The chapter starts by recalling the main pillars of the economic policy regime embedded in the Treaty and notably in its provisions on EMU (section 12.2). This framework sets restrictions on national economic policies and foresees (implicit) coordination through policy rules rather than (explicit) coordination in the form of common decisions on discretionary policy actions. Subsequently the chapter considers three main questions. First, is there a case for a fiscal transfer mechanism at the Community level to help euro area member states cope with country-specific disturbances or asymmetric shocks (section 12.3)? Second, does EMU call for action, including in the area of taxation and social security, with a view to strengthening the incentives to price and wage flexibility (section 12.4)? Third, would it be helpful – to avoid misalignments of the external value of the euro and for the sustainability of growth – to aim at coordination (beyond the SGP) so as to influence the aggregate stance of fiscal policy and the macroeconomic policy mix in the euro area as a whole (section 12.5)?

The answers to these three questions suggested in this chapter are roughly no, not really and yes. The answers are partly based on arguments of economic analysis, but they also reflect an assessment of some of the institutional, political and practical difficulties of implementation of policy coordination. The main arguments are summarised in the concluding comments (section 12.6).

12.2   POLICY COORDINATION AND THE ASSIGNMENT PRINCIPLE

Any discussion of policy coordination in EMU should recognise that the Treaty foresees coordination by assignment rather than by discretion. The EC Treaty and notably its Title VII (on economic and monetary policy) contains an 'economic policy constitution' based on certain fundamental principles. The subsidiarity principle is one of these. Also, economic policies must comply with the principle of the market economy with free competition. Furthermore, economic policies shall be geared to monetary and financial stability. These orientations embody key elements of a liberal economic doctrine.

More particularly, the EMU constitutes an economic policy regime based on three main pillars. First, the European Central Bank (ECB) is independent and its prime objective shall be to maintain price stability. The ECB shall also support the general economic policies in the Community, but only on the condition that this can be done 'without prejudice to the objective of price stability'. Second, governments retain competence for other economic policies, but these policies must respect certain Community rules, notably the provisions of the Excessive Deficit Procedure and the SGP (and of the internal market). This constrains the scope for policies leading to big budget deficits and public debts. Third, member states shall consider their economic policies to be of 'common concern' and shall coordinate them within the Council.

While the first two pillars of the economic policy regime of the EMU are spelled out with great clarity and detail in the Treaty and in the relevant secondary legislation, the third pillar is more difficult to characterise. A main instrument for economic policy coordination is set out in Article 99, which requires the Council to develop broad guidelines for the economic policies of the member states and the Community (BEPG), foresees that the implementation of these guidelines be monitored and assessed, and allows the Council to make recommendations if the economic policies of a member state deviate from the guidelines or risk jeopardising the proper functioning of EMU.

Article 99 is silent with regard to the content of the BEPG, and it could therefore be the basis for policy coordination with different ambitions (but only in the form of recommendations and without sanctions for failure to abide by them). Nevertheless, the BEPG cannot undo a fundamental feature of the EMU policy framework, which is that it embodies the particular assignment of instruments and responsibilities to specific actors set out above. The Treaty does not foresee policy actors deciding jointly on policy packages. Instead, the ECB and national governments are foreseen to act independently in their respective fields of competence, with their actions being coordinated only indirectly in that each policy actor respects the assignment of responsibilities as well as the rules defined in the Treaty and in the SGP.[3] The purpose of the framework is thus not to implement coordination in the ordinary sense of the word[4] but rather to reduce the need for discretionary coordination as compared to what would otherwise be necessary.

This set-up reflects the view that close coordination of discretionary economic policies would be extremely complex, might reduce the transparency of the policy regime, could create uncertainty with regard to policy assignments, and would thereby risk undermining the credibility of policies. EMU is, by and large, based on respect for national discretion within a framework of supranational rules.

The assignment principle limits the scope for discretionary coordination but does not preclude policy dialogue, or even some genuine coordination, between policy actors so as to improve the compatibility of decisions on timing and the size of policy changes. A close policy dialogue is indeed essential to avoid communication failures and to strengthen mutual understanding and confidence of decision-makers. It should pave the way for a successful implementation of the assignment principle by enhancing a common understanding of the economic situation as well as of policy problems and options. Also, there is no incompatibility between the assignment principle and coordination in the form of exchange of information and dialogue or multilateral surveillance and peer pressure based on identified 'good practices'.

In practice, economic policy coordination has evolved in such a way that it now amounts to a multitude of instruments and procedures. These include not only the SGP and the BEPG, but also an escalating set of policy processes, each with its own purposes and idiosyncrasies (notably the so-called Luxembourg, Cardiff, Cologne and Lisbon processes). The policy coordination activities involve the Commission, the ECB, numerous committees and Council formations as well as the European Council. The Euro Group, in particular, has emerged as an increasingly significant forum for much of the policy discussion.

Policy coordination is important and attracts much attention in the EU and the euro area. Nevertheless, there are severe constraints on what economic policy coordination can amount to and what it can achieve. This is partly due to uncertainty and forecasting difficulties as well as domestic political constraints. However, it also follows from the character of the policy regime as explained above. In particular, the possibilities for discretionary policy coordination are limited in an overall context of policy-making strongly conditioned by the subsidiarity and assignment principles.

12.3   FISCAL TRANSFERS

The heterogeneity of the EU is associated with risks for asymmetric shocks and divergent developments across countries. This has always been considered the Achilles heel of EMU. The standard argument consists of contrasting the USA and the EU with respect to the requirements of an optimum currency area. The USA has a flexible labour market with relatively high (interstate) mobility, facilitated by a common language, and the USA also has a large federal budget. In the EU, by contrast, labour markets are rigid because of regulations, compressed wage differentials, high taxes and (relatively) generous unemployment benefits. Also, language and other barriers continue to segment the EU into fifteen different labour markets. Furthermore, the EU budget is only a tiny 1 per cent of total GNP in the EU; there is no automatic stabilisation through a federal budget (leaving more of a burden on national stabilisation). The thrust of this reasoning is that Europe needs nationally differentiated monetary policies and flexible exchange rates to avoid the tensions which country-specific disturbances will otherwise give rise to.[5]

Alternatively, so the argument runs, the single currency and the single monetary policy need to be complemented by a mechanism at the euro area level for transfers between member states (amounting to an international insurance mechanism for reducing macroeconomic risks) and/or structural changes to enhance wage and price flexibility (see section 12.4 below). The policy conclusion of this observation used to be that national stabilisation needs the support of a sizeable budget at the Community level to help cushion the consequences of idiosyncratic macroeconomic disturbances in member states.[6]

It is indeed obvious that a large federal budget can function as a shock absorber for the states of which the union is composed. A state in recession relative to the rest of the federation will contribute less to the federal tax revenues and may benefit from increased federal transfers or expenditures on cyclical grounds. The resulting shift in the net flow of revenue should support income and activity in that state as compared to what would happen without federal redistributions. Available studies for the USA indicate that the stabilising effect of the federal budget is of considerable significance.[7] Another version of the argument is that the EU or EMU could usefully set up a specific Community transfer scheme to help countries with a high or increasing rate of unemployment by means of financial transfers from countries with a low or decreasing rate of unemployment.[8] This could take the form of, for example, a Community unemployment benefit system.

In the second half of the 1990s however, the literature on fiscal transfers has taken a more sombre or negative attitude to the usefulness of such redistributions, and has done so for several reasons. First, considerable stabilisation can and will take place already because private financial markets are highly integrated, notably in EMU, and this gives the private sector ample opportunities for diminishing risks by portfolio diversification. Second, automatic budget stabilisers are a key feature of the public finances of all EU member states, offering a degree of automatic stabilisation comparable to the role of the federal budget in the USA. Changes in budget positions caused by the cycle amount to a system of stabilisation through intertemporal redistribution of purchasing power. Third, member states may, if they so deem appropriate, complement the functioning of the automatic stabilisers with discretionary actions to change public expenditure, transfers or taxes in a countercyclical way. In EMU such fiscal policies would not, at the level of member states, lead to any significant counteracting repercussions of the exchange rate or interest rates. In principle, fiscal policy may be expected to be more effective in EMU than with pegged or flexible exchange rates.

Stabilisation can thus be achieved by intertemporal if not interregional redistributions, and one may therefore dispute the need for interregional transfers. Indeed, it has been shown that a scheme of fiscal transfers may in fact not help authorities of a member state to compensate for whatever monetary policy autonomy they may be giving up by adopting the euro.[9] This is not to deny that a system of international transfers might be effective in reducing macroeconomic risks; the point is rather that the value of such a scheme, if any, has nothing to do with EMU as such.

The argument that no Community-level scheme for fiscal transfers is called for because of EMU is weaker or different if the use of fiscal policy for domestic stabilisation is hampered by constraints associated with the functioning of financial markets or the budget deficit ceilings imposed by the SGP. In practice, fiscal policy can be successfully used for stabilisation only if a sufficient degree of budget discipline is maintained over the cycle. If not, a member state in a recession might be unable to relax its fiscal policy and might even have to tighten it in a situation with rising unemployment. Fiscal transfers could help countries in such situations, by allowing them to smooth the cycle in a way which is otherwise not feasible. However, this observation only brings out that a system of fiscal transfers to help countries with large budget deficits is difficult to reconcile with the SGP (as well as with the 'no bailout rule'); the one is in contradiction with the other.

The view that the SGP restricts fiscal policy autonomy excessively should be without foundation once member states have achieved the medium-term balance foreseen in the SGP, and provided that the SGP is subsequently implemented properly so as to ensure room for fiscal stabilisers to operate. But even if the criticism were accepted, it seems unjustified to conclude that there is a need to introduce a supranational scheme for fiscal transfers. The obvious conclusion, if the SGP is thought to hamper fiscal policy autonomy excessively, is to modify or abolish the SGP.

Anyway, a fiscal transfer scheme to reduce the macroeconomic consequences of asymmetric shocks will not come into existence. The arguments for the scheme are poor, it would be associated with very serious problems of moral hazard, the specifics of such a mechanism might easily lead to permanent redistributions and would be extremely difficult to negotiate, and any decision would have to be taken unanimously. This is a matter for theoretical debate, not for action on a proposal with a view to practical implementation.

While it is unlikely to lead to practical results, the sporadic discussion of transfer schemes nevertheless highlights a significant characteristic of EMU as a union. Member states in the euro area are strongly interrelated, and this interdependence is sometimes referred to euphemistically as a 'shared destiny' or a 'marriage contract'. However, EMU is a framework for competition and discipline, not for solidarity in the same sense as within a nation state. Such solidarity may be politically attractive on its own merits (despite problematic incentive effects) and it has a role in the Community (cf. the structural funds), but there is no compelling case that EMU would necessitate schemes giving expression to such solidarity in order to function properly.

12.4 FLEXIBILITY

The literature on optimum currency areas (OCA) assesses the merits of alternative exchange rate regimes. It argues notably that fixed rates (a currency area) are superior to flexible exchange rates in terms of macroeconomic stabilisation if monetary shocks are relatively frequent and real assymmetric shocks rare, if money wages adjust in a flexible manner (or if labour is mobile across frontiers), and if the constituent countries are highly open and have diversified production structures.[10]

As considerable cyclical divergence will no doubt continue to exist in the euro area, it is in this perspective important that each country can adjust flexibly to disturbances. Adjustment problems related to asymmetric shocks are bound to pose challenges to the government and its fiscal policies. Flexibility of labour and commodity markets is conditional on the legal and regulatory framework, but depends also on social security and tax systems. This could imply that governments in the euro area should take action, including in the area of taxation and social security (as well as in labour market policies), with a view to strengthening the incentives to cost adjustment, job creation and mobility on labour markets. In other words, EMU needs to be supported by structural reforms enhancing efficiency and flexibility.

It may also be argued that there is some 'common interest' to enhance the capacity of euro area member states to adjust to changes, since adjustment problems will have repercussions on other countries in the EMU. Policy trade-offs at both the national and the euro area level could worsen if adjustment problems (notably in large member states) were leading to more inflation or a process of cumulative divergence between member states. This might give rise to tensions and uncertainty with regard to the ways in which imbalances will in the end be resolved (reflected in risk premia and pressure on the currency). The importance of spillovers linked to the euro could thus justify concerted euro area action to enhance flexibility in labour and goods markets. Such action is called for notably if lack of flexibility in member states has systemic consequences, and if there is a 'free rider' problem in the sense that incentives for individual member states to promote flexibility are too weak from the point of view of the euro area as a whole.

It should be noted, however, that conditions in EMU are such as to reward flexibility and penalise rigidity. A member state in recession will find that relative cost reductions, notably in the competitive conditions prevailing in EMU, allow market shares to be gained within the euro area (as well as globally), and this should give decision-makers and economic agents strong incentives to accept and promote such flexibility. Indeed, the fear is occasionally expressed that competitive pressure in EMU will lead to 'excessive' flexibility in the form of deflationary nominal wage decreases or social dumping. Social partners therefore suggest that coordination is needed to reduce the scope for competitive adjustments. On the other hand, it is often thought that there is a political or institutional bias towards rigidity, and the flexibility induced by competition may be a useful counterweight to such a bias. The net effect of these forces will depend on country-specific circumstances.

Lack of adjustment will, for the member state in question, have serious consequences for competitiveness, growth and employment and there will be repercussions on other member states (more so if the member state in question is a big one). However, there need not be important systemic consequences, notably if the SGP and the relevant secondary legislation (including the 'no bail-out rule' and the safeguards of the independence of the central bank) are respected and credible. Adjustment problems may give rise to risk premia, but these should then be country-specific rather than generalised.

An important rebuttal to the view that EMU calls for money wage flexibility has been made by Willem Buiter,[11] who considers cyclical non-synchronisation and the associated adjustment problems as largely irrelevant for the EMU debate. The main elements of his argument are as follows. First, monetary policy has no real effects in the long run (neutrality), and focus should therefore be on the short- to medium-term effects. Second, the lags between monetary policy changes and their effects are not only long and variable but also highly uncertain, and monetary policy can therefore not be used successfully for 'fine-tuning'. Third, exchange rate changes do not in practice function as a shock absorber to trade balance or income changes, but are mainly driven by volatile flows of financial capital. As a consequence, autonomous monetary policies and exchange rate flexibility are not an effective response to adjustment problems, but are rather likely to add to the instability of the economy as a whole.

In short, the OCA theory of the 1960s is 'out of date, misleading and a dangerous guide to policy' (Buiter, 1999) in the circumstances now prevailing, which are characterised by unrestricted mobility of financial capital as well as by high risks for volatility and misalignments of exchange rates. Membership in a currency area therefore reduces macroeconomic instability as compared to monetary autonomy. An obvious corollary is that EMU as such cannot be considered to call for actions to promote flexibility.

Two further observations seem appropriate in this context. First, adjustment is obviously much more important in relation to permanent than temporary disturbances. Adjustments to permanent disturbances are likely to necessitate changes in relative wages and prices between sectors and regions as well as between countries, which means that the exchange rate is in any case a rather blunt mechanism. Also, such disturbances call for permanent adjustment in labour and product markets, while monetary policies as such have only transient effects related to nominal rigidities (unless 'hysteresis' is a significant phenomenon). It might be argued that EMU may facilitate the required adjustment as employers and employees know that they will pay the cost of bad decisions as there is no prospect of a monetary bail-out in the form of an injection of inflation through a devaluation.[12]

Second, the arguments of Buiter obviously do not amount to stating that monetary policy is irrelevant for output stabilisation; it can most likely be used to prevent extreme swings in economic activity. But this is essentially a question of the central bank acting as a lender of last resort to contain serious financial crises, and that can be done in a currency area as well as under monetary autonomy.

The essential argument is that adjustment in EMU should not be compared with what is conceivable with an idealised functioning of autonomous monetary policy and exchange rate flexibility, but rather with what is likely in the light of frequent monetary policy failures and problematic exchange rate turbulence. EMU is certainly likely to function better if costs and prices adjust smoothly, but adjustment problems related to nominal rigidities are a problem whatever the exchange rate regime, and it might be that the problems are worse with flexible exchange rates than in EMU.

This conclusion does not amount to denying the significance of the considerable work which has recently been done, as part of economic policy coordination in the EU, on structural changes or economic reforms to enhance flexibility and efficiency. The Cardiff process, in particular, sets common guidelines and national targets, uses national and Community reports to describe and evaluate the functioning of both real and financial market by the help of indicators and benchmarking, identifies 'best practices', and uses peer pressure to encourage member states to reform their policies.[13] This process enhances transparency of structural policies, facilitates a learning process, and underpins healthy competition between all EU member states.[14]

12.5   THE STANCE OF EURO AREA FISCAL POLICY AND THE MACROECONOMIC POLICY MIX

The stance of fiscal policy and the fiscal–monetary policy mix are key concepts of economic policy analysis (the use of which do not imply endorsement of fiscal fine-tuning). In the context of the euro area, however, the stance of fiscal policy plays a much less prominent role in analysis and debate. Yet it is clear that there is no reason to expect the sum of the fiscal policies of twelve individual member states always to be appropriate for the euro area. This gives rise to the following two questions. First, is there a case in principle for coordination[15] so as to ensure that the aggregate stance of fiscal policy and the macroeconomic policy mix is appropriate at the level of the euro area as a whole? Second, is it feasible – in other words, are there, in the light of the Treaty and other institutional considerations, practically enviseagable ways of achieving such coordination?

12.5.1 The Case for Coordination

The answer to the first question depends on the fiscal spillovers, that is, on the effects of fiscal policy in one euro area country on the economic situation in the other member states of the euro area. Fiscal expansion in one country will affect neighbour countries through both real and financial channels. Increased demand and activity in one member state will increase imports and thereby the level of demand and activity in the other euro area countries. However, higher income will also tend to raise the interest rate and may thereby lead to some appreciation of the euro, and the tightening of monetary conditions will offset some or all of the expansionary effects of the fiscal stimulus.[16]

A more precise assessment of the effects can thus be done only in terms of specific models. A natural benchmark model for such an analysis is the old workhorse of international macroeconomics, the Mundell–Fleming (MF) model. This model, which applies to an area which is small relative to the global economy and is based on a number of strong assumptions,[17] produces some strikingly simple results, in particular:

- Fiscal expansion (in one or several member states) will have no effect on total output in the euro area as a whole. This is just a restatement of the familiar conclusion that fiscal policy is ineffective under floating exchange rates; the expansionary effects of higher government expenditure or lower taxes on domestic demand are offset by the crowding-out of net exports due to an appreciation of the exchange rate. However, this conclusion holds only for the euro area as a whole.
- Fiscal expansion will increase activity in the country undertaking the expansionary measures, that is, for that country the effects on domestic demand are less than fully offset by the fall in net

exports. It follows that the reverse is true for the other member states; for them the positive demand effects are more than offset by the fall in net exports caused by the appreciation of the exchange rate.[18]

The significance of these conclusions will differ according to the covariation of the problems faced by countries within the monetary union. Assume first that the situation is *asymmetric* in that member states face different cyclical situations and problems. The use of fiscal policy for domestic stabilisation will in this case be valuable to the member state concerned (if the problems of fine-tuning, referred to below, can be avoided) and should pose no problems to the other member states. A deep recession in one member state, tending to lower interest rates, would induce a depreciation of the exchange rate and would thereby add to problems in member states suffering from inflationary pressure. Fiscal expansion by the member state concerned to counter the recession could help to limit or avoid these (harmful) repercussions. Similarly, an unconstrained boom in one part of the euro area will tighten monetary conditions with detrimental effects on countries suffering from recession. Tight fiscal policies in countries with strong activity would be cyclically appropriate in those member states and should ease monetary conditions to the benefit of countries with weak activity. (This consideration has for some time now suggested fiscal tightening in countries in the 'periphery' to the benefit of the 'core'.) Countercyclical fiscal policies are in the interest of the member state concerned as well as of the euro area as a whole. There is no obvious need for coordination, rather for encouraging member states to use (wisely and without violating the SGP) their fiscal policy autonomy.

Assume next that the situation is *symmetric* in the sense that all or most member states face a situation with excess capacity and high unemployment. Fiscal expansion will in this case be effective but also amount to a beggar-thy-neighbour policy: one country in recession may increase its activity by fiscal expansion, but this happens at the expense of activity in the other member states of the monetary union. The situation is similar if all or most member states experience high levels of activity and capacity utilisation (with risks for inflationary pressure): one member state may restrain aggregate demand by fiscal tightening, but this will increase external demand for the area as a whole by weakening the exchange rate. There will be effects on the composition of demand and output (which may have policy relevance) but total demand and activity are unaffected.

Obviously there may be a case for fiscal policy coordination. Also, coordination is unlikely to come about by itself and may be difficult to achieve. To see this, assume that the euro area were to consist of two countries which both may pursue either 'tight' or 'loose' fiscal policies. As just noted, the area-wide level of activity will always be the same, as fiscal policy (in the MF model) affects only the composition but not the level of activity for the monetary union as a whole. At the level of the individual country, however, the effects will depend on the relative stance of fiscal policies; country A will experience increased activity if it pursues a fiscal policy which is more expansionary than that of country B.

Assuming that the level of activity is lower than aspired to, the non-cooperative outcome may well be a ('prisoners' dilemma') situation, in which both countries pursue loose policies. Both countries may be worse off than if they chose a tight fiscal policy (as the composition of demand may be distorted), yet unproductive laxity may be the outcome unless there is a mechanism for agreeing to abstain from fiscal expansion.

The SGP will help to restrain fiscal policies but only to a limited extent, as it is operative mainly if countries are at or close to the deficit ceilings. These are more likely to become operative in a recession and will then restrict the scope for fiscal expansion. This may be perceived as unfortunate by member states, but would actually help avoid futile measures of fiscal expansion (futile in the sense of failing to stimulate activity in the euro area as a whole).

A more obvious problem is that the SGP may not ensure sufficient fiscal restraint when this is needed most, that is, when many countries in the euro area simultaneously experience a boom and budget balances are comfortable (partly due to the boom). No member state may then feel a need to tighten its fiscal policy, yet this tightening could be desirable to avoid a monetary tightening and an associated exchange rate appreciation with detrimental effects on external balance and long-term growth. Fiscal laxity could manifest itself as a tendency to (pro-cyclical) fiscal expansion in times of buoyant economic activity, and it could also have the consequence of delaying the easing of monetary policy when the area approaches recession. At worst a stalemate could arise, in which the ECB would hesitate to lower interest rates because of lax fiscal policies, while governments would hesitate to tighten fiscal policies because of concerns about weak demand associated with tight monetary policy.

The analysis above is compatible with the assignment of policy roles set out or allowed for in the Treaty: monetary policy should be pursued with a view to the euro area as a whole, while fiscal policies should help stabilise macroeconomic developments of individual member states.[19] Respect for the assignment should be helpful, but a main problem for coordination may remain: lack of sufficient incentives at the level of member states for fiscal restraint in situations of high activity in the area as a whole. Concerted action for fiscal restraint might then be called for to contain inflationary pressure and to induce a composition of demand (favourable to investment and exports) compatible with sustained growth. Otherwise each government may simply wait (acting as a 'free rider') for other member states to tighten their fiscal policies to support an appropriate area-wide policy mix.

The simplicity of the policy conclusions set out above largely follows from the fact that the MF model implies a separation, according to which fiscal policy affects only the composition of demand (while monetary policy has effects on overall developments). However, there are many reasons why the effects of fiscal policies may be more complicated than assumed above. First, fiscal policies will have effects on overall output if monetary policy is accommodating, offsetting the monetary repercussions of higher activity and bigger deficits. Monetary accommodation allows fiscal stabilisation to be effective and is (often implicitly) assumed in most of the occasional pleas for concerted fiscal reflation in the euro area.[20]

Second, fiscal policy will have area-wide effects on activity if the monetary union is big enough to affect the global level of interest rates.[21] It might still be desirable that monetary policy be the prime instrument for stabilisation of area-wide developments, but there would nevertheless be a choice to be made. Governments might conceivably be tempted to aim at coordinated fiscal expansion, particularly if the ECB were perceived to be insufficiently sensitive to the problem of unemployment and if it was seen as unduly disregarding the risks of a severe recession.

Third, time lags in the effects of competitiveness on exports imply that fiscal policy could be effective with regard to area-wide activity in the short run even if not in the medium or long term. Again, there would be a possibility of arguing for coordination between fiscal policies and monetary policy. For instance, in a generalised recession one could argue that both monetary expansion and a period of coordinated fiscal stimulus would be needed to achieve rapid effects, and that fiscal policies should subsequently be restricted as the effects of monetary expansion start to feed through.[22]

Fourth, and whatever the other transmission mechanisms, policy actions of individual member states may in practice affect market expectations concerning economic policy behaviour more generally and thereby the credibility of euro area policies and prospects. There is therefore a common interest to have at least a close monitoring of member states' policies (and a strict application of the SGP).

The external value of the euro is clearly a key variable in the transmission of spillovers (within the area and in relation to third countries), and the exchange rate is intimately related to the policy mix. The standard case is that expansionary fiscal policy leads to an appreciation,[23] as illustrated by the strong dollar related to the fiscal expansion of the Reagan administration and the appreciation of European currencies in the wake of German reunification.

However, fiscal expansion may raise concerns about inflation or future deficits and the sustainability of policies, and may for this reason lead to a depreciation of the exchange rate, possibly accompanied by a rise in long-term interest rates. This could amount to a stagflationary shock for other member states, that is, fiscal expansion would again have negative cross-border effects though the transmission mechanism would be a different one.

It is obvious that the whole issue of the fiscal–monetary policy mix would come into a very different light if policy-makers were to adopt an explicit exchange rate policy. Such a policy would be bound to have strong implications for monetary policy because of the close link between exchange rates and interest rates. It is a widely held view that sterilised interventions in foreign exchange markets are unlikely to be effective, whereas unsterilised interventions have consequences for liquidity, which may come into conflict with the objectives of monetary policy.

Given that both the USA and the euro area are relatively closed economic entities, and assuming that the monetary authorities in both areas focus primarily on the respective domestic situation, there is a risk for large swings in the euro–dollar exchange rate. This potential for misaligned exchange rates occasionally leads to demands for an explicit exchange rate policy to stabilise relations between the key currencies (the euro and the dollar). The mainstream view, however, is that the significance of short-term fluctuations (volatility) in exchange rates should not be overrated, and that exchange rate trends mostly reflect fundamentals, including the monetary–fiscal policy mix. The Council has taken the view that it should use its powers to decide on 'general orientations on exchange rate policy' only in exceptional circumstances, for example, in the case of a clear misalignment.[24]

In all, the domestic and cross-border effects of fiscal policies may differ significantly accordingly to initial conditions and the economic situation, the monetary and exchange rate policy pursued, relevant time lags and (not least) the effects on private sector anticipations of future policies and prospective imbalances. The policy conclusions will obviously differ from case to case. These complexities and uncertainties need to be considered when setting ambitions for fiscal policy coordination.

12.5.2   The Feasibility of Coordination

Given the significance of macroeconomic and financial spillovers in the euro area, there obviously are potential gains from policy coordination. However, there are several practical, institutional and political reasons why the potential may be difficult to exploit. Some of the conditions for successful policy coordination may be formulated as follows:

- Policy coordination must be compatible with the existing economic policy regime, which for EMU is the one set out in the Treaty (see section 12.2 above). Coordination always takes place within a given framework, and decisions on the former are to be kept separate from decisions on the latter. Otherwise there is a risk of lack of coherence and negative credibility effects.
- The methods of coordination should be robust in the sense of being compatible with a wide range of economic circumstances. As noted above, the character and significance of policy spillovers will differ according to factors which are not always well understood and are often difficult to predict. This constrains the scope for realistic policy aspirations.
- Coordination needs an operational framework with modalities allowing for good preparation, sufficient flexibility and reasonable effectiveness. The framework involves decision-makers and officials from Community institutions as well as from various ministries in member states, and to manage it effectively is a big challenge.
- The process should contribute to an articulation of policy positions which is coherent both internally (within the euro area) and externally (on the global level). To ensure that the euro area

'speaks with one voice' is, however, no easy task since representation cannot be dissociated from the assignment of policy competencies.

These requirements are general and yet helpful when assessing the possibilities for dealing successfully with the complexities and challenges of policy and policy coordination. By far the most important consideration is that the policy framework needs to be simple and the level of ambitions modest for the process to be manageable. Some conclusions on specific features of economic policy coordination would seem to be as follows.

Discretionary Coordination

Setting targets for the area-wide fiscal policy lacks clear meaning (and allows for 'free riding') unless there is agreement on actions by individual member states. However, it would be overly ambitious to aim at discretionary coordination, notably with formal or binding agreements, in order to attain an 'appropriate' aggregate stance of fiscal policy within the euro area. Experience of fine-tuning at the national level has seldom been encouraging, because of difficulties arising from time lags in decision-making, forecasting errors, political 'ratchet effects' and effects on private sector expectations. These difficulties would be much aggravated by negotiations at the level of the euro area, which would have to interact with domestic political processes, including those with national parliaments. Also, discretionary coordination might be perceived as being incompatible with the policy regime, and the information requirements of coordination would be formidable. Finally, fiscal policy measures are of limited usefulness if shocks are permanent rather than transitory, in which case adjustment of relative costs rather than financing is called for.

The Euro Group

The complexities of the issues strengthen the case for dialogue between ministers, and with the ECB, to enhance a common understanding of the economic situation and outlook as well as of policy risks and problems. There are several frameworks for this dialogue, but the Euro Group is clearly a forum of particular importance. Dialogue in the regularly held meetings of the Euro Group has great potential for clarifying the 'common interests' at stake and forging consensus views of the participants. This should reduce the risk of misunderstandings and build mutual thrust, thus paving the way for appropriate coordination while respecting the assignment of responsibilities. The Euro Group is likely to assume particular importance at times of economic stress; a common position of relevant decision-makers may then contribute importantly to maintaining confidence in policies and policy coordination.

Fiscal Policy Guidelines

Coordination in an area with a dozen or more members must, to a considerable extent, focus on rules or guidelines, and on monitoring their implementation by member states. The rules of the SGP are sometimes perceived as crude from an economic point of view, but politically they are quite helpful by giving a strong message about budget discipline. As noted above, the SGP might usefully be complemented by a set of orientations to encourage budget discipline in times of buoyant activity (when the SGP is unlikely to be operative). Guidelines recently suggested by the Commission are that tax reductions should be fully compatible with the SGP, should take into account the debt level and long-term budget sustainability, should not be pro-cyclical, and should form part of a comprehensive reform package.[25]

In particular, practical experience and anecdotal evidence suggest that politicians are tempted to make pro-cyclical tax decisions in times of strong economic growth and when the economic outlook is favourable. Empirical findings support the view that pro-cyclical fiscal decisions are a major problem.[26] The guideline that member states should avoid pro-cyclical tax changes could therefore usefully be elaborated upon and given operational content by, for instance, agreeing that member states commit themselves not to undertake major tax changes without first allowing for a presentation and discussion in the Council and/or the Euro Group. Such a discussion could result in an opinion or a recommendation,[27] which need not necessarily focus on the specific content of the envisaged tax reform, but should take a position on the appropriate timing of its implementation.

It would also be useful if member states committed themselves, more strongly than is presently the case, to abstain from public expenditure increases whenever growth turns out to be stronger than envisaged in their Stability Programmes. This would help automatic stabilisers operate and reduce the risks for pro-cyclical policies. High growth and activity levels should not only be associated with improvements in actual or recorded government balances; underlying or structural government financial balances should also improve or at least not deteriorate. This should be an essential ingredient of any code of conduct for fiscal policy.

Exchange Rate Policy

The exchange rate is, as noted above, a crucial link for interdependence and transmission of policy effects between the euro area and the global economy. An important provision in the EC Treaty stipulates that the Council may formulate 'general orientations' for exchange rate policy (and, in principle, even enter into formal exchange rate agreements) in relation to non-EC currencies (Article 111). As noted in the Resolution of the European Council adopted in Luxembourg in December 1997, interventions in foreign exchange markets (based on such orientations) may play some role in addressing situations with clearly 'misaligned' exchange rates. However, exchange rate orientations would, if implemented in practice, impose strong constraints on the monetary policy of the ECB. It is for this reason that the Luxembourg Resolution also reiterates Article 111 to the effect that 'These general orientations should always respect the independence of the ESCB and be consistent with the primary objective of the ESCB to maintain price stability'. This stipulation limits considerably the scope for exchange rate orientations issued at the discretion of the Council. Given the complexities of exchange rate behaviour and the potential difficulties of reconciling exchange rate policy with the Treaty assignment of policy responsibilities, it would seem prudent largely to abstain from (explicit) exchange rate policies. This does not preclude concerted interventions in specific situations, as in September 2000.

Mr Euro

The external value of the euro is intimately related to the policy mix, and coherence of euro area policy messages on this issue is of course of great significance. Close contacts between ministers and the ECB help decision-makers handle communication of sensitive topics (like exchange rates) both within the EU as well as in international fora (like the G7). It has been suggested that the Euro Group should be chaired by one and the same person for a period of, for example, two years, in order to facilitate systematic work, ensure continuity and visibility in external relations, and enhance internal coherence in the euro area. It has even been suggested to appoint a special 'High

Representative for economic policy' (Mr Euro) so as to have visibly 'a pilot in the plane'. However, the task of Mr Euro could be rendered difficult by the lack of a well-defined platform: monetary policy is the competence of the ECB, general economic policies fall within national subsidiarity, while the basis for policy coordination (and for a possible Mr Euro) is rather vague (see section 12.2). It is conceivable that Mr Euro would experience difficulties of 'cohabitation' with the ECB in times of tensions over exchange rates.

12.6   CONCLUDING COMMENTS

A key feature of the economic policy regime of EMU, often thought to be intriguing, is that power over monetary policy is centralised in the hands of a supranational central bank, while other policies remain mainly in the realm of national sovereignty. A more general way of making this observation is to note that the euro is 'a currency without a state'. Views continue to differ as to the economic and political significance of this asymmetry.

One view is that EMU is essentially a monetary arrangement. What matters is the independence of the ECB and the definition of a clear objective for its monetary policy, in combination with safeguards for budget discipline. This will foster a 'stability culture'. Markets can be assumed to function efficiently and adjust smoothly, notably if the public sector refrains from excessive regulations, if obstacles to competition are abolished, and if tax and social security systems are reformed to encourage flexibility. Centralised monetary policy not only can but should go hand in hand with decentralised fiscal and other policies so as to allow nationally differentiated responses to country-specific disturbances. Policy cooperation beyond the SGP, if any, should be non-binding, taking the form of, for example, exchange of information and mutual consultation.

Others think of EMU as an embryo of a political union. The asymmetry between monetary and fiscal policies is a fault of design, which will sooner or later lead to tensions between policy areas and member states. A good functioning of EMU will in this perspective require a further shift of policy competencies from the national to the Community level so as to reconcile the consequences of integration with aspirations for more ambitious policies. This would require changes to the Treaty (of a kind for which there is presently little inclination among member states).

The present trend is to strike a balance between these views and to focus on clarifying and reinforcing certain aspects of economic policy coordination within the institutional limits set by the Treaty. As suggested above, some important considerations with regard to this evolving coordination are as follows. First, economic policy coordination in the euro area is very much a process of learning by doing. It is conceivable that circumstances will arise in which high ambitions for discretionary coordination can be met, exchange rate coordination attracts a lot of international attention, and the euro area needs to appoint a person to represent its policy views. For the time being, however, political and practical considerations suggest relying on the SGP and simple assignments of policies, complemented by guidelines for fiscal policies (going beyond the SGP) and intense dialogue in the Euro Group.

Second, fiscal policy autonomy is appropriate (as long as the SGP is respected), and there is no need in EMU for a mechanism for fiscal transfers at the Community level to help member states deal with the consequences of idiosyncratic developments. Such a scheme would risk giving wrong incentives to economic agents and policy-makers and could therefore be counterproductive. EMU is not a transfer union.

Third, there is need for action in the area of structural policies to enhance the capacity of member states to adjust to changing circumstances, such as changes in technology and world markets. This emphasis is relevant for all member states in the EU (which is thus an appropriate context for Community discussions of structural reform). As argued above, the specific relevance for EMU of structural policies to enhance flexibility and efficiency may occasionally be overstated; EMU will function better to the extent that economic agents and markets adapt flexibly, but the need for supply-side measures is not necessarily stronger in EMU than under alternative monetary regimes.

Fourth, the Euro Group meets a genuine demand in providing ministers, the Commission and the ECB with a forum for debate of sensitive issues of common interest. Policy rules are very useful but also simplistic; discretion is essential for policies even if it would not lead to explicit coordination of decisions. Discussions in the Euro Group foster consensus and can be expected to forge a common position on key issues, particularly in times when this matters most (in times of high uncertainty and market turbulence).

Finally, while the SGP is a valuable framework for enhanced budget discipline (with a clear political message and balance between national sovereignty and Community obligations), it is reasonable to ask what will happen if and when its requirements are increasingly fulfilled. Comfortable budget positions could reflect sound fiscal policies, but may also be a consequence of strong economic growth and high activity levels. Unchecked growth risks trigger inflationary pressure, associated with high interest rates and an excessive strengthening of the euro. Such developments would compromise longer-term growth prospects by encouraging too much private and public consumption relative to exports and investment. To sustain growth it will therefore sooner or later be necessary to call for fiscal tightening. Experience suggests that the political will or capacity to implement tight fiscal policies is likely to be lacking just when it is most needed.

There is nothing in the SGP (nor in the other rules of EMU) to prevent member states from undertaking pro-cyclical expenditure increases and tax reductions during periods of strong growth. It would in this perspective make sense to develop fiscal policy guidelines, complementing the SGP, to encourage member states to avoid fiscal laxity in years of upswing and buoyant activity. This need not entail attempts at fiscal fine-tuning; the focus should rather be on avoiding pro-cyclical tax and expenditure changes and on ensuring a proper functioning of the automatic stabilisers.

There are indeed increasingly signs that fiscal policy in the euro area is presently (in the years 2000 and 2001), at a time of robust growth and increasingly high rates of capacity utilisation, becoming more expansionary when assessed in terms of cyclically adjusted or structural budget positions. It would be ironic if success of the SGP were to allow governments to repeat the frequently made historical mistake of pursuing excessively lax fiscal policies in good times to the detriment of prospects for healthy growth to be sustained.

Notes

1. See, for example, Werner *et al.* (1970), McDougall *et al.* (1977), Delors *et al.* (1989), European Commission (1990, 1993, 1994).
2. The favourable appreciation of the SGP is, unsurprisingly, more common among officials, ministers and central bankers than among those outside the decision-making process, notably the academic community; see, for example, Eichengreen and Wyplosz (1998); Muet (1998); Fitoussi *et al.* (1999).

3. This may be referred to as 'implicit coordination'; see Remsperger (1999) and Italianer (1999).
4. Coordination is in the international literature mostly understood to refer to mutual adjustment of policy parameters; see, for example, Bryant (1995). In EU discussions, however, coordination is increasingly used as a generic term covering, *inter alia*, exchange of information, dialogue, multilateral surveillance of common rules and agreements on discretionary action.
5. See, for example, Eichengreen (1997).
6. McDougall *et al.* (1977).
7. For various estimates see Sala-i-Martin and Sachs (1992), Bayoumi and Masson (1995), Italianer and Pisani-Ferry (1992), von Hagen (1992b).
8. Italianer and Vanheukelen (1993), Wyplosz (1991).
9. Kletzer (1998).
10. The origins of the OCA literature are Mundell (1961), McKinnon (1963) and Kenen (1969).
11. Buiter (1999).
12. An evaluation of this argument is presented by Calmfors (1998, 2000).
13. The Luxembourg process uses the same method to foster well-functioning labour markets and high employment. While there is some overlap of the Cardiff and Luxembourg processes, the former feeds into the BEPG and the latter results in the adoption at the Community level of employment guidelines. Also, the former tends to reflect the views of ministers of finance and economy, while the latter gives more attention to the views of ministers of social affairs and employment.
14. The issues covered by the Cardiff process will henceforth also be discussed by the European Council in its annual spring meeting (the Lisbon process). It is hoped that this will encourage structural reforms and policies so as to enhance the capacity of Europe to adjust to changes in world markets and technologies.
15. Another possible motive for budgetary discussions at the Community level, not covered here, would be to encourage institutional and procedural reform aimed at improving the quality of the national policy process; see von Hagen and Harden (1996).
16. The monetary repercussions are problematic particularly if the expansionary fiscal policy were also to fuel inflationary pressures and expectations, in which case the effect on interest rates could be more pronounced and the exchange rate could depreciate rather than appreciate. In practice, a major consideration will be the consequences of specific fiscal actions on financial market perceptions of prospective budget deficits (see below).
17. Key simplifying assumptions of the model are that wages and prices are treated as given, the complexities of exchange rate expectations are disregarded by assuming them to be static, and the area analysed is assumed to be too small to affect the global level of interest rates. See Krugman and Obstfeld (1997) or de Grauwe (1996).
18. See Kenen (1995) or, for a formal analysis of these conclusions, Hansen and Nielsen (1997) and Levin (1983).
19. Cf. Buti and Sapir (1998).

20. See, for example, Ambrosi (1999).
21. It is argued in Boyer (1999) that EMU is big enough to affect the global interest rate level and that concerted fiscal policy action therefore is effective.
22. For an exposition of the argument that time lags and uncertainty call for explicit (*ex ante*) coordination in the form of deals between ministers and the ECB see CEPS (1999). A strong plea for forceful and institutionalised macroeconomic policy cooperation was also put forward in a report by Notre Europe in March 1999.
23. See IMF (1995).
24. It is also consistent with this view that the ECB should intervene in the foreign exchange markets only when certain preconditions are met: the Council considers that the euro is misaligned, market sentiments are such as to allow interventions to make a difference, and other G7 partners are willing to participate in concerted interventions (as in September 2000).
25. See the European Commission (2000a).
26. See OECD (1999b) and Buti and Sapir (1998).
27. Such a recommendation could be based on Article 99(4). The Council could conceivably elaborate a procedure for such consultations (or, more broadly, for a code of conduct for fiscal policy) in the form of a Council Regulation based on Article 99(5).

Part VI
Public Debt Under the Stability and Growth Pact

13 Optimal Debt Under a Deficit Constraint

Massimo Rostagno, Javier Pérez-García and Paul Hiebert

13.1 INTRODUCTION

It has been consistently argued by many that European Union member states, in the context of significant demographic change in coming years, should pursue a more rigorous course of accelerated debt abatement in order to reduce the burden on future taxpayers. In this vein, these observers point to the need for a new fiscal paradigm more solidly based on the principles of sustainability and intergenerational responsibility. One tool to help in generating this outcome is the adoption of a rule-rather than discretion-based fiscal policy, given the success of this approach in the conduct of monetary policy. In order to produce a more credible and predictable path for future fiscal policy, there would be a need to curtail systematic discretionary policy and resuscitate the role of automatic stabilisers in government policy. In the past, the effectiveness of shock absorbers has been often severely reduced as the result of discretionary action, leading to a need for high interest spending and accompanied by recurrent spells of deficit and debt crises.

The constraint on the size of the deficit laid out in the Stability and Growth Pact (SGP) can be seen as a key contribution in this respect. In setting a clear limit upon the amount that governments can borrow on an annual basis, it provides a clear basis upon which the assessment of government policy can be based. As a general principle, the SGP implicitly prescribes that economies which are more prone to macroeconomic fluctuations and/or whose public budget is more sensitive to cyclical conditions should aim for a lower deficit on average in order to insure themselves against the risk of breaching the limit once at a trough of a severe recession (see Figure 13.1). This follows from the counter-cyclicality of budget deficits, keeping in mind that the deficit ceiling contained in the SGP has to be observed in nearly all states of nature, barring only extreme circumstances. Consequently, with a deficit limit – say, 3 per cent of GDP – an estimate of the degree to which the deficit ratio varies in response to cyclical fluctuations – denoted as a – and a measure of the maximum output gap likely to be realised – call it *MOG* – it is straightforward to estimate a deficit level, $d^* = 3\% - aMOG$, which, if consistently obeyed whenever the GDP is at its capacity level – that is, the output gap is zero – can insure the government against breaching the limit in the fact of 'normal' cyclical fluctuations (see Chapter 8 above).

Likewise, on the basis of the same reasoning, it is possible to pin down the debt/GDP ratio that a government should target in the long run, b^*. Indeed, if the deficit is to be equal to d^* on average for ever, then by compounding that numerical value at the expected growth rate of the economy n, it is easy to recover the ratio to which the debt as a percentage of GDP will gradually converge and around which it will fluctuate over the long haul, namely $b^* = -d^*/n$. Therefore, one can safely conclude that, given an estimate of a – along with an exogenous deficit limit – an associated debt level b^* is implied, consistent with sustaining a normal deficit of d^* for ever.

Nevertheless, this simple fiscal arithmetic – straightforward and nice as it may seem – does not suffice to pin down the debt norm within a more elaborated analytical context where fiscal quantities – b^*

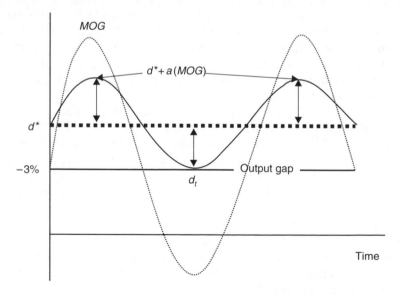

Figure 13.1   Cyclical developments and the budget balance

and a – were to be treated as the outcome of a policy choice. Were governments to decide over both their target debt level b^* and budgetary sensitivity a, then the simple stock–flow arithmetic outlined above – linking b^* to a via the deficit constraint – would not be sufficient to fully identify a fiscal regime. Reconciling the calls for a sustainable level of debt and an optimal degree of automatic stabilisation is accordingly a key issue, which cannot be addressed unless a fully specified optimisation problem is set up and solved.

In this chapter we propose a methodology under which it is possible to jointly determine an optimal budgetary target *and* a corresponding optimal level of budgetary sensitivity to cyclical movements. This methodology is based on an optimising model which is fully developed in Rostagno, Pérez-García and Hiebert (2001) – henceforth referred to as RPH. Our model is based on a dynastic overlapping generations framework along the lines of Weil (1989), augmented by random endowments and borrowing constrained households. It treats a small open economy in which the current taxpayer is assumed to live for ever and to receive at each date a gross income which is subject to random fluctuations around a stationary level, and in which population is expected to grow only by virtue of a steady inflow of likewise infinitely-lived immigrants. This can be thought of as a natural analytical setting for studying Europe's current situation, given its adverse endogenous demographics and its advanced stage of development in terms of attainable productivity levels.

The chapter shows that, under certain conditions, one generation of taxpayers would willingly accept to partially pay down debt rather than offload it entirely onto future generations. At first glance this seems surprising, given that the native household has no utility connection with any of the future new entrants – immigrants – and thus has no motive for intergenerational altruism. But the result becomes more transparent once the flip-side *taxing aspect* of the deficit is grasped. Maintaining a high debt over the long run, that is, choosing to stabilise, say, around the high current level of debt b_0, implies for the current taxpayers – who have to decide over the future course of fiscal policy – that they will be held responsible for a high tax – or primary surplus – for all the years to come. For, in order to prevent the debt from ever drifting away from b_0, the government has to levy a tax – or primary surplus – $s_0 = ((r - n)/(1 + r))b_0$ at all future dates. The higher b_0, the more onerous the primary surplus s_0 that is perennially required to sustain b_0.

This trade-off would not hurt a fully Ricardian taxpayer in the slightest. In fact, taxpayers who could easily borrow and lend without restrictions at the same interest rate would be completely indifferent between (1) stabilising at the current high level of debt – that is, bequeathing the entire amount of inherited debt b_0 to the future generations of immigrants – and having to pay a correspondingly high tax s_0 in the future: and (2) stabilising at some $b^* < b_0$, paying down the difference $(b_0 - b^*)$ – that is, offloading less of the current inherited debt burden onto future generations – and being, in turn, reassured that the future tax would be reduced from s_0 to $s^* = ((r - n)/(1 + r))b^*$. In other words, in an entirely frictionless world, the optimum problem whereby current taxpayers are requested to choose between alternative policy packages would have no solution.

But by introducing limits to the extent to which households can borrow against future income, the Modigliani–Miller-type indifference result discussed above vanishes. If current taxpayers were to be prevented from borrowing freely at the prevailing interest rate, they would anticipate possible future states of nature in which they would find themselves liquidity-constrained and thus unable to consume at the level consistent with their most preferred consumption-smoothing plan. Having to pay a higher or a lower tax under those circumstances would make a relevant difference.

Therefore, a different form of trade-off emerges whereby the current taxpayer has to balance off the advantages of bequeathing as much debt as possible to future taxpayers – whose welfare is attributed zero weight in their optimum problem – against the disadvantage of having to pay the high tax associated with a high steady-state amount of debt.

RPH solves this trade-off by casting the current taxpayer's choice exercise into the analytical terms of a standard 'income fluctuation problem', as popularised by Schechtman and Escudero (1977) and refined by a thriving successive body of literature. A benign government chooses an optimal degree of responsiveness of net taxes to individual incomes (a) along with an optimal measure of long-run public debt (b^*), in order to smooth households' consumption across states of nature – those in which the household is not liquidity-constrained and those in which it is – and never to violate the deficit restriction imposed by the SGP. We show that – under a certain scheme of accelerated debt repayment – the problem generally admits an interior solution for b^*. This means that current taxpayers would willingly choose to reimburse a portion of the inherited debt out of their own pockets in exchange for a permanently lower tax obligation in the future, s^*, and a permanently higher degree of responsiveness of deficits to current economic conditions, a. We interpret this result as suggesting that an accelerated policy of debt repayment by the currently living generation could represent a form of self-insurance whereby the down payment on debt made by current taxpayers constitutes the risk premium that they would consciously choose to pay in order to hedge personal incomes against future shortages. This hedge would take on two forms: a permanently reduced structural tax – or primary surplus – s^* to be paid on average, that is under zero output gap conditions, and a greater subsidy a to be received per each income unit in case of a negative output gap.

Our problem admits two kinds of solutions. The local solution is defined as a set $\{b^*, a\}$ that solves the constrained optimisation exercise *given the initial debt* inherited from history, b_0. The local solution thus answers the following question: what is the value of b^* and a which taxpayers would choose conditional on starting off from a given fiscal position identified by b_0? In contrast, the global solution is identified by a set $\{b^*, a\}$ which represents the fixed point of the optimum problem. In other words, conditional on starting off from a fixed-point couple b^* and a, taxpayers would not feel any incentive to move in any direction.

After solving the problem analytically, we calibrate our simple model by parameters capturing some characteristic features of a subset of EU countries, such as initial fiscal conditions, amplitude and frequency of income fluctuations and steady-state interest, growth and individual intertemporal discount rates. This allows us to characterise numerically both the local and global optima. We then interpret the numerical value of our global solution as providing a fully specified benchmark position at which the different countries under examination should aim in the very long run.

The chapter is organised as follows. Section 13.2 outlines the model, which is fully spelled out in RPH, going over the specification for households and the government. Section 13.3 explains the solution to the policy problem. Section 13.4 summarises the calibration of the model, while section 13.5 presents the results of an application of the model, explaining the local/global optima results for the countries under analysis along with the simulated transition to steady state. Concluding remarks are contained in section 13.6.

13.2   THE MODEL

13.2.1   Households

The model consists of an economy originally populated by one infinitely-lived household, which we call the 'native' household. While at
time zero the native household is the only one alive, from time 1
onwards population is expected to grow at a constant rate n by virtue
of a steady inflow of immigrants – all identical to the native household. Since everybody in the economy is endowed with the same
amount of consumption good per period, which is subject to random
fluctuations around a stationary amount, n denotes both the actual
growth rate of population and the trend growth rate of output.
Aggregate endowment fluctuations are the only source of private
income uncertainty within the economy: there is no idiosyncratic
source of income uncertainty. Preferences are defined over the utility
derived from the stream of future discounted consumption:

$$E_t \sum_{j=t}^{\infty} \left(\frac{1}{1+\delta} \right)^j U\big(c_j(g_j)\big) \tag{13.1}$$

where c_j is real consumption, δ the individual rate of time preference,
and g_j is considered as the individual – *and* aggregate – income (or
'output') gap, defined here as the random discrepancy between the
actual realisation of individual endowment at time j, y_j, and its stationary 'normal' level, y^*. The output gap is characterised by a first-
order autoregressive process, with shocks to the economy in any given
period drawn from a uniform distribution over the closed symmetric
support $[-\epsilon_e, +\epsilon_e]$ and $0 < \rho < 1$ measuring persistence.

Since all residents are equal and thus choose to insure themselves
against the same kind of uncertainty at the same time, there is no
scope for risk-pooling in this economy and, accordingly, no role for a
domestic capital market. Residents in this economy are assumed to
seek to finance a less variable profile of consumption relative to
national income by purchasing foreign assets.

A key assumption we make is that domestic households, while
having unlimited access to a world capital market as net suppliers of
saving, nevertheless face a borrowing limit. We formalise the latter in
its most extreme – but standard – form as an outright prohibition to
run wealth below zero.[1]

At the beginning of each period, after observing the shock to national – and individual – endowments, the resident households must decide how much to consume and how many financial claims to purchase or sell in the international capital market. A financial claim costs one unit of consumption and entitles its owner to $(1 + r)$ units next period, with $n < r < \delta.$[2] Consumption and accumulation decisions are made to satisfy a set of period flow budget constraints

$$c_t(g_t) + w_{t+1} - (y^* + g_t) + s_t - w_t(1 + r) + k_t \leq 0, \quad \forall t \geq 0$$

(13.2)

and a set of contemporary borrowing constraints for some predetermined w_t

$$w_{t+1} \geq 0, \quad \forall t \geq 0$$

(13.3)

In (13.2) and (13.3), w_t and w_{t+1} denote real wealth carried over from the earlier period and into the next period, respectively, $y^* + g_t$ is the realised level of individual endowment at time t, s_t, is a universal net tax paid by the entire population present at time t, and k_t is a non-negative tax levied solely on the 'native' household alive at time zero, which is positive or zero for the 'native' generation alive at time zero, and strictly zero for immigrants.

After observing the output gap at date zero, the native household decides over its preferred intertemporal allocation of consumption, with no concern for the welfare of any future generations of newcomers. In doing so, it is called upon to decide what share of current public debt should be repaid by itself and what share could be off-loaded onto future generations of alien taxpayers.

The choice problem facing the native household at time zero thus boils down to identifying the optimal intertemporal allocation of consumption in the presence of income fluctuations – drawn from a known distribution – which may involve it becoming liquidity-constrained in certain states of nature.[3] In RPH we conjecture that the analytical solution to this intertemporal choice problem can be well approximated by the following decision rule. The native household would set itself a consumption target equal to the 'unconstrained' level (c_0^{UC}) that would be chosen were it to operate in a complete markets world with no obstacles to borrowing against future income streams. It would then consume at that level – and save the difference between its actual disposable resources and consumption – in case the current realisation of income, net of taxes, and its accumulated wealth carried over from earlier dates were sufficient to finance it. Otherwise – that is, in the face of a particularly unfavourable gross income shock – consumption (c_0^C) would simply be set equal to total disposable resources – current disposable income plus any wealth carryover – driving its asset reserve to zero. In the latter case, the liquidity constraint would bind.

We specialise our analytical problem to one in which households maximise a quadratic period utility of the following form, in which consumption is saturated at some arbitrary value, which we normalise to the stationary level of normal income, y^*:[4]

$$U(c_t) = -(y^* - c_t)^2 \tag{13.4}$$

This form of the utility function invokes certainty equivalence, considerably simplifying the solution to the optimisation problem at hand. Quadratic utilities imply risk-averse and yet imprudent agents, that is, agents who do not save for precautionary motives. This removes a potential source of analytical bias since the main result of the model – that households would choose to purchase insurance by means of costly debt reduction – is strongly dependent on agents' attitude towards risk. After some manipulation, we obtain the decision rule for consumption at time zero as:

$$\hat{c}_0 = \min[c_0, y^*] \tag{13.5}$$

with:

$$c_0 = c_0^{UC} = y^* + \left[\frac{1+r-\beta}{1+r-\rho}\right] g_0 + (1+r-\beta)w_{-1}$$
$$- \left[\frac{1+r-\beta}{1+r}\right] \sum_{t=0}^{\infty} \left(\frac{1}{1+r}\right)^t E_t(s_t + k_t) \tag{13.6a}$$

if $y^* + g_0 + (1+r)w_{-1} - (s_0 + k_0) \geq c_0^{UC}$, and

$$c_0 = c_0^C = y^* + g_0 + (1+r)w_{-1} - (s_0 + k_0)$$

if the contrary happens. $\tag{13.6b}$

The 'Min' operator in (13.5) embodies the condition that, barring free disposal, optimal consumption at date zero cannot exceed the saturation point for consumption.

13.2.2 The Government

The form of market friction faced by the household, as outlined in the previous section, coupled with the government's ability under certain conditions to access the international financial market on behalf of its citizens, lends a key role to government as a financial intermediary. Assuming this role, it channels funds from international capital sources, inaccessible for unsecured borrowers, to its liquidity-constrained electorate in exchange for a claim on their electorate's future income. In doing so, however, the government itself must respect the conditions imposed by international financial markets.

At time zero the government, on behalf of its citizens, has an inherited level of debt, b_0, denominated in one-period risk-free real bonds issued on the international capital market. Given that at time zero citizens have mass one, b_0 stands for both total and per capita real public liabilities. At date zero the government asks the single native voter what is the level at which debt per capita should be stabilised. If the voter decides to stabilise at b_0, then each new entrant in the future will receive that same amount of debt to bear and to sustain with phased tax payments into eternity. If, on the other hand, the native voter were to decide to stabilise at a *lower* debt-per-taxpayer level, say $b^* < b_0$, this decision would imply that (i) each new entrant would be assigned, upon entry, a lower level of per capita debt to sustain, b^*, than outstanding at time zero and (ii) the native household would have to shoulder a higher debt than any other future generation of households and would consequently have to pay an excess tax – above that paid by all non-native future generations of immigrants – to cover the difference between b_0 and b^*. In other words, the initial level of debt b_0 can be considered as the sum of two components. The first one, b^*, is the amount of per head public debt which the native generation of taxpayers is going to share with each generation of newcomers, from the time in which these will settle into the country. The second component, $\bar{k}$, is the share of the actual outstanding debt borne by the native taxpayer which the latter accepts to shoulder *in excess of* the steady-state burden represented by b^* (see Figure 13.2).

The institutional framework under which the government forms policy decisions is constrained in three respects. First, the imposition of a solvency constraint effectively rules out the possibility of the government ever becoming engaged in Ponzi-type games in which some early investors would be paid off with money put up by later

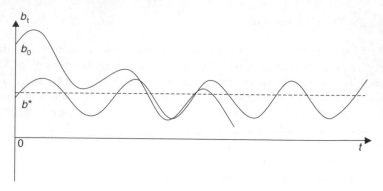

Figure 13.2   An illustrative path for the convergence of debt to its steady state value

ones. The second institutional constraint placed on the government is the overall deficit rule of the SGP. This restriction on the maximum amount of resources that the government can borrow at a time can be considered as one of the conditions placed on the government when acting as a financial intermediary in the foreign capital market on behalf of its citizens.[5] The third institutional constraint placed on government decisions imposes that taxes – or, equivalently in the present context, primary surpluses – have to be collected according to a contingent code which guarantees both flexibility of tax obliga-tions to households' income conditions, and the stationarity of future debt around the chosen norm $b^* \leq b_0$. The first and third institutional conditions can thus be summarised as follows:

$$b_0 = \sum_{t=0}^{\infty} \left(\frac{1+n}{1+r}\right)^t E_0(s_t) + \sum_{t=0}^{\infty} \left(\frac{1}{1+r}\right)^t E_0(k_t) \qquad (13.7a)$$

with:

$$b^* = \sum_{t=0}^{\infty} \left(\frac{1+n}{1+r}\right)^t E_0(s_t), \quad \bar{k} = \sum_{t=0}^{\infty} \left(\frac{1}{1+r}\right)^t E_0(k_t) \qquad (13.7b)$$

$$s_t(g_t) = s^* + ag_t + r(b_t^* - b^*) \qquad (13.8)$$

Notice that (13.7a) and (13.7b) together impose solvency in that they make b^* equal to – that is, backed by – the present value of the infinite stream of future taxes – primary surpluses – levied on all future generations of taxpayers, including the only one currently alive; and

$\bar{k}$, namely the share of current debt to be exclusively borne by the native generation, backed by the present value of the (possibly finite) stream of taxes to be levied on the native generation only.

The rule for taxes – or primary surpluses – outlined in (13.8) has the standard built-in countercyclical automatic stabiliser features of fiscal policy, whereby net revenues typically rise as the realised output gap widens, captured by ag_t. This rule also embodies important stability properties. In this respect, notice two things. First, that the systematic component of primary fiscal balances – denoted by s^* in (13.8) – uniquely pins down the level at which the authorities want to stabilise their per capita debt – or, equivalently in the present context, as a share of GDP, namely the b^* of (13.7a) and (13.7b). This can be readily seen by substituting (13.8) into (13.7b) under zero-output gap conditions, to obtain:

$$b^* = \left(\frac{1+r}{r-n}\right)s^* \tag{13.9}$$

Second, the last term in (13.8) – the discrepancy between the actual interest payments at any t and those that would be due were the contemporary actual debt to be exactly equal to its 'target' b^* – guarantees that future debt ratios will always fluctuate randomly around the target for any shocks that happen to hit the economy. In other words, the latter term makes sure that any over- or under-shooting in interest payments caused by past random departures of the actual debt from its long-run norm would be made good by – or repaid to – taxpayers. This is what guarantees stationarity of the debt ratios b_t^* around a long-term target b^*.

RPH studies a solution to our policy problem under an arbitrary 'opportunistic' reimbursement schedule of the following type:[6]

$$k(\bar{k},\, g_t) = \begin{cases} y^* + g_t - c_t^*(g_t) - s_t(g_t), y^* + g_t - s_t(g_t) \geq c_t^*(g_t) \\ 0, y^* + g_t - s_t(g_t) < c_t^*(g_t) \end{cases}$$

$$\tag{13.10}$$

The repayment schedule above is opportunistic in that the government takes advantage of good states of nature, when the native household's disposable resources suffice to finance at least $c_t^{UC}(g_t)$, to tax income heavily, in order to mitigate – and possibly temporarily lift altogether – the burden of the excess tax k_t in periods in which the household is liquidity-constrained. In any case, the native household is always taxed – against its $\bar{k}$ exclusive obligation – in a way to extract the excess of its income net of the universal tax $s_t(g_t)$ over its optimal target consumption $c_t^{UC}(g_t)$, for all g_t.

Given (13.10) and substituting (13.7b), (13.8) and (13.9) into (13.6a) and (13.6b), and assuming for simplicity a zero wealth carry-over from one period earlier into time zero, we can express the optimal reaction rule for the native household in the following terms:

$$
\hat{c}_0 = \begin{cases} c_0^{UC} = y^* + \left[\dfrac{(1-a)(1+r-\beta)}{1+r-\rho}\right]g_0 + \left[\dfrac{1+r-\beta}{r(1+r)}\right][nb^* - rb_0] \\[2ex] c_0^C = y^* + (1-a)g_0 - s^* = y^* + (1-a)g_0 - b^*\left(\dfrac{r-n}{1+r}\right) \end{cases}
$$

(13.11)

(13.11) highlights the fundamental tension existing between the policy preferences that the native household would advance under a *good* and a *bad* state. If the native household were to express its preferences over the split of b_0 into b^* and $\bar{k}$ conditionally on being in a favourable situation (given by the upper part of (13.11)), it would decide to set $\bar{k}$ to zero and to offload as much debt as possible to future generations. Households – even at times in which they behave *as if* they were operating under complete markets – are *not* indifferent to the burden of the debt and the timing of its abatement.[7] In this respect, note that c_0^{UC} is a positive function of b^* only if n is positive. If the population is expected to be sustained by a positive stream of immigrants, offloading more of b_0 onto these newcomers becomes a natural choice for the native household living in a good state of nature.

However, the native household is not going to always find itself in a good state of nature. In fact, if it were to formulate its policy preferences under binding credit restrictions, it would choose as low a value for b^* (and thus as high a $\bar{k}$ compared to b_0) as possible – c_0^C is a decreasing function of b^*. This is because choosing a low b^* would imply reducing the non-contingent fraction s^* of the universal tax $s_t(g_t)$ which is due in support of the chosen b^*. Further, having to pay a milder tax on average would help precisely in periods of distress, in which disposable resources are badly needed and the marginal propensity to consume out of a tax cut is one. Having to sustain a larger b^* would subtract from disposable resources in all circumstances, with particularly negative consequences when gross income is low and the output gap is largely negative – making the occurrence of the bad state more likely.

As such, *ex ante* there might be demand for a form of insurance which trades the payment of premia levied in good income conditions according to the 'opportunistic' schedule $k(\bar{k}, g_t)$ against a reduction of the non-contingent 'core' of tax obligations s^*. Since s^* and b^* are positively related via (13.8), this form of insurance requires a policy of debt reduction.

Of course, self-insurance payable through debt reduction is not the only insurance package made available by government in this economy, as apparent from (13.8). In principle, debt could very well be stabilised at its current level b_0 and yet an effective source of insurance could be offered by boosting the semi-elasticity of primary surpluses to the output gap, a. The latter measures the subsidy that households receive when endowments are below normal levels and the additional tax that they pay when endowments are above normal. A value of a close to 1 can both mitigate the consequences of a bad shock once it occurs and make the bad state less likely to occur in the first place. It is certainly a preferable form of self-insurance against a bad occurrence, since – all else equal – it is provided *ex post* and, as such, it need not be paid in advance.

13.3 SOLUTION TO THE POLICY PROBLEM

Finding the optimum amount of self-insurance demanded by the native household and trading off available packages – debt reduction versus *ex post* automatic stabilisation – is the ultimate goal of the government's optimisation problem in this economy. While the native household at date zero makes its choices after observing g_0, the government has to draw out its plan for fiscal policy over the foreseeable future and along the steady state before anyone can observe actual income conditions.

The benign government is modelled in such a way that it credibly commits to a sequence of possibly state-contingent policies which maximises the lifetime welfare of the native household with respect to b^* and a:

$$\max_{\{b^*, a\}} \sum_{t=0}^{\infty} \left(\frac{1}{1+\delta}\right)^t E_t(\hat{c}_t(g_t)) \tag{13.12}$$

subject to the conditions for individual optima given by (13.5), (13.6a) and (13.6b), to the constraints (13.7a), (13.7b), (13.8), (13.9), conditional on (13.10) and, finally, constrained by the two deficit conditions applicable over the steady state and the transition to the steady state, respectively:

$$\lfloor s^* + a\varepsilon(\omega - 1)\rfloor - rb^* = -0.03\lfloor y^* + \varepsilon(\omega - 1)\rfloor \tag{13.13}$$

$$[s^* + a\varepsilon(\omega - 1)] - rb^* + (1 + n)^{-t}\left[k(\bar{k}, \varepsilon(\omega - 1))\right.$$

$$\left. - r\left(\bar{k} - \sum_{i=0}^{t-1}\left(\frac{1}{1+r}\right)^i k_i\right)(1 + r)^{t-1}\right] = -0.03[y^* + \varepsilon(\omega - 1)]$$

$$\tag{13.14}$$

As regards the alternative forms given to the deficit constraint in (13.13) and (13.14) respectively, two remarks are worthwhile. The first touches upon the issue of how *soft* the constraint should be allowed to be in our model. Normally, provided it is credible, a deficit limit must be observed in virtually *all* circumstances of nature to which a positive probability, no matter how small this might be, is attached. In our context, such a *hard* constraint would dictate that fiscal variables be calibrated so as to insure against a breach of the rule even under the worst possible realisation of output, no matter how unlikely that might be. However, in the real practice – and notably in the light of the implementation arrangements put in place by the SGP – credible deficit rules can still leave scope for contingent provisions tolerating breaches of the deficit limit under particularly unfavourable circumstances.[8] Consequently, in the above formalisation of the deficit limit, the parameter ω denotes the stringency of the constraint.

The second remark on the deficit constraint concerns the distinction we draw between a deficit rule applying over the steady state and the more stringent rule which would bind along the transition to the steady state. The key difference between (13.13) and (13.14) lies in the terms related to the excess tax liability borne by the native household. Clearly, we define the steady state, as portrayed by (13.13), as a state of affairs in which the original excess liability shouldered by the native taxpayer, $\bar{k}$, has been repaid in full, so that all taxpayers are subject to a uniform fiscal regime, represented by (13.8). By contrast, along the transition, there coexist two categories of taxpayers, sustaining debt burdens of different magnitudes. Whereas all residents at time t (for some $t \geq 0$) are co-responsible for the 'kernel' or steady-state tax burden indicated by b^* and represented by the first two terms on the left-side of (13.14), only the native household bears the additional tax obligations related to the redemption of the time-t residual value of the bonds originally associated with the excess liability $\bar{k}$. The third term on the left-hand side of (13.14) provides the accounting of such redemption. At each time t, the residual of the financial claims originally associated with $\bar{k}$ compounds interest on the international capital market – the second term within the squared brackets of (13.14). At the same time, however, the native household relinquishes a certain amount of its current resources as an additional tax k_t earmarked for the buy-back of a portion of the native household's compounded residual obligation. This tax should diminish – or at least keep constant – over time the residual liability hanging over its head.[9]

Notice that we allowed for this tax paid under unfavourable circumstances to be some function of the realised output gap, $k\{\bar{k}, \varepsilon(\omega-1)\}$, on the presumption that – not unlike the universal tax $s_t(g_t)$ – the authorities might choose to graduate disbursements on the basis of the native household's capacity to pay under those circumstances. Notice, finally, that both deficit constraints are calibrated in real per capita output terms, by multiplying the deficit threshold 0.03 by $\{y^*+\varepsilon(\omega-1)\}$, to make them applicable to an institutional setting close to that defined by the SGP.

The solution to the government policy problem is a complicated analytical object, which is fully spelled out in RPH. Here we represent its generic form as a pair of conditions including a reduced form expression for optimal b^* as a quadratic function of structural and institutional parameters only, and a linear function relating a to b^*:

$$B_1(b^*)^2 + B_2 b^* + B_3 = 0$$
$$a = 1 - C_1 - C_2 b^* \tag{13.15}$$

where coefficients C contain only those parameters appearing in the deficit constraint, and the terms denominated with B are more elaborated functions of all parameters, including, most notably, the initial debt burden b_0.

In words, at the optimum the marginal rate of substitution between the two available forms of self-insurance – that 'purchased' through a cut in b^* and that acquired by augmenting a – must equate the marginal rate of transformation of the one into the other, given the deficit condition. Just as we need a condition such as that provided by the upper condition in (13.15) to pick one particular combination of

b^* and a among the many pairs which satisfy the deficit restriction, we need a deficit restriction to attach a shadow price to automatic stabilisation – a-based insurance – which otherwise, without the lower section of (13.15), would simply be costless.[10]

The solution to the model provides both *local* and *global* optima. In terms of local optima, the initial conditions, and particularly that of b_0, are of paramount importance in generating the results. Obviously, an economy with the same structural parameters as another but starting off from a relatively higher debt burden would obtain a quite different indication in terms of the appropriate target for fiscal policy. Thus we take local optima as identifying the value of b^* and a which taxpayers would choose conditional on starting off from a given inherited debt ratio b_0. In contrast, the global solution is identified by a couple $\{b^* = b_0 = b_G, a\}$ which represents the fixed point of the optimum problem. In other words, conditional on starting off from a fixed-point couple b^* and a, taxpayers would not feel any incentive to move in any direction and the solution to the government problem would thus be precisely $\{b^*, a\}$. As regards global optima, they do exist in our model and are relatively easy to characterise, simply by setting.[11] Analysing globally optimal figures has the dual advantage that discrepancies across countries are a function of only structural parameters unrelated to the initial position, and helps side-step important problems of time consistency.

13.4   CALIBRATION OF THE MODEL

The model is applied to all European Union member countries with the exception of Greece, Ireland, Luxembourg and Portugal.[12] Some model parameters (such as y^*, r, n, b_0, and ω) are calibrated, while other parameters related to the output gap (γ, ε) are estimated on the basis of econometric methods.

The initial debt ratios, b_0, are calibrated to estimates for 2000 of general government consolidated gross debt (Maastricht definition) as a percentage of gross domestic product at market prices, as contained in the *Spring 2000 Forecasts* of the European Commission. The use of debt in terms of GDP rather than in per capita terms was possible as the rate of population growth, n, is also a proxy for economic growth in the RPH model. The value of n is taken as fixed at 1.5 per cent, while the interest rate, r, is set equal to 3.5 per cent for all countries, in line with long-run observations for long-term real interest rates. Estimates of the real rate of time preference, β, are taken as fixed at 1 for the baseline scenario. The degree of tolerance with respect to the institutional deficit constraint, ω, is set to zero in the baseline scenario for all countries, implying a stringent interpretation of the SGP in the steady state. As regards y^*, its value was normalised to 100 in order to interpret output gap realisations as deviations in percentage points.

Country-specific estimates of the persistence (γ) and magnitude (ε) of output gaps are based on annual data for actual and trend output contained in the Spring 2000 AMECO database of the European Commission over the period 1960–99. Estimates of the output gap for the eleven countries under analysis are based on the percentage deviation of actual output from trend output, with the Commission measure of g_t based on an estimation of trend output using the Hodrick–Prescott filter.[13] An important drawback of the filter is its inability to cope with structural breaks. This results in a biased measure of trend output in countries where clear structural breaks are evident in historical observations of GDP, such as Finland and Sweden in the 1990s. An obvious problem is also evident in Germany, where the structural break in the series in the early 1990s has led the Commission to omit estimates of real growth domestic product prior to 1991 in its Spring 2000 AMECO release. For this reason, the estimates for output gaps in Germany are based on a series chained backwards using pre-1991 data from the Autumn 1999 AMECO release.

Country-specific estimates of γ are obtained by estimating a first-order autoregressive model of g_t.[14] Estimates of ε were obtained by taking the average of the maximum and minimum values of the observed output gap over the sample period. In order to compensate for the absence of an adequate treatment of structural breaks in the Commission estimates of trend output, the maximum amplitude of maximum output gaps was censored for observed output gaps in excess of 7.5 per cent. This resulted in a censoring of ε for output gap observations only for Finland (1989 and 1993). Nevertheless, it should be noted that the maximum observed output gap using Commission data was also lower than may have been initially expected in some cases, most notably for France. Table 13.1 summarises the baseline parameters used in the simulation exercise.

In order to gauge the extent to which the results are dependent on the chosen baseline parameterisation, RPH contains an extensive sensitivity analysis exercise with respect to the calibrated parameters. The exercise confirms that the results are fairly resilient to changes in

Table 13.1   Baseline parameterisation

	$b_0(1)$	$\rho(2)$	$\varepsilon(3)$	$r(4)$	$\omega(5)$	$n(6)$	$\beta(7)$
Belgium	110.01	0.526	3.21	0.035	0.00	0.015	1.00
Denmark	49.27	0.598	4.95	0.035	0.00	0.015	1.00
Germany	60.66	0.576	3.97	0.035	0.00	0.015	1.00
Spain	62.27	0.732	4.91	0.035	0.00	0.015	1.00
France	58.17	0.681	2.59	0.035	0.00	0.015	1.00
Italy	110.82	0.456	3.20	0.035	0.00	0.015	1.00
Netherlands	58.67	0.625	2.90	0.035	0.00	0.015	1.00
Austria	63.99	0.593	2.99	0.035	0.00	0.015	1.00
Finland	42.65	0.728	5.53	0.035	0.00	0.015	1.00
Sweden	61.31	0.640	4.28	0.035	0.00	0.015	1.00
United Kingdom	42.36	0.615	4.60	0.035	0.00	0.015	1.00

the calibrated parameters r and n, while values of the rate of time preference different from the interest rate tend to produce more pronounced effects.

13.5   RESULTS

13.5.1   Local Optima

First, *local* measures of 'optimal debt' and 'optimal sensitivity' of primary surpluses to general economic conditions were obtained using (13.15), which summarises the target level of debt and the desired degree of automatic stabilisation that electorates would vote for when starting off from their current fiscal situations. A straightforward by-product of this solution was the calculation of the total excess burden (that is, $\bar{k} = b_0 - b^*$) that the current generations of resident taxpayers in the various countries would accept to shoulder over the amount of debt b^* to be shared with future generations.

Table 13.2 illustrates the steady-state local and global solutions. The first two columns of the table summarise the starting point for the countries under analysis, while columns 3 to 6 summarise the implications of the *locally* optimal fiscal policy for the debt ratios of our selection of EU countries under the baseline parameterisation. As expected, countries experiencing large output fluctuations on average are assigned a lower local target for debt. A particularly striking example can be found with the parameterisation of Finland, in which the native electorate would be ready to accept a total bill exceeding a quarter of their gross income in normal times (fifth column) in order to have the non-contingent primary surplus reduced in the steady state. Voters in Denmark and the UK would be as ambitious as the Finnish, although their final target debt would be higher. Not surprisingly, the three countries have a record of strong cyclicality, as apparent from Table 13.1 (third column), which reports the maximum values of the country-specific output gap residuals in our GDP regressions – as presented in the previous section. In contrast, other electorates with less volatile GDP and/or with larger initial debt burdens would content themselves with a more measured approach to fiscal stabilisation.

Column 7 of Table 13.2 illustrates the local targets for the semi-elasticities of the primary surpluses to output gaps. These sensitivities are quite substantial and considerably larger than the current values as estimated in the literature. Indeed, while recent studies by Wyplosz (1999) and Mélitz (2000) estimate a at around 0.2 for the area as a whole, the electorates modelled here would be content to pay a tax for having the automatic subsidy accruing from the budget in bad times increased to between 50 and 80 per cent of realised income shortfalls. Again, countries with smooth output fluctuations, such as France, Austria and the Netherlands, would target a higher semi-elasticity than countries at the opposite extreme. This can be easily explained by noting that for them, the cost of this (more efficient) form of insurance, based on an *ex post* rather than an *ex ante* arrangement, would be lower in terms of the needed down payment on debt in terms of the fiscal adjustment required to have the deficit constraint hold in all circumstances.

By implication, the converse would hold true for countries displaying more pronounced instability of income conditions. As for these countries – notably the Nordic member states – the anticipated absolute amplitude of normal income fluctuations to be cushioned through a is larger than for other countries, which translates into a higher price of this type of insurance *vis-à-vis* the alternative one of cutting the debt burden through an accelerated debt redemption – that is, via a lower b^*. This, in turn, is reflected in both a lower b^* and a.

As an illustration of the optimality conditions described in Table 13.2 and recent actual developments, Figure 13.3 selects two pairs of countries at the opposite extreme of our spectrum measuring incentives to reduce debt. The figure is highly suggestive of a key result of our study, namely that economies such as those of Finland and Denmark with strong self-insurance motives have indeed embarked on

Table 13.2 Steady-state values under baseline parameterisation

	Initial debt (b_0)	Associated primary surplus needed to stabilise at b_0	Locally optimal debt (b^*)	Associated primary surplus needed to stabilise at b^*	$\bar{k}$	$\bar{k}/b_0$	Locally optimal sensitivity	Global optimum for debt, $b^*(G)$	Global optimum $a^*(G)$
	(1)	(2)	(3)	(4)	(5a)	(5b)	(6)	(7)	(8)
Belgium	110.01	2.13	81.16	1.57	28.85	26.23	0.51	−1.47	0.91
Denmark	49.27	0.95	9.35	0.18	39.92	81.01	0.55	−19.00	0.64
Germany	60.66	1.17	32.31	0.62	28.35	46.74	0.60	−9.14	0.76
Spain	62.27	1.20	21.91	0.42	40.36	64.81	0.51	−17.05	0.64
France	58.17	1.12	51.18	1.99	6.99	12.02	0.82	5.50	1.00
Italy	110.82	2.14	81.55	1.58	29.27	26.42	0.51	−1.63	0.92
Netherlands	58.67	1.13	46.82	0.90	11.85	20.20	0.75	2.07	0.99
Austria	63.99	1.24	49.50	1.96	14.49	22.64	0.72	1.06	0.97
Finland	42.65	0.82	−2.19	−0.04	44.84	105.14	0.52	−23.30	0.58
Sweden	61.31	1.18	28.87	0.56	32.44	52.91	0.57	−11.82	0.72
United Kingdom	42.36	0.82	9.39	0.18	32.97	77.84	0.59	−15.29	0.68

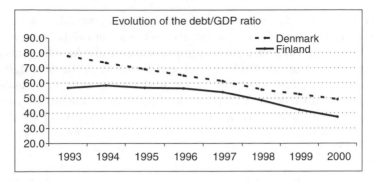

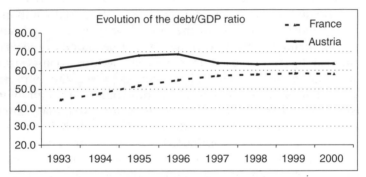

Figure 13.3   Evolution of the debt ratio, 1993–present
Source: European Commission, AMECO database, Autumn 1999 release.

a precipitous reduction of their debt levels over the recent past. By contrast, other member states, such as France and Austria, with less risky aggregate income profiles – and consequently fewer incentives toward fiscal retrenchment according to our line of reasoning – could indeed afford a more relaxed time schedule for redemption.

13.5.2   Global Optima

We also provide a *global* measure for both these target variables, which is independent from initial conditions and entirely induced by institutional constraints, such as the numerical deficit limit imposed by the SGP, and structural features of the economy, such as the long-run real rates of interest and growth, the individual rate of time preference and the degree of persistence in the stochastic processes driving gross incomes. In conjunction with structural parameters, the relative diversity of initial fiscal positions is responsible for the wide range of debt ratios that the same optimisation problem would indicate to different governments as the local target for policy. Therefore, an interesting question to answer quantitatively is whether the convergence trajectories that the various governments would have to start at the current juncture according to our model would eventually lead to a more contained set of fixed points for b_G and a_G in the *very* long run. The answer we give to this question is positive and the set of numbers corresponding to the global attractors for fiscal policy under our various parametric assumptions is provided in the two last columns of Table 13.2.

The results point to the existence of a quite substantial pent-up demand for automatic stabilisation at the current configuration of starting positions. If freed from the burden of their inherited debts, electorates would be willing to trade off a large chunk of their consumption in favourable conditions in exchange for robust income subsidisation in unfavourable circumstances. Once the impact of initial conditions is almost entirely netted out as a result of the imposition of a fixed-point condition, electorates would ask governments to guarantee that no less than two-thirds of their envisaged income shortfalls be compensated by an endogenous correction of taxes and transfers. And they would be ready to foot the cost of turning a debt into an asset position, if that is what the frequency and severity of recessions would require them to do in order to respect the fiscal code of the SGP.

Notice that such a strong and unambiguous finding has been derived on the basis of a model which, if anything, biases the final results *against* the voluntary purchase of insurance through debt repayment. Indeed, our households are risk-averse – which is why they choose to self-insure anyway – but act in a totally imprudent manner in the face of the uncertainty that looms ahead. Although they dislike uncertainty, they basically act as if there were none. More prudent households – saving *also* against the possibility of being liquidity-constrained in the future – would demand larger amounts of automatic stabilisation and would be willing to pay more in exchange for it.

The targets for b_G that we obtain are indeed less dispersed than their local counterparts. In our baseline scenario these net asset positions would numerically be between 25 per cent of GDP – under Finland's extreme output volatility – and zero, with five out of eleven countries clustering around a balanced net asset position, and two other countries – Germany and Sweden – not far from there.

On the whole, countries expecting output fluctuations of moderate amplitude would afford targeting a less ambitious – that is, non-negative – debt even in the *very* long run. This notwithstanding, they would be able to target a very high value for a_G. Conversely, countries subject to more pronounced cycles would have to settle for *both* less automatic stabilisation ($a_G < 1$) *and* a negative debt position in the *very* long run.[15] The threshold between countries belonging to the two different groupings is traced by the numerical deficit limit.

13.5.3 The Transition to Steady State

The time path of transition to steady state was simulated whilst checking to which extent the restriction constraining government borrowing over the transition to the steady state, (13.14), was met in the transition. Two considerations framed the exercise. First, in order to provide for the most stringent interpretation of the deficit ceiling, ω entering both (13.13) and (13.14), and determining the width of the confidence interval to the right of the worst possible gap realisation was set to zero, implying that the 3 per cent deficit rule would be not suspended for any conceivable observation of the output gap drawn from the uniform distribution over the support $[-\varepsilon, \varepsilon]$. The second factor related to the percentage of observations that, during the simulated transition, a breach of the 3 per cent deficit limit would be tolerated on the grounds of a host of factors, ranging from the existence of an escape clause for deficits run under severe recessions to purely statistical reasons calling for a probabilistic interpretation of the allowable degree of slack in the constraint. Correspondingly, breaches of the deficit ceiling were tolerated during the transition, provided that they occurred less frequently than in 5 per cent of the total number of simulated periods.

A relatively more stringent adherence to the rule over the steady state than over the transitional period was required for two reasons. First, notice that our formulation of the deficit limit valid over the steady state, (13.13), is only an approximation to the 'true' limit that should be observed when total debt *fluctuates around b** in a random fashion and need not necessarily be *always equal to b** in all states of nature. The difference can be crucial, as actual interest spending, equivalent to $rb_t^*(-\varepsilon)$, that the government would have to sustain at the trough of a recession along the stochastic steady state would be higher than interest expenditure at the level rb^*, due when the debt level is *exactly equal* to its zero-output-gap steady-state target b^*, because $rb_t^*(-\varepsilon) \geq rb^*(0) = rb^*$. As the latter condition was introduced into the steady-state condition used for calculating the optimal values $\{b^*, a\}$, a more cautious approach in other respects was adopted in compensation. Second, in tolerating infrequent and mild breaches during the transition, it was taken into account that the fiscal burden plaguing current generations of taxpayers is generally more onerous than that which newcomers would bear in the steady state. There is, in other words, an issue of horizontal equity which we tried not to ignore by setting the tolerance interval equal to zero in the steady state and to 5 per cent during the transition.

Each simulation round involved some 500 replications, based on uniformly distributed independent random shocks to the period-t output gap. For each simulation we computed the transition path from b_0 to the steady state, the number of breaches during the transition and during the steady state, and we then calculated averages over the simulated paths, to get reference statistics.

The results show that no country violated the deficit ceiling more frequently than 5 per cent of the total observations while approaching their steady-state optimal values – see the second column of Table 13.3. Nevertheless, it should be noted that the number of periods required to attain steady state for any particular parametrisation varied considerably, as summarised by the high standard deviations in column two of the table. The reason is simple. As outstanding debt

Table 13.3   Summary statistics for the transition

	Average length (1)	Standard deviation (2)	Average percentage of breaches (3)
Belgium	311	220	2.1
Denmark	305	223	1.2
Germany	298	224	0.8
Spain	269	226	0.9
France	228	227	0.0
Italy	333	233	1.8
Netherlands	262	225	0.1
Austria	260	225	0.3
Finland	290	233	0.8
Sweden	296	240	0.8
United Kingdom	305	237	0.7

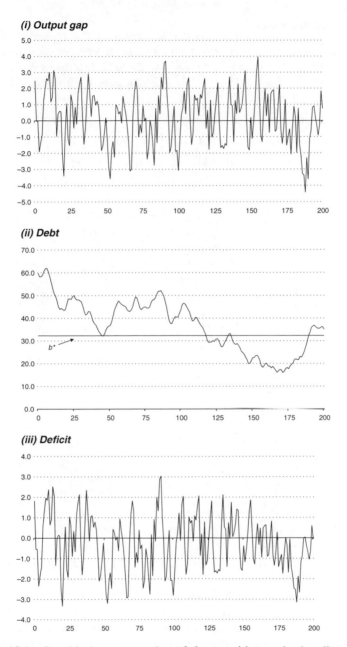

Figure 13.4   Graphical representation of the transition under baseline para-meterisation for *Germany*

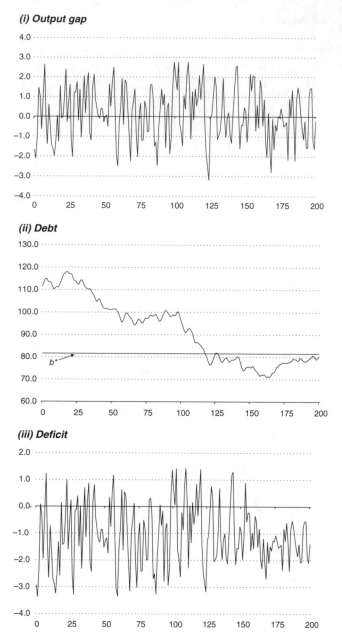

Figure 13.5 Graphical representation of the transition under baseline parameterisation for *Italy*

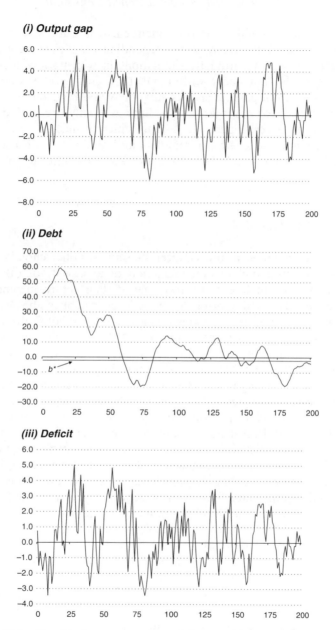

Figure 13.6   Graphical representation of the transition under baseline parameterisation for *Finland*

is accruing interest, a delay in repayment early on can result in a very lengthy transition to steady state, depending on the sequencing of economic shocks. Accordingly, simulations in which convergence to steady state did not occur within one thousand periods were discarded. A series of positive shocks early on would reduce the number of years it takes to convergence to as little as twenty-five periods. For illustrative purposes, Figures 13.4–13.6 depict an illustrative case for the transition to the locally optimal debt indicated in the third column of Table 13.2 for a selection of countries with differing baseline parameter values.

13.6   CONCLUSIONS

The model presented in this chapter shows that policy choices faced by governments entail the reconciliation of a basic trade-off when households are not free to borrow against their future income and an excess tax designed to bring down the level of debt can be designed in such a way as not to excessively penalise the household's disposable resources in low-endowment conditions. Although stabilising debt at current levels implies placing no excess burden on current taxpayers, it also boosts the 'core' tax needed to sustain per capita debt at that (high) level in the long run in *all* states of nature. This would of course have negative consequences for households, as having to pay a high non-contingent tax is painful when liquidity is scarce and credit restrictions bind. If, instead, current taxpayers were to choose to pay for a reduction in liabilities in order to stabilise per capita debt below currently prevailing levels, they would also reduce the non-contingent tax required to keep debt at its steady state value for ever. In contrast to maintaining the status quo level of debt, a paydown in debt would in general be beneficial for a household facing liquidity restrictions in the future, as it would free spendable resources at times in which borrowing would be desirable, but prohibited.

This balancing of the pros attached to a low-debt stabilisation option (the fact that the native household would in this way insure itself against income shortfalls in periods of distress) against the relative cons (the fact that it would have to pay an excess tax in good times compared to future generations) is at the heart of the model outlined in this chapter. This methodological approach achieved several goals. First, it extracted normative advice directly from first principles, without resorting to arbitrary formulations of social welfare objectives. Although the model is not invulnerable to the Lucas critique (1976) by virtue of its micro foundations,[16] it yields a normative policy course in terms of primitive factors and has some merit in at least allowing the conduct of meaningful sensitivity analysis.

The policy indication from a purely *normative* standpoint is quite unambiguous. The current generation of European taxpayers, with no exception, regards its current fiscal situation as unsatisfactory for several reasons. First, current public liabilities are too burdensome to be considered sustainable in periods of economic distress, when the payment of taxes detracts directly from consumption. From this perspective, lower debt levels are desirable because they imply that lower taxes can be maintained in the long run and help to free resources at times when these are scarce. Second, budgets are too rigid to be of help in smoothing consumption across states of nature. The degree to which net contingent taxes are allowed to vary in accordance with individual income conditions at current debt levels is considered too low compared to an ideal situation of optimal self-insurance. Again, agents appear to be ready to pay a risk premium to 'purchase' a more effective hedging of personal income uncertainty by means of more active fiscal stabilisers. On both accounts, the amount of resources that the mildly risk-averse, selfish agents defined by this model would forfeit in order to bring about more balanced and more flexible and responsive public finances is potentially quite sizeable. In addition, from the standpoint of a *positive* interpretation of the results, this chapter might be taken to provide an explanation for why different countries in Europe have recently embarked on policies of debt reabsorption of such different intensities, with electorates facing particularly erratic income conditions more likely to elect for dramatic debt cutbacks than voters who feel less pressing motives to be concerned about income riskiness.

While we would not regard these policy prescriptions as definitive before conducting further analysis on the basis of a richer model – notably including physical capital – they are nevertheless very suggestive in pointing to a univocal direction. Namely, that countries expecting output fluctuations of moderate amplitude will target a less ambitious debt reduction both in the short run – that is, looking forward from their current initial conditions – and in the *very* long run and will always afford a more responsive system of fiscal stabilisers. Conversely, countries subject to more pronounced cycles will always be willing to accept a more aggressive policy of debt repayment, in the short run as well as in the very long haul.

Notes

1. This is also broadly the strategy adopted by, *inter alia*, J. Schechtman and V. Escudero (1977), F. Hayashi (1985), R. Hubbard and K. Judd (1986, 1987) and P. Krusell and A. Smith (1998). A more general setting, allowing agents to accumulate a limited amount of net financial liabilities, is studied by *inter alia*, Clarida (1987) and Aiyagari (1994).
2. This is consistent with Clarida (1990).
3. This problem has been originally studied by Schechtman and Escudero (1977). For more recent contributions, see Clarida (1987, 1990), Deaton (1991) and Aiyagari (1994).
4. This utility function has been used by Hall (1978), Hayashi (1985) and Abel (1990). Blanchard and Mankiw (1988) review the arguments in favour of more plausible approaches to the formalisation of preferences. Caballero (1990) provides a closed-form solution to a stochastic optimal consumption problem (without borrowing constraints) using an exponential utility, which in our case, however, would not guarantee a bounded process of wealth accumulation.
5. RPH provides a deeper rationale for a budget constraint limiting the ability of governments to borrow at any date t. Indeed, RPH proves that the imposition of a total deficit rule is a necessary condition for the policy problem to have a solution over a feasible set of policy parameters.
6. In order to minimise notational clutter, the above case is presented in which the native household begins history with no accumulated wealth, that is, $W_{t-1} = 0$.
7. This anti-Modigliani – Miller feature of our model is simply a reflection of the basic non-Ricardianness of a framework in the vein of Weil (1989) where eternal dynasties overlap without motives for mutual altruism.
8. Indeed, the Stability and Growth Pact has an escape clause in the event of extraordinary economic conditions.
9. Notice that the squared brackets containing the compounded residual of the native household's tax obligation is deflated by the size of the population alive at t, $(1 + n)^t$ as the deficit condition has to hold in per capita terms and the incidence of the native household on total tax-payers at t is the inverse of total population.
10. In fact, RPH shows that, without a deficit constraint and conditional on a being close enough to 1, the native household would always choose to stabilise the debt ratio at its current level b. In essence, that would be a situation in which one insurance package would cost nothing in terms of forgone consumption, making a potentially painful policy of debt reduction unnecessary.
11. RPH discusses the time-consistency pitfalls of the policy exercise described in our model. If the government were allowed to reoptimise at some later date before the native household had fully repaid its excess debt burden, the mere anticipation of this later action by the native household at time zero would suffice to distort its policy preferences at the same point of history and the whole policy exercise outline above would thereby unravel.

12.   With the exception of Luxembourg, these countries represent those in a 'catching up' phase, in which special factors could distort a comparison with other EU countries.

13.   Note that the measurement of the output gap is equivalent in either per capita or level terms, as an offsetting adjustment must be made for population growth to both actual output and trend output, cancelling out in the computation of the output gap.

14.   Detail on the rationale behind this choice of autoregressive specification can be found in RPH.

15.   On the theoretical possibilities of a gross *asset* ratio for a government, see Barro (1979), pp. 940–71.

16.   The advantages of micro-founded models for (monetary) policy exercises have been emphasised by Rotemberg and Woodford (1997) and Woodford (1990).

14 Public Debt Management and the SGP*

Alessandro Missale

14.1 INTRODUCTION

No mention is made of debt management in the Stability and Growth Pact, but a careful choice of debt instruments is needed to control interest payments and budget deficits. Interest-cost minimisation is important especially in countries where interest payments absorb a large share of the budget. In the same countries avoiding the risk that interest rate shocks lead to large payments on short-term and floating-rate debt is equally important.

This chapter examines how the public debt should be managed to minimise the risk that the deficit/GDP ratio exceeds the 3 per cent limit of the Stability and Growth Pact. In particular, we want to examine whether the Stability Pact justifies the lengthening of debt maturity that has occurred in EMU member states. We are also interested in assessing the scope for inflation-indexed bonds that are issued only in France in EMU.

Over the 1990s the duration of the debt has indeed lengthened, especially in countries where it was shortest. Figures 14.1 and 14.2 (taken from Favero, Missale and Piga, 2000) show that both the maturity of fixed-rate conventional debt and the maturity which corrects for the short duration of floating-rate bonds are either very long or have substantially increased. A number of explanations are possible for this evidence. First, the lengthening of debt duration may only be apparent; it may just reflect the increasing use of interest rate swaps.[1]

* I wish to thank Gustavo Piga with whom the idea of this paper was shared. I am also grateful to Marco Buti and Carlo Favero for insightful discussions on the Stability Pact and monetary policy. I thank Michael Artis, Winfried Koeniger, Roberto Perotti and Riccardo Rovelli for their helpful comments.

Second, the anti-inflationary policy of countries like Italy, Portugal and Spain has gained credibility, thus leading to a reduction of the term premium on long-term bonds. Finally, the increasing integration and liquidity of securities markets for long benchmark bonds have made such bonds relatively cheaper (see Favero, Missale and Piga, 2000). All explanations thus point to the importance of interest-cost minimisation which should also play an important role in light of the Stability Pact. A reliance on long-term debt – if not undone by interest rate swaps – is likewise consistent with a concern for minimising interest rate risk and possibly the risk of exceeding the 3 per cent deficit limit. However, as argued by Piga (1999), for the Stability Pact the relevant object of risk management is the budget deficit: attention should be redirected from interest payments to deficit stabilisation.

The idea that the Stability Pact makes deficit stabilisation a main goal of debt management is formalised in this chapter. It is shown that debt instruments can be used to hedge against inflation and output shocks to the budget so as to stabilise the deficit/GDP ratio. For instance, if interest rates and output were negatively correlated, a long maturity debt would insulate the budget from interest rate shocks, thus avoiding higher than expected interest payments at times of cyclical downturns. Inflation-indexed bonds provide a perfect hedge against the budgetary effects of deflation which arise because of the nominalistic features of tax systems and spending programmes. The message is that the debt can be designed to provide flexibility to fiscal policy; to create room in the budget for the automatic stabilisers or counter-cyclical fiscal policy to operate.

We present a simple three-period model where the government trades off the cost of exceeding the 3 per cent deficit limit against the costs of fiscal adjustment. The budget is affected by cyclical conditions, namely by output growth and inflation, while an increase in the interest rate leads to higher interest payments on the part of the debt which has a short maturity or variable coupons. The debt composition, which stabilises the deficit, thus depends on the stochastic relations between output, inflation and the interest rate as determined by the monetary policy of the European Central Bank (ECB). The relevant correlations are derived from a multi-country model where the ECB reacts to inflationary pressure due to average EMU demand and supply shocks.

We explore how monetary policy and the ECB preferences for output relative to inflation stabilisation may affect the correlations of the interest rate with output and inflation and thus the optimal choice of debt instruments. We also examine how the debt composition changes when asymmetric shocks and differences in the impact of monetary policy are taken into consideration. We find that a longer maturity structure of conventional debt is optimal if the ECB assigns less weight on output stabilisation (relative to price stability) than the national monetary authorities and if EMU member states are hit by asymmetric shocks. Short-term and floating-rate debt should instead be issued by countries which experience a relatively higher output and inflation uncertainty and exhibit a lower sensitivity of aggregate demand to interest rate changes. The optimal share of inflation-indexed debt is largest in a strict inflation-targeting regime; the greater the weight on price stability the more attractive is indexation for deficit stabilisation.

The analysis is structured as follows. After this Introduction, section 14.2 introduces a simple model of fiscal adjustment which motivates the objective of deficit stabilisation. In section 14.3 the optimal debt composition is derived as a function of the risk premia on government bonds and the stochastic relations between output, inflation and the interest rate. Monetary policy is introduced in section 14.4 and the implications of supranational policy by the ECB are investigated. The analysis shows how the optimal debt structure depends on the preferences of the ECB and on asymmetries across EMU economies. Section 14.5 concludes.

14.2   THE GOVERNMENT OBJECTIVE

In this section we present a simple model where debt management helps to maintain the deficit/GDP ratio within the 3 per cent limit set by the Stability and Growth Pact. This task is accomplished by choosing the debt composition which minimises the expected cost of debt service and provides a hedge against variations in the primary budget due to cyclical effects and inflation. Indeed, reducing the variability of deficits across states of nature, for any given expected deficit, is valuable in that it lowers the probability that the deficit may exceed the 3 per cent limit because of a bad shock to the budget. The optimal debt composition thus trades off the minimisation of interest costs with the insurance obtained with deficit stabilisation.

The stabilisation of budget deficits calls for issuing instruments whose interest payments are positively correlated with primary surpluses. In the absence of GDP-indexed bonds, debt managers must rely on the limited insurance offered by conventional instruments and inflation-indexed bonds. In choosing debt instruments, they must consider the stochastic relations between output, inflation and the interest rate which arise from the shocks affecting the economy and the policy response by the monetary authority. Indeed, the monetary regime plays a key role in determining the relevant correlations on which the optimal debt composition is based.

We look at the interaction between debt management and monetary policy in a three-period model where the timing of policy decisions and events is as follows. In period $t-1$ the government decides the debt composition: that is, the relative amounts of one-period conventional bonds (or floating-rate bonds), two-period conventional bonds and two-period inflation-indexed bonds. Then, in period t, the monetary authority sets the interest rate as a reaction to inflationary pressure from macroeconomic shocks. This determines the interest rate at which the short-term debt is refinanced and hence the interest payments on such debt at time $t+1$. The interest rate along with new shocks affects output and inflation in period $t+1$ and thus the cyclical component of the budget. In turn, the inflation rate determines the interest payments on inflation-indexed bonds. The fiscal correction aimed at maintaining the deficit within the 3 per cent limit is implemented in period $t+1$ after the government observes the realisation of output and inflation. However, whether the government is able to contain the deficit remains uncertain, since it also depends on a shock which hits the budget at the end of period $t+1$.

The government decides the fiscal correction facing a trade-off between the cost of the adjustment and the probability of incurring the penalties of the Stability Pact. In fact, the outcome of the stabilisation is uncertain because the budget is subject to a shock, X, which occurs after the fiscal adjustment, F_{t+1}, has been carried out.

Assuming that budget cuts are increasingly costly, the government loss is given by

$$L_{t+1} = \frac{1}{2}F_{t+1}^2 + \int_{D^T+F_{t+1}-G_{t+1}}^{\infty} K\phi(X)dX \tag{14.1}$$

where D^T denotes the 3 per cent deficit limit, G_{t+1} is the deficit/GDP ratio in the absence of government intervention, that is, the trend component of the deficit, and $\phi(X)$ is the probability density function of the shock X. Finally, K is the fixed cost of failure due to the loss of reputation and the penalties for violating the Stability Pact.[2]

The first term of equation (14.1) represents the cost of the fiscal adjustment while the second term is the expected cost of exceeding the deficit limit. The latter is given by the fixed cost, K, times the probability that the shock, X, exceeds the deficit ceiling augmented by the planned surplus; that is, the probability that $X > D^T + F_{t+1} - G_{t+1}$.

Hence, stabilisation objectives are assumed away; output, inflation and the interest rate are determined by monetary policy before the fiscal correction is implemented. The model is therefore admittedly simple as it entails a complete separation of fiscal and monetary policy.

The composition of the debt is important since it determines the interest payments which affect the trend component of the deficit together with cyclical conditions and inflation:

$$G_{t+1} = g - \eta_y y_{t+1} - \eta_\pi \pi_{t+1} + R_{t+1} b$$

where g is the deterministic component of the deficit, y_{t+1} is the growth rate of output, π_{t+1} is the rate of inflation, η_y is the semi-elasticity of the government budget with respect to output, and η_π is the semi-elasticity of the budget with respect to the price level.[3] Finally, b denotes the debt/GDP ratio and $R_{t+1} b$ is the flow of interest payments relative to GDP.[4]

The deficit/GDP ratio is affected by cyclical conditions, that is, by output growth y_{t+1}, and by the rate of inflation π_{t+1}. While the impact of economic activity on the budget is well-known from a number of studies,[5] inflation also helps to reduce the deficit because tax systems and spending programmes are not fully indexed. The effects on net lending of an increase in output by 1 per cent are reported in the *OECD Economic Outlook* (1999a). With the notable exceptions of Austria, Denmark, Ireland, the Netherlands and Sweden, OECD countries have elasticities in the 0.4 to 0.7 range. The effects of inflation on government budgets have not been measured to the same extent, but appear substantial. For Sweden, Persson, Persson and Svensson (1998) estimate a budget improvement of 0.4 per cent of GDP on a yearly basis for a 1 per cent increase in the inflation rate.

The flow of interest payments, $R_{t+1} b$, on the outstanding debt depends on the interest rates and on the composition of public debt as determined by past decisions. To model the interest payments it is sufficient to consider the interest rate, i_t, set at the end of period t and prevailing in period $t + 1$. This is because the interest rate, i_{t-1}, prevailing in period t is known at the time of debt issuance. As we are interested in the relative cost of alternative debt instruments, the exact level of i_{t-1} is irrelevant and is thus set equal to zero to simplify the notation.

Denoting with E_{t-1} the expectations conditional on the information available at period $t - 1$, the interest payments relative to GDP in period $t + 1$ are equal to

$$R_{t+1}b = sbi_t + (1 - s - h)b(E_{t-1}i_t + p_L) \\ + hb[E_{t-1}(i_t - \pi_{t+1}) + \pi_{t+1} + p_I] \tag{14.2}$$

where s is the share of one-period conventional bonds (or floating-rate bonds) and h is the share of two-period inflation-indexed bonds, both issued in period $t - 1$. The interest payments in period $t + 1$ on one-period debt depend on the nominal interest rate, i_t, set at the end of period t. The interest rate on two-period bonds is given by the expectation of i_t and by the constant term premium, p_L. The payments on two-period inflation-indexed bonds depend on the real interest rate as expected in period $t - 1$, on the inflation rate, π_{t+1} and on the premium p_I over one-period bonds.

The interest rate, i_t, plays a key role in the choice of debt maturity. Having set i_{t-1} equal to zero, the cost of long-term debt is equal to the expectation, at period $t - 1$, of the one-period interest rate, i_t; that is, to the forward rate $E_{t-1}i_t$. While the nominal cost of long-term debt is predetermined, the cost of short-term (or floating-rate) debt is uncertain, since it depends on the interest rate, i_t, at which such debt will be refinanced in period t. This interest rate, which is chosen by the central bank, determines the interest payments on short-term (and floating-rate) debt, besides output and inflation in period $t + 1$.

14.3 THE CHOICE OF DEBT MATURITY AND INDEXATION

In this section we characterise the choice of debt maturity and indexation as a function of the stochastic relations between output, inflation and the interest rate. We solve the government problem backward in time, first deriving the fiscal correction, F_{t+1}, and then the choice of debt instruments.

The government decides the fiscal correction, F_{t+1}, to minimise the loss function (14.1) before knowing the realisation of X, but after observing output, inflation, the interest rate and thus the interest payments on public debt. Deriving (14.1) with respect to F_{t+1}, yields the first-order condition

$$F_{t+1}^* = K\phi(D^T + F_{t+1}^* - G_{t+1}) \tag{14.3}$$

which implicitly defines the optimal adjustment, F_{t+1}^*, as a function of the trend component of the deficit, G_{t+1}, and the deficit ceiling D^T. Intuitively, the optimal adjustment equals the marginal cost of the correction to the change in the expected cost of violating the Stability Pact due to the reduction in the probability of exceeding the deficit limit.

In what follows, we assume that the probability density function $\phi(X)$ decreases with X for $X > 0$, namely that bad shocks to the budget are less likely to occur the greater is their size. We also assume that the cost, K, is high relative to the trend deficit, G_{t+1}, so that the optimal fiscal adjustment implies an expected deficit below the deficit limit, that is, $F_{t+1}^* > G_{t+1} - D^T$, and the limit is exceeded only for bad shocks $X > 0$. Though weak, these restrictions ensure that the adjustment, F_{t+1}^*, minimises the government's loss (14.1) and imply that F_{t+1}^* is an increasing function of the trend component of the deficit, G_{t+1}.

We can now turn to the choice of debt maturity and indexation. Substituting F_{t+1}^* in the loss function (14.1) and taking expectations conditional on the information at time $t - 1$, we obtain the expected value of the government loss at the time when it decides the debt composition. The government chooses s and h to minimise:

$$E_{t-1}L_{t+1} = E_{t-1}\left[\frac{1}{2}F_{t+1}^{*2} + \int_{D^T+F_{t+1}^*-G_{t+1}}^{\infty} K\phi(X)dx\right] \tag{14.4}$$

Deriving (14.4) with respect to s and h and using condition (14.3), yields

$$E_{t-1}[(i_t - E_{t-1}i_t - p_L)F_{t+1}^*] = 0 \tag{14.5}$$

$$E_{t-1}[(\pi_{t+1} - E_{t-1}\pi_{t+1} + p_I - p_L)F_{t+1}^*] = 0 \tag{14.6}$$

Equations (14.5) and (14.6) have an intuitive interpretation: they show that the choice of a debt instrument is optimal only if its interest costs (relative to long-term debt) are uncorrelated with the fiscal correction. Indeed, if this were not the case, the government could modify the debt structure (for example, substitute short- for long-term debt and vice versa), so as to reduce the fiscal adjustment needed to maintain the deficit within the 3 per cent limit.[6]

An explicit solution for the optimal shares of debt can be obtained by a linear approximation of the fiscal rule F^*_{t+1}. Substituting $F^*_{t+1} \sim \alpha + \beta(G_{t+1} - D^T)$ for its value in equations (14.5) and (14.6) gives the optimal shares of short-term conventional debt, s^*, and long-term inflation-indexed debt, h^*, which minimise the expected loss (14.4)

$$s^* = \frac{\eta_y}{b}\frac{\mathrm{Cov}(y_{t+1}i_t)}{\mathrm{Var}(i_t)} + \frac{\eta_\pi}{b}\frac{\mathrm{Cov}(\pi_{t+1}i_t)}{\mathrm{Var}(i_t)} - h^*\frac{\mathrm{Cov}(\pi_{t+1}i_t)}{\mathrm{Var}(i_t)} + p_L\frac{E_{t-1}F^*_{t+1}}{\beta b\mathrm{Var}(i_t)}$$

(14.7)

$$h^* = \frac{\eta_y}{b}\frac{\mathrm{Cov}(y_{t+1}\pi_{t+1})}{\mathrm{Var}(\pi_{t+1})} + \frac{\eta_\pi}{b} - s^*\frac{\mathrm{Cov}(\pi_{t+1}i_t)}{\mathrm{Var}(\pi_{t+1})} - (p_I - p_L)\frac{E_{t-1}F^*_{t+1}}{\beta b\mathrm{Var}(\pi_{t+1})}$$

(14.8)

where $\mathrm{Var}(\cdot)$ and $\mathrm{Cov}(\cdot)$ denote variances and covariances conditional on the information available at time $t - 1$.[7]

There are two determinants of the optimal shares of short-term and indexed debt. The first component concerns the hedging role of debt instruments against variations in the primary budget due to output and inflation uncertainty. The second component, that is captured by the last terms in the right-hand side of equations (14.7) and (14.8), refers to the differences in risk premia, more precisely, in the expected returns between debt instruments.

In the following sections we first examine the implications of expected return differentials and then focus on insurance considerations.

14.3.1 Minimising the Expected Cost of Debt Service

The expected return on the various debt instruments and thus their relative cost may differ for a number of reasons. For instance, with risk-averse investors, expected return differentials may reflect (properly called) risk premia arising because of inflation uncertainty, the risk of default, preferred holding periods, and so on. Differentials may also be determined by liquidity premia due to the different liquidity and efficiency of the markets in which they are traded.

Finally, credibility problems regarding, say, the anti-inflationary stance of monetary policy may also lead to expected cost differentials which are not justified from the viewpoint of the government.

The deficit limit set by the Stability Pact clearly induces a preference for debt instruments with a lower expected return. Equation (14.7) shows that the optimal share of short-term debt increases with the expected return differential between long- and short-term debt, p_L. Likewise, equation (14.8) shows that the optimal share of inflation-indexed debt decreases with its expected return relative to long-term debt, $p_I - p_L$.

In principle, the Stability Pact may distort the choice of debt managers in favour of cheaper debt instruments. This happens when return differentials reflect properly called risk premia. In this case interest-cost minimisation may not be optimal since it increases tax distortions and shifts risk from debt-holders onto taxpayers or future generations (see Missale, 1997, 1999). In practice, however, it is unlikely that the Stability Pact may change the behaviour of debt managers, given that the minimisation of interest costs has long been their priority. If anything, as we discuss below, the Stability Pact is likely to induce a greater concern for risk minimisation. Therefore, the interesting issue to address is how expected return differentials may have changed with the advent of EMU, namely as a consequence of common euro denomination of government bonds and the move to a supranational monetary policy.

Three factors may have changed the relative cost of long- relative to short-term debt. First, common euro denomination and the loss of an autonomous monetary policy have reduced expected inflation and/or expected currency depreciation in countries affected by credibility problems and thus the spread of their long-term interest rates over German rates.[8] Second, the development of deeper and more integrated European securities markets may reduce the liquidity premium on long-term bonds. Although liquidity gains appear relatively more important for large issuers, the cost of long- versus short-term debt is likely to have fallen in other countries as well, thus favouring long-term bonds versus short-term instruments (see Favero, Missale and Piga, 2000). Third, as some economists have claimed, notwithstanding the Stability Pact, the loss of monetary policy autonomy may increase the risk of default for highly indebted countries. If credit risk were important it would make a case for short-term debt (as far as cost minimisation is concerned), since the credit-risk premium appears to increase with the term to maturity (see Favero, 1999).

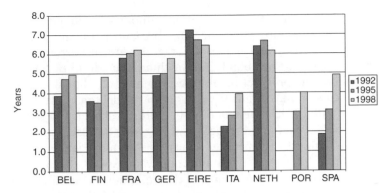

Figure 14.1   Convergence of average remaining term to maturity – marketable domestic currency debt: fixed-rate securities

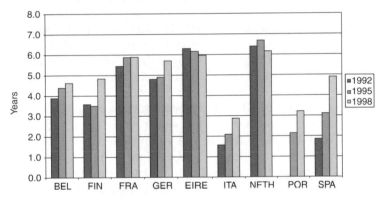

Figure 14.2   Convergence of term to maturity corrected for variable debt before swaps – marketable domestic currency debt: all securities

Focusing on the relative cost of inflation-indexed debt, two factors are important: the inflation-risk premium and the liquidity premium. Although the credibility of the anti-inflationary stance is not an issue as it was before EMU, a properly called inflation risk remains and so does a demand for protection. In fact, as shown in section 14.4.2 asymmetric shocks and asymmetries in the transmission mechanisms of monetary policy may have increased local inflation variability and thus the attractiveness of inflation-indexed bonds. So far, inflation-indexed bonds have been issued only in France (among EMU member states), probably because of liquidity problems (see

Townend, 1997, and Persson, 1997). Although an illiquid market could be a temporary phenomenon, the launch of an indexation programme is costly and may discourage sovereign borrowers from experimenting with such bonds.[9] If anything, the advent of EMU has not worsened the prospect for the development of a liquid market.

The discussion thus points to an evolution of debt maturity which is consistent with the lengthening of debt maturity observed in Belgium, Finland, Italy, Spain and Portugal and its relative constancy or slight decrease in other EMU member states, as shown in Figures 14.1 and 14.2. Indeed, interest-cost minimisation can explain the increasing reliance on fixed-rate long-term bonds, especially by those countries whose maturity structure was shortest in the early 1990s (see Favero, Missale and Piga, 2000).

14.3.2 Minimising the Uncertainty of Budget Deficits

The composition of public debt would matter even if all types of debt had the same expected return, that is, if $p_L = p_I = 0$, so that the expected cost of debt service was independent of the debt structure. Equations (14.7) and (14.8) show that, in order to minimise the expected loss (14.5), the debt must be designed to reduce the volatility of the deficit/GDP ratio. For any given interest cost, the government should choose the debt composition which minimises the uncertainty of the deficit/GDP ratio: that is, the composition that smoothes the deficit across states of nature. The intuition for this result is that a government which expects to succeed will not take bets on interest payments: an increase in the trend deficit raises the probability of exceeding the 3 per cent limit by a larger amount than a decrease of the deficit (of the same size) reduces it. This is because the probability of a bad shock to the budget decreases with the size of the shock.[10] Hence, the government chooses the debt composition which offers the best insurance against the risk of cyclical downturns and deflation.

For $p_L = p_I = 0$, equation (14.7) shows that short-term debt is optimal when the interest rate and thus the interest payments are positively correlated with unanticipated inflation and economic activity. Put simply, it is optimal for the government to pay lower interest at times when output and inflation are lower than expected and the primary deficit is unexpectedly high. On the other hand, the benefits of short-term debt are clearly reduced by the volatility of the interest rate, since (independently distributed) variations of the interest rate produce unnecessary fluctuations in interest payments. Except for the consideration of the impact of inflation, the implications for debt management are interestingly similar to those of tax-smoothing (see, for example, Bohn, 1990, Barro 1995, 1997, and Missale, 1997). The main insight of this literature, that debt instruments provide insurance against macroeconomic shocks to the budget and thus allow tax-smoothing across time and states of nature, is applied here to a situation where the constraint imposed by the Stability and Growth Pact induces a greater attention to insuring against current unfavourable events as opposed to tax-smoothing over the future ahead. Specifically, the Stability Pact extends tax-smoothing implications of permanent output variations to temporary output changes.

Equation (14.7) shows that the optimal share of inflation-indexed debt increases with the covariance between output growth and inflation. If this covariance is positive, inflation-indexed debt provides an insurance against unexpected slowdowns in economic activity, since lower interest payments on such debt partly offset the cyclical deficit. Inflation-indexed bonds are less attractive as the conditional variance of inflation increases. Implications of deficit stabilisation are again remarkably similar to implications of tax-smoothing (see, for example, Bohn, 1988, 1990). However, equation (14.7) points out that issuing inflation-indexed debt is optimal even when the covariance between output and inflation is zero. The reason is that we consider the positive impact of inflation (when it is low) on the primary deficit due to several nominalistic features of the tax system and spending programmes (see Persson, Persson and Svensson, 1998). This implies that inflation-indexed debt provides the perfect hedge against unexpected deflation.

While the result that the optimal debt composition relates to the stochastic structure of the economy is not new in the literature, in what follows we take a step further by explicitly investigating the role of monetary policy in determining the relations between the macroeconomic variables affecting the government budget.

14.4 MONETARY POLICY AND DEBT MANAGEMENT

The stochastic relations between output, inflation and the interest rate depend on the reaction of the monetary authority to macroeconomic shocks affecting the economy.[11] Therefore, we expect the monetary regime to play an important role in the choice of debt maturity and indexation.

In this section we study a simple model of the domestic economy and the group of other EMU member states where the ECB reacts to the average output gap and average inflation. We consider two groups of countries – the domestic economy and the other EMU member states – with relative weights in the ECB's loss function equal to $q < 0.5$ and $1 - q > 0.5$, respectively. The domestic economy, besides being of smaller size, differs for variance of shocks and parameter values.

The ECB aims at maintaining price stability and possibly at stabilising output, so that it chooses the interest rate to minimise

$$L_t^{ECB} = E_t[q\pi_{t+i} + (1 - q)\pi_{t+i}^* - \pi^T]^2 + \lambda E_t[qy_{t+i} + (1 - q)y_{t+i}^*]^2$$

(14.9)

where λ is the (publicly known) weight given by the ECB to output stabilisation relative to the inflation target. An asterisk indicates a variable of the group 'other EMU member states'.

The central bank controls aggregate demand and thus output and inflation – with a lag – through the choice of the nominal interest rate, i_t, at the end of period t. The aggregate demand of each country is equal to

$$y_{t+1} = \rho y_t - a(i_t - E_t\pi_{t+1} - r) + v_{t+1}$$

(14.10)

where y_{t+1} is the output gap and $(i_t - E_t\pi_{t+1})$ is the real interest rate between period t and $t + 1$. The impact of the interest rate is measured by the parameter a, while ρ measures output auto-correlation. Finally, v_{t+1} is an i.i.d. demand shock with mean zero and variance equal to σ_v^2. We do not consider interactions, in particular, the impact of aggregate EMU output on the demand of the domestic economy.

The supply side of each economy is modeled as a backward-looking Phillips curve:

$$\pi_{t+1} = \pi_t + cy_{t+1} + u_{t+1}$$

(14.11)

where c measures the impact of the output gap on inflation. Inflation is affected by an adverse supply shock, u_t, with mean zero and variance equal to σ_u^2.

Equation (14.11) implies important nominal rigidities and backward-looking behaviour in that the current inflation rate entirely depends on lagged inflation as opposed to expected inflation.[12] The backward-looking Phillips curve has been introduced by Buiter and Jewitt (1989), Fuhrer and Moore (1995) and Obstfeld (1995) and its empirical performance is quite satisfactorily (see, for example, Fuhrer, 1997).[13]

The ECB sets the short-term interest rate, i_t, to minimise the loss function (14.9) subject to equations (14.10) and (14.11) for both the domestic economy and the other EMU member countries. This leads to the following interest rate rule:

$$
\begin{aligned}
i_t = r + \pi^T &+ \frac{P(I + I^*) + a\lambda P(P + P^*)}{a(I + I^*)^2 + a\lambda(P + P^*)^2}(\pi_t - \pi^T) \\
&+ \frac{I(I + I^*) + \lambda P(P + P^*)}{a(I + I^*)^2 + a\lambda(P + P^*)^2}\rho y_t \\
&+ \frac{P^*(I + I^*) + a^*\lambda P^*(P + P^*)}{a^*(I + I^*)^2 + a^*\lambda(P + P^*)^2}(\pi_t^* - \pi^T) \\
&+ \frac{I^*(I + I^*) + \lambda P^*(P + P^*)}{a^*(I + I^*)^2 + a^*\lambda(P + P^*)^2}\rho^* y_t^*
\end{aligned}
\tag{14.12}
$$

where

$$
P = \frac{qa}{1 - ac}; \quad P^* = \frac{(1 - q)a^*}{1 - a^*c^*}; \quad I = \frac{qac}{1 - ac}; \quad I^* = \frac{(1 - q)a^*c^*}{1 - a^*c^*}
$$

and where we must assume that $1 - ac > 0$ and $1 - a^*c^* > 0$ to ensure that an increase in the interest rate has a negative impact on the inflation rate of the domestic economy and of the other EMU member states. As expected, the reaction to current inflation is stronger the lower is the weight, λ, assigned to output stabilisation.

The interest rate rule (14.12) can be combined with the aggregate demand (14.10) and the aggregate supply (14.11) of the domestic economy to derive the conditional covariances between output, inflation and the interest rate. In the next section we examine how such covariances are affected by the preferences of the ECB regarding output stabilisation.

14.4.1 The Monetary Regime

A main issue is how the debt structure that stabilises the deficit is related to the monetary regime and, in particular, to the weight that the monetary authority assigns to output relative to price stabilisation. In this section we explore how the monetary policy shapes the relations between output, inflation and the interest rate which are relevant for debt management. Moreover, the analysis shows how the debt composition that stabilises the deficit may have changed with the advent of EMU because of different preferences of the ECB and the local authorities.

In what follows we abstract from differences across countries and focus on the change in the preferences of the monetary authority; that is, on a change in λ. When countries are alike the interest rate rule (14.12) collapses to

$$i_t = r + \pi^T + \frac{c + a\lambda}{ac^2 + a\lambda}(\pi_t - \pi^T) + \frac{\rho}{a}y_t \qquad (14.13)$$

and it is equal to the interest rate rule for a single country under a national monetary policy.

The effect of monetary policy on debt management depends on the covariances between output, inflation and the interest rate conditional on the information available at time $t-1$, when the government chooses the composition of the debt. The (two-period ahead) unanticipated components of inflation, output and the interest rate are equal to

$$\pi_{t+1} - E_{t-1}\pi_{t+1} = \frac{\lambda}{c^2 + \lambda}(\pi_t - E_{t-1}\pi_t) + u_{t+1} + cv_{t+1} \qquad (14.14)$$

$$y_{t+1} - E_{t-1}y_{t+1} = -\frac{c}{c^2 + \lambda}(\pi_t - E_{t-1}\pi_t) + v_{t+1} \qquad (14.15)$$

$$i_t - E_{t-1}i_t = \frac{c + a\lambda}{ac^2 + a\lambda}(\pi_t - E_{t-1}\pi_t) + \frac{\rho}{a}(y_t - E_{t-1}y_t) \qquad (14.16)$$

Recalling that $\text{Cov}_{t-1}(y_t\pi_t) = c\sigma_v^2$, $\text{Var}_{t-1}(y_t) = \sigma_v^2$ and $\text{Var}_{t-1}(\pi_t) = c^2\sigma_v^2 + \sigma_u^2$, we can compute the correlation coefficients of equations (14.7) and (14.8). They are not reported here since the main forces at work can be discussed with reference to equations (14.14)–(14.16).

Focusing on the choice of debt maturity, we observe that the coefficient $\text{Cov}_{t-1}(y_{t+1}i_t)/\text{Var}_{t-1}(i_t)$ is always negative and increases with λ. The conditional covariance between the output gap and the interest rate is negative because the interest rate lowers inflation through a contraction of aggregate demand. This negative correlation weakens as the inflation targeting becomes more flexible (as λ increases) because of the weaker reaction of the interest rate to inflationary pressure. From equation (14.7) it follows that short-term debt may have a role in stabilising the deficit only if the conditional covariance between the interest rate and future inflation is positive. However, the coefficient $\text{Cov}_{t-1}(\pi_{t+1}i_t)/\text{Var}_{t-1}(i_t)$ is positive (and increases with λ) only if the monetary authority cares about output stabilisation. The reason is that, in strict inflation targeting – that is, for $\lambda = 0$ – the interest rate is set so as to fully stabilise inflation. As equation (14.14) shows, with $\lambda = 0$ inflation may differ from its expectation two periods earlier only because of contemporaneous shocks. Intuitively, if monetary policy has only one objective, at time $t - 1$ inflation is expected to be uncorrelated with the policy instrument, i_t, otherwise the monetary authority would intervene. On the other hand, if the authorities care about output stabilisation, the interest rate is not raised enough to eliminate inflation and a positive covariance between inflation and the interest rate emerges.

Focusing on the choice of inflation-indexed debt, we observe that the coefficient $\text{Cov}_{t-1}(y_{t+1}\pi_{t+1})/\text{Var}_{t-1}(\pi_{t+1})$ is positive for $\lambda = 0$; it increases with the variance of demand shocks relative to the variance of supply shocks and decreases with λ.[14] The intuition for this result is as follows. The covariance between output and inflation at time $t + 1$ conditional on the information at time $t - 1$ is uncertain because it depends on both demand and supply shocks occurring at time $t + 1$ and by the correlation induced by monetary policy. Contemporaneous shocks lead to a positive covariance which increases with the magnitude of demand relative to supply shocks. On the other hand, the effect of monetary policy depends on the weight assigned to output stabilisation. In strict inflation targeting unanticipated inflation only depends on contemporaneous shocks and the policy effect vanishes. In flexible inflation targeting the reaction of the monetary authority tends to reduce the covariance between output and inflation, as shown by equations (14.14) and (14.15). The effect is stronger the greater the weight, λ, assigned to output stabilisation.

The analysis offers interesting insights for debt management. It suggests that neither short-term debt nor floating-rate debt should be issued in strict inflation targeting for the purpose of stabilising the budget deficit. When the monetary authority only cares about price stability, the debt should either have a long maturity or be indexed to the inflation rate. As implied by tax-smoothing, the optimal share of indexed debt increases with the variance of demand relative to supply shocks. On the contrary, a concern for output stabilisation unambiguously favours short-term and floating-rate debt since it induces a positive covariance between inflation and the interest rate and increases the covariance between output and the interest rate (though the latter covariance remains negative). Interestingly, a greater concern for output stabilisation also reduces the opportunity to issue inflation-indexed bonds. This happens for two reasons. First, the variance of inflation rises. Second, the covariance between output and inflation falls, since the authorities give up inflation stability in exchange for output stabilisation.

The analysis also provides insights in how the optimal debt structure for deficit stabilisation may have changed along with the monetary authority, as policy-making moved from national central banks to the ECB. Clearly, if the ECB were less concerned with output fluctuations than the national authority, everything else being equal, lengthening debt maturity would be the optimal policy. In this case EMU participation would also call for a larger share of inflation-indexed debt.

These results are derived for the unrealistic case when member states are all alike, but provide useful benchmarks to evaluate the implications of asymmetries regarding the type of shocks and the transmission of monetary policy.

14.4.2 Asymmetric Shocks and Monetary Policy Transmission[15]

The traditional concern with supranational monetary policy is the loss of monetary autonomy to counter asymmetric real shocks. To investigate the implications of internationally uncorrelated shocks for the choice of debt maturity and indexation we assume that EMU economies are hit by supply and demand shocks that are not perfectly correlated – that is, $\mathrm{Cov}(uu^*) < [\mathrm{Var}(u)\mathrm{Var}(u^*)]^{1/2}$ and $\mathrm{Cov}(vv^*) < [\mathrm{Var}(v)\mathrm{Var}(v^*)]^{1/2}$ – while we maintain the hypotheses that member economies are characterised by the same parameter values and are hit by shocks of the same size: that is, that $\mathrm{Var}(v) = Var(v^*)$ and $\mathrm{Var}(u) = \mathrm{Var}(u^*)$.

The optimal debt composition can be derived by using equations (14.10), (14.11) and (14.12) to compute the conditional variances and covariances in equations (14.7) and (14.8). We find that, if the domestic economy is sufficiently small, that is, if $2q < ac$, the fact that shocks are not perfectly correlated lowers the conditional covariance between output and the interest rate. The intuition is that changes in interest rates, being triggered by foreign demand shocks, have now little relation to domestic conditions but they still adversely affect domestic output. However, the economy must be small for its output gap to weigh little in the ECB decisions.[16]

Asymmetric shocks to output and inflation also reduce the conditional covariance between inflation and the interest rate. The reason is that, if the ECB does not react to the same euro shocks, changes in the interest rate tend to be unrelated to domestic inflationary pressure but they still reduce the inflation rate. The lack of correlation between shocks thus suggests that the maturity structure which stabilises the deficit is longer in a monetary union than under a national monetary policy.[17]

Whether the asymmetry of shocks in a monetary union favours conventional or inflation-indexed debt depends on the preferences of the ECB and other factors. In strict inflation targeting, the effect on the conditional covariance between output and inflation is uncertain. If the domestic economy is small and changes in the interest rate have a strong impact on inflation, that is, if $q < ac$, then the covariance of output and inflation is greater than under symmetric shocks (and hence than under a national policy). However, the conditional variance of domestic inflation also increases because inflationary pressure is not fully countered by the ECB, while the reaction of the interest rate to euro shocks may destabilise domestic inflation. To conclude, without further information on the characteristics of the economy, it is difficult to ascertain whether in a monetary union inflation-indexed debt may play a greater role in deficit stabilisation.

So far we have assumed that domestic supply and demand shocks have the same magnitude as those of other EMU economies. An interesting issue is how the debt should be managed when a country experiences a greater macroeconomic uncertainty. For instance, we can think of common euro shocks displaying a different impact on output and inflation across member states. To capture such effect, let us assume that the variance of domestic shocks is greater than the variance of foreign shocks, that is, that $\sigma_u^2 \geq \sigma_u^{2*}$ and $\sigma_v^2 \geq \sigma_v^{2*}$.

With greater macroeconomic uncertainty the covariance of output with the interest rate, though it may remain negative, unambiguously increases relative to the symmetric case. This follows either from a weaker interest rate reaction to lower EMU inflation uncertainty or from the higher volatility of domestic output for any given interest rate.

The effect on the conditional covariance of inflation and the interest rate depends on the monetary regime. In strict inflation targeting, that is, for $\lambda = 0$, the covariance between domestic inflation and the interest rate becomes positive since the ECB reaction is not sufficient to stabilise domestic inflation if the magnitude of the shocks, and thus the inflationary pressure, is greater than in the other economies. By contrast, in flexible inflation targeting, that is, for $\lambda > 0$, the effect is ambiguous because the covariance between inflation and the interest rate is positive and the ECB underreaction to inflationary pressure has two opposite effects. On the one hand, it increases inflation volatility, on the other hand, it implies excessive interest rate smoothing, so that the combined effect is uncertain.

Finally, the variance of the interest rate is unambiguously lower than it would be if average EMU shocks had the same magnitude as those experienced by the domestic economy.

It follows that a greater macroeconomic uncertainty should favour short-term (or floating-rate) debt over long-term conventional debt. The role for short maturity is suggested by the positive correlation between the interest rate and inflation which arises when the ECB cares little about output stabilisation. The covariance between output and the interest rate is also higher under the common monetary policy, though it may remain negative.

The effect of macroeconomic uncertainty on the optimal share of inflation-indexed debt is instead uncertain, since the covariance between output and inflation may rise or fall depending on the impact of the interest rate on economic activity. Focusing on the case of strict inflation targeting, that is, for $\lambda = 0$, we observe that in the new regime inflation will no longer be stabilised while the effect of (larger than EMU average) demand shocks on output may or may not be reversed by monetary policy. While the same conclusion holds true for flexible inflation targeting, that is, $\lambda > 0$, it is more likely that demand shocks will not be offset, thus raising the covariance between output and inflation.[18] However, the optimal share of inflation-indexed debt may fall even in the latter case, since a greater uncertainty unambiguously translates into higher inflation volatility than under the national policy. Therefore, it is unlikely that economies experiencing higher output and inflation volatility should issue more inflation-indexed debt.

Important implications for debt management also emerge from the asymmetric effects of monetary policy. Asymmetries may arise either because of differences in the impact of the interest rate on aggregate demand or in the transmission mechanism, due to different financial

structures, goods and labour markets. In order to examine the implications of a stronger impact of the interest rate on the aggregate
demand of the domestic economy relative to the EMU average, let
us assume that $a > a^*$. Then, we can derive the optimal debt composition by computing the conditional variances and covariances in equations (14.7) and (14.8), under the assumption that shocks are
symmetric and parameter values are the same except that $a > a^*$.

When the domestic economy is more sensitive to interest rate
variations than the EMU average, it suffers more output variation
than needed to counter inflationary pressure. For any given interest
rate, output falls more than under the symmetric case, so that the
covariance between output and the interest rate decreases.

Too high interest rates and unnecessary contraction of economic
activity also imply a strong effect on inflation. In particular, if no
weight were given to output stabilisation, prices would settle below
target, generating a negative covariance between inflation and the
interest rate. Although this is likely to be the case also in flexible
inflation targeting, in principle a higher covariance between inflation
and the interest rate cannot be excluded when monetary policy is
accommodating. The reason is that the overreaction of the interest
rate has two opposite effects on the positive covariance between
inflation and the interest rate. Although inflation is lower for any
given interest rate, the volatility of the interest rate increases (relative
to the symmetric case) and possibly raises the covariance of inflation
with the interest rate. Indeed, the conditional variance of the interest
rate is greater than in the symmetric case.

To conclude, the maturity of conventional debt should be lengthened in the new regime by countries where aggregate demand is more
sensitive to the interest rate than the EMU average, provided that the
ECB does not place too much weight on output stabilisation.

With regard to inflation-indexed debt, we observe that the covariance between output and inflation is higher in the EMU in so far as
the ECB is not concerned with output stabilisation. In strict inflation
targeting a strong negative impact of the interest rate on economic
activity would be associated with unanticipated deflation leading to a
positive covariance between output and inflation. However, a reduction in the covariance between output and inflation cannot be
excluded if the authorities care about output stabilisation and the
aggregate supply is relatively flat.[19]

The effect on the variance of inflation is also uncertain, since it
depends on how strict is inflation targeting. If the authority aims at

stabilising inflation at any output cost, then excessive interest rate variation destabilises inflation, raising its conditional volatility. However, if the monetary policy is more accommodating, a stronger impact of the interest rate on economic activity might help to stabilise inflation. Therefore, without specific information on the parameter values, no indication can be given regarding the opportunity to issue inflation-indexed debt.

14.5   FINAL CONSIDERATIONS

We have shown that the Stability and Growth Pact provides a rationale for taking deficit stabilisation as a goal of debt management. The debt composition which is optimal for deficit stabilisation depends on the monetary regime and in particular on the preferences of the ECB. A long-maturity structure of conventional debt is optimal if the ECB assigns a low weight to output stabilisation relative to inflation stabilisation. In such a case, the optimal share of inflation-indexed debt is largest: the greater the concern for price stability, the more attractive is inflation indexation for deficit stabilisation. The optimal debt composition also depends on the correlation of supply and demand shocks across member states, on differences in the size of such shocks and in the transmission mechanism of monetary policy. Long-maturity debt is optimal if EMU economies are hit by asymmetric shocks. Short-term and floating-rate debt are useful only if shocks are correlated across countries and generate a higher uncertainty in domestic output and inflation than in other EMU economies. The maturity of conventional debt should also be relatively shorter in countries where the interest-rate sensitivity of aggregate demand is lower than the EMU average.

Although the analysis offers important indications for debt management, one may wonder whether the empirical evidence supports the theoretical relations on which these indications are based. To answer this question Missale (2001) estimates the correlation coefficients of equations (14.7) and (14.8) for OECD economies for the period preceding EMU.[20]

The correlation coefficients, reported in Table 14.1, are remarkably consistent with those predicted using the monetary policy model presented in section 14.4. As expected, the coefficients of output growth on the interest rate are negative and significant for all countries considered except for Greece, Portugal, Spain and Sweden. The

Table 14.1   Correlation coefficients and debt composition

	$\dfrac{Cov(y_{t+1}i_t)}{Var(i_t)}$	$\dfrac{Cov(\pi_{t+1}\pi_{t+1})}{Var(i_t)}$	$\dfrac{Cov(y_{t+1}\pi_{t+1})}{Var(\pi_{t+1})}$	Short-maturity	Fixed long-maturity	Inflation-indexed
Austria	−0.43**	0.12	−0.03	0	53	47
1967–97	(2.16)	(0.77)	(0.14)			
Belgium	−0.44**	0.57**	−0.16	0	75	25
1960–97	(3.20)	(3.71)	(1.17)			
Denmark[a]	−0.75**	0.72**	−0.52**	0	100	0
1960–97	(2.97)	(3.80)	(2.68)			
Finland	−0.63**	0.31	0.14	0	45	55
1970–97	(2.08)	(1.17)	(0.61)			
France	−0.45**	0.46**	−0.42**	0	84	16
1970–97	(3.65)	(3.42)	(2.56)			
Germany	−0.39**	0.36**	−0.10	0	53	47
1960–97	(2.27)	(3.46)	(0.39)			
Greece	−0.09	1.03**	−0.31**	28	72	0
1960–97	(0.42)	(2.40)	(5.37)			
Ireland	−0.70**	0.66*	−0.15	0	53	47
1975–97	(3.37)	(1.87)	(1.05)			
Italy	−0.67**	0.22	0.12	0	75	25
1971–97	(4.86)	(1.01)	(0.73)			
Japan	−0.37*	0.26	−0.25**	0	73	27
1969–97	(2.05)	(0.88)	(2.18)			
Netherlands	−0.47**	0.25	−0.01	0	58	42
1960–97	(3.67)	(1.60)	(0.07)			
Portugal	−0.41	1.13**	−0.24**	55	45	0
1966–97	(1.36)	(2.56)	(2.17)			
Spain[a]	−0.20	0.03	0.02	0	59	41
1960–97	(0.54)	(0.08)	(0.15)			
Sweden[a]	0.40	1.39**	0.05	72	28	0
1960–97	(1.07)	(3.33)	(0.37)			
UK	−0.43**	0.42	−0.27**	0	73	27
1969–97	(2.85)	(1.44)	(2.73)			
USA	−0.65**	0.60**	−0.32**	0	64	36
1960–97	(3.52)	(2.82)	(2.20)			

Note: *t*-statistics in parentheses.
* Significant at the 10 per cent level.
** Significant at the 5 per cent level.
[a] The long-term interest rate has been used to estimate the coefficients. the debt composition is derived from equations (14.7) and (14.8) assuming a price elasticity of 0.3 for all countries (0.4 for Sweden) and using statistically significant coefficients. The debt composition is computed assuming that debt shares cannot be negative.

correlation coefficients of inflation on the interest rate are not significantly different from zero in Austria, Finland Italy, Japan, the Netherlands and the UK, as we would expect in strict inflation targeting. The other group of countries, which includes, perhaps surprisingly, Germany, presents instead a significant positive correlation which should emerge in monetary regimes with a concern for output stabilisation. Within this group Greece, Portugal and Sweden show coefficients greater than 1, consistently with informal evidence for the sample period. Finally, the correlation coefficient of output on inflation, though negative for all countries considered, is significant only in a few cases.

This evidence provides support to the monetary policy approach to the identification of the relevant correlations and suggests a further investigation of the debt composition which would have stabilised the deficit in the period before EMU. The last three columns of Table 14.1 show the optimal debt composition corresponding to equations (14.7) and (14.8) when the expected return differentials, p_L and p_I, are set equal to zero.[21] For most countries fixed-rate long-term debt appears the optimal choice. Short-term and floating-rate debt should have been issued only in Greece, Portugal and Sweden. Although the role of inflation-indexed debt is limited to the insurance that it provides against unexpected deflation, its optimal share appears substantial.

This evidence suggests that the long maturity of conventional debt that is currently observed in the euro area (see Figures 14.1 and 14.2) should provide a sufficiently good insurance against macroeconomic shocks and thus reduce the risk that the deficit limit of the Stability Pact is exceeded. However, the evidence also suggests that inflation-indexed bonds have a positive role for deficit stabilisation that is clearly at odds with failure to issue such instruments.

Notes

1. See Missale and Piga (2000) for a discussion of the problems created by interest rate swaps.
2. That the costs are fixed is clearly a simplifying assumption since the amount that the government must place in a deposit bearing no interest increases with the excess deficit. However, reputation costs, which are arguably more important, are of a fixed nature.

3. It can be argued that for the fiscal correction only unanticipated output and inflation matter, since the effects of anticipated movements in output and inflation should be taken care of in advance, and thus should be included in the deterministic component, g, of the trend deficit. However, the consideration of unanticipated output and inflation does not affect the results.

4. It is worth noting that we consider nominal as opposed to real interest payments, that is, we do not deflate $R_{t+1}b$ by nominal output growth. The justification is that this effect of nominal output growth and thus inflation is arguably small, that is, smaller than the direct effect on the other components of the deficit. For example, even if the interest expenditure were as large as 5 per cent of GDP, an increase in nominal output growth from 4 per cent to 10 per cent would lead to a deficit reduction smaller than 0.03 per cent of GDP. This should be compared with a deficit reduction of 1.5 per cent of GDP for a 3 per cent real output growth or for a fall in the interest rate of 300 basis points when all the debt has maturity within one year.

5. See, for example, Giorno, Richardson, Rosevaere and van den Noord (1995), European Commission (2000a) and van den Noord (2000).

6. The argument assumes that there are non-negative constraints to the choice of debt instruments.

7. It is worth noting that $E_{t-1}F^*_{t+1}$ is also a function of s and h. The explicit solution is not reported here since results and discussion would not be affected.

8. A reduction of the inflation-risk premium associated with a strong preference for price stability by the ECB may also favour long-term debt.

9. See Pecchi and Piga (1999) for alternative explanations.

10. This is to say that, in the region we are considering, the probability density function, $\phi(X)$, decreases with X.

11. See Clarida, Galí and Gertler (1999) for a presentation of the monetary policy model and a discussion of the literature.

12. As shown in Missale (2001), results are not affected by the extent of backward-looking behaviour.

13. However, Galí and Gertler (1999) provide evidence in favour of a forward-looking Phillips curve.

14. More precisely, this coefficient is positive and decreases with λ for $c^2\sigma_v^2 < \sigma_u^2$. When this condition is not satisfied the coefficient decreases with λ until it reaches a negative minimum.

15. This section borrows from Missale (2001).

16. This result holds for a higher q as λ increases.

17. However, since the ECB tends to react less aggressively to shocks that hit only a fraction of EMU member states, the variance of the interest rate is also lower in the new regime. Although this weakens the case for long-maturity debt in flexible inflation targeting, it can be shown that a longer-maturity structure is optimal if the correlation of shocks across countries is sufficiently low or if the correlation of demand shocks is not greater than that of supply shocks.

18. A sufficient condition for the covariance to increase for any λ is that $q < ac$: that is, that the economy is small and the impact of the interest rate on output and inflation is sufficiently strong.
19. A sufficient condition for the covariance to increase is $c^2 > \lambda > 0$.
20. Conditional covariances are estimated using the residuals of two-period-ahead forecasting regressions of output growth, inflation and the short-term interest rate on the second lags of the same variables. The ratios between covariances and variances are obtained as the coefficients of OLS regressions of, say, the residuals of output growth and inflation on the residual of the interest rate (see Missale, 2001, for details).
21. The optimal composition is obtained from the estimated correlation coefficients (set to zero when not significant), reported in columns 1 to 3. The debt shares are computed using the debt/GDP ratios of 1998 and OECD estimates of the semi-elasticity of the government deficit with respect to output (see OECD, *Economic Outlook*, 1999a) and a tentative 0.3 for the semi-elasticity with respect to the price level.

Part VII
Were There Possible Alternatives?

15 The SGP and the 'Golden Rule'*

Fabrizio Balassone and Daniele Franco

15.1 INTRODUCTION

The slowdown in growth in 1998 and its possible implications for the level of unemployment raised worries and doubts concerning the fiscal rules set in the Treaty of Maastricht and in the Stability and Growth Pact. It has been argued that these rules may represent an excessively binding constraint for appropriate counter-cyclical action and that the attempt to reach rapidly a budget position 'close to balance or in surplus' may worsen the slowdown. The risk that the rules may permanently reduce the public sector's contribution to capital accumulation has also been pointed out.

In this framework the adoption of a 'golden rule' has been suggested. The rule would exclude investment spending from the computation of the fiscal parameters relevant to the Excessive Deficits Procedure.[1] In the opinion of those supporting the amendment, this would allow EU member states to loosen their fiscal stance while positively affecting long-run growth: debt finance would thus not harm future generations. Underlying the debate there are several issues. It is important to separate problems concerning the current economic situation from those concerning the design of EMU's fiscal constitution *per se*. The solution to the potential conflict between the objective of moving towards a close-to-balance position and the need to avoid a worsening of short-term economic prospects may not

* The views expressed in this chapter are those of the authors and do not commit the Banca d'Italia. The authors wish to thank Marc Robinson and two anonymous referees for helpful comments and for suggesting improvements. All remaining mistakes are ours. This chapter is a reprint of a paper published in *Fiscal Studies*, vol. 21, no. 2, (2000), pp. 207–29.

371

require changes to the rules set in the Treaty and in the Pact. Furthermore, the risk that a revision of the rules could harm the credibility of the commitment to fiscal sustainability, which in turn may prevent the adoption of the appropriate policy mix, must be taken into account.

Also the need to allow more room for counter-cyclical budgetary action and the need to increase public investment should be dealt with separately. As to the public sector's contribution to capital accumulation, one cannot simply assume that an increase in public investment spending is always superior to a cut in taxes, an increase in current outlays for human capital formation or a reduction in the deficit.

Finally, it is necessary to evaluate whether the golden rule is consistent with the objectives underlying present European fiscal rules. These rules aim at reducing the risk that unbalanced budgets in some member states may harm other members of the Union, and even endanger EMU, through financial instability and inflationary pressures. The rules also aim at allowing countries to adopt the appropriate policy mix when dealing with both symmetric and asymmetric shocks. The reduction of deficits and debts, necessary for reaching both objectives, may find an obstacle in the golden rule depending on the way the rule is implemented.

Starting from this debate, this chapter tackles two issues: (a) the implications of the Pact for public investment, and (b) the pros and cons of introducing a golden rule in EMU's fiscal framework, given the objectives of low public debts and adequate margins for stabilisation policy. The analysis suggests that the rules set in the Treaty and in the Pact may negatively influence public investment. However, the golden rule, although intuitively appealing, does not seem to be an appropriate solution to the problem.

The chapter is organised as follows. Section 15.2 examines the implications of a balanced budget for public investment both in the long run, when the debt reaches the new equilibrium level, and during the transition towards such equilibrium. Section 15.3 reviews the empirical evidence on the link between fiscal consolidations and reductions in public investment. Section 15.4 reviews the literature on the effects of public investment on growth in order to assess the possible consequences of a reduction in investment spending. Section 15.5 highlights the difficulty in reconciling different specifications of the golden rule with EMU's fiscal framework. Section 15.6 summarises the main conclusions.

15.2   THE STABILITY AND GROWTH PACT AND PUBLIC INVESTMENT

The achievement of budget positions 'close to balance or in surplus' implies that most capital expenditure will have to be funded from current revenues. Hence it will no longer be possible to spread the cost of an investment project over all the generations of taxpayers who benefit from it. This has two main implications which are analysed below:

(a) there is a disincentive to undertake large projects producing deferred benefits and entailing a significant gap between current revenues and current expenditures;
(b) the disincentive will be stronger while the deficit is being reduced.[2] The above-mentioned gap will grow if the flow of investment stays unchanged; the gap will remain larger than the initial level until the decline in interest expenditure induced by the reduction of the debt equals the decline in the deficit.

Concerning the first consequence, in Balassone and Franco (1999a) we show how the introduction of a deficit ceiling can imply a reduction in investment in a two-period model where a policy-maker with a finite horizon maximises disposable income and the latter is positively affected by investment with a lag. The finite horizon suggests a political economy interpretation of the result. Without a ceiling, the policy-maker, who cares about economic performance only when he or she is in power, can run deficits and invest in the first period without reducing disposable income. With a ceiling, investment will reduce disposable income in the first period, and the policy-maker invests less.

However, the introduction of a ceiling implies a reduction of investment also in the case of a benevolent planner aiming at maximising social welfare. In Barro (1979), given an expenditure profile, the efficiency loss caused by distortionary taxation is minimised if the tax rate is constant (tax-smoothing). If a budget constraint is introduced, indivisible investment projects may have welfare costs (the tax profile is no longer smooth); if the expenditure profile is not given, these costs may induce a reduction in investment.

Finally, since investments produce deferred benefits, the means of financing them (tax rather than debt) also affect intergenerational equity. Tax financing implies a welfare loss for the current generation and favours future ones: the former fully pays for a project whose benefits will partly accrue to the latter. When a budget constraint is introduced, it is then possible that voters will prefer a reduction in capital expenditure to an increase in taxes or a reduction in current outlays (from which they fully benefit).

The disincentive would mainly apply to projects with very uneven cost distributions. With a homogeneous expenditure flow the difference between tax and debt financing is limited:[3] only those generations living when the earliest projects are undertaken suffer a loss under tax finance; future generations will have to pay more or less the same, be it to finance interest on past debt (while new projects are financed via new debts) or to finance new projects (while past ones have already been paid for by past generations).

The transition to a lower deficit level is equivalent to an expenditure peak. If the flow of investment is unchanged, current generations will have to pay part of the new projects (the whole if the budget is balanced) while also paying interest on debts: taxes will have to be raised or current expenditures cut. For these generations the transition would be less burdensome if the level of investment (producing deferred benefits) was reduced, so that a smaller tax increase (or current outlays reduction) would be needed.[4]

The problem can easily be seen with reference to the budget constraint:

$$T + B = G = C_p + I(D) + K \quad \Rightarrow \quad T - C_p = K + I(D) - B$$

$$(15.1)$$

where T is taxes, B the deficit, G overall outlays (made up by interest I, other current outlays C_p, and investment K). The burden for current generations is $T - C_p$, since they give up resources (T) in excess of the transfers and services that they receive (C_p). This burden is compensated by the flow of services produced by investment projects which were undertaken in the past and financed by deficit. The burden is a positive function of interest payments (and hence of past debt, D) and of present investment spending; it is reduced by the deficit, so that the transition to a lower deficit implies an increase in the burden, which is higher the higher are K and D; *ceteris paribus* it will be higher in those countries where deficit finance has also been used to pay for current expenditures.

The double burden issue is exemplified in Figure 15.1, which is drawn assuming both nominal GDP growth rate and nominal interest

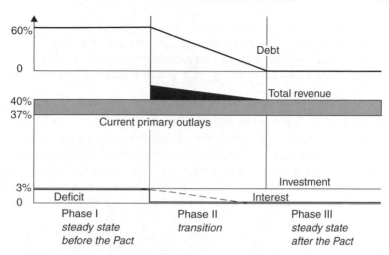

Figure 15.1   The burden of transition

rate at 5 per cent, and an initial debt/GDP ratio at 60 per cent of GDP. The initial deficit ratio is 3 per cent of GDP; thereafter a balanced budget is attained. Three phases can be separated:

(a) The first, labelled 'steady state before the Pact', is a situation in which the overall deficit is constant at 3 per cent of GDP; this implies a balanced primary budget and a constant debt/GDP ratio. The primary balance is assumed to result from a 40 per cent revenue to GDP ratio, a 37 per cent current primary expenditure ratio and a 3 per cent capital expenditure ratio. There is a 3 per cent of GDP gap between revenues and current primary expenditures (the light-shaded area) which is assumed to be balanced by the flow of services produced by past public investments.

(b) The second phase ('transition') opens with the abrupt reduction of the deficit to zero. This is obtained via an increase of 3 percentage points of GDP in the revenue ratio (a reduction in current primary outlays would have the same effect[5]). The gap between revenues and current primary outlays doubles. As the debt ratio gradually declines, so do interest expenditures and the revenue ratio can slowly move back to 40 per cent. The additional burden induced by the reduction of the deficit during the transition phase corresponds to the dark-shaded triangle.

(c)   The third phase ('steady state after the Pact'), begins when the debt ratio and interest expenditures are nil. The gap between revenues and current primary outlays is again at 3 per cent, balanced again by the flow of services produced by past investments.

The problems involved in the transition from deficit to tax financing of public investment are similar to those involved in the transition from a pay-as-you-go to a funded pension scheme.[6] In both cases the burden on current generations depends on the speed of the transition and on the stock of debt. In countries where a shift to funded schemes is under way, the burdens determined by the two transitions will be summed.

15.3   FISCAL CONSOLIDATION AND PUBLIC INVESTMENT REDUCTION: THE EMPIRICAL EVIDENCE

The link between fiscal consolidation and cuts in capital spending is confirmed by the experience of EU countries. In 1992, the year of the Treaty, the deficit ratio exceeded 3 per cent in nine countries. In 1997, for all these countries but Greece the ratio was at or below the threshold; all had reduced the investment/GDP ratio; all but Greece and the Netherlands had lowered the investment/primary outlays ratio (Table 15.1). Over the same period investment ratios increased in three of the six countries that met the deficit criterion in 1992.

In some countries the reduction of investment may reflect the privatisation process or changes in the classification of public utilities and other units (from the general government to the private sector); for Austria the latter factor accounts for half of the reduction between 1993 and 1997. In the UK the use of public finance initiatives (involving private capital in the realisation of projects of public interest) may explain about one-third of the reduction in public investment expenditure between 1993 and 1997. The contribution from sales of public real estate, which are recorded as negative investment outlays by general government, appears less relevant.

Similar evidence emerges when considering data from the 1980s and 1990s. Between 1980 and 1997, we identify 32 episodes of lasting and significant budget consolidation in EU countries: in 25 cases the ratio of investments to GDP decreased; in 23 the ratio of investment to primary outlays decreased (Table 15.2).[7]

Table 15.1   Deficit and public investment in EU countries
(1992–97; ESA-79 data)

	Deficit (% of GDP)		Investment (% of GDP)		Investment (% primary outlays)	
	1992	1997	1992	1997	1992	1997
Italy	9.6	2.7	3.0	2.4	6.8	5.7
France	3.9	3	3.5	3.1	6.9	6.1
Germany	2.6	2.7	2.8	1.9	6.1	4.3
UK	6.2	1.9	2.1	1.1	5.2	3.0
Spain	3.8	2.6	4.1	3.1	9.7	7.9
Belgium	6.9	2.1	1.5	1.4	3.4	3.2
Denmark	2.1	−0.7	1.7	1.8	3.2	3.4
Greece	12.8	4	3.5	3.3	10.1	10.2
Eire	2.5	−0.9	2.0	2.2	5.9	7.1
Luxembourg	−0.8	−1.7	5.4	4.9	n.d.	n.d.
Netherlands	3.9	1.4	2.1	1.9	4.2	4.2
Portugal	3.0	2.5	3.8	4.3	10.7	10.9
Austria	2.0	2.5	3.3	2.6	6.9	5.3
Finland	5.9	0.9	3.5	2.7	6.0	5.5
Sweden	7.7	0.8	2.7	2.4	4.3	4.2

With the exception of Greece, Portugal and Spain, which however benefited from particular conditions (for example, EU support for infrastructure development), the ratio of investment to GDP and primary outlays decreased in the EU between the first half of the 1980s and the 1995–97 period. With the exception of Greece, the larger reductions occurred in high-debt countries (Belgium, Ireland and Italy), where the investment/GDP ratio declined from an average of 3.7 per cent in 1980–84 to 2.3 per cent in 1995–97; at the same time the deficit/GDP ratio decreased from 9.8 to 4.2 per cent. In the rest of the EU, while the deficit decreased from 3.9 to 3.4 per cent of GDP, investment was reduced from 3.2 to 2.6 per cent (Figure 15.2). A similar picture emerges for the investment/primary outlays ratios (Figure 15.3). The growth of deficit and investment in low-debt countries in the first half of the 1990s may reflect expansionary policies implemented in response to a cyclical downswing: this opportunity was not available to countries where fiscal consolidation was still under way. During the 1990s the investment/GDP ratio in high-debt countries was significantly lower than in low-debt countries.

Table 15.2   Deficit reduction and changes in public investment: EU countries
(1980–97; ESA-79 data)

Country	Period	Deficit improvement	Changes in ratios	
			Investment/ GDP	Investment/ primary expenditure
Italy	1985–89	2.5	−0.4	−0.9
	1990–97	8.4	−0.9	−1.7
France	1985–89	1.7	0.2	0.8
	1994–97	2.8	−0.1	−0.1
Germany	1981–85	2.5	−0.6	−1.4
UK	1984–89	4.9	−0.3	0.0
	1993–97	6.0	−0.8	−1.7
Spain	1985–87	3.8	−0.3	−0.4
	1995–97	4.7	−0.7	−1.2
Belgium	1983–85	2.6	−0.8	−1.2
	1986–90	3.7	−1.0	−1.7
	1993–97	5.0	−0.2	−0.4
Denmark	1982–86	12.5	−0.8	−1.7
	1994–97	3.5	0	0.3
Greece	1985–87	2.0	−1.0	−2.4
	1995–97	6.3	0	0.7
Eire	1982–84	3.8	−1.2	−2.4
	1985–89	8.9	−2.0	−3.5
	1995–97	3.1	0	0.4
Netherlands	1982–85	3.0	−0.6	−0.8
	1995–97	2.6	−0.1	0.0
Portugal	1985–89	4.1	0.6	1.8
	1993–97	3.6	0.3	0.3
Austria	1983–85	1.5	−0.2	−0.6
	1987–90	1.8	−0.2	−0.1
	1995–97	2.7	−0.2	−0.2
Finland	1983–86	2.4	−0.5	−1.6
	1987–89	5.3	−0.7	−1.1
	1993–97	7.1	−0.1	0.6
Sweden	1982–84	4.1	−0.5	−1.0
	1985–87	8.0	−0.5	−0.1
	1993–97	11.4	1.3	−0.9

15.4   THE EFFECTS OF A REDUCTION IN PUBLIC INVESTMENT EXPENDITURE

The reduction in public investment is a problem if, as implicitly assumed in the previous sections, it reduces the productive and

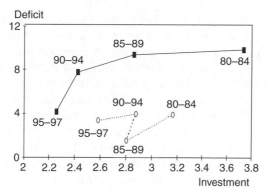

Figure 15.2   Investment and deficit in EU countries (% GDP; ESA-79 average over 1980–84; 1985–89; 1990–94; 1995–97)

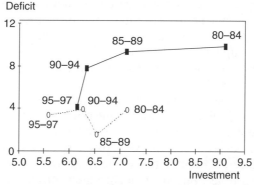

Figure 15.3   Deficit (% GDP) and investment (% primary expenditures) in EU countries (ESA-79 average over 1980–84; 1985–89; 1990–94; 1995–97)

growth potential of the economy. However, the empirical evidence on the effects of public investment is not unequivocal.[8]

Various techniques have been used to measure the impact of public capital. Direct estimation of a production function dates back to Mera

(1973) and Ratner (1983).[9] Using this approach Aschauer (1989) revived the debate. He found that non-military public capital is a significant input to a national production function for the USA and that the implied marginal product of public capital is high; he argued that the slowdown in public capital growth in the USA during the 1970s and the 1980s explains the decline in productivity growth that occurred over the same period. Aschauer's work spurred a literature aimed at refining his method and results (see the reviews in Eberts, 1990; Munnel, 1992; and Gramlich, 1994). Many studies initially confirmed (in sign if not in value) Aschauer's results also using US state-level panel data. However, subsequent efforts have found that when controlling for state fixed effects the positive infrastructure – output link found in OLS and random effects models disappears (Holtz-Eakin, 1994; Garcia-Milà et al., 1996; Kelejian and Robinson, 1997); similar results have been obtained by Evans and Karras (1994) using a panel of seven OECD countries.[10]

The statistical measurement of the effect of public capital on private production encounters several problems: the causality direction is difficult to assess; there is potential endogeneity of inputs and outputs; time-series may not be stationary; the proper treatment of fixed and random effects in an unsettled issue; the measurement of the stock of public capital or of the net addition to the stock generated by the annual flow of public investment is often inadequate (see the review in Hurst, 1994).

To this effect, the Italian experience clearly indicates that the ratio of investment to GDP is not a good indicator of variations in the stock of public capital: the Italian ratio has long been among the highest in Western countries without improving Italy's relative position in terms of infrastructures.[11] Besides the obvious issue of amortisation, the result may also reflect improper management or any other source of inefficiency.

Furthermore a large part of the infrastructures presumably affecting productivity and growth is not included among general government investment as the institutions responsible for such infrastructures are not part of the general government (this is frequently the case for energy, telecommunications and railways).

Hence, while there is a consensus that private sector production of goods and services depends crucially upon an adequate infrastructure of roads, electricity, telecommunications, water and other similar facilities, the public investment/GDP ratio cannot be the sole indicator of year-to-year changes in the stock of public capital.

The problem of efficiency of public investment is also stressed by Girard *et al.* (1994, 1995) who argue that 'the different quality of investment has played a significant role in the different economic growth experiences of the EU, Japan and USA' (1995, p. 731) and by Girard and Hurst (1994), who argue that a suboptimal public capital stock is consistent with a too high rate of public capital accumulation, that is, 'that there is some maximum rate at which viable projects can be prepared' (p. 53).[12]

15.5   WHICH 'GOLDEN RULE' FOR THE MONETARY UNION?

The usefulness of a dual budget has been long debated, since the 1930s, when a dual budget was proposed in order to foster the acceptance of using public debt to finance investment. It is still an unsettled issue, which has been tackled in different ways in different countries and at different times.[13] Sweden, for example, introduced the dual budget in 1937 and suppressed it in 1980.

The separation of current and capital operations is attractive for various respects. One of its main advantages is the possibility of spreading the costs of durables over the years during which they will be used. However, it has been noted that it is necessary to be careful about which expenditures should be included in the capital account otherwise the dual budget would result 'in a preference for expenditures on physical assets rather than greater spending for intangibles such as health or education' (Colm and Wagner, 1963, p. 125). Clearly there are current expenditures, such as those increasing human capital, that can give a relevant contribution to growth.[14] Moreover, the possibility to borrow, without strict limits, in order to finance investments can lower the attention paid when evaluating the costs and benefits of each project. Contrary to what happens in the private sector, there would be no mechanism to penalise public institutions investing in low-revenue projects.

Besides taking into account the above-mentioned aspects, the proposal to introduce such a rule in EMU's fiscal framework must be evaluated with regard to its consistency with the objectives of EMU's fiscal rules and to its impact upon the effectiveness of the surveillance procedure set to safeguard their enforcement.

The reference values and the targets defined in the Maastricht Treaty and in the Stability and Growth Pact do not distinguish between current and capital outlays. The latter are only mentioned among the other relevant factors for evaluating excessive deficits (Article 104c(3)); investment expenditure must be specified in the Convergence Programmes that each member state will submit annually to the Council and the European Commission.

As discussed in previous chapters, the objectives of the Treaty and the Pact are a sound fiscal stance (to this end quantitative limits are set for the deficit/GDP and the debt/GDP ratios) and sufficient room for counter-cyclical action (to this end, given the above-mentioned limits, a medium-term target of a budget position close to balance or in surplus is set).

The ECOFIN Council has subsequently made clear that such a medium-term target is to be obtained 'over the cycle'; in other words, it may be thought of as applying to structural budgets, around which automatic stabilisers will be operating and, if necessary, discretionary interventions will be made. The lower this budget balance with respect to the 3 per cent threshold, the wider the margins for counter-cyclical policy. The actual value set by each country for the medium-term target depends on three elements: the size of foreseeable recessions; the elasticity of the budget to the cycle; and the size of discretionary interventions that may be needed to supplement automatic stabilisers.[15] Countries with debt ratios above 60 per cent of GDP should also take into account the need to decrease such ratios, at a satisfactory pace, towards the threshold. Moreover, an increase in the debt ratio during recessions should be avoided.[16]

Some indications can be drawn from the analysis of past output gaps. According to the European Commission's estimates, over the period 1960–97 the maximum output gap among EU member states was on average 4 percentage points. Budget elasticity ranged from 0.4 for Greece to 0.9 in Sweden; on average it was 0.6. For output gaps no larger than in the past, in most EU countries a cyclically adjusted budget between 0 and 1 per cent of GDP would allow full operation of automatic stabilisers with no risk of breaching the 3 per cent threshold (Buti *et al.*, 1997, 1998). Countries with cycles of lower amplitude and lower budget elasticity could stay closer to the upper part of this 'safety zone'.

A stylised version of the EMU fiscal constitution can be drawn as follows: the reference parameter is general government deficit (*DEF*); the parameter is subject to an upper ceiling (3 per cent of GDP) and to a medium-term objective of a position close to balance or in surplus (to allow stabilisation policy without breaching the upper ceiling):

$$(DEF/GDP)_t \leq 0.03 \quad \forall t$$
$$(DEF_s/GDP)_t \in (0.00\,0.01) \quad \forall t \tag{15.2}$$

where DEF_s is the structural deficit and the medium-term objective of a position of close to balance or in surplus is operationalised in terms of the 'safety zone' defined above.

This characterisation allows us to distinguish three ways to introduce the 'golden rule'.

(a) changing the reference parameter;
(b) changing the upper limit;
(c) changing the medium-term objective.

For each option both the kind of investment outlays considered and the time span to which one refers need to be specified.

The implications of the three types of reform can be explained by looking at solutions already adopted in some countries or proposed in the debate:

(a) the proposal made by Modigliani *et al.* (1998), suggesting the use of a deficit net of net investment, represents a reform of the first type;
(b) in Germany (Article 115 of the Constitution), yearly deficits are allowed up to the level of gross investment in the federal budget (this includes items which differ from those considered in national accounts[17]); the adoption of this solution at EMU level would represent a reform of the second type;
(c) in the UK public borrowing cannot exceed the level of net investment over the cycle (HM Treasury, 1997); the adoption of this solution for EMU member countries would represent a reform of the third type.

To evaluate the consistency of each solution with the objectives of the Treaty and the Pact it is useful to refer to Figure 15.4a–d where the effects of each proposal on the structural deficit and on the margins for stabilisation policy are stylised. The curves show the level of the balance; they are traced assuming a 4 per cent of GDP difference between the position at the top of the upswing and the position at the bottom of the downswing (this is assumed to be sufficient for stabilisation purposes). The straight lines show the limits set to the deficit. Figure 15.4a depicts the present situation. The two curves refer to a balanced structural budget and a 1 per cent structural deficit. To simplify the analysis in the next subsections reference is made only to the latter situation.

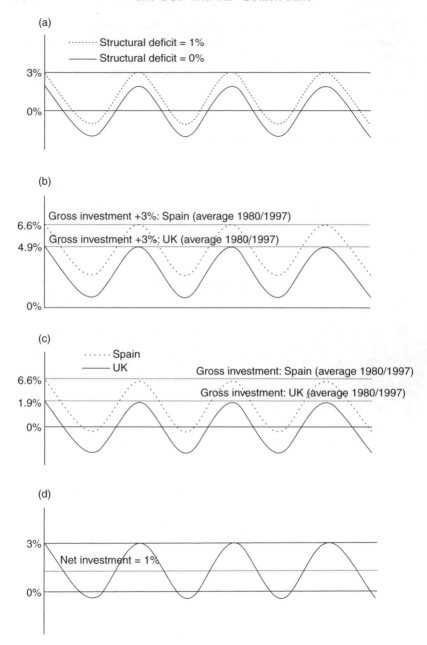

Figure 15.4   (a) The stability pact, (b) Excluding gross investment, (c) Golden rule: German model, (d) Golden rule: UK model

15.5.1 The Proposal by Modigliani *et al.*

Changing the reference parameter as proposed by Modigliani *et al.* the conditions in (15.2) would change into:

$$\{[DEF - (INV - AMM)]/GDP\}_t \leq 0.03 \qquad \forall t$$

$$\{[DEF_s - (INV - AMM)]/GDP\}_t = 0.01 \qquad \forall t \tag{15.3}$$

where *INV* and *AMM* stay for gross investment and amortisation respectively. These conditions amount to an increase in the upper limit and the medium-term objective presently set for the overall deficit. The increase depends on the country's level of net investment. In fact, (15.3) can be rewritten as

$$(DEF/GDP)_t \leq \{0.03 + [(INV - AMM)/GDP]_t\} \qquad \forall t$$

$$(DEF_s/GDP)_t = 0.01 + [(INV - AMM)/GDP]_t \qquad \forall t \tag{15.3a}$$

The margins for counter-cyclical action are unchanged with respect to (15.2). However, this proposal would determine an increase in the structural deficit which, for high-enough values of net investment, may be incompatible with the reduction of debt.

Reference to net investment is what a proper application of the dual budget requires. It has the merit of making the deficit level conditional upon the level of that part of expenditures that actually can increase a country's productive potential.[18] However, it also poses some problems for evaluation: (a) amortisation would have to be evaluated item by item with high administrative costs; and (b) this would be complicated by the fact that public infrastructures have multiple functions and no market value. Furthermore, the margins for opportunistic behaviour may widen.[19] These problems are all the more relevant for the multilateral surveillance procedure.

The use of gross investment would not be in line with the correct application of a double budget but would avoid the above-mentioned difficulties. The elements for the computation of the modified reference parameter (overall deficit and gross investment) are already available and communicated to the EU by member states within the Excessive Deficits Procedure.[20] There would not be extra administrative costs and the leeway for opportunistic behaviour would be less pronounced.[21] However, the monitoring of results during the year would become more difficult.[22]

The constraints in (15.3a) would change to

$$(DEF/GDP)_t \le [0.03 + (INV/GDP)_t] \quad \forall t$$
$$(DEF_s/GDP)_t = 0.01 + (INV/GDP)_t \quad \forall t$$

(15.3b)

In this case, if gross investment remain at the levels recorded on average over the 1980s and 1990s, the resulting structural deficit would not be consistent with the objective of a sound fiscal stance. In Figure 15.4b two lines are traced corresponding to the limits to the overall deficit resulting from the minimum and maximum value of the gross investment/GDP ratio recorded on average in the 1980–97 period in EU countries (respectively 1.9 per cent in the UK and 3.6 in Spain). The structural deficit would lie between 1.9 and 4.6 per cent of GDP (considering fluctuation margins respectively equal to 3 and 2 percentage points).[23] Such values, given the present low inflation environment, would only be consistent with the limit set for the debt ratio (60 per cent of GDP) under sustained real growth rates; for a country with a structural deficit of 3 per cent and a debt ratio of 60 per cent, growth rates higher than 5 per cent would be required. For Italy, a nominal growth rate of 4.5 per cent and structural deficit of 3 per cent would imply a debt ratio still at 100 per cent in the year 2010.

15.5.2   The German Model

The German model would meet difficulties similar to those mentioned above from the point of view of multilateral surveillance (again, gross investment is used). The constraints in (15.2) would change to

$$(DEF/GDP)_t \le (INV/GDP)_t \quad \forall t$$
$$(DEF_s/GDP)_t = (INV/GDP)_t - 0.02 \quad \forall t$$

(15.4)

where, as in (15.3a), it is assumed that the change in the upper ceiling of the reference parameter also determines a change in the medium-term objective allowing stabilisation policy without breaching the upper limit (the margins are left unaltered to 2 per cent).

As for the consistency with the objectives of the Treaty and the Pact, if the same level of expenditure experienced in the past were to prevail in the future, this solution would not imply a significant change with respect to the present situation for most EU member states. On average between 1980 and 1997 the ratio of gross investment to GDP in EU countries was slightly below 3 per cent; only in a few countries and for very limited periods of time did it go above 4 per cent; so, in order to have sufficient margins for counter-cyclical action, most countries would have to target a structural balance between 0 and 1 per cent of GDP. In Figure 15.4c two examples are depicted concerning the countries with the lowest and the highest gross investment/ GDP ratio in the EU (again the fluctuation margins are set to 2 per cent of GDP).

15.5.3 The UK Model

The UK model refers to results over the cycle; thus it appears to be better suited to be consistent with the objectives of soundness and flexibility of the budget. Adopting this model in EMU would imply the following constraints:

$$(DEF/GDP)_t \leq [(INV - AMM)/GDP]_a + 0.02 \quad \forall t$$
$$(DEF_s/GDP)_t \leq [(INV - AMM)/GDP]_a \quad \forall t \tag{15.5}$$

where the upper ceiling on the reference parameter has been defined so as to leave the fluctuation margins for the budget unaltered and $[(INV - AMM)/GDP]_a$ is the average level of the net investment/ GDP ratio over the cycle.

The actual determination of the reference period (the length of the cycle) may encounter some difficulties both on theoretical and practical grounds. It also adds to the complexity of the multilateral surveillance process. As already mentioned, additional problems stem from the reference to net investment.

Depending on the level of net investment, the medium-term target consistent with the UK model may or may not fall in the 'safety zone'.[24] In the first case, the UK model would only differ from the present situation in that a structural deficit could only be incurred if net investment were under way; it would leave unaltered both the margins for stabilisation policy and the safeguard of a structural budget consistent with a sustainable debt level. In the second case, both objectives could be compromised. Considering the investment undertaken by EU countries between 1980 and 1997, the structural deficit would lie between $(1.9 - x)$ and $(3.6 - x)$, where $x = AMM/GDP$; these levels are lower than those allowed by the proposal in Modigliani *et al.* (1998) $(1.9 - x; 4.6 - x)$, but they could still be inconsistent with a reduction of the debt ratio.[25] Furthermore, if the 3 per cent threshold for the overall deficit is kept (Figure 15.4d), net investment larger than 1 per cent would imply shrinking margins for stabilisation policy.

In conclusion, the adoption of the 'golden rule' cannot change significantly the policy options open to EU countries without conflicting with the objective of a sound fiscal stance and without making the multilateral surveillance process more complex.[26]

15.6   CONCLUSION

The Maastricht Treaty defines the soundness of public finances as a necessary condition for the success of EMU and sets quantitative limits to deficit and debt in EU member countries. The centralisation of monetary policy and the impossibility of using the exchange rate as a policy instrument make fiscal policy all the more important. Indeed, fiscal policy together with structural policy becomes the main instrument of national economic policy. Fiscal policy must deal with asymmetric shocks and with situations in which the national cycle diverges from that of the Union as a whole. This requires sufficient margins of fluctuation for the budget. In order to avoid flexibility conflicting with soundness, a structural budget close to balance is called for.

This arrangement is not without problems: (a) the transition to a balanced budget can have negative effects on conjunctural developments;[27] (b) the long process of debt reduction brings significant costs in terms of primary surpluses to current generations; (c) there is limited scope to using debt in order to finance investment and this in turn can determine a reduction in investment.

The first problem is undoubtedly relevant. In the event of extremely unfavourable conjunctural developments, a prudent tuning of the transition may be considered. However, a large part of the needed adjustment has already been completed: in 1999, the average deficit in EU countries was 0.6 per cent of GDP, compared with the 6.2 per cent peak in 1993. It should also be noted that in several countries the interest/GDP ratio tends to decrease as the reduction in interest rates affects the average cost of debt and as the debt ratio itself declines, making the needed effort in terms of primary surplus less demanding.

The effect of the transition to a balanced budget could be lessened by increasing the degree of competition and of flexibility in product and factor markets. A loosening of the rules designed to govern the system after the transition docs not seem necessary; it may damage the credibility of the commitment to sustainable public finances; monetary policy may be called to take a restrictive stance. Moreover, the 'golden rule' does not help during downswings: investment decisions only translate into actual expenditure with a significant delay.

The second problem cannot be avoided. The burden in terms of primary surplus is the price to pay to gain budget flexibility and soundness. In some countries the reduction of the debt can break the vicious cycle between high debt and high interest rates which has conditioned economic policy in the 1980s and 1990s (for Italy see Sartor, 1998). Furthermore, it allows margins for counter-cyclical action, avoiding the risk that an expansionary policy may be perceived as a threat to sustainability.[28] Finally, it permits tackling, from a sounder financial position, the coming phase of intense ageing and compensating with lower interest payments the ensuing increase in expenditure (see, for example, Franco and Munzi, 1999). If the introduction of the golden rule implied a reduction in primary surpluses, it could endanger the objectives of soundness and flexibility set for government budgets.

Previous sections have explained how the third problem evolves: a broadly balanced budget reduces the possibility of spreading investment costs over the generations benefiting from investment and can negatively affect the investment level. This effect can be especially relevant during the transition to the low debt levels consistent with the chosen structural balance. The reduction in deficit recorded in EU countries during the 1990s benefited from cuts in investment spending; in relative terms these cuts have often been higher than the corresponding cuts in other items. The problem may be more serious for countries and regions with a lower stock of public capital. However, a reduction in investment as measured in the general government accounts should not be too worrisome since this is not the most appropriate measure of change in public capital.

Should a golden rule be introduced into EMU fiscal framework to avoid the reduction in investment? The analysis above points to a negative answer. Some of the solutions proposed may be an obstacle to deficit and debt reduction, others meet practical difficulties, such as the evaluation of amortisation. Generally, leeway for opportunistic behaviour would increase and the surveillance of outcomes and trends would be more complex.

Perhaps it is better to search for different solutions. While an exhaustive list is certainly not the aim of this chapter, some ideas can be put forward. At the national level, one may consider safeguard clauses to avoid fiscal consolidation efforts translating into investment cuts. The adoption of the UK model at the national level may be a useful self-discipline mechanism warranting a minimum level of investment; if the mechanism has no relevance at EU level, no surveillance problem will arise. In adopting this model, the actual use of the margins for a structural deficit allowed by the EU fiscal constitution will become conditional on the realisation of infrastructure. As noted in section 15.5, in order to avoid an excessive reduction of the margins for counter-cyclical action and to make sure that EU fiscal rules are not breached, the structural deficit should not be above 1 per cent of GDP; this is a modest amount which should also limit the relevance of the conceptual problems posed by the double budget system.

In order to ensure a larger flow of resources available for public investment, other measures are necessary. For example, especially for smaller projects, the decentralisation of investment decision and financing may help to reduce the disincentive for projects with deferred benefits. At the local community level intergenerational altruism may be stronger and people may be more willing to bear a larger gap between taxes and immediate benefits. More generally, private capital will have to be involved in funding projects of public interest. Most infrastructure networks are already the responsibility of institutions and firms outside the general government.

Notes

1. This point of view is taken by Modigliani *et al.* (1998). Opinions in favour of some kind of golden rule have also been expressed by European Commissioner Mario Monti. It should be noted that when defining an excessive deficit the Treaty does not discriminate between current and capital outlays; however, it provides for the Commission's Report on Excessive Deficits to take into account a list of relevant factors and, among those, 'whether government deficit exceeds government investment expenditure' (Article 104c(3)).
2. The idea that investment is reduced more than other items during fiscal consolidations is largely shared in the literature. For example, Oxley and Martin (1991) point to 'the political reality that it is easier

to cut back or postpone investment spending than it is to cut current expenditure' (p. 161); de Haan *et al.* (1996) argue that investment '[is] the least rigid component of expenditure' (p. 108).

3. Let us express all variables in real terms and assume that the deficit is equal to investment expenditure (I) and constant as a ratio to GDP (Y): $I_t/Y_t = i_t = i \; \forall t$. If i is such that the debt (D) to GDP ratio converges (that is, if $i = (g/1+g)d$, where $d = d_t = D_t/Y_t \; \forall t$ and g is the growth rate of GDP), then since taxes (T) must equal interest outlays $(rD_{t-1}$ – where r is the interest rate) plus primary current expenditure (C) we have $T_t/Y_t = rD_{t-1}/Y_t + C_t/Y_t = rD_{t-1}/(1+g)Y_{t-1} + C_t/Y_t = (r/1+g)d + c_t \; \forall t$; where $c_t = C_t/Y_t$. If the same level of i were to be financed by taxes, we would have $T_t/Y_t = i + c_t = (g/1+g)d + c_t$. The difference between the two cases once the debt ratio is stable would then be negligible if $r \cong g$ (that is, if the real interest rate were close to the real GDP growth).

4. See Kitterer (1994) for an analysis based on an overlapping generations –general equilibrium model. The Central Planning Bureau of the Netherlands estimates that the shift from deficit to tax finance would entail a welfare loss for current generations equal to 34 per cent of GDP (van Ewijk, 1997).

5. If capital expenditures were reduced, the burden of transition would be shifted onto future generations who would suffer from the lower accumulated stock of public capital.

6. Budgetary problems involved in this second transition are analysed in Holzmann (1999).

7. By 'lasting and significant improvement' we mean a reduction of the deficit ratio for at least two years and by at least 1.5 percentage points of GDP. Luxembourg is not included in the analysis. Similar evidence is also reported by Roubini and Sachs (1989a) and by de Haan *et al.* (1996) with reference to different time spans and using a sample of OECD countries.

8. The implications of deficit financing of public investment also raise doubts from a theoretical point of view. Among the relevant issues, the possibility of crowding out should be mentioned. A review of the theory is provided by Dalamagas (1995).

9. Cost function estimations have also been used (see the references in Dalenberg *et al.*, 1998). In Dalenberg *et al.* (1998) the analysis focuses on the relationship between public infrastructure and private employment using a labour demand function: 'public highway capital is significantly related to state employment growth in all specifications' (p. 46). Also the effects of public investment on private investment have been investigated; Erenburg (1993) finds a significant positive relationship between the two variables at state level for the USA. Overall the results are ambiguous.

10. The production function method is based on an aggregate production function where public capital (G) is a factor of production (Q) together with private capital (K) and labour (L):

$$Q = MFP^*f(K,L,G)$$

where *MFP* (multifactor productivity) is the residual after subtracting from the growth in total output the direct contributions from capital and labour. Subsequent to the specification of the function (usually a Cobb–Douglas) and of the error term (a typical structure for a panel would be $\varepsilon_{it} = f_i + g_t + m_{it}$; where f is a country specific effect, g is a time-specific component and m is an identically and independently distributed error), a regression analysis is conducted to check whether the coefficient of G is positive and significant. The literature shows that the results of the analysis are strongly dependent upon the assumptions concerning f and g; specifically the presence of significant productivity effects from public capital seems to depend on the hypothesis that $f = 0 \; \forall i$.

11.   Comparative analyses show that the stock of infrastructure in Italy is currently 10 per cent lower than the EU average; a similar gap was estimated for the mid-1980s. See, for example, Pontolillo (1998).

12.   De la Fuente (1997), using a sample of OECD countries, finds that the elasticity of GDP with respect to investment expenditure decreases rapidly as outlays increase and can even assume negative values as a consequence of distortions and crowding out induced by public intervention.

13.   Proposals to exclude capital outlays from the operating budget and to include depreciation of government capital stock date back at least to Musgrave (1939). The issue is reviewed, for example, in Goode and Birnbaum (1955), Steve (1972), Premchand (1983), Poterba (1995) and Robinson (1998, 1999).

14.   The inclusion in the capital account (which can be debt-financed) of all expenditures contributing to human capital accumulation would imply high levels of deficits and pose serious classification problems. One should also take into account that part of expenditures replaces existing capital. Modigliani and Padoa Schioppa Kostoris (1998) estimate that in Italy gross public expenditure for 'development' amounts to 15 per cent of GDP; the corresponding net figure would be 5 per cent.

15.   We follow the definitions of the IMF, the OECD and the European Commission: structural is a synonym of cyclically adjusted and only automatic reactions to the cycle (that is, those induced by existing legislation) are considered (see Banca d'Italia, 1999, for a review of methodologies and practices). It is common in the literature to term 'elasticity' rather than 'semi-elasticity' the relation between point changes in the deficit/GDP ratio and percentage changes in output.

16.   Article 104c of the Treaty says that when the ratio is above 60 per cent of GDP it must 'diminish sufficiently' and approach 60 per cent 'at a satisfactory pace'. If the ratio increases, the Excessive Deficit Procedure begins. It should be noted that, while the Treaty allows exceptions to the 3 per cent deficit criterion, it does not for the criterion concerning the debt ratio. The implications for stabilisation policy of the interaction between the deficit and the debt rule are analysed in Balassone and Monacelli (2000). Other relevant issues concerning the stabilisation function of fiscal policy in EMU are discussed in Buti and Sapir (1998).

17. 'Borrowing cannot exceed the total investment expenditure in the budget; exceptions are only allowed to avoid disturbances to the overall economic equilibrium.'
18. On this, see HM Treasury (1998).
19. For example: how would one distinguish between maintenance and new investment?
20. In the procedure, investment is defined as 'gross fixed capital formation'.
21. It would be different if all capital expenditure were excluded from the deficit. Among these expenditures payments aimed at covering current deficits of public enterprises or at settling past debts would be included.
22. In several countries general government accounts are only available on a yearly basis. Monitoring of overall balances is often based on more readily available financial data (for example, borrowing requirement), which do not provide indications concerning the composition of balances and, more specifically, investment expenditure.
23. In Figure 15.4b fluctuation margins are always equal to 2 percentage points of GDP.
24. In the UK net investment to GDP is likely to be below 1 per cent (the gross ratio is just above 1 per cent).
25. In HM Treasury (1997) a safeguard clause is included for the stability of the debt/GDP ratio over the economic cycle.
26. These problems become more relevant when referring to the overall contribution of public sector outlays to human and physical capital accumulation. Estimates by Modigliani and Padoa Schioppa Kostoris (1998) clearly show how high the deficit could reach (see note 15) and the complexity of evaluating that contribution; the latter would be further compounded at the EU level.
27. According to the ECOFIN decision on 12 October 1998 the objective should be attained by 2002.
28. It has been suggested that the effects of expansionary policies diminish with the level of debt and that an increase in deficit may even have restrictive effects. See, for example, Bertola and Drazen (1993) and Giavazzi and Pagano (1990 and 1996).

16 Tradable Deficit Permits*

Alessandra Casella

16.1 INTRODUCTION

The current provisions of the Stability and Growth Pact (hereafter, SGP) advocate balanced budgets in the longer term and specify a ceiling for deficit spending of 3 per cent of GDP for each member of the European Monetary Union. A violation of the ceiling will trigger warnings and eventually penalties (unless exceptional circumstances can be invoked). In this form, the Pact suffers from several short-comings that will limit its effectiveness and impose exceptional costs on at least some of the member countries.

This chapter will discuss a scheme for achieving the objective of overall fiscal moderation embodied in the SGP at lower costs to countries' growth. It will not question whether the SGP is itself needed, but, taking the intent to regulate the fiscal position of member countries as established, present an efficient mechanism for the implementation of this regulation. Unemployment is still too high and the political will to maintain fiscal discipline will weaken if the costs are too large. If balancing the fiscal accounts is considered a worthwhile goal, reaching it may well depend on our ability to design a better mechanism.

The weaknesses of the SGP have been widely discussed:

- The imposition of the same criterion for each country leaves no room for differences, either in countries' initial fiscal positions

---

* This chapter is a short version of a longer study (Casella, 1999) where several issues touched upon here (especially those related to the experience of environmental market-able permits) were analysed thoroughly.

394

(which may be intended) or in countries' cyclical phases. For some economies at least the room for manoeuvre required for the functioning of the automatic stabilisers during the cycle is almost certainly missing.

- The arbitrariness left in the criteria creates uncertainty about the application of the penalties and is sure to generate difficult negotiations with individual countries. Compliance will be affected. Especially when times are hard (but not hard enough to qualify for exceptions automatically), the incentive to violate the deficit limit and then negotiate will be high.
- There is no reward for virtue. While an exposed fiscal position by any one country is considered a weakness for the whole system, a particularly solid position must be its own reward: 'The problem with the Pact as presently framed is that it is all stick and no carrot: rewarding good fiscal behavior in booms ... in addition to punishing bad behavior in slumps would surely make better sense' (Bean, 1998, p. 106).
- Politically the Pact seems designed to be unpopular. Combining a draconian criterion with discretion in the application of the penalties, it emphasises the countries' loss of sovereignty. It is likely to be an obstacle if and when the UK decides to join the Monetary Union.

The thesis of this chapter is that all these limitations can be overcome if we combine the overall objective of fiscal discipline with sufficient flexibility for individual countries. Borrowing from the experience of environmental markets, we should design a system of tradable deficit permits: having set an overall ceiling and an initial distribution of permits, EMU countries could be allowed to trade rights to deficit creation. The scheme need not treat all countries identically and could be designed to penalise countries with higher debt/GDP ratios. Its fundamental virtue is that it exploits countries' incentives to minimise their costs to ensure that the final goal is achieved as efficiently as possible. The next section clarifies the logic behind the proposal, and section 16.3 discusses options and obstacles in adapting the simplest design to the fiscal concerns of the Monetary Union.

16.2 THE BASIC IDEA

The starting point of the SGP must be the belief that markets alone are unable to impose sufficient discipline on the fiscal position of individual EMU members. High deficit spending by any one country has costs for the other members that the country itself fails to internalise: a high deficit in Italy affects negatively Germany, France and the other members of the Union. We can then think of deficits as a form of pollution, originating in one country's activity, but having repercussions for all. Once the problem is stated in these terms, we see that the arguments that have been developed for environmental regulations can be adapted to our purposes.

In a world where a benevolent and perfectly informed central planner existed, a centralised solution would be possible. All decisions would be deferred to the centre: in the same way as countries have relinquished their monetary policy, they would also lend their fiscal powers to a European-wide body. At least in the short run, neither the institutions nor the political will are in place to make such a scenario feasible or in fact desirable. Alternatively, countries running fiscal deficits could be charged a tax per unit of new debt equivalent to the social cost of their issues, a direct parallel to the Pigouvian tax advocated for environmental problems. But the information required to calculate the tax correctly is very difficult to obtain: a tax scheme imposes a daunting task on the regulator, with the likely result that the realised deficits could be seriously different from the desired objectives. In the presence of uncertainty, fixing the aggregate ceiling to fiscal expansion limits this risk, but must be complemented by an allocation mechanism that distributes the responsibility for fiscal austerity in the most efficient manner. Analogously to pollution permits, a system of tradable deficit permits sets a total limit to fiscal deficits but uses the market to allocate them across the different countries at minimum cost. This is the scheme recommended and discussed in this chapter.[1]

Most traditional forms of pollution control take the form of quantitative limits on pollution sources, typically imposing the same limit on all sources. But because different sources utilise different production technologies, have different access to cleaner inputs and different scope for capital investment in pollution reduction, the same pollution limit imposes widely diverging costs. In a market for pollution permits, instead, while the regulatory authority sets the overall pollution limit – the total stock of permits available on the market – it is the market itself that ensures that all pollution sources will act to equalise their marginal costs of pollution reduction, achieving the target decrease in pollution at minimum total cost.

The parallel with our fiscal problem is immediate: the scheme currently envisioned by the SGP consists of uniform quantitative constraints on each country's deficit (not more than 3 per cent of GDP, barring a serious recession), and the observance of this limit is likely to be associated with very different costs, depending on the country's structure, debt overhang and cyclical phase. The dispersion in costs is a sign of the scheme's inefficiency: a system of tradable deficit permits would allocate deficits there where their value is higher, making it possible to implement the desired fiscal discipline much more efficiently.

There are of course a number of potential difficulties with applying a system of tradable permits to fiscal discipline, and they are discussed below in section 16.3. For the moment, let us consider how the scheme would work in its simplest realisation. Each year each country is allocated a number of deficit permits, equivalent, for example, to 3 per cent of its GDP. In practice, these permits could simply be entries in special accounts maintained by each country at the ECB or at the European Commission. The permits are denominated in euros and freely tradable. At the time final fiscal statistics are made public, for example by the end of April of the following year, each country must have in its account a sufficient number of permits to cover the year's deficit, and these permits are withdrawn from the system.[2] If a country is found not in compliance, it faces a steep fee for each of the missing permits and must relinquish a corresponding number of permits from the following year's allocation. Following the example of existing environmental markets, it seems advisable to let countries bank permits for future use while not allowing them to borrow from future allocations. This leaves some room for intertemporal planning and smoothing of anticipated shocks, but limits temptations for governments with too short horizons. In practice, this means that deficits can be offset by permits carrying a date contemporaneous with or preceding the year of the deficit.

An unusual feature of the scheme is its finances. Buying the permit is buying the right to issue a unit of debt; but since the permit must be paid, part of the new debt is in fact devoted to the purchase of the permit itself. If p is the price of the right to issue one euro of debt, a government can devote only a share $1-p$ of the value of each permit to the purchase of new resources; in other words, the right to borrow one euro of new resources for national expenditure requires the purchase of $1/(1-p)$ euros of permits, that is, costs the government $p/(1-p)$. This multiplicative factor implies that the price of the right to issue one euro of debt must always be smaller than 1 (as intuition suggests), and creates a wedge between total new debt and those borrowed resources that can be devoted to national expenditure, but has no other implications, and in particular does not affect the theoretical optimality of the scheme.[3]

It is true of course that each government would be faced with an extra expense – the purchase of the permits – exactly when it is already surpassing its 3 per cent deficit allocation. But this occurs in the current system too, if the penalties are applied. The important difference is that in the scheme suggested here the fee is not fixed arbitrarily, but determined by the market. In particular, consider a country affected by an asymmetric negative shock, the type of idiosyncratic shock that would put the existing system under stress. If the other countries do not anticipate a need for fiscal expansion, the price of the permits will be low (the price is positive only if the total unconstrained deficit of the EMU countries is larger than 3 per cent of their total GDP), and the shock can be countered by fiscal policy at low cost. More generally, the cost of going above the 3 per cent limit at any given time is the market valuation of a fiscal expansion at that time, taking into account the overall ceiling and, possibly, the option of banking permits for the future. If the ceiling has been chosen correctly, this is exactly what the cost should be.

Thus the first important advantage of the scheme is the flexibility it provides to individual countries – the performance of all countries need not be the same, nor need the performance of each country at different times. Notice, and this is a second benefit, that the increased flexibility works both through imposing the correct costs to fiscal expansion and through creating the correct rewards for fiscal cuts. A country choosing to sell some of its permits collects resources, again according to the value of those permits in their best alternative use. Contrary to the current writing of the SGP, good behaviour is rewarded. Finally, flexibility means that a country can intervene *before* experiencing a severe contraction – as opposed to the present plan where exceptions to the fiscal constraint are only triggered when a very serious recession has been experienced, and thus when, by definition, stabilisation policy has already failed.

As all regulatory mechanisms, this too will function well if the aggregate ceiling is appropriate. In the case of an unexpected Europe-wide negative shock, the supply of permits may need to be increased to prevent an undesirable and contractionary increase in their price. More generally, the supply of permits should be adjusted to take into account the state of the European economy. This allows the system to overcome two further limitations of the SGP. First, in the case of a symmetric negative shock, the quantitative constraints on fiscal deficits at present leave all responsibility for stabilisation policy with the Central Bank. At least until deficits remain close to their upper limits there can be no meaningful discussion of an optimal policy mix. Second, while the SGP advocates the medium-term objective of a balanced budget, there is no mechanism that encourages countries to bring it about. Individual countries are given no inducement to reduce deficits below the limit, and imposing a lower limit would be extremely difficult in the absence of any room for individual deviations. A system of tradable permits, on the contrary, allows enough flexibility to accommodate anticipated declines in supply. Indeed this is one of the reasons that have made the system acceptable to environmental groups in the USA.

If changes in permits' supply are planned, however, it is important to make them as predictable and as transparent as possible: the scheme functions if the market functions, and the market requires predictability. Thus there is a trade-off between the possibility of fine-tuning the supply of permits and the need to minimise interference with the market. Again as in the case of the environmental markets, there should be an automatic rule that specifies how supply is determined over time, and the rule should be as simple as possible, focusing on indicators that countries' policies cannot manipulate.

One of the fundamental advantages of a system of tradable permits over the current Pact is its transparency, and it should not be compromised. It would be a system regulated by rules as opposed to a system open to political exceptions, and as such much easier to understand, predict and enforce. A standard finding in the literature on environmental regulation is the decline in litigation following the substitution of a system of tradable permits for quantitative constraints. The lack of flexibility that defines the latter makes it necessary to allow for exceptions, and the presence of exceptions makes it often desirable for a firm to violate the constraint first, and litigate later. A significant part of the increase in compliance predicted (and observed) with tradable permits comes from a decline in violations whose legitimacy could conceivably be defended in a murkier system (Tietenberg, 1985; Stavins, 1998).

Finally, the theoretical superiority of the scheme suggested here is also its main practical advantage: at equal enforcement, it is guaranteed to cost less. No matter how desirable fiscal discipline may appear ideally, it will not be pursued if its costs are too high. This is particularly true at the time of writing when other painful reforms must be tackled – to labour markets, to pension systems, to social benefits in general – and people's impatience with further fiscal austerity has been expressed at the polls and is shared by many of their representatives. If a scheme of fiscal discipline is to be imposed at all, then its only chance of implementation comes from being as efficient as possible.

The example of environmental regulation has been mentioned frequently because it is the main field where alternative schemes for controlling externalities were devised, studied and compared. Beyond the theoretical work, what is really exceptional about environmental regulation is that economists' schemes were in fact put into practice as policies. Thus not only the theoretical studies but the practical experience of existing permits markets can be used as a benchmark for quite different applications.[4]

16.3   HOW TO IMPLEMENT THE SCHEME

The basic system of tradable deficit permits can be amended to capture more faithfully the concerns of European policy-makers and ensure that it can be implemented. The purpose of this section is to show that potential problems can be faced, not to claim definitive answers. Most of the points raised here will eventually require more detailed analyses.

16.3.1   Deficits and Debts

A serious concern at the start of the sulphur dioxide emissions programme in the USA was the possibility that trade would lead to 'hot spots', geographical concentrations of pollutants in specific areas. Theoretically, a system of emission permits is optimal only when it concerns an 'assimilative pollutant', that is, a substance that mixes perfectly in the atmosphere and whose precise geographical origin is therefore irrelevant. Only in this case are emissions from all sources perfect substitutes and thus justified to trade at one price. 'Hot spots' could develop in the case of sulphur dioxide, but apparently have not, at least to any important extent (Ellerman *et al.*, 1997).

A very similar problem exists for a system of deficit permits. The system described in section 16.2 is the efficient way to implement an aggregate constraint on EMU countries' deficits, as a percentage of EMU GDP. But it assumes that the distribution of deficits among the different countries is irrelevant, because all individual deficits are perfect substitutes. If the source of the fiscal externality is interest rate spillovers when the market considers all countries' debts perfect substitutes, then the design of the system is appropriate. But if on the contrary the fear is that a country's excessive exposure can trigger a crisis for the Union as a whole, then Italy's new debt issues, for example, are not perfect substitutes for Germany's, because their outstanding debt volumes are different. Since heavier debt service means higher costs of deficit reduction, purchases of permits could be concentrated among countries with larger stocks of debt, creating 'hot spots' of new debt creation exactly where deficits are more costly for the Monetary Union. The distribution of deficits matters.

What is the appropriate design in such a case? Once again the intuition becomes particularly clear when we phrase the problem in terms of pollution. Consider two sources of pollution located at different distances from a town. The policy target is air quality in the town, and air quality is affected by emissions from the two sources in inverse proportion to distance. A system of emission permits is not well-suited to the problem because it values emissions from the two sources at the same price, whereas the two sources' impact on the target is different. The correct system should be instead one of *pollution* permits, as distinct from *emission* permits, where the two sources are allocated and trade permits to create pollution as measured at the receptor point, that is, in the town (an 'ambient permits system'). If one source is twice as distant from the town as the other, then two units of its emissions will have the same effect on air quality as one from the second source. Hence pollution permits trading at 1 to 1 translate into emissions permits trading at 2 to 1: the same level of emissions must cost the source closer to town twice as much. The solution, proposed and studied formally by Montgomery (1972), is simple and elegant: property rights should be created for the targeted externality and not for its origin, because the latter is one step removed from the policy problem.

In the case of environmental regulation, the simplicity of the theoretical solution translates into an impossibly difficult problem of implementation. Even if the impact of each source of emissions at a target point could be estimated accurately, each source affects environmental quality at a number of target points, and affects each of them differently. Thus each point should correspond to a different market, and each source should be active on all of them. But in fact if a source emits several pollutants, as typically the case, then it should be active on a different set of markets for each pollutant, and all these trades should happen contemporaneously and be interdependent. It seems highly implausible that firms could navigate such a system in practice.

For the purposes of our problem however, the essential intuition can be applied much more simply. The policy objective is to control the impact of each country's fiscal choices on the financial stability of the Monetary Union. This latter variable is equivalent to town air quality in the simple example discussed above; because it is the only relevant objective, a single market will be sufficient to achieve it, and it should be a market in 'permits to increase the financial fragility of the Union'. Thus what we need is an index of financial fragility and a measure of the impact that different countries' deficits have on such an index.

Consider the following plausible implementation. The proxy for aggregate financial fragility is given by the average squared deviation of Union countries' debt/GDP ratios from a fixed reference level; the policy objective is maintaining the rate of growth of that index below a specified target (that could be negative). Under reasonable assumptions this amounts to holding the weighted sum of all countries' deficits below the target, using as weight each country's debt/GDP ratio.[5] Again, such a policy can be efficiently implemented through a system of marketable permits: at the end of the year, each country must hold an amount of permits proportional to the year's deficit, using the country's debt/GDP ratio as a factor of proportionality. Exactly as in the case of the two sources of pollution at different distances from town, if country A's debt/GDP ratio is double that of country B, then country A will have to hold twice as many permits to issue the same amount of new debt, or equivalently will pay twice the price for each euro of deficit. And this is just as it should be, since the marginal impact of country A's deficit on the Union's financial fragility is twice as large as that of country B's.

The simple example comes close to real policy concerns. But of course different indexes of financial fragility could be constructed, taking other variables into account. As shown by Montgomery (1972) the only important constraint is that the policy target be expressed as a linear function of each country's deficit. Any such policy, choosing freely the factor of proportionality, can be implemented at minimum cost through a system of permits.

Environmental economists, on the other hand, have been forced to consider different approximations to the optimal system, given its forbidding complexity in the applications that are relevant to their concerns (see, for example, Krupnick, Oates and van de Verg (1983), and the discussion in Chapter 4 of Tietenberg (1985)). When undesirable geographical concentrations of pollutants are a possibility, a natural option to consider is that of 'zonal permits' where free trading of emission permits is allowed within each zone, but not across zone borders. Such a system guarantees that pollution levels in each zone do not exceed target levels, but does so by raising aggregate costs, because it interferes with the equalisation of marginal compliance costs produced by free trade. For our purposes, an analogous system would divide the member countries into different groups, according to their likelihood of triggering a fiscal crisis, fix a maximum deficit/GDP ratio for each group and a corresponding distribution of permits among all countries in the group, and allow trading only within the group. Given the small number of countries, the partition should probably not be finer than two groups, and again a plausible criterion for selecting group members could be debt/GDP ratios.[6] Individual countries would move between the two groups as their debt/GDP ratios change. To the extent that similar debt/GDP positions do not imply perfect correlation of shocks, some individual disturbances could still be smoothed through trading. It is clear however that the main purpose of a 'zonal' system is to reduce trade, and thus the system will be inefficient, unless the ceilings have been chosen exactly right. In addition, the scheme could be politically very unpopular, because it would subject different countries to different constraints, with permits trading at different prices within each group. We have discussed above how a better scheme can be designed for our problem with relative ease; thus the only reason to consider a 'zonal' system at all is its simplicity. It would be very transparent, easy to explain to the public, and a possible compromise between the current regime and a more desirable, fully flexible scheme.

It may be important to clarify at this point that our entire discussion follows from the maintained assumption that the fiscal externality takes the form of global, not local effects. The geographical analogy that allows us to borrow directly from the environmental literature should not be misleading. In our analysis, each country cares only about an overall measure of the Union's fiscal health, be it a straightforward aggregate variable – for example, the Union's aggregate deficit/GDP ratio – or a more complex function of member countries' policies – the probability that a financial crisis may be triggered, or that the ECB may be pressured into an inflationary path. We are not considering the alternative case where each country has preferences over the precise distribution of fiscal spending, independently of any aggregate measure of fiscal stability (as would happen, for example, if a country were affected exclusively by the fiscal stance of its main trading partners, or its geographical neighbours). The logic of our approach generalises to this scenario, but the appropriate trading mechanism could not be a simple market for permits. With a unique market price and anonymous trading, a country has no instrument with which to impose differential discipline on other member countries. We would need to devise more complex exchange mechanisms where countries could bid over specific distributions of fiscal spending across Union members, a 'menu auction' *à la* Bernheim and Whinston (1986). I am confident that the correct scheme could be designed, at least in theory, but neither the current formulation of the SGP nor the discussions that have accompanied it suggest that local effects are a central concern (see, for example, Eichengreen and Wyplosz (1998), and the discussion that follows the paper). All attention is focused on the possible influence of individual countries' fiscal mismanagement on Union-wide indicators: interest rates, inflation, the euro exchange rate. Thus studying a simple mechanism that can provide a solution to these global effects seems to be of particular importance and is the only issue addressed in this chapter. Even in this case the institution through which countries exchange permits requires some attention, and we turn to it now.

16.3.2   How Should Trade Be Organised?

If the theoretical answer is the creation of a competitive market, how do we make sure that transactions between the governments of eleven countries will indeed be competitive? There are two main difficulties. First, eleven is a small number, and since countries have very different sizes, the impact on the market of a large transaction by one of the big countries could *a priori* be important. Hahn (1984) has shown that the active presence of a monopsonist in the permits market distorts the equilibrium price and leads to higher compliance costs than in the competitive case. Hahn's result does not apply directly to our case because we have several large countries who are likely to find themselves on opposite sides of the market, not a single monopsonist, and a small number of players is not a guarantee of anti-competitive behaviour (think, for example, of Bertrand's model of price competition in a duopoly). Nevertheless, trusting that a deficit permits market in general will be competitive requires considerable faith.

One particular reason for concern, the second difficulty mentioned above, is that EMU countries' governments interact continuously on a large set of issues, and there would be scope for bundling purchases of permits with other bilateral transactions. Again, bilateral bargaining need not be inefficient in principle, but the terms of trade are bound to reflect the two parties' relative strength. Direct negotiations between any two countries cannot be prevented, but the deviation from competition will be minimised if we can design a parallel market where a country can always buy or sell permits at the competitive price. Is it possible to design realistic trading rules that would fulfil this function?

Based on the experience of environmental markets, a continuous double auction, where the current highest bid and lowest ask prices, and corresponding quantities, are posted on all terminals of connected agents (and with some delay on the Internet), appears a suitable option for organising trading in deficit permits.

A continuous double auction (often oral, with increasing frequency computerised) is the trading mechanism followed by most organised exchanges around the world and governing transactions of stocks, bonds, metals, commodities and derivative securities. Because of its practical importance, its intuitive resemblance to the abstract idea of 'the market', and the extreme difficulty of characterising its properties theoretically, it has been the object of a large volume of experimental work. In laboratory experiments, double auctions quickly converge to competitive outcomes with full efficiency even when the number of participants is as small as three players on each side of the market. The conclusion is surprising and very robust, insensitive to the exact details of the mechanism.

In line with developments in all financial markets, the continuous double auction should be computerised, a feature that reduces transaction costs and to some extent protects anonymity. Thus exchanges would then take place through a two-tier system: direct bilateral negotiations between countries, and a simultaneous electronic and anonymous double auction. A similar dual structure exists in most financial markets: for example the 'upstairs' and 'downstairs' market of the New York Stock Exchange. The downstairs market is the main market, organised as a (partially) computerised double auction; the upstairs market is reserved for very large trades that could not be concluded without delay through the main market, but are closed

through the dealers' personal negotiations. If the downstairs market is
sufficiently liquid, it can exercise the necessary disciplinary effect on
the upstairs market.[7]

To maximise the liquidity of the continuous double auction, we
need to consider which role, if any, should be played in it by
market-makers, and who these market-makers might be. Although
in theory the auction could function without intermediaries,[8] the
presence of market-makers actively speculating on their own
accounts, and thus acting to maximise the volume of trades, provides
liquidity. This is particularly important in a new market, and certainly
would be in a market where the number of traders is expected to be
small. In addition, transactions in deficit permits could well be lumpy,
with countries entering the market only to purchase or sell relatively
large volumes of permits.

The continuous nature of the auction, together with the year-long
horizon over which countries can plan for necessary acquisitions of
permits, is meant to alleviate the problem, but we cannot exclude that
the market may be required to accommodate large trades, or risk
losing all relevance. A hybrid system, where the auction's order
book is supplemented by a dealer ready to close large transactions
at price quotes that cannot be more favourable to traders than the
current best prices in the order book, is a possible solution.

16.3.3   Who Should Trade?

We need to face explicitly an issue we have avoided so far: who should
be allowed to trade on the permits market? There are two parts to
the question. First, should trading be open to all, or should it be
restricted to the agents required to hold permits? Second, even if we
decide for the latter, should these agents be exclusively the central
governments of the member countries, or should we extend the programme to state, provincial and local governments? Neither answer is
obvious.

In environmental permits markets, anybody can trade. Two arguments support this design: first, the larger the number of traders, the
more likely that the outcome of the market will be competitive;
second, participation in the market by consumers and environmental
groups can lead to a better approximation of the socially desirable
total pollution ceiling. In reality the presence of consumers in the
permits market remains very limited, but the first argument has
proven important: the market would not have developed as it has

without the presence of brokers who have acted as market-makers and engineered new contracts.

In the case of fiscal permits, the logic is unchanged. The more dispersed the ownership and trading of the permits, the more likely that the market will be thick and efficient. A fully developed market for deficit permits should not be any more fragile or manipulable than a market for, say, government bonds. If anything, the yearly allocation of permits to the member countries should offer a partial buffer from market instability.[9] In the government bonds market, the presence of large financial intermediaries, private agents, central banks and foreign governments is not seen as a threat but as an important contribution to the volume, liquidity and efficiency of the markets.

The problem, however, is that the market would not be born fully developed. Given the political sensitivity of the assets traded, opening a thin tentative market to all – and particularly to large foreign players – would probably rely too much on the competitive features of the double auction and would certainly be very controversial. Even within Europe, allowing the ECB to be an active trader would raise the concern that the bank could control both monetary and fiscal policies for the Union. A more realistic alternative is to begin by restricting entry to the players directly bound by the programme and to regulated brokers. Private intermediaries would be monitored, but should be allowed to trade because their objectives are more closely aligned with profit maximisation than governments', and thus their presence will improve the functioning of the market. Opening the market further should be considered at a later stage.

Which agents then should be bound by the programme? The discussion so far has assumed that only national governments would be required to hold permits. But the SGP specifies ceilings for general government deficit, thus including deficits incurred by state, provincial and local governments. In all member countries a sizable share of general government expenditure is channelled through state and local governments (the average share was 24 per cent in 1995). If we look at the four largest economies alone – accounting for more than 80 per cent of the Union's GDP in 1997 – not only does this remain true, but, what is most significant, state and local governments have consistently borrowed directly on financial markets.

The most likely outcome at present is an arbitrary partition of the total allowed deficit between central and local governments. But the deficit permits scheme suggests a superior alternative: if local governments are allowed to borrow, they should also be required to hold permits. After having received its initial allocation of permits, a national government should distribute it among its different jurisdictions. All jurisdictions would then be allowed to intervene in the permits market, so that the final allocation of permits, and the pattern of borrowing, would reflect the different costs of fiscal austerity. Efficiency would be enhanced through two channels: first, with a competitive permits market, the marginal costs of the borrowing constraint would be equalised not only across countries, but also within each country, among its local governments. Second, and equally important, the increase in the number of players and the reduction in the size of each player would improve the functioning of the market and increase the chance that its outcome would indeed be competitive. Because the initial allocation of permits does not impinge on efficiency, each country would be free to decide on the appropriate distribution across states or regions. Thus without preventing redistributive schemes within a country, the programme could further a policy of fiscal federalism, in line with the often enunciated principle of subsidiarity.

16.3.4 Enforcement and Political Economy

In the current version of the SGP, penalties for countries violating their deficit ceiling are not automatic, and it is hard to escape the impression that compliance with the Pact may not be enforced. In a market for deficit permits, enforcement will still be at the arbitrium of the collective will of the Union members, but there are some additional elements that should make enforcement easier. First, as emphasised earlier, the costs of compliance would be lower, and extenuating circumstances meriting exceptions would be harder to claim. In addition, suppose a country is found in violation of the scheme. If penalties are not enacted, the price of the permits immediately falls to zero; if the trading price was positive, any country who has saved permits for future use, or who has emitted debt to finance permits purchases suffers a capital loss. Thus not only is the Union affected by the negative externality attached to excessive deficit spending, as in the case of violation of quantitative limits in the SGP, but the market imposes a direct financial penalty on those countries who played by the rules.

Even if penalties are imposed and collected, under both schemes countries will constrain their behaviour only if they indeed bear the final responsibility for such penalties. If countries expect that their obligations will eventually be shared among Union members (directly or through inflationary pressures on the ECB), then enactment of the penalties is irrelevant. Although the possible expectation of a debt bail-out is one of the original motivations for the SGP, the Pact does not address the problem directly, beside taking the important step of making a country's fiscal imbalances very visible. Again, the same general reasoning holds in the case of a market for permits. As in the case of enforcement of penalties for non-compliance, here too the only real differences are the added flexibility enjoyed by all countries and the additional capital loss that a fiscal bail-out imposes on the other Union members.

Within any one country, taking full advantage of the flexibility allowed by the programme should mean being able to trade permits freely across time. Rational players choosing their series of deficits over an infinite horizon should be allowed not only to save permits, but also to borrow them so as to smooth the costs of fiscal contraction over time.[10] On the other hand, in a world of democratic governments with short horizons and strong electoral pressures, allowing a government to spend with no effective restrictions while imposing constraints on (remote) successors seems rather unwise.

The more pragmatic approach recommended in this chapter, such that governments would be allowed to save but not to borrow permits from their future allocations, is still consistent with some intertemporal trade. As discussed in the case of environmental markets, swaps of current permits in exchange for future ones among market participants may still emerge. They are a form of intertemporal borrowing with two main advantages: first, the desired aggregate fiscal ceiling is satisfied each period; second, the terms of the contract are decided by the market, and thus no contract will emerge if future repayments are not credible. If the alternation of different, competing governments makes past obligations unlikely to be honoured, then no borrowing will occur. The market would be so new that it is impossible to tell now whether the permits will acquire the status of 'standard' financial assets, mostly insensitive to government changes, or not. Thus leaving this matter open for market participants to resolve seems correct. In addition, preventing governments from borrowing directly from their own future permits limits the mistakes that initial inexperience with the programme is sure to produce, an important benefit in its own right.[11]

16.5 CONCLUSIONS

This chapter has discussed the creation of a market for tradable deficit permits as an efficient mechanism for the implementation of fiscal constraints in the European Monetary Union. When compared to the current provisions of the Stability and Growth Pact, a system of deficit permits would have a number of advantages. First of all, it would be much more flexible – individual countries could decide to incur larger deficits by purchasing permits on the market. Thus, for example, a negative idiosyncratic shock could be overcome at low cost, since the market price of the permits would reflect low demand by the other Union members. At the aggregate level, supply could be adjusted in the case of Europe-wide recessions.

Second, because of its flexibility, a system of tradable permits minimises the aggregate costs of compliance with the fiscal target. Given the high rates of unemployment in the four largest countries of the Union, ensuring that the costs of fiscal discipline are as low as possible is particularly important. And, if such discipline is indeed desired, the probability of enforcing it should be higher the lower the cost of doing so.

Third, by allowing countries to save or sell their unused permits, the present scheme gives them the incentive to reduce their deficit below the fixed 3 per cent ceiling of the SGP. The Pact's recommendation of a balanced budget in the medium run becomes much more likely to be implemented if it is accompanied by appropriate rewards for doing so.

Finally, given the general idea of a system of tradable permits, the design of the market can vary to reflect the specific policy concerns that have inspired the call for fiscal discipline. For example, countries with different debt positions can be treated differently, mirroring the fear that deficits from economies with larger outstanding debts may be particularly destabilising for the Union as a whole.

Will countries accept a deficit permits market as an alternative to the current provisions of the SGP? In the aggregate the costs of compliance would be lower; individually, countries that remain below the bound of the 3 per cent deficit/GDP ratio and have an equivalent initial allocation of permits would gain, by being able to sell their unused permits. Countries that go above their initial allotment would have to purchase permits on the market; we expect that the cost of doing so would be lower than the very high penalties foreseen by the SGP, if the purchase is not too large, but a more precise answer to this question must wait for a quantitative estimate of the permits market equilibrium price.

The real difficulty in comparing the costs that countries would sustain under the two schemes is assessing the probability that the SGP will indeed be enforced. It is quite possible that when the Pact was agreed upon, policy-makers believed that political considerations, more than economic ones, would finally determine whether or not fiscal discipline would be imposed on Union members. The fixed quantitative targets, together with the possible exceptions, create strong temptations for political settlements concluded outside the public view. In an enlightening discussion of political obstacles to environmental regulation, Robert Stavins describes how difficult it was to go beyond fixed ceilings for individual sources of pollution (Stavins, 1998). 'Old style' ceilings were popular with the public, because they sounded severe and unforgiving; they were popular with polluting firms, because firms knew that exceptions could and would be negotiated out of the limelight; they were popular with politicians because politicians maintained final control and benefited from the exceptions they were able to grant.[12] But international capital markets are not very forgiving of ambiguities. At the time of writing this (May 1999), five months after the introduction of the euro, the markets appear to demand compliance with the fiscal targets, demonstrating a loss of confidence in the European currency in response to any indication of a softening fiscal stance. Enacting a market in deficit permits, with its predictability, its transparency and its realistic requirements, could be an important step towards gaining the international role for the euro that we all expect.

Notes

1. It is possible to derive rigorous conditions that determine whether a tax or a quantity ceiling is the superior policy in the presence of uncertainty (Weitzman, 1974). Weitzman concludes generally in favour of quantity constraints, because he believes that small deviations from the optimal quantity are associated with steep reductions in benefits. For a very balanced discussion, see Baumol and Oates (1988), ch. 5.

2. As remarked by Peter Birch Sørensen, both the SGP and a system of tradable deficit permits induce countries to under-report their deficits. In the case of tradable permits, the incentive to under-report exists even when a country is below the 3 per cent limit, because it benefits from selling or banking its permits. But it seems unlikely that countries could indefinitely resort to accounting legerdemain, or that over time the difference in under-reporting between the two schemes would be of significant magnitude.

3. The point is analysed more formally in the Appendix to Casella (1999). Because the market price p is always smaller than 1, setting the penalty for non-compliance at or above 1 for each missing permit guarantees

that the fee is higher than the market price. Alternatively, the fee can be set equal to a stated multiple of the price, again exploiting the ceiling at 1 to ensure that the market price never follows an explosive path.

4. A different proposal for a permits market targeted, like the one discussed in this chapter, to macroeconomic policy, was never enacted but is too interesting not to be mentioned. Concern with inflation in the 1970s triggered the idea that individual nominal price increases caused an externality through their impact on inflation. Hence they could be curbed through appropriate taxes: TIPS (tax-based income policy schemes) would use penalties or subsidies to induce firms to refrain from granting wage increases and raising prices (Wallich and Weintraub, 1971; Seidman, 1976; Okun, 1977). The customary difficulties of a tax scheme led to the suggestion of a market for licences to increase prices (Lerner, 1977; Lerner and Colander, 1980; Vickrey, 1986). A special issue of the *Brooking Papers on Economic Activity* (1978) was devoted to the mechanisms, and Vickrey was sufficiently intrigued by the idea to return to it in his presidential address to the American Economic Association (Vickrey, 1993). In principle, the scheme was meant to apply to all firms and makes the proposal in this chapter appear very moderate.

5. See the Appendix to Casella (1999). For comparison, the simple case discussed in section 16.2 is equivalent to holding the unweighted sum of the Union's countries deficits below a target level.

6. For example, using as threshold a ratio of debt to GDP of 65 per cent, the two groups would be: Belgium, Italy, the Netherlands and Spain, as high-debt countries; and Austria, Finland, France, Germany, Ireland, Luxembourg and Portugal, as low-debt countries.

7. In most European exchanges, this dual structure takes the form of a computerised continuous auction for trades of smaller size, and a quote-driven dealers' market for large trades (Pagano, 1998). A trading system that protects a trader's identity is useful because lack of anonymity in the permits market could create two problems. First, competing countries could collude and artificially raise (or lower) the price at which transactions take place. At least partly, this difficulty is mitigated by those features of a double auction that appear to curb collusion. Second, although governments' baseline demand for permits will be written in the budget plans, and thus be public information, revisions during the fiscal year will become known abroad only with a lag. Thus knowing where sales or purchases of permits originate would transmit information about future demand and could result in large bid – ask spreads for large players, perceived as insiders.

8. Some existing proprietary trading system, for example, provide institutional investors with direct access to the order book (see Tradepoint in the London market).

9. It may seem at first that the market could be more volatile than the market for bonds, possibly subject to bubbles and crashes: contrary to bonds, the permits would not have an expiration date with a fixed redemption value. However the market price of the permits can never exceed 1, and this is sufficient to rule out the possibility of bubbles.

10. The correct dynamic plan depends on whether the target aggregate ceiling for the regulator includes only deficits or only debts or both.

11. Of course, a government can still shift the costs of its fiscal spending on the future administration by not complying with the programme. Two factors though may limit this temptation: first, the government must be sure to lose the elections, in which case the political gains from excessive spending would be few; second, the violation would be very visible.

12. The difficulty seems common to all new market-based regulations: Riker and Sened (1991) discuss identical problems in introducing tradable rights to airport time slots. As in the environmental case, the final adoption of marketable permits occurred only when the inefficiencies of the previous system became too large to bear.

Glossary

Adjustment path   The adjustment path is the profile of budgetary adjustment projected over a medium-term horizon. As defined in the Stability and Growth Pact, it refers to the planned evolution of the general government budget balance in the national Stability or Convergence Programmes.

Automatic stabilisers   Various features of the tax and spending regime react to the economic cycle and serve to reduce fluctuations in economic activity. As a result of the automatic stabilisers, the budget balance tends to improve in years of high growth and deteriorate during economic slowdowns. See *Cyclical component of the budget balance*.

Broad Economic Policy Guidelines (BEPG)   The BEPG constitute the main instrument for general coordination of the economic policies of the EU. They are adopted annually by the ECOFIN Council following a recommendation from the Commission and a discussion in the European Council, and contain recommendations on budgetary as well as structural policies. Their relevance for the SGP arises from the fact that the BEPG contain recommendations on the medium-term budgetary strategies to be pursued by the member states. According to the SGP the Council shall consider whether the policies of the member states are consistent with these recommendations when carrying out the annual assessment of the national Stability and Convergence Programmes. See also *Multilateral surveillance*.

Budget balance   This is the balance between total public expenditure and revenue in a specific year, with a positive balance indicating a surplus and a negative balance indicating a deficit. For the monitoring of member state budgetary positions, the EU uses consolidated aggregates for the general government sector. See also *Structural budget balance*, *Primary budget balance*, *Primary structural budget balance* and *General government sector*.

'Close to balance or in surplus'   See *Medium-term budgetary objective*.

Code of Conduct   The requirements that were set out in the SGP regarding the contents and format of the Stability and Convergence Programmes have been supplemented by a non-binding Code of Conduct, endorsed by the ECOFIN Council in the autumn of 1998.

Convergence Programme   See *Stability and Convergence Programmes*.

Council opinion   According to the SGP, the Council shall issue an opinion on each national Stability or Convergence Programme. It does so on the basis of a separate recommendation from the Commission. If the Council finds that a programme should be strengthened, it shall invite the member state concerned to adjust its programme. While the SGP does not oblige the Council to give opinions on the annual updates of the Stability and Convergence Programmes, it may nevertheless do so. The updates are in any case to be assessed by the Commission and examined in the Economic and Financial Committee.

Council recommendation   The Council may issue various kinds of recommendations to member states under the SGP. A distinction should be made between recommendations under the multilateral surveillance procedure and under the Excessive Deficit Procedure. In the former case, the Council shall issue a recommendation whenever it identifies an actual or expected *significant slippage* from the medium-term budgetary objective in a member state. The aim is here to avoid an excessive deficit from occurring by giving 'early warning' to the member state concerned. In the case of the Excessive Deficit Procedure, on the other hand, recommendations are issued when the Council decides that an excessive deficit already exists in a member state. The two kinds of recommendation differ markedly in their implications for the member state. See *Multilateral surveillance* and *Excessive Deficit Procedure*.

Council Regulation   The legally binding part of the Stability and Growth Pact consists of two Council Regulations. One concerns the strengthening of the surveillance of budgetary positions and the surveillance and coordination of economic policies. The other aims at speeding up and clarifying the Excessive Deficit Procedure. Regulations are directly applicable in the member states. Unlike Directives they do not need to be transposed into national legislation, and they therefore constitute a strong form of Community legislation. Those parts of the SGP that could not be included in secondary legislation are embodied in two Resolutions of the European Council in Amsterdam, June 1997: see *European Council Resolution*.

Cyclical component of the budget balance   This refers to that part of a change in the budget balance that follows automatically from the economic cycle, due to the reaction of public revenue and expenditure to changes in the output gap. See *Automatic stabilisers*, *Tax smoothing* and *Structural budget balance*.

Cyclically adjusted budget balance   See *Structural budget balance*.

ECOFIN Council   The Council of Ministers for Economic and Financial Affairs (ECOFIN Council) meets on average every month, and it is here that all the most important decisions are made relating to the SGP. Since June 1998, a special informal forum has been created for those member states that participate in the euro area. In July 2000 it was decided in future to call this forum the 'Euro Group'. In contrast to the ECOFIN Council, the Euro Group has no formal decision-making authority and is not even an official organ of the Community. Nevertheless, it is a significant change in the working practices of the ECOFIN Council.

Economic and Financial Committee   The Economic and Financial Committee (EFC), until 1999 called the Monetary Committee, consists of high-ranking officials from national ministries of finance or economic affairs and central banks as well as from the Commission and the European Central Bank. The EFC is responsible for preparing recommendations and assessments for the ECOFIN Council on a wide range of issues, including all matters related to the SGP. On these issues it replaces the Committee of Permanent Representatives (Coreper) in a number of important functions related to meetings in the Council.

'**Effective action**'   When the Council issues *recommendations* under the Excessive Deficit Procedure, the member state concerned is required to take 'effective action' within a deadline of no more than four months. The Council assesses the actions of the member state on the basis of policy measures announced by the government, and holds the procedure in *abeyance* wherever these measures are judged sufficient to correct the deficit within a certain time period. In the event that the measures are not implemented, or if it later appears that they are inadequate to correct the excessive deficit within the specified time period, the Council proceeds to the next step in the procedure. This implies *giving notice* to the member state to take measures within a deadline of no more than two months. Again the procedure may be held in *abeyance* by reference to measures announced by the government. It can later be reactivated according to the same principles as described above, in which case the Council proceeds to impose *sanctions* on the member state.

ESA-95/ESA-79   The European system of accounts (ESA) are harmonised systems of accounting standards used for the reporting of economic data by the member states to the EU. As from 2000, ESA-95 has replaced the earlier ESA-79 standard with regard to the comparison and analysis of national public finance data.

Euro area   The euro area consists of those member states that have adopted the single currency. They are referred to individually as 'participating Member States' or 'Member States without a derogation'. As from January 2001 Greece joins the euro area, and there will be twelve participating member states. While the SGP is mainly concerned with the budgetary policies in each individual member state, the Treaty stipulates that the Council carry out regular overall assessments of the economic policies of the member states and the Community. Furthermore, as part of the multilateral surveillance process, the Commission regularly reports on the overall budgetary stance of the euro area as well as of the Community and each member state.

European Commission (role in the SGP)   The role of the European Commission, as set out in the SGP, is to assist the ECOFIN Council in monitoring the budgetary positions of the member states and the euro area, primarily by preparing independent assessments of the Stability and Convergence Programmes as well as of current economic and budgetary developments in the Community. In case of a deficit above 3 per cent of GDP occurring in one of the member states, the Commission is also responsible for initiating the Excessive Deficit Procedure by addressing a report to the Council of Ministers on the relevant member state.

European Council Resolution   The Stability and Growth Pact includes two Resolutions of the European Council in Amsterdam 1997, giving political guidance to the member states, the Commission and the Council of Ministers in applying the provisions of the Pact. The first Council Resolution embodies various commitments of the Commission and of the member states pertaining to the strict implementation of the Pact. The second Resolution confirms the commitment of the European Council to give employment and growth a central place on the European agenda. While the Resolutions are not legally binding in the same way as Council Regulations, they do carry strong political weight as statements of intent on behalf of the member states and the Commission. The role of the European Council in defining such general political guidelines for the Union was formally recognised in the Maastricht Treaty.

'Exceptional and temporary' conditions According to the Treaty, a deficit on the general government balance is excessive wherever it exceeds 3 per cent of GDP, unless the excess is both exceptional and temporary and stays close to the reference value. In the SGP, some further clarifications are provided. A deficit is *exceptional* if it results from an unusual event outside the control of the member state or from a severe economic downturn. A severe downturn is defined as an annual fall in GDP of at least 2 per cent, or, in light of further evidence, of more than 0.75 per cent. The excess is *temporary* if Commission forecasts indicate that it will fall below the 3 per cent reference value the year after the end of the unusual event or economic downturn. The 'closeness' condition has not been further specified.

Excessive Deficit Procedure According to the Treaty the Commission and the Council are to monitor the budgetary developments in the member states in order to identify and act upon the occurrence of 'excessive deficits'. An excessive deficit is identified by the Council on the basis of a Commission recommendation. Wherever an excess is identified, the Council will proceed to issue recommendations to the member state with a view to bringing the deficit down within a certain time limit. In the final instance, if a member state does not address the excessive deficit in spite of several warnings from the Council, sanctions may be imposed. The Treaty leaves some discretion to both Commission and Council in the assessment of whether a given deficit is 'excessive', but in the SGP the concept has been further clarified and now all deficits above 3 per cent of GDP will normally be regarded excessive, subject to certain limited exemptions. See *'Exceptional and temporary' conditions*, *Council recommendation* and *Sanctions*.

Fiscal stance The fiscal stance is a measure of the discretionary (as opposed to cyclical) fiscal policy component. It is often defined as the change in the primary structural budget deficit relative to the preceding period. When the deficit increases (falls) the fiscal stance is expansionary (contractionary). See *Cyclical component of the budget balance* and *Primary structural budget balance*.

General government sector When monitoring member state budgetary developments under the Excessive Deficit Procedure and multilateral surveillance the Community uses a special definition of deficits and debt, based on the concept of the 'general government' sector. General government includes national government, regional government, local government and social security funds. Public enterprises are excluded, as are transfers to and from the EU budget. In the Excessive Deficit Procedure consolidated figures are used so that any internal balances and debt positions among the four sub-sectors are netted out against each other. In this way, the national government is held accountable for the overall deficit and debt position of the entire general government sector *vis-à-vis* the private and foreign sectors.

Government budget constraint   The government budget constraint is a basic condition applying to the public finances, according to which total public expenditure in any one year must be financed by either taxation, government borrowing, or changes in the monetary base. In the context of EMU, the ability of governments to finance spending through money issuance is prohibited. See also *Stock–flow adjustment*.

Maastricht criteria   See *Reference values*.

Medium-term budgetary objective   Under the SGP member states are to pursue an objective for the general government budgetary position 'close to balance or in surplus' over the medium term. In this way, room is created to let the budget react to the economic cycle in an economic slowdown without breaching the 3 per cent reference value for the general government deficit. The exact value of the medium-term budgetary objective should depend on expected output volatility and the average sensitivity of the budget to the cycle in each member state as well as national preferences for fiscal stabilisation and any challenges to long-run budgetary sustainability. Each member state defines its own medium-term objective in the national Stability or Convergence Programme, including a projected three-year adjustment path for the budget balance of general government. However, the Commission has estimated minimal benchmarks for each member state, allowing the budgetary stabilisers to work unhindered during normal economic slowdowns. See also *Multilateral surveillance* and *Minimal benchmarks*.

Minimal benchmarks   These are medium-term reference values estimated for each member state. They indicate the budget balances that would provide sufficient safety margins for the automatic stabilisers to operate freely during normal economic slowdowns without leading to an excessive deficit. The benchmarks ensure only a *minimal* safety margin between the 3 per cent reference value and the structural budget balance, based on individual estimates of output volatility and budgetary sensitivity in the various member states (European Commission, 1999). See *Cyclical component of the budget balance* and *Medium-term budgetary objective*.

Multilateral surveillance   Multilateral surveillance is a process whereby the Council of Ministers examines member state economic policies with a view to facilitate coordination and ensure adherence to the Broad Economic Policy Guidelines and the policy rules of the SGP. Surveillance of the budgetary policies takes place on the basis of Stability and Convergence Programmes, which are updated annually by the member states and submitted to Commission and the Council for examination. On the basis of assessments by the Commission and the Economic and Financial Committee, the Council of Ministers examines whether the medium-term budgetary objective of each programme provides for a safety margin to ensure the avoidance of an excessive deficit, whether the macroeconomic assumptions employed in the programme are realistic, and whether the measures envisaged by the government are sufficient to achieve the targeted adjustment path for the budget balance. The Council invites the member state to strengthen the programme wherever it finds it appropriate to do so. It also monitors the subsequent implementation of the programmes with a view to identifying significant divergence from the medium-term objective. See *'Significant divergence'* and *Stability and Convergence Programmes*.

Output gap   The output gap is the difference between actual output and estimated potential output at any particular point in time. When it is positive, the economy is running above its long-term capacity which may have inflationary consequences. The output gap has consequences for fiscal policy through the workings of the automatic stabilisers. See also *Cyclical component of the budget balance*.

Peer review   Peer review is a process of mutual monitoring among independent authorities, where argument and persuasion is used in order to ensure compliance with agreed goals. This form of monitoring is a central feature of the multilateral surveillance of national budgetary policies under the Stability and Growth Pact.

Primary budget balance   The budget balance net of interest payments on government debt.

Primary structural budget balance   The structural (or cyclically adjusted) budget balance net of interest payments on government debt.

Pro-cyclical fiscal policy   Fiscal policy is pro-cyclical if the fiscal stance amplifies the economic cycle by increasing the structural primary deficit during an economic upturn, or by decreasing it in a downturn. Such a policy can be contrasted with counter-cyclical policy which has the opposite effects. Finally, a neutral fiscal policy keeps the cyclically adjusted budget balance unchanged over the economic cycle but lets the automatic stabilisers work unhindered. See *Tax-smoothing*.

Public debt   The EU uses consolidated gross debt for the general government sector as the key indicator of public debt. This concept includes the total nominal value of all debt owed by public institutions in the member state, except that part of the debt which is owed to other public institutions in the same member state. See also *General government sector*.

Reference values   The Maastricht Treaty stipulates reference values (or 'criteria') for general government deficit and debt, which are to be considered when deciding on accession of a member state to the single currency and when assessing national budgetary positions under the Excessive Deficit Procedure. The levels of these reference values (3 and 60 per cent of GDP respectively) are defined in a protocol annexed to the Treaty. In the SGP, further provisions have been set out regarding the application of the deficit criterion in the Excessive Deficit Procedure. See *'Exceptional and temporary'* conditions.

Sanctions   The Treaty envisages a number of sanctions that can be imposed on member states that persistently refuse to address an excessive deficit (see *Excessive Deficit Procedure*). Most importantly, the SGP stipulates that, whenever imposed, sanctions will include a non-interest-bearing deposit to be lodged by the member state with the European Commission. The deposit will include a fixed component of 0.2 per cent of GDP as well as a variable component equal to one-tenth of the actual excess of the budget deficit over the 3 per cent reference value. Each year that the excessive deficit persists, a new deposit is imposed equal to the variable component. Each deposit is capped at 0.5 per cent of GDP. After two years the deposit is converted into a fine, if the excessive deficit has not in the meantime been corrected. The proceeds of the sanctions are to be distributed among the participating member states without an excessive deficit. Other sanctions, besides deposits and fines, are also mentioned in the Treaty and may be used at the discretion of the Council.

'Significant divergence' As part of the multilateral surveillance procedure, the Council of Ministers regularly examines the national budgetary positions with a view to identifying 'actual or expected significant divergence' from the medium-term budgetary objective or the adjustment path towards it. It does so on the basis of assessments provided by the Commission and the Economic and Financial Committee. Wherever the Council finds that a significant divergence exists or may develop it addresses a recommendation to the member state concerned in order to give early warning and prevent an excessive deficit from occurring. Subsequently, if the divergence persists or worsens, the Council issues a new recommendation to the member state to take 'prompt corrective measures'. It may also decide to make its former recommendation public, in case it has not already been made public by the member state itself. See also *Council recommendation*.

Snow-ball effect The 'snow-ball effect' is the self-reinforcing effect of public debt accumulation (or decumulation) arising from a positive or negative differential between the interest rate paid on public debt and the growth rate of the national economy. The concept captures the phenomenon that, when the interest rate exceeds the growth rate, the debt/GDP ratio will rise over time unless the government runs an off-setting surplus on the primary budget balance.

Stability and Convergence Programmes Stability Programmes are multi-annual budgetary strategies prepared by member states in the euro area and submitted to the Commission and Council with a view to facilitating multi-lateral surveillance of their budgetary policies. For each member state, the programme contains information on the medium-term budgetary objective for the general government deficit, including projections three years ahead for deficit and debt. It also sets out the macroeconomic scenarios on which the projections are made, including measures adopted or envisaged by the national government. Finally, it assesses the likely effect of changes in key macroeconomic variables on the budgetary objective and the debt position. Further information may be included as defined in a separate Code of Conduct which has been agreed concerning the format and contents of the programmes. Member States outside the euro area submit Convergence Programmes on a similar basis to that of the Stability Programmes, although these include additional information on national monetary policies and their likely effect on inflation and exchange rate stability. See *Code of Conduct*.

Stock–flow adjustment   The stock–flow adjustment (also known as the debt–deficit adjustment) ensures consistency between net borrowing (flow) and total debt (stock) on an annual basis. It includes the effect of accumulation of financial assets by the public sector, changes in the value of debt denominated in foreign currency, and remaining statistical adjustments.

Structural budget balance   The actual budget balance adjusted for its cyclical component. The structural balance gives a measure of the underlying trend in the budget balance, when taking into account the automatic effect on the budget of the economic cycle. It is often referred to as the cyclically adjusted budget balance. See *Automatic stabilisers.*

Tax-smoothing   The idea that tax rates should be kept stable while leaving it for the automatic stabilisers to smooth the economic cycle. See *Cyclical component of the budget balance.*

References

Abel, A. B. (1990) 'Consumption and Investment', in Friedman, B. M. and F. H. Hahn, *Handbook of Monetary Economics* (Amsterdam: North-Holland).

Ariyagari, S. R. (1994) 'Uninsured Idiosyncratic Risk and Aggregate Saving', *Quarterly Journal of Economics*, vol. 109: 659–84.

Alesina, A. and T. Bayomi (1996) 'The Costs and Benefits of Fiscal Rules: Evidence from the U.S. States', NBER Working Paper, No. 5614.

Alesina, A. and R. Perotti (1995) 'Fiscal Expansions and Adjustments in OECD Countries', *Economic Policy*, vol. 21: 205–48.

Alesina, A. and G. Tabellini (1990) 'A Positive Theory of Fiscal Deficits and Government Debt', *Review of Economic Studies*, vol. 57: 403–14.

Alesina, A., Ardagna, S., Perotti, R. and F. Schiantarelli (1999) 'Fiscal Policy, Profits and Investment', NBER Working Paper, No. 7207.

Alesina, A., Broeck, M., Prati, A. and G. Tabellini (1992) 'Default Risk on Government Debt in OECD Countries', *Economic Policy*, vol. 15: 428–51.

Allsopp, C., McKibbin, W. and D. Vines (1999) 'Fiscal Consolidation in Europe: Some Empirical Issues', in Hughes Hallett, A., Hutchison, M. and S. Hougaard Jensen (eds), *Fiscal Aspects of European Monetary Integration* (Cambridge: Cambridge University Press).

Alt, J. E. and R. C. Lowry (1994) 'Divided Government, Fiscal Institution, and Budget Deficits: Evidence from the States', *American Political Science Review*, vol. 88: 811–28.

Ambrosi, G. M. (1999) 'Economic Policy Co-ordination and the Euro', in Louis, J. V. and H. Bronkhorst (eds), *The Euro and European Integration* (BRUSSELS: Euro Institute).

Amisano, G. and C. Giannini (1997) *Topics in Structural VAR Econometrics*, 2nd edn (Heidelberg: Springer-Verlag).

Artis, M. J. and M. Buti (2000) 'Close to Balance or in Surplus – A Policy Maker's Guide to the Implementation of the Stability and Growth Pact', *Journal of Common Market Studies*, vol. 34: 563–92.

Artis, M. J. and M. Marcellino (1998) 'Fiscal Solvency and Fiscal Forecasting in Europe', CEPR Discussion Papers, No. 1836.

Artis, M. J. and M. Marcellino (1999) 'Fiscal Forecasting: The Track Record of the IMF, OECD and EC', CEPR Discussion Papers, No. 2206, August.

Artis, M. J. and B. Winkler (1997) 'The Stability Pact: Safeguarding the Credibility of the European Central Bank', CEPR Discussion Papers, No. 1688.

Aschauer, D. A. (1989) 'Is Public Expenditure Productive?', *Journal of Monetary Economics*, vol. 23: 177–200.

Backus, D. and J. Driffill (1985) 'Inflation and Reputation', *American Economic Review*, vol. 75: 3.

Balassone, F. and D. Franco (1999a) 'Public Investment in the Stability Pact Framework', in Bordignon, M. and D. Da Empoli (eds), *Concorrenza fiscale in un'economia internazionale integrata* (Milano: Franco Angeli).

Balassone, F. and D. Franco (1999b) 'Fiscal Federalism and the Stability and Growth Pact: A Difficult Union', paper presented at the Conference 'I controlli di gestione delle Amministrazioni pubbliche', Banca d'Italia, Perugia, December.

Balassone, F. and D. Monacelli (2000) 'EMU Fiscal Rules: Is There a Gap?', *Temi di discussione*, no. 375, July.

Banca d'Italia (1999) *Indicators of Structural Budget Balances* (Rome: Banca d'Italia).

Barrell, R. and A. Pina (2000) 'How Important are Automatic Stabilisers in Europe?', EUI Working Papers, ECO, No. 2000/2.

Barrell, R. and J. Sefton (1997) 'Fiscal Policy and the Maastricht Solvency Criteria', *The Manchester School*, June, vol. 65: 259–79.

Barrell, R., Dury, K. and I. Hurst (1999a) 'An Encompassing Framework for Evaluating Simple Monetary Policy Rules', National Institute Discussion Paper, No. 156.

Barrell, R., Dury, K. and I. Hurst (1999b) 'International Monetary Policy Coordination: An Evaluation of Cooperative Strategies Using a Large Econometric Model', paper presented at the ESRC Global Economic Institutions workshop, June.

Barrell, R., Dury, K. and N. Pain (2000) 'Decomposing Forecast Uncertainty', National Institute Discussion Paper, forthcoming, London.

Barro, R. J. (1979) 'On the Determination of Public Debt', *Journal of Political Economy*, vol. 87: 940–71.

Barro, R. J. (1995) 'Optimal Debt Management', NBER Working Paper, No. 5327. Published as 'Optimal Funding Policy', in Calvo, G. and M. King (eds) (1998) *The Debt Burden and its Consequences for Monetary Policy*, IEA Conference Volume No. 118 (London: Macmillan).

Barro, R. J. (1997) 'Optimal Management of Indexed and Nominal Debt', NBER Working Paper, No. 6197.

Barro, R. J. and D. B. Gordon (1983) 'Rules, Discretion and Reputation in a Model of Monetary Policy', *Journal of Monetary Economics*, vol. 12: 101–21.

Baumol, W. J. and W. E. Oates (1988) *The Theory of Environmental Policy* (Cambridge: Cambridge University Press).

Bayoumi, T. and B. Eichengreen (1995) 'Restraining Yourself: The Implications of Fiscal Rules for Economic Stabilisation', *IMF Staff Papers*, vol. 42: 32–48.

Bayoumi, T. and P. Masson (1995) 'Fiscal Flows in the United States and Canada: Lessons for Monetary Union in Europe', *European Economic Review*, vol. 39: 253–74.

Bayoumi, T., Eichengreen, B. and J. von Hagen (1997) 'European Monetary Unification: Implications of Research for Policy, Implications of Policy for Research', *Open Economies Review*, vol. 8: 71–91.

Bean, C. R. (1992) 'Economic and Monetary Union in Europe', *Journal of Economic Perspectives*, vol. 6: 31–52.

Bean, C. R. (1998) 'Discussion', *Economic Policy*, No. 26: 104–07.

Becker, T. (1997) 'An Investigation of Ricardian Equivalence in a Common Trends Model', *Journal of Monetary Economics*, vol. 39: 405–31.

Beer, J. de and L. van Wissen (eds) (1999) *Europe: One Continent, Different Worlds. Population Scenarios for the 21st Century* (Dordrecht: Kluwer Academic Publishers).

Beetsma, R. and A. L. Bovenberg (1998) 'Monetary Union without Fiscal Coordination May Discipline Policymakers', *Journal of International Economics*, vol. 45: 239–58.

Beetsma, R. and H. Jensen (2000) 'Contingent Deficit Sanctions and Moral Hazard with a Stability Pact', mimeo, Universities of Amsterdam and Copenhagen.

Beetsma, R. and H. Uhlig (1999) 'An Analysis of the Stability and Growth Pact', *Economic Journal*, vol. 109: 546–71.

Bergin, P. (1998) 'Fiscal Solvency and Price Level Determination in a Monetary Union', mimeo, UC Davis.

Bernheim, D. B. and M. D. Whinston (1986) 'Menu Auctions, Resource Allocation, and Economic Influence', *Quarterly Journal of Economics*, vol. 101: 1–32.

Bertola, G. and A. Drazen (1993) 'Trigger Points and Budgetary Cuts: Explaining the Effects of Fiscal Austerity', *American Economic Review*, vol. 38: 11–26.

Blake, A. (2000) 'Optimality and Taylor Rules', *National Institute Economic Review*, No. 174: 80–91.

Blanchard, O. (1990) 'Suggestions for a New Set of Fiscal Indicators', OECD Economics and Statistics Department Working Papers, No. 79.

Blanchard, O. (1999) 'Commentary', Economic Policy Review Federal Reserve Bank of New York, vol. 6: 69–73.

Blanchard, O. and G. Mankiw (1988) 'Consumption: Beyond Certainty Equivalence', *American Economic Review*, vol. 78: 173–7.

Blanchard, O. and R. Perotti (1999) 'An Empirical Characterization of the Dynamic Effects of Changes in Government Spending and Taxes on Output', NBER Working Paper, No. 7269.

Blanchard, O. and D. Quah (1989) 'The Dynamic Effect of Aggregate Demand and Supply Disturbances', *American Economic Review*, vol. 79, no. 4: 655–73.

Bohn, H. (1988) 'Why Do We Have Nominal Government Debt?', *Journal of Monetary Economics*, vol. 21: 127–40.

Bohn, H, (1990) 'Tax Smoothing with Financial Instruments', *American Economic Review*, vol. 80: 1217–30.

Bohn, H. and R. P. Inman (1995) 'Constitutional Limitation and Public Deficits: Evidence from the U.S. States' University of California, Working Papers in Economics, 18/95.

Boyer, R. (1999) *Le gouvernement economique de la zone euro*, La Documentation française, Paris.

Brainard, W. (1967) 'Uncertainty and the Effectiveness of Policy', *American Economic Review, Papers and Proceedings*, vol. LVII: 11–25.

Brandner, P., Diebalek, L. and H. Schuberth (1998) 'Structural Budget Deficits and Sustainability of Fiscal Positions in the European Union', Österreichische Nationalbank Working Paper, No. 26.

Branson, W., Frenkel, J. and M. Goldstein (eds) (1990) *International Policy Coordination and Exchange Rate Fluctuations* (Chicago, Ill.: University of Chicago Press).

Brookings Papers on Economic Activity. Special Issue (1978) *Innovative Policies to Slow Inflation*, vol. 2 (Washington, DC: The Brookings Institution).

Bruneau, C. and O. de Bandt (1997) 'Fiscal Policy in the Transition to Monetary Union: A Structural VAR Model', unpublished conference paper.

Bryant, R. (1995) *International Coordination of National Stabilization Policies* (Washington, DC: The Brookings Institution).

Bryant, R. C., Hooper, P and C. L. Mann (1993) *Evaluating Policy Regimes: New Research in Empirical Macroeconomics* (Washington, DC: The Brookings Institution).

Bryant, R., Henderson, D., Holtham, G., Hooper, P. and S. Symansky (1988) *Empirical Macroeconomics for Interdependent Economies* (Washington, DC: The Brookings Institution).

Buiter, W. (1999) 'Six Months in the Life of the Euro. What Have We Learnt?', paper prepared for seminar in Utrecht, June.

Buiter, W. and I. Jewitt (1989) 'Staggered Wage Setting with Real Wage Relativities: Variations on a Theme of Taylor', in *Macroeconomic Theory and Stabilization Policy* (Ann Arbor: University of Michigan Press).

Buiter, W. and R. Marston (1985) *International Economic Policy Coordination* (Cambridge: Cambridge University Press).

Buiter, W. and A. Sibert (1997) 'Transition Issues for the European Monetary Union', *De EMU in Breed Perspectief, Preadviezen 1997, Koninklijke Vereniging voor de Staatshuishoudkunde*, 1–17.

Buiter, W. H., Corsetti, G. and N. Roubini (1993) 'Excessive Deficits: Sense and Nonsense in the Treaty of Maastricht', *Economic Policy*, no. 8: 57–100.

Buti, M. (2000) 'Comments', in *Fiscal Sustainability* (Rome: Banca d'Italia).

Buti, M. and B. Martinot (2000) 'Open Issues in the Implementation of the Stability and Growth Pact', *National Institute Economic Review*, no. 174: 92–104.

Buti, M. and A. Sapir (eds) (1998) *Economic Policy in EMU: A Study by the European Commission Services* (Oxford: Oxford University Press).

Buti, M. and M. Suardi (2000) 'Cyclical Convergence or Differentiation? Insights from the First Year of EMU', *Revue de la Banque*, no. 2–3: 164–72.

Buti, M., Franco, D. and H. Ongena (1997) 'Budgetary Policies during Recessions – Retrospective Application of the Stability and Growth Pact to the Post-War Period in the European Commission', *Recherches Economiques de Louvain*, vol. 63: 321–66.

Buti, M., Franco, D. and H. Ongena (1998) 'Fiscal Discipline and Flexibility in EMU: The Implementation of the Stability and Growth Pact', *Oxford Review of Economic Policy*, vol. 14: 81–97.

Caballero, R. J. (1990) 'Consumption Puzzles and Precautionary Savings', *Journal of Monetary Economics*, vol. 25: 113–36.

Cabral A. (1997) 'The Stability and Growth Pact', *Zentrum für Europäische Integrationsforschung (ZEI) Papers*, No. B97-01, University of Bonn.

Calmfors, L. (1998) 'Macroeconomic Policy, Wage Setting and Employment – What Difference Does the EMU Make?', *Oxford Review of Economic Policy*, vol. 14: 125–51.

Calmfors, L. (2000) 'EMU och arbetslösheten', *Ekonomisk Debatt*, vol. 28.

Canzoneri, M. B. and B. T. Diba (1991) 'Fiscal Deficits, Financial Integration, and a Central Bank for Europe', *Journal of Japanese and International Economics*, vol. 5: 381–403.

Canzoneri, M. B. and B. Diba (1998) 'Fiscal Constraints on Central Bank Independence and Price Stability', in J. L. Malo de Molina J. Vinals, and F. Gutierrez (eds), *Monetary Policy and Inflation in Spain* (New York: St Martin's Press).

Canzoneri, M. B. and J. Gray (1985) 'Monetary Policy Games and the Consequences of Non-cooperative Behaviour', *International Economic Review* vol. 26: 547–64.

Canzoneri, M. B. and D. Henderson (1998) 'Is Sovereign Policymaking Bad?', in K. Brunner and A. Meltzer (eds), *Stabilization Policies and Labor Markets*, Carnegie–Rochester Conference on Public Policy 28 (Amsterdam: North-Holland).

Canzoneri, M. B. and P. Minford (1998) 'When International Policy Coordination Matters: An Empirical Analysis', *Applied Economics*, vol. 20: 1137–54.

Canzoneri, M. B., Cumby, R. and B. Diba (1998) 'Is the Price Level Determined by the Needs of Fiscal Solvency?', NBER Working Paper, no. 6471.

Canzoneri, M. B., Nolan, C. and A. Yates (1997) 'Mechanisms for Achieving Monetary Stability: Inflation Targeting vs the ERM', *Journal of Money, Credit and Banking*, vol. 29: 46–60.

Casella, A. (1999) 'Tradable Deficit Permits: Efficient Implementation of the Stability Pact in the European Monetary Union', *Economic Policy*, no. 29: 323–61.

Catenaro, M. and P. Tirelli (2000) 'Reconsidering the Pros and Cons of Fiscal Policy Coordination in a Monetary Union: Should We Set Public Expenditure Targets?' mimeo, University of Milan-Bicocca.

Centre for European Policy Studies (CEPS) (1999) *Macroeconomic Policy in the First Year of Euroland: 1st Annual Report of the CEPS Macroeconomic Policy Group*, Brussels.

Chang, R. (1990) 'International Coordination of Fiscal Deficits', *Journal of Monetary Economics*, vol. 25: 347–66.

Chari, V. V. and P. J. Kehoe (1990) 'International Coordination of Fiscal Policy in Limiting Economics', *Journal of Political Economy*, vol. 98: 617–36.

Chari, V. V. and P. J. Kehoe (1998) 'On the Need for Fiscal Constraints in a Monetary Union', Federal Reserve Bank of Minneapolis Working Paper, No. 589.

Chari, V., Christiano, L. and P. Kehoe (1993) 'Optimal Fiscal Policy in a Business Cycle Model', Federal Reserve Bank of Minneapolis, Research Department Staff Report, No. 160.

Clarida, R. (1987) 'Consumption, Liquidity Constraints, and Asset Accumulation in the Presence of Random Income Fluctuations', *International Economic Review*, vol. 28: 339–51.

Clarida, R. (1990) 'International Lending and Borrowing in a Stochastic, Stationary Equilibrium', *International Economic Review*, vol. 31: 543–58.

Clarida, R., Galí, J. and M. Gertler (1999) 'The Science of Monetary Policy: A New Keynesian Perspective', *Journal of Economic Literature*, vol. 37: 1661–1707.

Cohen, D. and G. Follette (1999) 'The Automatic Stabilisers: Quietly Doing Their Thing', *Economic Policy Review*, vol. 6: 35–67.

Colm, G., and P. Wagner (1963) 'Some Observation on the Budget Concept', *Review of Economic Studies*, vol. 45: 122–6.

Committee for the Study of Economic and Monetary Union (1989) *Report on Economic and Monetary Union in the European Community* (the Delors report) (Luxembourg: EC Publications Office).

Corsetti, G. and N. Roubini (1993) 'The Design of Optimal Fiscal Rules for Europe after 1992', in Torres, F. and F. Giavazzi (eds), *Adjustment and Growth in the European Monetary System* (Cambridge: Cambridge University Press).

Cukierman, A., Edwards, S. and G. Tabellini (1992) 'Seignorage and Political Instability', *American Economic Review*, vol. 82: 537–55.

Dalamagas, B. (1995) 'Growth, Public Investment and Deficit Financing', *Australian Economic Papers*, vol. 65: 244–62.

Dalenberg D. R., Partridge M. D. and D. S. Rickman (1998) 'Public Infrastructure: Pork or Jobs Creator?', *Public Finance Review*, vol. 1: 24–52.

Dalsgaard, T. and A. de Serres (1999) 'Estimating Prudent Budgetary Margins for 11 EU Countries: A Simulated SVAR Model Approach', OECD Economics Department Working Papers, No. 216.

Deaton, A. (1991) 'Saving and Liquidity Constraints', *Econometrica*, vol. 59: 1221–48.

Debrun, X. (2000) 'Fiscal Rules in a Monetary Union: A Short-Run Analysis', *Open Economies Review*, vol. 11, no. 4: 323–58.

Duisenberg, W. (1998) *A Stability Oriented Monetary Policy for the ESCB* (Frankfurt: European Central Bank).

Dur, R. (2000) 'Political Institutions and Economic Policy Choice', PhD thesis, Erasmus University, Rotterdam.

Dury, K. and A. Pina (2000) 'European Fiscal Policy After EMU: Simulating the Operation of the Stability Pact', EUI Working papers, ECO, No. 2000/3.

Eberts, R. (1990) 'Public Infrastructure and Regional Economic Development', *Economic Review of the Federal Reserve Bank of Cleveland*, vol. 26: 15–28.

Economic Policy Committee (2000) 'The Impact of Ageing Populations on Public Pension Systems', Working Group on Ageing Populations, Brussels.

Eichengreen, B. (1997) *European Monetary Unification: Theory, Practice and Analysis* (Cambridge, MA: MIT Press).

Eichengreen, B. and C. Wyplosz (1998) 'The Stability Pact: More than a Minor Nuisance?', in Begg, D. *et al.* (eds), *EMU: Prospects and Challenges for the Euro*, pp. 65–114. (Oxford: Blackwell).

Ellerman, A. D., Schmalensee, R., Joskow, P. L., Montero, J. P. and E. M. Bailey (1997) 'Emission Trading Under the U.S. Acid Rain Program: Evaluation of Compliance Costs and Allowance Market Performance', Special Report, MIT, CEPR, October.

Elmendorf, D. and G. Mankiw (1998) 'Government Debt', NBER Working Paper, No. 6470.

Erenburg, S. J. (1993) 'The Real Effects of Public Investment on Private Investment', *Applied Economics*, vol. 25: 831–7.

European Commission (1990) 'One Market – One Money', *European Economy*, No. 44.

European Commission (1993) 'Stable Money – Sound Finances', *European Economy*, No. 53.

References

European Commission (1994) 'Towards Greater Fiscal Discipline', *European Economy: Reports and Studies*, No. 3.

European Commission (1999) 'Budgetary Surveillance in EMU: The New Stability and Convergence Programmes', *European Economy: Reports and Studies*, Supplement A, No. 3.

European Commission (2000a) 'Public Finances in EMU – 2000', *European Economy: Reports and Studies*, No. 3.

European Commission (2000b) 'Communication on the Contribution of Public Finances to Growth and Employment: Improving Quality and Sustainability', COM(2000)846, December.

Evans, P. and G. Karras (1994) 'Is Government Capital Productive? Evidence from a Panel of Seven Countries', *Journal of Macroeconomics*, vol. 16: 271–9.

Ewijk, C. van (1997) 'Infrastructure, Intergenerational Conflict and the *Golden Rule* of Finance', *De Economist*, vol. 145, no. 3: 447–60.

Fair, R. (1979) 'On Modeling the Economics Linkages Among Countries', in Dornbush, R. and J. Frenkel (eds), *International Economic Policy: Theory and Evidence* (Baltimore, Md: Johns Hopkins University Press).

Favero, C. (1999) 'Credit Risk in the European Union', mimeo, IGIER.

Favero, C., Missale, A. and G. Piga (2000) 'EMU and Public Debt Management: One Money, One Debt?', CEPR Policy Paper, No. 3.

Fitoussi, J.-P. *et al.* (1999) *Rapport sur l'état de l'Union Européenne 1999* Fayard Presses de Sciences Po.

Franco, D. and T. Munzi (1999) 'Ageing and Fiscal Policies in the European Union', in Buti, M., Franco, D. and L. R. Pench (eds), *The Welfare State in Europe – Challenges and Reforms* (Cheltenham, UK: Edward Elgar).

Frenkel, J. and A. Razin (1985) 'Fiscal Expenditures and International Economic Interdependence', in Buiter, W. and R. Marston (eds), *International Economic Coordination* (Cambridge: Cambridge University Press).

Frenkel, J. and A. Razin (1992) 'Fiscal Policy in Open Economies', in Newman, P., Milgate, M. and J. Eatwell (eds), *The New Palgrave Dictionary of Money and Finance*, vol. 2 (London: Macmillan).

Fuente, A. de la (1997) 'Fiscal Policy and Growth in the OECD', CEPR Discussion Paper, No. 1755.

Fuhrer, J. C. (1997) 'The (Un)Importance of Forward Looking Behavior in Price Setting', *Journal of Money Credit and Banking*, vol. 29: 338–50.

Fuhrer, J. C. and G. R. Moore (1995) 'Inflation Persistence', *Quarterly Journal of Economics*, vol. 110: 127–59.

Galí, J. and M. Gertler (1999) 'Inflation Dynamics: A Structural Econometric Analysis', *Journal of Monetary Economics*, vol. 44, no. 2: 195–222.

Garcia-Milà, T., McGuire, T. J. and R. H. Porter (1996) 'The Effect of Public Capital in State-Level Production Functions Reconsidered', *Review of Economics and Statistics*, vol. 78: 177–80.

Giavazzi, F. and M. Pagano (1990) 'Can Severe Fiscal Contractions Be Expansionary? Tales of Two Small European Countries', CEPR Discussion Papers, No. 417.

Giavazzi, F. and M. Pagano (1996) 'Non-Keynesian Effects of Fiscal Policy Change: International Evidence and the Swedish Experience', *Swedish Economic Policy Review*, vol. 3: 67–105.

Giavazzi, F., Jappelli, T. and M. Pagano (1998) 'Searching for Non-Keynesian Effects of Fiscal Policy: Evidence from Industrial and Developing Countries', mimeo, IGIER.

Giorno, C., Richardson, P., Rosevaere, D. and P. van den Noord (1995) 'Potential Output, Output Gaps and Structural Budget Balances', *OECD Economic Studies*, no. 24: 167–209.

Giovannetti, G., Marimon, R. and P. Teles (1997) 'If You Do what You Should Not: Policy Commitments in a Delayed EMU', mimeo, European University Institute, Florence.

Girard, J. and C. Hurst (1994) 'Investment and Growth: Quality versus Quantity', *Cahiers BEI-EIB Papers*, vol. 23: 13–19.

Girard, J., Gruber, H. and C. Hurst (1994) 'A Discussion of the Role of Public Investment in Economic Growth', *Cahiers BEI-EIB Papers*, vol. 23: 39–55.

Girard, J., Gruber, H. and C. Hurst (1995) 'Increasing Public Investment in Europe: Some Practical Considerations', *European Economic Review*, vol. 39: 731–8.

Goode, R. and E. A. Birnbaum (1955) *Government Capital Budgets* (Washington, DC: IMF).

Gramlich, E. M. (1994) 'Infrastructure Investment: A Review Essay', *Journal of Economic Literature*, vol. 32: 1147–75.

Granger, C. and T. Teräsvirta (1993) *Modelling Nonlinear Economic Relationships* (Oxford: Oxford University Press).

Grauwe, P. de (1996) *International Money* (Oxford: Oxford University Press).

Grauwe, P. de (2000a) *The Economics of Monetary Union*, 4th edn (Oxford: Oxford University Press).

Grauwe, P. de (2000b) 'The Challenge of Monetary Policy in Euroland', paper presented at the Flemish conference 'EMU: The Challenge', Ghent, March.

Haan, J. de., Sturm, J. E. and B. J. Sikken (1996) 'Government Capital Formation: Explaining the Decline', *Review of World Economics*, vol. 132: 55–74.

Hagen, J. von (1992a) 'Budgeting Procedures and Fiscal Performance in the EC', *Economic Papers*, vol. 96 (Brussels: European Commission).

Hagen, J. von (1992b) 'Fiscal Arrangements in a Monetary Union: Evidence from the US', in Fair, D. E. and C. de Boissieu (eds), *Fiscal Policy, Taxation and the Financial System in an Increasingly Integrated Europe*, Financial and Monetary Studies, vol. 22 (Dordrecht: Kluwer Academic Publications).

Hagen, J. von and I. Harden (1994) 'National Budget Processes and Fiscal Performance', *European Economy – Reports and Studies*, no. 3: 311–418.

Hagen, J. von and I. Harden (1996) 'Budget Processes and Commitment to Fiscal Discipline', IMF Working Paper, WP 96/97.

Hagen, J. von, Hughes Hallet, A. and R. Strauch (2001) 'Budgetary Consolidation In EMU', DG ECFIN Economic Papers (forthcoming).

Hahn, R. W. (1984) 'Market Power and Transferable Property Rights', *Quarterly Journal of Economics*, vol. XCIX: 753–165.

Hall, D. (1978) 'Stochastic Implications of the Life Cycle-Permanent Income Hypothesis: Theory and Evidence', *Journal of Political Economy*, vol. 86: 971–87.

Hallerberg, M. and J. von Hagen (1999) 'The Common Pool Problem in European Parliaments: The Interrelationship of Electoral and Legislative

Institutions', in Strauch, R. and J. von Hagen (eds), *Institutions, Politics, and Fiscal Policy*, ZEI Studies in European Economics and Law (Boston, Mass: Kluwer).

Hamada, K. (1985) *The Political Economy of International Monetary Independence* (Cambridge, Mass.: MIT Press).

Hansen, J. and J. Nielsen (1997) *An Economic Analysis of the EU* (Maidenhead: McGraw-Hill). Hayashi, F. (1982) 'The Permanent Income Hypothesis: Estimation and Testing by Instrumental Variables', *Journal of Political Economy*, vol. 90: 895–916.

Hayashi, F. (1985) 'The Permanent Income Hypothesis and Consumption Durability: Analysis Based on Japanese Panel Data', *Quarterly Journal of Economics*, vol. 100: 1083–113.

Helliwell, J. and T. Padmore (1985) 'Empirical Studies of Macroeconomic Interdependence', in Jones, R. and P. Kenen (eds), *Handbook of International Economics*, vol. II (Amsterdam: Elsevier Science Publishers).

HM Treasury (1997) *A Code for Fiscal Stability* (London).

HM Treasury (1998) *The Public Sector Balance Sheet* (London).

Holtz-Eakin, D. (1994) 'Public Sector Capital and the Productivity Puzzle', *Review of Economics and Statistics*, vol. 76: 12–21.

Holzmann, R. (1999) 'On Economic Benefits and Fiscal Requirements of Moving from Unfunded to Funded Pensions', in Buti, M., Franco, D. and L. R. Pench (eds), *The Welfare State in Europe – Challenges and Reforms* (Cheltenham, UK: Edward Elgar).

Hubbard, R. and K. Judd (1986) 'Liquidity Constraints, Fiscal Policy, and Consumption', *Brooking Papers on Economic Activity*, vol. 1: 1–50.

Hubbard, R. and K. Judd (1987) 'Social Security and Individual Welfare: Precautionary Saving, Borrowing Constraints, and the Payroll Tax', *American Economic Review*, vol. 77: 630–46.

Hughes Hallett, A. and P. McAdam (1999) 'Implications of the Stability and Growth Pact: Why the "Growth" Element is Important', in Hughes Hallett, A., Hutchison, M. and S. Hougaard Jensen (eds), *Fiscal Aspects of European Monetary Integration* (Cambridge: Cambridge University Press).

Hurst, C. (1994) 'Infrastructure and Growth: A Literature Review', *Cahiers BEI-EIB Papers*, vol. 23: 57–66.

IMF (1995) 'Exchange Rate Effects of Fiscal Consolidation', *World Economic Outlook*, Annex.

IMF (1998a) *World Economic Outlook*.

IMF (1998b) 'France: Selected Issues. Fiscal Stabilizers under EMU', *IMF Staff Country Report*, No. 98/132, December.

Italianer, A. (1997) 'The Excessive Deficit Procedure: A Legal Description', in Aderas, M., L. Gormley, C. Hadjiemmanuil and I. Harder (eds), *European Economic and Monetary Union: The Institutional Framework* (Dordrecht: Kluwer Law International).

Italianer, A. (1999) 'The Euro and International Economic Policy Cooperation', *Empirica*, vol. 26: 201–16.

Italianer, A. and J. Pisani-Ferry (1992) 'Regional Stabilisation, Properties of Fiscal Arrangements: What Lessons for the Community?', paper presented in CEPS Conference on Economic and Social Cohesion in the EC, June.

Italianer, A. and M. Vanheukelen (1993) 'Proposals for Community Stabilisation Mechanisms: Some Historical Applications', *European Economy – Reports and Studies*, No. 5.

Keereman, F. (1999) 'The Track Record of the Commission Forecasts', DG ECFIN Economic Papers, No. 137, October.

Kehoe, P. (1987) 'Coordination of Fiscal Policies in a World Economy', *Journal of Monetary Economics*, vol. 19: 349–76.

Kehoe, P. (1988) 'Policy Cooperation Among Benevolent Governments May Be Undesirable', *Federal Reserve Bank of Minneapolis*.

Kelejian, H. H. and D. P. Robinson (1997) 'Infrastructure Productivity Estimation and Its Underlying Econometric Specification: A Sensitivity Analysis', *Papers in Regional Science*, vol. 72: 297–312.

Kenen, P. (1969) 'The Theory of Optimum Currency Areas: An Eclectic View', in Mundell, R. A. and S. Swoboda (eds), *Monetary Problems of the International Economy* (Chicago: Chicago University Press).

Kenen, P. (1995) *Economic and Monetary Union in Europe* (Cambridge: Cambridge University Press).

Kiander, J. and M. Virén (2000) 'Do Automatic Stabilisers Take Care of Asymmetric Shocks in the Euro Area?', Government Institute for Economic Research Working Paper, No. 231, Helsinki.

Kitterer, W. (1994) 'Tax- versus Debt-Financing of Public Investment: A Dynamic Simulation Analysis', *Kredit und Kapital*, vol. 2: 163–87.

Kletzer, K. M. (1998) 'Macroeconomic Stabilisation with a Common Currency: Does European Monetary Unification Create a Need for Fiscal Insurance or Federalism?, in Eichengreen, B. and J. Frieden (eds), *Forging an Integrated Europe* (Michigan: The University of Michigan Press).

Koren, S. and A. Stiassny (1998) 'Tax and Spend, or Spend and Tax? An International Study', *Journal of Policy Modelling*, vol. 20: 163–91.

Krugman, P. and M. Obstfeld (1997) *International Economics, Theory and Policy* (Reading, MA: Addison–Wesley).

Krupnick, A. J., Oates, W. E. and E. van de Verg (1983), 'On Marketable Air Pollution Permits: The Case for a System of Pollution Offsets', *Journal of Environmental Economics and Management*, vol. 10: 233–47.

Krusell, P. and A. Smith (1998) 'Incomes and Wealth Heterogeneity in the Macroeconomy', *Journal of Political Economy*, vol. 106, no. 5: 867–96.

Laursen, S. and L. Metzler (1950) 'Flexible Exchange Rates and the Theory of Employment', *Review of Economics and Statistics*, vol. 32: 281–99.

Lerner, A. P. (1977) 'Stagflation – Its Causes and Cure', *Challenge*, vol. 20: 14–19.

Lerner, A. P. and D. C. Colander (1980) *MAP: A Market Anti-Inflation Plan* (New York: Harcourt Brace Jovanovich).

Levin, J. H. (1983) 'A Model of Stabilization Policy in a Jointly Floating Currency Area', in Bhandari, J. S. and B. H. Putnam (eds), *Economic Interdependence and Flexible Exchange Rates* (Cambridge, Mass.: MIT Press).

Lucas, R. J. (1976) 'Econometric Policy Evaluation: A Critique', *Journal of Monetary Economies*, vol. 1, no. 2, Supplementary Series, 19–46.

Lucas, R. J. and N. Stokey (1983) 'Optimal Fiscal and Monetary Policy in an Economy with Capital', *Journal of Monetary Economics*, vol. 12: 55–93.

McDougall, D. *et al.* (1977) *Report of the Study Group on the Role of Public Finance in European Integration*, vols. I–II (the McDougall report) Brussels: Commission of the European Communities).

McKinnon, R. I. (1963) 'Optimum Currency Areas', *American Economic Review*, vol. 53: 717–25.

Marston, R. (1985) 'Stabilization Policies in Open Economies', in Jones, R. and P. Kenen (eds), *Handbook of International Economics*, vol. II (Amsterdam: Elsevier Science Publishers).

Mayes, D. and M. Virén (2000) 'Asymmetry and the Problem of Aggregation in the Euro Area', Bank of Finland Discussion Papers, No. 10.

Mäki, T. and M. Virén (1998) 'Fiscal Policy Coordination in OECD Countries', Government Institute for Economic Research Discussion Paper, No. 160, Helsinki.

Mäki, T. and M. Virén (1999) 'Practical Experiences from Computing Fiscal Policy Indicators', *Government Institute for Economic Research*, VATT memorandum 42 (in Finnish).

Mélitz, J. (1997) 'Some Cross-Country Evidence about Debt, Deficits and the Behaviour of Monetary and Fiscal Authorities', CEPR Discussion Paper Series, No. 1653.

Mélitz, J. (2000) 'Some Cross-Country Evidence about Fiscal Policy Behavior and Consequences for EMU', mimeo, June.

Mera, K. (1973) 'Production Functions and Social Overhead Capital: An Analysis of the Japanese Case', *Regional and Urban Economics*, vol. 3: 297–312.

Milesi-Ferretti, G. M. (1998) 'Good, Bad or Ugly? On the Effects of Fiscal Rules with Creative Accounting', mimeo, IMF.

Missale, A. (1997) 'Managing the Public Debt: The Optimal Taxation Approach', *Journal of Economic Surveys*, vol. 11, no. 3: 235–65.

Missale, A. (1999) *Public Debt Management* (Oxford: Oxford University Press).

Missale, A. (2001) 'Optimal Debt Management with a Stability and Growth Pact', *Public Finance and Management*, vol. 1, forthcoming.

Missale, A. and G. Piga (2000) 'Public Debt Management, Challenges and Prospects in the EMU', in Eijffinger, S., Koedijk, K. and S. Yeo (eds), *Fiscal Policy Imbalances, the Monetary Transmission Mechanism and Prudential Supervision: Issues Facing Europe's Central Bankers* (CEPR and European Summer Institute).

Modigliani, F. and F. Padoa Schioppa Kostoris (1998) *Sostenibilità e solvibilità del debito pubblico in Italia* (Bologna: II Mulino).

Modigliani, F., Fitoussi, J. P., Moro, B., Snower, D., Solow, R., Steinherr, A. and P. Sylos Labini (1998) 'Manifesto contro la disoccupazione nell'Unione Europea', *Moneta e Credito*, vol. 51, no. 203: 375–412.

Montgomery, W. D. (1972) 'Market Licenses and Efficient Pollution Control Programs', *Journal of Economic Theory*, vol. 5: 395–418.

Muet, P. A. (1998) 'Deficit de croissance européen et defaut de coordination: une analyse retrospective' in *Coordination européenne des politiques economiques*, Report of the Conseil d'analyse economique (Paris).

Mundell, R. A. (1961) 'Optimum Currency Areas', *American Economic Review*, vol. 51: 657–65.

Munnel, A. H. (1992) 'Infrastructure Investment and Economic Growth', *Journal of Economic Perspectives*, vol. 6: 189–98.

Musgrave, R. A. (1939) 'The Nature of Budgetary Balance and the Case for a Capital Budget', *American Economic Review*, vol. 29: 260–71.

NIESR (1999) 'The National Institute of Economic and Social Research: The National Institute Global Econometric Model (NiGEM)', *The World Model Manual*, January 2000 version (London).

NIESR (2000) 'World Model Manual', mimeo, NIESR, London.

Noord, P. van den (2000) 'The Size and Role of Automatic Fiscal Stabilisers in the 1990s and Beyond', OECD Economics Department Working Papers, No. 230.

Notre Europe (1999) 'Reussir l'Union Economique et Monetaire (UEM)', *Etudes et Recherches de Notre Europe*, March.

Obstfeld, M. (1995) 'International Currency Experience: New Lessons and Lessons Relearned', *Brookings Papers on Economic Activity*, no. 1: 119–96.

Obstfeld, M. and K. Rogoff (1996) *Foundations of International Macroeconomics* (Cambridge, Mass.: MIT Press).

OECD (1997) *Economic Outlook 62*, December (Paris).

OECD (1999a) *Economic Outlook 66*, December (Paris).

OECD (1999b) *EMU: Facts, Challenges and Policies* (Paris).

OECD (2000) *Economic Outlook 67*, June (Paris).

Okun, A. M. (1977) 'The Great Stagflation Swamp', *Challenge*, vol. 20: 60–13.

Oudiz, G. and J. Sachs (1984) 'Macroeconomic Policy Coordination among the Industrial Economies', *Brookings Papers on Economic Activity* no. 1: 1–64.

Oxley, H. and J. P. Martin (1991) 'Controlling Government Spending and Deficits: Trends in the 80s and Prospects for the 90s', *OECD Economic Studies*, vol. 17: 145–89.

Pagano, M. (1998) 'The Changing Microstructure of European Equity Markets', in Ferrarini, G. (ed.), *European Securities Markets: The Investment Services Directive and Beyond* (Dordrecht: Kluwer Law International).

Pecchi, L. and G. Piga (1999) 'The Politics of Index-Linked Bonds', *Economics and Politics*, vol. 12: 201–12.

Peletier, B. D., Dur R. and O. Swank (1999) 'Voting on the Budget Deficit: Comment', *American Economic Review*, vol. 89: 1377–381.

Perotti, R. (1999) 'Fiscal Policy in Good Times and Bad', *Quarterly Journal of Economics*, vol. 114: 1399–1436.

Perotti, R., Strauch, R. and J. von Hagen (1998) 'Sustainability of Public Finances', Centre for Economic Policy Research (CEPR) Zentrum für Europäische Integrationsforschung, London.

Persson, M. (1997) 'Index-Linked Bonds: The Swedish Experience', in De Cecco, M., Pecchi, L. and G. Piga (eds), *Managing Public Debt: Index-Linked Bonds in Theory and Practice* (Cheltenham: Edward Elgar).

Persson, M., Persson T. and L. E. O. Svensson (1998) 'Debt, Cash Flows and Inflation Incentives: A Swedish Example', in Calvo, G. and M. King (eds), *The Debt Burden and its Consequences for Monetary Policy*, IEA Conference Volume No. 118 (London: Macmillan).

Persson, T. and G. Tabellini (1990) *Macroeconimic Policy, Credibility and Politics* (Chur: Harwood Academic Publishers).

Piga, G. (1999) 'Forward to the Swedish Guidelines on Public Debt Management', *Rivista Italiana degli Economisti*, vol. 1: 137–41.

Pontolillo, V. (1998) 'Aspetti economico-istituzionali del *project financing*. Problematiche ed esperienze in Italia', *Documenti* no. 589, Banca d'Italia.

Poterba, J. M. (1994) 'State Responses to Fiscal Crises: The Effects of Budgetary Institutions and Politics', *Journal of Political Economy*, vol. 102: 799–821.

Poterba, J. M. (1995) 'Capital Budgets, Borrowing Rules and State Capital Spending', *Journal of Public Economics*, vol. 56: 165–87.

Poterba, J. M. (1996) 'Budget Institutions and Fiscal Policy in the U.S. States', *American Economic Review, Papers and Proceedings*, vol. 86: 395–400.

Premchand, A. (1983) *Government Budgeting and Expenditure Controls: Theory and practice* (Washington, DC: IMF).

Ratner, J. B. (1983) 'Government Capital and the Production Function for U. S. Private Output', *Economics Letters*, vol. 13: 213–17.

Remsperger, H. (1999) 'The Role of Monetary Policy and the Macro Policy Mix', in *Möglichkeiten und Grenzen der Geldpolitik, 27. Volkswirtschaftliche Tagung 1999* (Vienna: Oesterreichische Nationalbank).

Restoy, F. (1996) 'Interest Rates and Fiscal Discipline in Monetary Unions', *European Economic Review*, vol. 40: 1629–46.

Riker, W. H. and I. Sened (1991) 'A Political Theory of the Origin of Property Rights: Airport Slots', *American Journal of Political Science*, vol. 35: 951–69.

Robinson, M. (1998) 'Measuring Compliance with the Golden Rule', *Fiscal Studies*, vol. 19: 447–62.

Robinson, M. (1999) 'The Role and Nature of Public Sector Balance Sheets', Queensland University of Technology Discussion Papers in Economics, Finance and International Competitiveness, No. 49, February.

Rogoff, K. (1985) 'Can International Monetary Policy Coordination be Counterproductive?', *Journal of International Economics*, vol. 18: 199–217.

Roodenburg, H., Janssen, R. and H. Ter Rele (1998) 'Assessing a Safety Margin for the Fiscal Deficit *vis-à-vis* the EMU Ceiling', *De Economist*, vol. 146: 501–07.

Rose, A. (1999) 'One Money, One Market', *Economic Policy*, no. 30: 7–46.

Rostagno M., Pérez-García, J. J. and P. Hiebert (2001) 'On Debt Optimality Under Borrowing Constraints', mimeo, April, Frankfurt.

Rotemberg J. and M. Woodford (1997) 'An Optimization-Based Econometric Framework for the Evaluation of Monetary policy', in Bernanke, B. S. and J. J. Rotemberg (eds), *NBER Macroeconomics Annual 1997* (Cambridge and London: MIT Press).

Roubini, N. and J. D. Sachs (1989a) 'Government Spending and Budget Deficits in the Industrial Countries', *Economic Policy*, no. 8: 99–132.

Roubini, N. and J. D. Sachs (1989b) 'Political and Economic Determinants of Budget Deficits in the Industrial Economies', *European Economic Review*, vol. 33: 903–38.

Sala-i-Martin, X. and J. Sachs (1992) 'Fiscal Federalism and Optimum Currency Areas: Evidence for Europe from the United States', CEPR Discussion paper, No. 632.

Sargent, T. (1987) *Dynamic Macroeconomic Theory* (Cambridge, Mass.: Harvard University Press).

Sargent, T. and N. Wallace (1981) 'Some Unpleasant Monetarist Arithmetic', *Quarterly Review of the Minneapolis Federal Reserve Bank*, vol. 5: 1–17.

Sartor, N. (ed.) (1998) *Il risanamento mancato – La politica di bilancio italiana: 1986–90* (Roma: Carocci).

Schechtman, J. and V. Escudero (1977) 'Some Results on an Income Fluctuations Problem', *Journal of Economic Theory*, vol. 16: 151–66.

Schinasi, G. and M. Lutz (1992) 'Fiscal Impulse', *Journal of International Economics*, vol. 18: 199–217.

Seidman, L. S. (1976) 'A New Approach to the Control of Inflation', *Challenge*, vol. 19: 39–43.

Sims, C. (1999) 'The Precarious Fiscal Foundations of EMU', De Economist, vol. 147: 415–36.

Stavins, R. (1998), 'What Can We Learn from the Grand Policy Experiment? Lessons from SO2 Allowance Trading', *Journal of Economic Perspectives*, vol. 12: 69–88.

Steve, S. (1972) *Lezioni di scienza delle finanze* (Padova: Cedam).

Svensson, L. (1997) 'Inflation Forecast Targeting: Implementing and Monitoring Inflation Targets', *European Economic Review*, vol. 41: 1111–46.

Svensson, L. (1999) 'Monetary Policy Issues for the Euro-system', *Carnegie–Rochester Conference Series on Public Policy*, vol. 51: 79–136.

Svensson, L. (2000) 'Open-Economy Inflation Targeting', *Journal of International Economics*, vol. 50: 155–83.

Tabellini, G. and A. Alesina (1990) 'Voting on the Budget Deficit', *American Economic Review*, vol. 80: 37–49.

Tanzi, V. and L. Schuknecht (1997) 'Reconsidering the Fiscal Role of Government: The International Perspective', *American Economic Review, Papers and Proceedings*, vol. 87: 164–8.

Taylor, J. B. (1985) 'International Co-ordination in the Design of Macro-economic Policy Rules', *European Economic Review*, vol. 28: 53–81.

Taylor, J. B. (1993) *Macroeconomic Policy in a World Economy* (New York: Norton).

Taylor, J. B. (1999) 'The Robustness and Efficiency of Monetary Policy Rules as Guidelines for Interest Rate Setting at the European Central Bank', *Journal of Monetary Economics*, vol. 43: 655–79.

Tietenberg, T. H. (1985) *Emissions Trading: An Exercise in Reforming Pollution Policy* (Washington, DC: Resources for the Future, Inc.).

Townend, J. (1997) 'Index-Linked Government Securities: The UK Experience', in De Cecco, M., Pecchi, L. and G. Piga (eds), *Managing Public Debt: Index-Linked Bonds in Theory and practice* (Cheltenham: Edward Elgar).

Vickrey, W. (1986) 'Design of a Market Anti-Inflation Program', in Colander, D. C. (ed.), *Incentives-Based Incomes Policies* (Cambridge, Mass.: Ballinger).

Vickrey, W. (1993) 'Today's Tasks for Economists', *American Economic Review*, vol. 83: 1–10.

Virén, M. (1998) 'Do the OECD Countries Follow the Same Fiscal Policy Rule?', Government Institute for Economic Research Discussion Paper, No. 186.

Virén, M. (2000a) 'Measuring the Effectiveness of Fiscal Policy in OECD Countries', *Applied Economics Letters*, vol. 7: 29–34.

Virén, M. (2000b) 'How Sensitive is the Public Budget Balance to Cyclical Fluctuations in the EU?', Government Institute for Economic Research Discussion Paper, No. 230.

Wallich, H. C. and S. Weintraub (1971) 'A Tax-Based Income Policy', *Journal of Economic Issues*, vol. 5: 1–17.

Walsh, C. E. (1995) 'Optimal Contracts for Independent Central Bankers', *American Economic Review*, vol. 85: 150–67.

Weil, P. (1989) 'Overlapping Families of Infinitely-Lived Agents', *Journal of Public Economics*, vol. 38: 183–9.

Weitzman, M. L. (1974) 'Prices vs. Quantities', *Review of Economic Studies*, vol. 41: 479–89.

Werner, P., Ansiaux, H., Brouwers, G., Clappier, B., Mosca, U., Schöllhorn, J. B. and G. Stammati (1970) 'Report to the Council and the Commission on the Realisation by Stages of Economic and Monetary Union in the community' (the Werner Report), Supplement to Bulletin II–1970 of the European Communities (Brussels).

Willett, T. D. (1999) 'A Political Economy Analysis of the Maastricht and Stability Pact Fiscal Criteria', in Hughes Hallett, A., Hutchison, M. M. and S. E. Hougaard Jensen (eds), *Fiscal Aspects of European Monetary Integration* (Cambridge: Cambridge University Press) pp. 37–68.

Woodford, M. (1990) 'Public Debt as Private Liquidity', *American Economic Review*, vol. 80: 382–88.

Woodford, M. (1996) 'Control of the Public Debt: A Requirement for Price Stability?', NBER Working Paper, No. 5684.

Wyplosz, C. (1991) 'Monetary Union and Fiscal Policy Discipline', CEPR Discussion Paper, No. 488.

Wyplosz, C. (1999) 'Economic Policy Coordination in EMU: Strategies and Institutions', ZEI Policy Paper, B11.

Index